MW00635651

LATTER-DAY ★SAINTS★ IN WASHINGTON

EDITED BY KENNETH L. ALFORD,
LLOYD D. NEWELL, AND ALEXANDER L. BAUGH

REGIONAL STUDIES IN LATTER-DAY SAINT HISTORY

RSC
BYU

DESERET
BOOK

Published by the Religious Studies Center, Brigham Young University, Provo, Utah, in cooperation with Deseret Book Company, Salt Lake City, Utah.
Visit us at rsc.byu.edu.

© 2021 by Brigham Young University. All rights reserved.
Printed in the United States of America by Sheridan Books, Inc.

DESERET BOOK is a registered trademark of Deseret Book Company.
Visit us at DeseretBook.com.

Any uses of this material beyond those allowed by the exemptions in US copyright law, such as section 107, "Fair Use," and section 108, "Library Copying," require the written permission of the publisher, Religious Studies Center, 185 HGB, Brigham Young University, Provo, UT 84602. The views expressed herein are the responsibility of the authors and do not necessarily represent the position of Brigham Young University or the Religious Studies Center.

Editor's note: Careful readers will note minor inconsistencies in the way the term *DC* appears. We have followed the editorial preference of *The Chicago Manual of Style* in omitting periods and including commas, except in the names of official Church units or buildings, which include periods and omit commas.

Cover and interior design by Emily V. Strong

ISBN: 978-1-9503-0403-5
Library of Congress Cataloging-in-Publication Data

Names: Alford, Kenneth L., 1955- editor. | Newell, Lloyd D., 1956- editor.
| Baugh, Alexander L., editor.
Title: Latter-day Saints in Washington, DC : history, people, and places /
edited by Kenneth L. Alford, Lloyd D. Newell, and Alexander L. Baugh.
Other titles: Regional studies in LDS Church history.
Description: Provo, Utah : Brigham Young University, Religious Studies
Center ; Salt Lake City, Utah : Deseret Book Company, [2021] | Series:
Regional studies in Latter-day Saint History | Includes index. |
Summary: "This volume takes a fresh look at the history, people, and
places in Washington, DC, that have affected the Church. Beginning with
Joseph Smith's earliest interactions with the federal government in the
1830s, the Church's progress has been shaped by leaders and members
interacting in Washington. This volume is filled with essays on many
topics about the Church's history, people, and places of the Latter-day
Saints in Washington, DC. It also chronicles many of the Saints and
statesmen who have worked to bring the Church out of obscurity and onto
a national and international stage"-- Provided by publisher.
Identifiers: LCCN 2020037128 | ISBN 9781950304035 (hardcover)
Subjects: LCSH: Church of Jesus Christ of Latter-day Saints--Washington
(D.C.)--History. | Mormons--Washington (D.C.)--History. | Mormon
Church--Washington (D.C.)--History.
Classification: LCC BX8615.W37 L38 2021 | DDC 289.3/753--dc23
LC record available at https://lccn.loc.gov/2020037128

CONTENTS

SECTION 2: PEOPLE

SECTION 3: PLACES

INTRODUCTION

The Church of Jesus Christ of Latter-day Saints has an important history in Washington, DC. Beyond cities like Salt Lake City, Logan, and St. George in its traditional western footprint, or communities like Palmyra, Kirtland, and Nauvoo that were central to its founding narrative, no U.S. city has had a more significant influence across the history of the Church than the nation's capital. The Church's presence in the District of Columbia spans nearly the entirety of the faith's history. Significant influence exerted on the Church by individuals and agencies associated with the federal government make a study of the Church in Washington, DC, a rich endeavor.

As early as August 1833, Latter-day Saints were directed "in befriending . . . the constitutional law of the land" (Doctrine and Covenants 98:6). Responding to growing violence in Missouri, the Lord instructed Saints to "continue to importune for redress, and redemption, by the hands of those who are placed as rulers and are in authority over you," including the governor and the president of the United States (Doctrine and Covenants 101:76; see also v. 88). Following the Prophet's release from Liberty Jail, Joseph Smith visited Washington, DC, in the winter of 1839–40, seeking redress for the Saints' suffering in Missouri. Later, a revelation directed that a proclamation be written "to the honorable president-elect," calling upon him and other leaders of nations "to give heed to the light and glory of Zion" by coming "with your gold and your silver, to the help of my people" (Doctrine and Covenants 124:3, 6, 11).

From those earliest interactions with the federal government, the story of the Church has been shaped by leaders and members interacting in Washington, DC. In 2019 the faculty of the Department of Church History and Doctrine at Brigham Young University traveled to DC to study the intersection between the nation's history and the Church and hosted a symposium in the Washington D.C. Temple Visitors' Center, visiting archives, historic sites, relevant museums, and networking with local members, historians, and dignitaries. This volume is filled with essays representing some of the many topics explored during their regional studies.

The book is divided into three sections. The first section, "History," examines episodes occurring in or involving Washington, DC, including Joseph Smith's 1839–40 visit, Latter-day Saints petitioning for redress, the federal government's role in Latter-day Saints fleeing persecution, and Orson Pratt's publishing of *The Seer*. In the twentieth century, it recounts the placement of a Nauvoo Sunstone in the Smithsonian Institution, participation by the Tabernacle Choir at Temple Square in national celebrations, the development of the proclamation on the family, and ways Latter-day Saints have been characterized on the pages of the *Washington Post*.

The next section, "People," details prominent individuals affiliated in a variety of ways with Latter-day Saints in the District of Columbia. Included are elected officials like Senators Reed Smoot, Elbert D. Thomas, and President Theodore Roosevelt; cabinet secretaries Ezra Taft Benson and T. H. Bell; public affairs director Beverly Campbell; the Marriott family; and dedicated Church leaders who provided leadership as Church membership began to increase in the DC area. Through the lives of these men and women, Latter-day Saint life in the DC area is examined, especially across the twentieth century.

The final section, "Places," begins with an examination of how Joseph Smith's portrait came to be placed in the National Portrait Gallery. It explores prominent sites associated with Latter-day Saints in the DC area, including the Washington Chapel and the temple, as well as Latter-day

Saints interred in Arlington National Cemetery. It also considers the influence of federal agencies like the National Park Service who extend their reach beyond Washington to influence Latter-day Saint historic sites across the country and concludes with an annotated photo essay of historic sites in Washington.

Latter-day Saints in Washington, DC helps readers appreciate the sometimes complicated, yet cooperative, relationship between the Church and the United States federal government. It chronicles Saints and statesmen who have worked to bring the Church out of obscurity and onto both a national and international stage. We hope you enjoy this volume!

★ HISTORY ★

Figure 1. *Sutcliffe Maudsley,* Lt. General Joseph Smith, *1842. Church History Library.*

IMAGES OF JOSEPH SMITH'S
1839-40 VISIT TO WASHINGTON, DC

BYRAN B. KORTH

Byran B. Korth is an associate professor of Church history and doctrine at
Brigham Young University.

In the summer of 1839, Latter-day Saints began gathering in Commerce,
Illinois, to regroup following their exile from Missouri. During the May
and October conferences, they agreed to send a group of delegates to
Washington, DC, "to importune the President and Congress of the United
States for redress."[1] With many members of the Quorum of the Twelve
Apostles serving missions, Joseph Smith Jr. (age thirty-four), Elias Higbee
(age forty-four, a former Caldwell County, Missouri, judge), Sidney Rigdon (age forty-six, a counselor in the First Presidency), and Porter Rockwell (age twenty-five, Joseph's friend and bodyguard) were called to take
the cause of the Saints to Washington.

Much research has been done by historians and the Joseph Smith Papers Project regarding Joseph's visit to Washington.[2] This essay contrib-
utes to this work by providing actual images of drawings, paintings, lithographs, and other artistic representations of the main locations at or near
the time of his visit. A letter written upon their arrival by Elias Higbee
to Hyrum Smith and the Nauvoo city council on 5 December 1839[3] will
be a primary historical source for this chapter. By conducting historical

and archival research with the Library of Congress to identify images pertaining to dates and locations referred to in Higbee's letter, this chapter will focus on images that depict the overall layout of Washington and the National Mall in 1839–40 and the possible location of where Joseph and company boarded, as well as time-period images of the White House and Capitol Building that were central to their visit.

HISTORICAL BACKGROUND OF THE MISSION TO WASHINGTON, DC

To appreciate the significance, purpose, and outcome of Joseph's visit to Washington, DC, it is helpful to briefly highlight significant events of the suffering Saints leading up to the trip and to describe the circumstances that were demanding the attention of the government in the nation's capital at that time. During 1838–39, the so-called Mormon War resulted in Saints being expelled from Missouri with an accompanying loss of life, land, and goods. From November 1838 to March 1839, Joseph and several other Church leaders were incarcerated in the Missouri cities of Independence, Richmond, and Liberty. By May 1839, many of the Saints had relocated to eastern Illinois and western Iowa. At Joseph's direction, the struggling Saints gathered in the area of Commerce, Illinois, a bend in the Mississippi River that would later be named Nauvoo. Also during this time, the members of the Quorum of the Twelve were being called as missionaries to the British Isles.

The nation's capital was still in its infancy. In 1790, just fifty years before Joseph's visit, the District of Columbia was created by an act of Congress to be "a meaningful expression of America's new political and social order [giving] the country a governing structure symbolized in the location, construction, [and] design of government buildings."[4] The city was very much a work in progress with about twenty-three thousand residents when Joseph arrived.[5] Figure 2 is a map of the United States around 1839.

The following are important events and government policies that were occupying the time and energy of the federal government in the United States during the late 1830s. "The weighty matters occupying America's

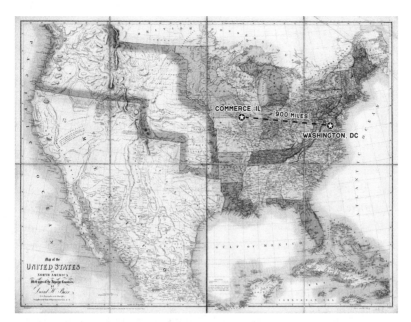

Figure 2. John Arrowsmith and David H. Burr. Map of the United States of North America with Parts of the Adjacent Countries *(London: John Arrowsmith, 1839). Library of Congress.*

citizenry [during this time] subordinated the catastrophe consuming the Latter-day Saints in America's westernmost state, Missouri."[6]

- The president of the United States at the time of Joseph Smith's visit was Martin Van Buren. He had succeeded Andrew Jackson in 1837 as the eighth president.
- The early Saints were not the only group who were dealing with the injustice of being forced from their homes and lands. In 1838, under the direction of the federal government, the Cherokee Indians were forced to leave their homes and land in Alabama, Georgia, North Carolina, and Tennessee and emigrate west to Indian Territory (modern-day Oklahoma).
- The United States and governmental officials were still dealing with the effects of the Panic of 1837, a financial crisis in the United States that touched off a major recession and lasted until the mid-1840s.

• As prelude to the Civil War (1861–65), the divisiveness of slavery could be felt and observed in the halls of Congress as early as the mid-1830s, with the first abolitionist elected to the House of Representatives in 1838.

DEPARTURE TO AND ARRIVAL AT WASHINGTON, DC

Joseph and the others departed from Commerce on 29 October 1839 (see table 1, p. 25, which provides a list of significant dates and events regarding Joseph's overall journey). In his history, Joseph wrote, "I left Nauvoo in a two horse carriage for the City of Washington to lay before the Congress of the United States, the grievances of the Saints in Missouri accompanied by Sidney Rigdon[7], Elias Higbee and Orin P. [Orrin Porter] Rockwell."[8] As further evidence of the purpose and motivation to make this long journey in the late fall and winter to Washington, Joseph stated in a 9 November 1839 letter to his wife Emma, "But shall I see so many perish and <not> seek redress no I will try this once in the <name> of the Lord."[9] Joseph and his companions arrived in Washington, DC, on 28 November 1839. The prophet stayed in the area for three weeks, primarily working with the Illinois delegation regarding his cause. Joseph then left to conduct a ministry tour in Pennsylvania and New Jersey, leaving Elias Higbee to continue seeking sympathy for the cause among members of Congress. Joseph returned to Washington for a time before returning to Nauvoo.[10]

In his letter to Hyrum and the Nauvoo council, Higbee states, "We arrived in this City on the morning of the 28th of November."[11] An 1838 artistic rendition of Washington from a distance provides a perspective of what Joseph might have seen as he drew near to the city on the other side of the Potomac River (see figure 3). This image emphasizes what Washington, DC, would have looked like to Joseph and company: a prominent city—with the monumental buildings of the White House and U.S. Capitol Building—that is still emerging from a largely country area.

Figure 4 includes a circa 1839 map of the city of Washington, and figure 5 is a magnification of the 1839 map that overlays a current satellite image of the same location focusing on the National Mall and various significant buildings. These figures further demonstrate how Washington,

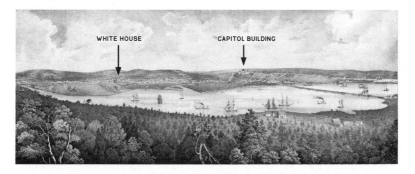

Figure 3. Philander Anderson and Fitz Henry Lane, View of the City of Washington, the Metropolis of the United States of America, Taken from Arlington House, the Residence of George Washington P. Custis Esq. *(Boston: T. Moore's Lithography, 1839). Library of Congress.*

DC, would have been laid out in 1839 compared to today. The arrow line of figure 5 shows the approximate 1839 city border to the Potomac River, and the dotted line shows today's border to the river. At the time of Joseph's visit, the location of the National Mall was known. The White House, U.S. Capitol Building, and Lockkeeper's House were prominent buildings of the time (see large black circles in figure 5). In 1815 the Washington City Canal was built and was intended to be a grand avenue (shown by the striped line in figure 5). Memorials that would not have existed during Joseph's 1839 visit would have included the Washington Memorial (foundation stone laid in 1848 and completed in 1884), the Smithsonian Castle, the Lincoln Memorial, and the Jefferson Memorial (see large black squares in figure 5). The entrance to the canal was managed by the Lockkeeper's House, built in 1837, which regulated entry and traffic and collected tolls from those coming into the canal. It still stands today and is considered one of the oldest buildings on the National Mall. It is unknown where Joseph and his companions would have entered the city, but it is possible that they crossed the Potomac River and entered through the canal, passing the Lockkeeper's House. The mudflats and marshland to the west of the 1839 National Mall were called the Potomac Flats for most of the 1800s. In 1870 the Army Corps of Engineers began dredging the Potomac to remove sediment and silt in order to deepen the canal's ship channel so

Figure 4. *William James Stone,* Map of the City of Washington in the District of Columbia: Established as the Permanent Seat of the Government of the United States of America *(Washington?: n.p., 1839). Library of Congress.*

that Washington could be better accessed by water. Dredged material was dumped onto the tidal flats along the Washington waterfront. The work continued until 30 August 1911. After over forty years of dredging, more than twelve million cubic yards of material had been moved from the river to the waterfront, extending the National Mall to where the Lincoln Memorial (completed in 1922), the Jefferson Memorial (completed in 1943), and other national memorials and monuments stand today.[12]

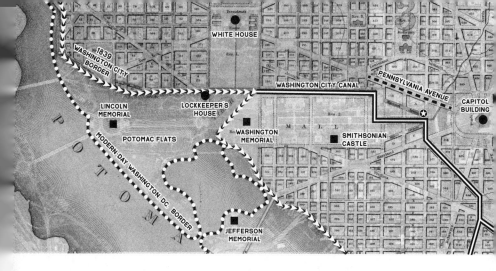

Figure 5. *Overlay of 1839 map (see figure 4) and current satellite image of Washington, DC. Satellite image retrieved from maps.apple.com, 6 November 2019. Solid black circles indicate prominent locations that existed at the time of Joseph's visit. Solid black squares indicate prominent locations that were built after Joseph's visit. Striped line indicates the Washington City Canal. Arrow line indicates the approximate Washington, DC, border in 1839. Dotted line indicates the approximate border of modern-day Washington, DC.*

"CORNER OF MISSOURI & 3D STREET"

In Higbee's 5 December 1839 letter, he states that upon their arrival to Washington, DC, they "spent the most of that day in looking up a boarding house which we succeeded in finding. We found as cheap boarding as can be had in this city."[13] In the heading of his letter it indicates the location was "Washington City Corner of Missouri & 3d Street" (see figure 6).

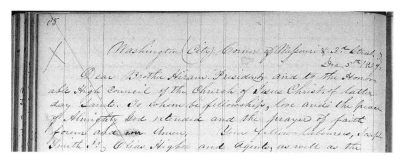

Figure 6. *Heading of Higbee Letter to Hyrum Smith, 5 December 1839. Joseph Smith and Elias Higbee, Letter, Washington, DC, to Hyrum Smith and Nauvoo High Council, Commerce, IL, 5 December 1839; in JS Letterbook 2, pp. 85–88; handwriting of Howard Coray; Church History Library.*

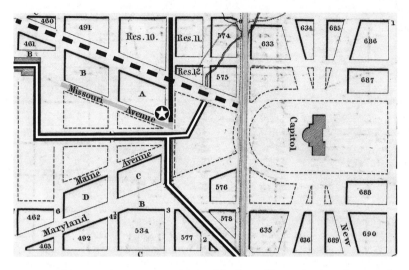

Figure 7. *"Corner of Missouri & 3d Street" (indicated by star). Magnification of 1839 map (see figure 4). Striped line: Washington Canal; solid vertical line: 3rd Street; diagonal gray line: Missouri Avenue; diagonal dashed line: Pennsylvania Avenue.*

Magnifying the circa 1839 map of Washington in figure 4, figure 7 shows the location of Missouri Avenue (gray diagonal) in relation to the Capitol Building and how Missouri Avenue parallels Pennsylvania Avenue (dashed diagonal) and intersects with Third Street (solid vertical line). This relationship of streets culminates with the "corner of Missouri & 3d Street" and is indicated by the star.

An 1843 city directory of Washington, DC,[14] describes Missouri Street as running "north of and near the canal, running from 3d to 6d street, west." It runs parallel with and is one block to the south of Pennsylvania Avenue, the main thoroughfare connecting the Capitol Building at First Street and the White House at Fifteenth Street. The National Park Service notes, "Much history transpired within the walls of private homes as well as in the hotels and boarding houses of the Pennsylvania Avenue district."[15] According to city directories in the 1840s and 1850s and in line with other historical information about the avenue during this time period, Pennsylvania Avenue was a prime location for boardinghouses, hotels, restaurants, and entertainment. This was a place where government leaders and dignitaries resided while

Figure 8. *1843 image of Pennsylvania Avenue from Capitol Hill. Library of Congress.*

they conducted their public and political business at the Capitol Building and White House. Figure 8 is the earliest known photograph (1843) of Pennsylvania Avenue with boardinghouses and hotels in the foreground.[16]

There was a concentration of such establishments on Pennsylvania Avenue between Third and Sixth Street, given the close proximity to the Capitol Building. One such prominent hotel around in the 1830s and 1840s was The National, which was located on the corner of Sixth Street and Pennsylvania. Others prestigious hotels were located nearby, including The United States Hotel and The Indian Queen Hotel. Given the likely higher cost of boardinghouses and hotels on Pennsylvania Avenue, places which offered members of Congress easy access to the legislative halls, it is logical that Joseph and company desired to stay in the vicinity but found cheaper lodging on Missouri Avenue and off of the main artery (Pennsylvania Avenue) of Washington, DC.

Professor Kirk Savage has written extensively on public monuments within the larger theoretical context of collective memory and identity. In his book on the history of the Washington, DC, monuments, he explains the history of Missouri Avenue as follows:

A quasi memorial to Congress's bargain with slavery emerged in the very center of the Mall near the Capitol. Completely unrecognized in histories of the city, this intervention in the landscape marked the outcome of the first of the grand bargains struck by Congress to solve the problems created by slavery's expansion into new territories. The Compromise of 1820, or Missouri Compromise, admitted Maine as a free state and Missouri as a slave state, and prohibited slavery in the Louisiana Purchase everywhere north of the 36° 30' parallel, excepting Missouri. The memorial came in the form of two street names created after some Congressional wheeling and dealing to raise money for public works. Congress had authorized the city to sell off some of the public land at the east end of the Mall and create several large new residential blocks. The deal created two new diagonal avenues within the Mall, each one an inner spoke that shrank the boundaries of the Mall between Third and Sixth Streets. . . . In the 1820s the city council named the new avenues after the two new states that had been admitted to the Union by the 1820 Compromise: Missouri, the slave state, and Maine, the free state. For reasons unknown, the northern street was named Missouri and the southern street Maine. For more than a hundred years, this pair of radiating avenues framing the east entrance to the Mall marked the ultimately futile effort to contain the political crisis wrought by slavery.[17]

Given the history of the Saints, the purpose of Joseph's visit, and the overarching politics of slavery, the irony of staying in a boardinghouse on Missouri Avenue cannot be left without acknowledgment. Although historical letters do not mention it, one can imagine Joseph and his companions conversing of this irony. Savage goes on to explain that "these diagonal streets and the resulting blocks of mostly residential buildings were all razed in the early 1930s." The location of Missouri Avenue is now occupied by the National Gallery of Art on the National Mall (see figure 9).

Further historical and archival investigation reveals additional details of the possible area where Joseph and his companions stayed. An 1888 *Sansborn Fire Insurance Map* provides detail of the plat layout (see figure 10). Although created nearly fifty years later, the map gives an idea of how the residential area between Pennsylvania and Missouri Avenues looked with an alleyway between the two.

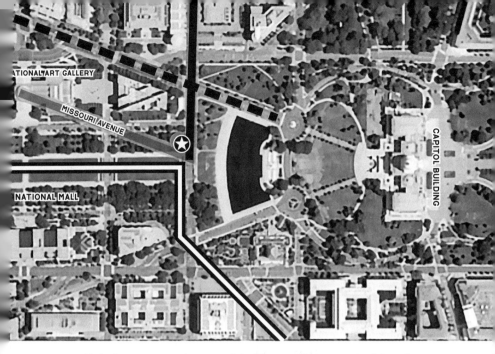

Figure 9. Today's approximate location of the "Corner of Missouri & 3d Street" (indicated by star). Satellite image retrieved from maps.apple.com, 6 November 2019.

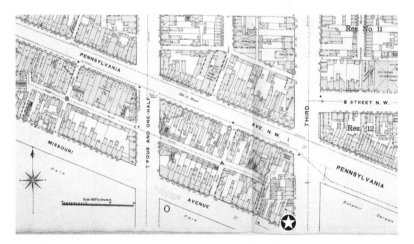

Figure 10. Sanborn Fire Insurance Map from Washington, District of Columbia *(District of Columbia: Sanborn Map Company, 1888). Library of Congress. Corner of Missouri Avenue and Third Street indicated by star symbol.*

This layout is evident in earlier bird's-eye view[18] renditions of Washington. In an 1880 bird's-eye view from the Potomac looking north (see figure 11), we see additional detail depicted of this residential area west of the Capitol Building, including the corner of Missouri Avenue and Third Street (see figure 11 inset). An 1850s print showing a bird's-eye view of the U.S. Capitol Building looking west gives additional insight into how the area may have looked closer to the time of 1839 (see figure 12). The most intriguing bird's-eye artist rendition is a circa 1852 image looking west up Pennsylvania Avenue (see figure 13). Magnification of this image shows even more detail in relation to this residential area of Missouri Avenue (see inset of figure 13). Furthermore, an 1843 *Washington Directory* further indicates that the only boardinghouse listed in this area was "Mrs. Pierce, boarding-house, Missouri St, btw 3 and 4 and 1/2 w, nr 3"[19] (see figure 14)—referring to the possible location of the boardinghouse Joseph and company stayed at on Missouri Avenue between Third and 4½ Street, near Third Street.

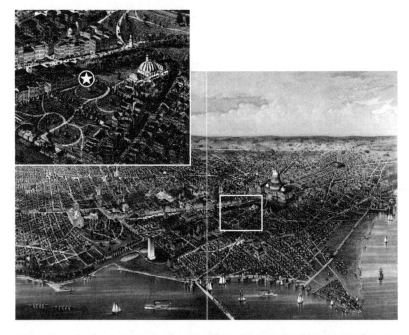

Figure 11. *Charles R. Parsons.* The City of Washington Bird's-Eye View from the Potomac, Looking North *(New York: Currier & Ives, ca. 1880). Library of Congress. Inset: magnification showing corner of Missouri Avenue and 3rd Street indicated by star symbol.*

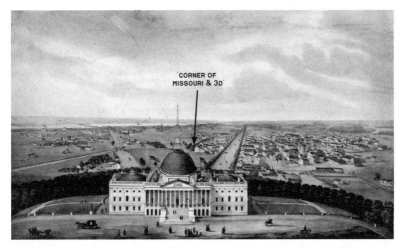

Figure 12. Robert Pearsall Smith. 1850 Bird's-Eye View of the U.S. Capitol Building Looking West. *View of Washington (ca. 1850). Library of Congress.*

Figure 13. Edward Sachse. 1852 Bird's-Eye View of Washington, DC, Looking West with the U.S. Capitol in the Foreground (*Baltimore: E. Sachse & Co*). *Library of Congress. Inset: magnification showing the corner of Missouri Avenue and 3rd Street.*

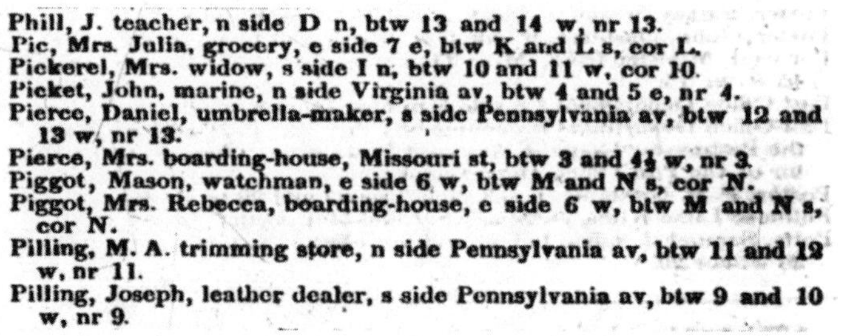

Phill, J. teacher, n side D n, btw 13 and 14 w, nr 13.
Pic, Mrs. Julia, grocery, e side 7 e, btw K and L s, cor L.
Pickerel, Mrs. widow, s side I n, btw 10 and 11 w, cor 10.
Picket, John, marine, n side Virginia av, btw 4 and 5 e, nr 4.
Pierce, Daniel, umbrella-maker, s side Pennsylvania av, btw 12 and 13 w, nr 13.
Pierce, Mrs. boarding-house, Missouri st, btw 3 and 4½ w, nr 3.
Piggot, Mason, watchman, e side 6 w, btw M and N s, cor N.
Piggot, Mrs. Rebecca, boarding-house, e side 6 w, btw M and N s, cor N.
Pilling, M. A. trimming store, n side Pennsylvania av, btw 11 and 12 w, nr 11.
Pilling, Joseph, leather dealer, s side Pennsylvania av, btw 9 and 10 w, nr 9.

Figure 14. 1843 Washington Directory—"Pierce, Mrs. boarding-house."

VISIT TO THE WHITE HOUSE

Higbee's letter then indicates, "On Friday morning [November] 29th, [the day after they arrived] we proceeded <to> the house of the President—We found a very large and splendid palace, surrounded with a splendid enclosure decorated with all the fineries and elegancies of this world we went to the door and requested to see the President."[20] Construction of the White House began in 1792, with John Adams being the first president to take residency there. Following a fire in 1814 (a result of the War of 1812), it was restored in 1817. North and south porticos were added in 1825 and 1829, with water and central heat being added in 1833 and 1837. Thus the White House was still new in its prominence when Joseph and Elias went to the door to see the president. A common image included in writings describing Joseph's visit is an 1846 image showing the south side of the White House (see figure 15). However, paintings and drawings during the 1830s and 1840s give additional visual detail regarding the open landscape, proximity to waterways of the time, and accessibility to visitors and dignitaries because it was intended to be an impressive monument of the country. For example, figure 16 is an 1833 painting of Washington, DC, that looks northeast across the Anacostia River toward the Navy Yard with the Capitol Building in the center of the painting and the White House off to the left. Other etchings from the 1830s give additional perspectives (see figures 17–18).

The visit to the White House and the meeting with President Van Buren was discouraging, given the description by Elias Higbee in his 5 December letter. He first describes Van Buren as follows: "He is a small man, sandy complexion, and ordinary features; with frowning brow and

Figure 15. John Plumbe, President's House, *ca. 1846. Library of Congress.*

Figure 16. W. J. Bennett and G. Cooke, View, probably 1833, from Anacostia, *showing Navy Yard and Capitol in center, Arsenal and White House at left (New York: Lewis P. Clover). Library of Congress.*

Figure 17. 1830s view of White House. Library of Congress.

Figure 18. 1830s north view of the President's House with Potomac River directly behind. Library of Congress.

considerable body but not well proportioned, as his arms and legs—and to use his own words is quite fat— . . . and in fine to come directly to the point, he so much a fop or a fool, (for he judged our cause before he knew it,) we could find no place to put truth into him."[21] Common images of the president show him as an older man (see figure 19). Another image from an 1839 print possibly reflects how Van Buren looked at the time of Joseph

Figure 19. President Martin Van Buren, half-length portrait *(photographed between 1840 and 1862). Library of Congress.*

Figure 20. Charles Fenderich and Peter S. Duval. Martin Van Buren, President of the United States *(Philadelphia: P. S. Duval, 1839). Library of Congress.*

and Elias's meeting with him when he was fifty-seven (see figure 20). Of their visit, Higbee states, "We presented him with our Letters of introductions;— as soon as he had read one of them, he looked upon us with a kind of half frown and said, what can I do? I can do nothing for you,—if I do any thing, I shall come in contact with the whole State of Missouri—But we were not to be intimidated, and demanded a hearing and constitutional rights— Before we left him he promised to reconsider what he had said."[22]

THE U.S. CAPITOL BUILDING

With the first congressional sessions being held in 1800, the Capitol Building quickly became a familiar icon throughout America. Numerous printings were included in travel accounts beginning in the 1810s, depicting an architecturally magnificent building that represented the vital and ambitious institutions it housed (see figures 21–23).[23] Architecture and construction were an intentional conveyance of political structure and social order, a symbol of power. Joseph and company likely had seen these images prior to their 1839 visit and anticipated viewing the building and were hopeful in participating in what it stood for.

As Joseph and the group approached Washington, DC, on the day of their arrival, they would have noticed the prominence of the U.S. Capitol Building both from a distance and up close. As they spent that first day searching for boarding just west of the Capitol, the building would have been impressive as they prepared to speak with government officials in the halls of Congress. An online exhibition by the Library of Congress titled "Temple of Liberty: Building a Capitol for a New Nation," explains that the Capitol Building was meant to be a symbol, a symbol that Joseph may have interpreted as a hope for the liberty of his people. Artistic renditions from the 1830s and 1840s often captured the more popular west-side view from Pennsylvania Avenue showing "the newly planted trees that covered the

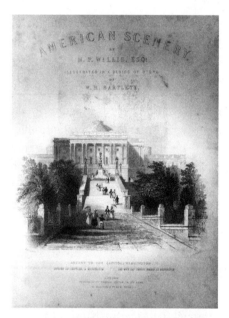

grounds and provided a dark base upon which the white building seemed to float"[24] (see figures 24–25). Joseph and company would have spent much time here pleading their case in the hall and rooms of the Capitol,[25] portrayed as the "center and heart of America" (see figures 26–27).

Figure 21. W. H. Bartlett, *View of the Capitol at Washington.* Nathaniel P. Willis, American Scenery, vol. 1 *(London: Virtue, 1840), frontispiece. Library of Congress.*

Figure 22. Bandbox with Wallpaper View of the Capitol, ca. 1840. From J. and D. Louv, Mizzentop Farm Antiques. *Library of Congress.*

Figure 23. *William A. Pratt and Charles Fenderich,* Elevation of the Eastern Front of the Capitol of the United States *(Philadelphia: P. S. Duval, 1839). Library of Congress.*

Figure 24. *John Rubens Smith,* West Front of the Capitol with Cows in the Foreground *(Washington, DC, ca. 1831). Library of Congress.*

Figure 25. *West view of the Capitol from Pennsylvania. Alfred Jones,* Capitol of the United States at Washington *(New York: Burton, ca. 1846–1855). Library of Congress.*

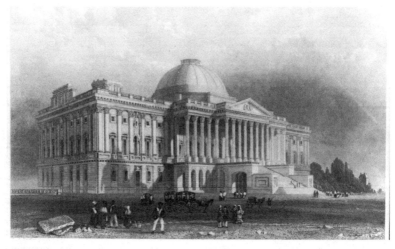

Figure 26. *Robert Brandard and W. H. Bartlett.* Principal Front of the Capitol, Washington *(Washington, DC, 1839). Library of Congress.*

Figure 27. *August Köllner.* Washington—Capitol East View *(New York & Paris: Goupil, Vibert & Co., 1848). Library of Congress.*

IMPACT OF THE WASHINGTON, DC, MISSION ON JOSEPH AND THE CITY OF NAUVOO

By providing actual images of paintings, sketches, lithographs, and other artistic representations of the main locations at or near the time of Joseph's visit, this essay has enhanced our ability to visualize Joseph's historic visit to Washington, DC, to seek redress for the suffering Saints. At the same time, it also opens up other possible connections and outcomes of his visit.

First, it is likely that the experiences of this trip planted and nurtured a seed for Joseph and the Saints to get involved in government and politics, including a presidential campaign. In response to his own presidential campaign, Joseph stated, "If I ever get in the presedental [presidential] chair— I will protect the people in their rights & libe[r]ties."[26] On another occasion Joseph declared, "As to politics I care but little about the Presidential Chair, I would not give half as much for the office as I would for the one I now hold, but as the world have used the power of Government to oppress & persecute us, it is right for us to use it for the protection of our rights. when I got hold of the eastern paper & see how popular I am I am afraid myself that I shall be elected, But if I should be, I would not say that your cause is just & I could not do any thing for you."[27] These statements allude to the response Joseph received from President Van Buren in response to Joseph's plea for justice: "What can I do? I can do nothing for you,— if I do any thing, I shall come in contact with the whole State of Missouri."[28]

Second, given the purposeful visual expression of America's governing structure symbolized in the location and design of the buildings and monuments of Washington, DC, a question that deserves further study is whether this experience influenced Joseph in his design and layout of the city of Nauvoo—namely, his purposeful placement and location of the city's buildings. This includes the Nauvoo House as a place to welcome and host guests (similar to the purpose of the White House) and the location of the temple on the top of the hill where it could be seen from a distance by visitors as a symbol of the religious government that had been restored (similar to the symbolic placement of the Capitol Building). Joseph had prior experience in city planning with Kirtland. However, by comparing the consistent and unique patterns used in Kirtland and Nauvoo, it may be possible to identify the parallels between what Joseph saw in Washington and what he wanted to visually incorporate in the building of Nauvoo. Figures 28–30 support this possible connection.

Figure 28. Nauvoo, Illinois (ca. 1855). Library of Congress.

Figure 29. Henry Lewis, Nauvoe, Illinois *(1854). New York Public Library.*

CONCLUSION

After more than three months, Joseph's party decided to end their mission to Washington, DC, and turn their attention to building their own monumental city, Nauvoo. In a letter to Joseph, Elias shared, "I feel now, as though that we have made our last appeal to all earthly tribunals; that we should now put our whole trust in the God of Abraham, Isaac, and Jacob— We have a right now which we could not heretofore so fully claim— That is of asking God for redress and redemption; as they have been refused us by man."[29] Disappointed and discouraged with the country that claimed to protect the freedoms for all, and despite the hope they had had in their government to provide justice for what had happened in Missouri, Elias's letter shows the determination of Joseph and the Saints to once again put their reliance and trust in God.

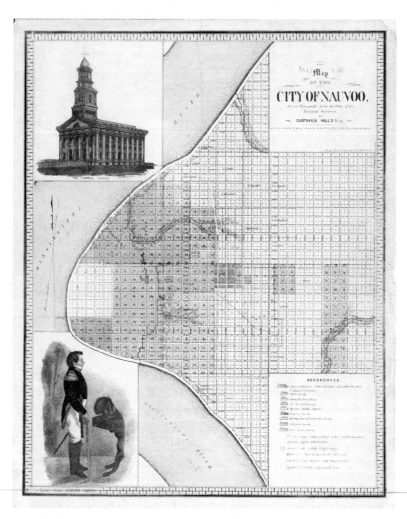

Figure 30. Map of Nauvoo with profile of Joseph Smith *(Lithograph, John Childs, 1844, from a plat by Gustavus Hills, 1842; inset of temple by William Weeks, 1842; inset of Joseph Smith by Sutcliffe Maudsley, 1842). Church History Library.*

TABLE I. SIGNIFICANT DATES AND EVENTS REGARDING JOSEPH SMITH'S VISIT TO WASHINGTON, DC

DATE	EVENT
May & October 1839	Conferences appoint delegates to go to Washington, DC.
29 October 1839	Delegates depart Commerce, Illinois (in a carriage).
8 November 1839	In Springfield, Missouri, a physician joins group to care for Sidney Rigdon, who is suffering from malaria.
18 November 1839	Stop in Columbus, Ohio, to allow Sidney some relief. Group continues without Sidney.
28 November 1839	Arrive at Washington, DC, and spend the day looking for boarding.
29 November 1839	Visit White House and President Martin Van Buren.
End of November and early December 1839	Meet with state representatives to prepare to bring case to the House of Representatives.
January 1840	Joseph visits Saints in Pennsylvania and New Jersey while Elias remains in Washington, DC.
January-March 1840	Case is made to government.
March 1840	Joseph arrives back in Nauvoo. Elias concludes efforts in Washington, DC, and also returns to Nauvoo.
7 April 1840	Joseph reports trip at the general conference.

NOTES

1. "History, 1838–1856, volume C-1 [2 November 1838–31 July 1842]," 972, The Joseph Smith Papers (website).

2. See the following sources: Ronald O. Barney, "Joseph Smith Goes to Washington," in *Joseph Smith, the Prophet and Seer*, ed. Richard Neitzel Holzapfel and Kent P. Jackson (Provo, UT: Religious Studies Center, Brigham Young University; Salt Lake City: Deseret Book, 2010), 391–420; R. Scott Lloyd, "Joseph Smith's Unsuccessful Visit to White House for Redress Still Inspiring, Editor Says," *Church News*, 1 May 2018; *Saints*, vol. 1, *Standard of Truth, 1815–1846* (Salt Lake City: The Church of Jesus Christ of Latter-day Saints), chap. 34; for letters and accounts, see The Joseph Smith Papers.

3. "Letter to Hyrum Smith and Nauvoo, Illinois, High Council, 5 December 1839," 85, The Joseph Smith Papers.

4. "Temple of Liberty: Building the Capitol for a New Nation," Exhibitions, Library of Congress (website).

5. "1840 United States Census," Wikipedia.

6. Barney, "Joseph Smith Goes to Washington," 391–420.

7. Before their departure, Sidney was suffering from malaria. His condition worsened during the first part of the journey and thus was unable to continue with Joseph and company. See Barney, "Joseph Smith Goes to Washington," 391–420.

8. "History, 1838–1856, volume C-1 [2 November 1838–31 July 1842]," 972.

9. "Letter to Emma Smith, 9 November 1839," 1, The Joseph Smith Papers.

10. Barney, "Joseph Smith Goes to Washington," 391–420.

11. "Letter to Hyrum Smith and Nauvoo, Illinois, High Council, 5 December 1839," 85.

12. www.mallhistory.org.

13. "Letter to Hyrum Smith and Nauvoo, Illinois, High Council, 5 December 1839," 85.

14. "1843 Washington City Directory, A–K," DCGenWeb Project.

15. National Park Service, *The Pennsylvania Avenue District in the United States History: A Report on the National Significance of Pennsylvania Avenue and Historically Related Environs, Washington, D.C.* (1965), 41.

16. National Park Service, "Pennsylvania Avenue District," 41.

17. Kirk Savage, *Monument Wars: Washington, D.C., the National Mall, and the Transformation of the Memorial Landscape* (Berkeley: University of California Press, 2011), 46–48.

18. Between the mid-1800s and the early 1900s, panoramic or bird's-eye-view maps of cities and towns captured the imagination of Americans because air flight was uncommon. These perspective drawings gave the view of a popular location from both ground level and high elevations.

19. National Park Service, "Pennsylvania Avenue District," 41.

20. "Letter to Hyrum Smith and Nauvoo, Illinois, High Council, 5 December 1839," 85.

21. "Letter to Hyrum Smith and Nauvoo, Illinois, High Council, 5 December 1839," 85–86.

22. "Letter to Hyrum Smith and Nauvoo, Illinois, High Council, 5 December 1839," 85.

23. "Temple of Liberty: Building the Capitol for a New Nation."

24. "Temple of Liberty: Building the Capitol for a New Nation."

25. See Elias Higbee letters dated 5 December; 20, 21, 22, 26 February; 9, 24 March, josephsmithpapers.org.

26. "Journal, December 1842–June 1844; Book 3, 15 July 1843–29 February 1844," 248, The Joseph Smith Papers.

27. "Discourse, 7 March 1844-B, as Reported by Wilford Woodruff," 203, The Joseph Smith Papers.

28. "Letter to Hyrum Smith and Nauvoo, Illinois, High Council, 5 December 1839," 85.

29. "History, 1838–1856, volume C-1 [2 November 1838–31 July 1842]," 1022, The Joseph Smith Papers.

work. We have the law of 1819, which fixes the prices those who do the work shall receive, and that law was passed by a Congress as competent to understand the subject, and who had the good of the country as much at heart as this. But suppose, in carrying out the intentions of this resolution, the CLERK confines his efforts to the city of Washington. In that case, what is to prevent a combination from being formed among the printers here to raise the prices higher than those allowed by the law of 1819? The resolution, as amended, did not provide for the manner in which the work should be done. It only provided that the CLERK should get the work done on the cheapest terms, without regard to time and without regard to the quality of the work. This was another reason operating with him for moving the reconsideration. No man, Mr. D. said, should go ahead of him in any measure of economy, where economy was practicable; but he did not conceive it to be so in this case. Another objection to the adoption of the resolution arose from the fact that they must soon go into the election of Printer. The interests of the country demanded it, and their duty demanded that these interests should no longer be neglected. Why, then, should we at this time introduce into this resolution, which can only be a temporary measure, provisions which, so far from performing its objects, are only calculated to defeat them? He was not (Mr. D. said) favorable to previous questions. He had assigned, so very briefly, his reasons for moving the reconsideration, as not to render a reply necessary, and he would, therefore, for the second time in his life, move the previous question.

Mr. PETRIKIN moved to lay the whole subject on the table.

The SPEAKER was of opinion that that motion was not in order; but that the gentleman could move to lay the motion for reconsideration on the table, and that motion would, if it prevailed, carry the whole subject with it.

Mr. PETRIKIN then moved to lay the motion for reconsideration on the table.

Mr. LEWIS WILLIAMS called for the yeas and nays; which were ordered, and were—yeas 106, nays 111.

So the House refused to lay it on the table.

The question then recurring on the motion to reconsider it was decided in the negative—yeas 108, nays 100.

The question recurred on the adoption of the resolution as amended; on which

Mr. EVERETT demanded the yeas and nays; which were ordered, and were—yeas 115, nays 97, as follows:

YEAS—Messrs. Adams, Alford, John W. Allen, Simeon H Anderson, Andrews, Baker, Barnard, Bell, Bond, Botts, Boyd, Briggs, Brockway, Anson Brown, Sampson H. Butler, Calhoun, William B. Campbell, Carter, Casey, Chittenden, Clark, Connor, J. Cooper, M. A. Cooper, Corwin, Crabb, Cranston, Curtis, Cushing, Edward Davies, John W. Davis, Garret Davis, Dawson, Deberry, Dillett, Edwards, Evans, Everett, Fillmore, Fisher, James Garland, Rice Garland, Gates, Gentry, Giddings, Goggin, Goode, Graham, Granger, Graves, Green, Griffin, Grinnell, Habersham, Hall, Wm. S. Hastings, Hawes, Henry, Hill of Virginia, Hoffman, Hook, Hopkins, Hunt, James, Jenifer, C. Johnston, William Cost Johnson, Kempshall, Lawrence, Lincoln, McCarty, Marvin, Mitchell, Monroe, Montgomery, Morgan, Calvary Morris, Naylor, Nisbet, Ogle, Osborne, Palen, Peck, Pickens, Pope, Proffit, Randall, Randolph, Rariden, Ridgway, Reed, Russell, Saltonstall, Sergeant, Shepard, Simonton, Slade, Truman Smith, Stanly, Storrs, Stuart, Taliaferro, Waddy Thompson, Tillinghast, Toland, Triplett, Trumbull, Underwood, Peter J. Wagner, Warren, John White, Lewis Williams, Joseph L. Williams, Christopher H. Williams and Sherrod Williams—115.

NAYS—Messrs. J. Allen, H. J. Anderson, Atherton, Banks, Beatty, Beirne, Black, Blackwell, Brewster, Aaron V. Brown, Albert G. Brown, Burke, William O. Butler, Bynum, Carr, Carroll, Chapman, Clifford, Coles, Craig, Crary, Dana, Davee, John Davis, Doan, Doig, Dromgoole, Duncan, Earl, Eastman, Ely, Fine, Fletcher, Floyd, Fornance, Gerry, Hammond, Hand, J. Hastings, Hawkins, Holleman, Howard, Hubbard, Jackson, Jameson, Joseph Johnson, Nathaniel Jones, Keim, Kemble, Leadbetter, Leet, Leonard, Lowell, Lucas, McClellan, McCulloh, McKay, Marchand, Medill, Miller, Montanya, Samuel W. Morris, Newhard, Parmenter, Parris, Paynter, Petrikin, Prentiss, Ramsey, Reynolds, Rives, Robinson, Edward Rogers, James Rogers, Samuels, Shaw, Albert Smith, John Smith, Thomas Smith, Starkweather, Steenrod, Strong, Sweeny, Taylor, Francis Thomas, Philip F. Thomas, Jacob Thompson, Turney, Vanderpoel, David D. Wagener, Watterson, Weller, Wick, Jared W. Williams, Henry Williams, and Worthington—97,

So the resolution was adopted.

Mr. JOHNSON, of Maryland, then proceeded in his remarks on the proposition to amend the rules. He made a strong constitutional argument against the movements of the Abolitionists, a synopsis of which there is not room in this day's paper, but the speech will be given hereafter at length. Mr. J. before concluding, yielded the floor to Mr. PETRIKIN, on whose motion,

The House adjourned.

IN SENATE,

TUESDAY, January 28, 1840.

The CHAIR presented a message from the President of the United States, communicating a supplement to the annual report of the Chief Engineer; which was referred to the Committee on Military Affairs, and ordered to be printed.

Also, a communication from the Secretary of War, transmitting a report from the Commissioner of Indian Affairs of the persons employed by that bureau, with their compensation, during the last year; which was laid on the table, and ordered to be printed.

Also, a memorial of the Legislative Assembly of the Territory of Iowa, that settlers on the sixteenth sections be allowed a pre-emption right to the same, and that other lands be set apart as school lands; and

A memorial from the same body, praying that settlers on the mineral lands may be allowed the right of pre-emption; and

A memorial from the same body, praying that the commissioners of Lee county be authorized to enter a quantity of school lands in the Sac and Fox reservation; which were severally referred to the Committee on the Public Lands.

Also, a memorial of the same body, praying that Congress provide for that Territory three six-pounder cannon and other munitions of war; which was referred to the Committee on Military Affairs.

Mr. MERRICK presented a memorial of Jacob Greaves for a pension; which was referred to the Committee on Naval Affairs.

Also, a memorial of the Howard Institution of the city of Washington, praying for assistance; which was referred to the Committee on the District of Columbia.

Also, the memorial of the president and directors of the Bank of the Metropolis, in the city of Washington, praying for a renewal of their charter; which was referred to the Committee on the District of Columbia.

Mr. STURGEON presented the memorial of the administrator of George Simpson, deceased; which was referred to the Committee on Finance.

Mr. CALHOUN presented the petition of Mathew Irvine Keith; which was referred to the Committee on Claims.

Mr. CLAYTON presented a petition of citizens of the State of Delaware, praying for the construction of a steam revenue cutter for Delaware bay; which was referred to the Committee on Commerce.

Mr. PRESTON presented the memorial of the heirs of Dr. Thomas Cooper, praying the repayment of a fine exacted under the Alien and Sedition laws; which was referred to the Committee on the Judiciary.

Mr. WRIGHT presented the petition of a number of inhabitants of Westchester county, New York, for a reduction of the rates of postage; which was referred to the Committee on the Post Office and Post Roads.

Mr. TALLMADGE presented the memorial of the executors of Henry Eckford; which was referred to the Committee on Naval Affairs.

Mr. RUGGLES presented the memorial of Samuel E. Smith and others, of Wiscasset, praying for a reduction of postage; which was referred to the Committee on the Post Office and Post Roads.

Mr. YOUNG presented the memorial of Joseph Smith, jr. Sidney Rigdon, and Elias Higbee, in behalf of "The Latter Day Saints," commonly called Mormons, praying for a redress of grievances, inflicted on them by the people of the State of Missouri.

Mr. Y. moved that it be printed, and referred to the Committee on the Judiciary.

After some remarks from Mr. LINN,

Mr. NORVELL moved to lay the whole subject on the table.

Mr. YOUNG called for the reading of the memorial, and it was accordingly read.

After some further remarks from Messrs. BENTON, PRESTON, and CLAY, of Kentucky, the motion to lay on the table was agreed to, with the understanding that it would be called up at an early day.

Mr. STRANGE presented the petition of Susannah R. Pickett; which was referred to the Committee on Pensions.

Also, the petition of William Hawkins; which was referred to the Committee on Claims.

Mr. HUBBARD, from the Committee on Claims, reported

A bill for the relief of Joseph M. Hernandez; and

A bill for the relief of George W. Paschall; which were severally read and ordered to a second reading.

Mr. SEVIER, from the Committee on Indian Affairs, reported a bill for the relief of John C. Reynolds, late disbursing agent of the Indian Department; which was read, and ordered to a second reading.

Mr. MERRICK, from the Committee on the District of Columbia, to which was referred

A bill concerning the estates of idiots or lunatics and infants in the District of Columbia; and

A bill giving the assent of Congress to the acts of the General Assembly of Virginia, incorporating the Falmouth and Alexandria Railroad Company, and for other purposes;

Reported the same without amendment.

Mr. M. also, from the same committee, reported a bill authorising the granting of letters testamentary, and of administration to aliens in the District of Columbia; which was read, and ordered to a second reading.

Mr. WALKER, from the Committee on Public Lands, reported an act for the relief of William Osteen; which was read, and ordered to a second reading.

The resolution submitted by Mr. MERRICK, to admit the District Attorney and the Reporter of the Supreme Court on the floor of the Senate, was taken up and disagreed to.

Mr. PRESTON submitted the following resolution:

Resolved, That the President of the United States be requested to communicate to the Senate the cause of the removal of General Call from the government of the Territory of Florida, and the correspondence connected therewith; and also the correspondence between the Department of War and Governor Call, concerning the war in Florida.

The bill for the relief of certain persons therein named; and

The bill for the relief of Samuel R. Slaymaker, were severally read a third time, and passed.

BOARD OF COMMISSIONERS.

The bill to establish a Board of Commissioners to hear and examine claims against the United States, was taken up as in Committee of the Whole.

Mr. SEVIER offered an amendment excluding private land claims from the jurisdiction of the bill; which was not agreed to—ayes 10, noes 31.

Mr. PRENTISS offered an amendment excluding such cases as were within the jurisdiction of the judicial tribunals and the officers of the General Government; which was agreed to.

Mr. WALKER moved a new section, making the action of the board, when adverse to the claimants final, but not so when against the United States, and that nothing in the bill should compel claimants to present their claims before this board; which was disagreed to—ayes 12, noes 31.

After some further unimportant amendments, which, with those preceding, were debated by Messrs. HUBBARD, SEVIER, TAPPAN, WALKER, CLAY, of Alabama, PRENTISS, GRUNDY, and HENDERSON, the bill was ordered to be engrossed—ayes 25, noes 16, as follows:

YEAS—Messrs. Clayton, Crittenden, Cuthbert, Davis, Dixon, Grundy, Hubbard, King, Knight, Linn, Merrick, Nicholas, Pierce, Prentiss, Preston, Roane, Robinson, Smith, of Connecticut, South-

Coverage of congressional discussions about the Latter-day Saints memorial and abolition petitions in the Congressional Globe, *28 January 1840. Library of Congress.*

THE REVELATORY SOURCES OF EARLY LATTER-DAY SAINT PETITIONING

JORDAN T. WATKINS

Jordan T. Watkins is an assistant professor of Church history and doctrine at Brigham Young University.

In December 1833, the Lord instructed members of the Church of Christ to petition government for assistance. This instruction came soon after Joseph Smith learned that mobs had driven members from their homes in Jackson County, Missouri. In commanding those members to seek governmental support, the Lord identified the Constitution as the inspired legal basis for their petition efforts. This revelation made sacred both the Constitution and the act of seeking redress.[1]

But if that act was sacred, it also was freighted with political meaning. While the revelation came as a direct response to the particular circumstances in Missouri, it also appeared in the midst of a charged national debate over slavery. The slavery issue overshadowed the era's other political concerns, including congressional consideration of Church members' petition efforts. During the mid-1830s, when abolitionists flooded Congress with petitions, anxious Southern politicians led a successful charge to stem the tide. Southern fears of federal meddling with their peculiar institution stood to undermine the prospect of federal intervention in Missouri and on behalf of the Missouri members.

The divine direction to petition seemed doomed by human failure, but Smith's 1833 revelation anticipated governmental indifference and warned that the Lord would "come forth out of his <hiding> place & in his fury vex the nation."[2] This checked the members' reliance on government and even qualified their view of the Constitution as sacred. In other words, by promising godly retribution in the face of human failure, the same source that instructed members to cherish the Constitution and petition government discouraged them from fully trusting in those institutions.

In the pages that follow, I identify the divine origins of early Latter-day Saint petition efforts and outline the ways in which political debates over slavery undermined those efforts. I also track how the very revelation that sanctioned the members' constitutionalism and commanded their petitioning directed them to look to God when those petition efforts failed. These developments occurred in relationship to the Missouri members' experiences and the Saints' petition efforts in the District of Columbia.

Revelation indicating that the Lord had established the Constitution and instructing the members to appeal to government for assistance, 16–17 December 1833, Revelation Book 2, Kirtland Revelation Book, Revelations Collection, ca. 1829–1876. Church History Library.

The failure of these efforts encouraged a crucial change in approach. While members continued to petition the government throughout Smith's life, in the 1840s he shifted their focus from human legislatures to the divine lawmaker. The members' early acceptance of the revelatory command to petition anticipated this late development; in relying on the Lord's direction about human government, Smith's followers demonstrated their ultimate loyalty to God's legislation.

In the 1830s, members sacralized the Constitution. The process by which they envisioned the Constitution as sacred both corresponded to and diverged from broader developments. The nation's founding legal document was not born as *the* Constitution. At the time of its ratification, James Madison thought of the document less as a complete legal text and more as an imperfect system of government. However, over the course of the next decade, congressional debate recast the document as fixed, static, and even sacred.[3] The generation that followed the Founders adopted and advanced this view. Indeed, the passage of time and the passing of the founding generation bestowed a new sacredness on the Constitution.

Church members sacralized the Constitution while falling victim to some Southerners' insecurities about their slave property. Although the Missouri members who opposed slavery did little to publicize their views, in the summer of 1833 a Jackson County mob cited perceived antislavery sentiment in order to justify the destruction of the Church's press and the tarring and feathering of Bishop Edward Partridge and Church member Charles Allen. News of rising tensions troubled Smith, whose revelations had promised the establishment of a millennial Zion.[4] In response to his concerned cries, the Lord directed Missouri members to uphold "constitutional" law.[5] A few weeks later Smith wrote from Kirtland, urging members to remain in Jackson County. He also prophesied that "god will send Embasadors to the authorities of the government and sue for protection and redress."[6]

Smith's followers recognized that prophetic success required human effort. In September, Missouri Church leaders petitioned Governor Daniel Dunklin. Introducing themselves as "citizens of the republic . . . residents of Jackson county" and "members of the church of Christ," they laid claim to "rights, privileges, immunities and religion, according to the Constitution." The petitioners informed Dunklin that, based on the perceived

C. C. A. Christensen, Mobbers Raiding Printing Property Store at Independence, Mo., July 20, 1833. *Church History Library.*

threat of losing land and slaves, Jackson County residents had destroyed the petitioners' property and warned them that any effort to obtain redress would be met with violence. The members argued that such intimidation jeopardized the republic as a whole, noting that when "the poorest citizen's person, property or rights and privileges, shall be trampled upon by a lawless mob with impunity, that moment a dagger is plunged into the heart of the Constitution." They then petitioned Dunklin to raise troops to help them defend their rights, sue for damages, and try the mob "for treason."[7] This marked the beginning of a Latter-day Saint constitutionalism forged in the fires of religious persecution.

Church members had no reason to believe that their petition would fail. In his response, Dunklin wrote, "I should think myself unworthy the confidence with which I have been honored by my fellow citizens did I not promptly employ all the means which the Constitution and laws have placed at my disposal, to avert the calamity with which you are threatened." After referencing what seemed to be wide-ranging executive powers, Dunklin proceeded to encourage a narrow judicial solution. He advised

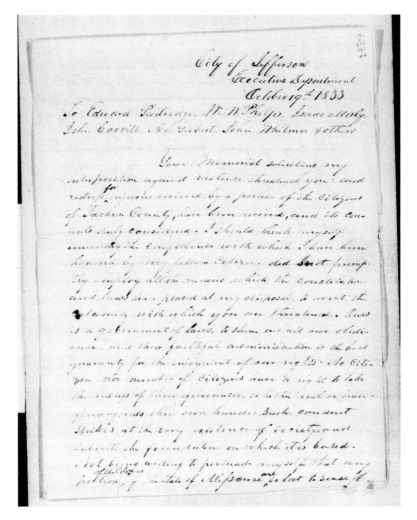

Letter from Governor Daniel Dunklin to Church leaders in Missouri, 19 October 1833.
W. W. Phelps Collection of Missouri Documents, 1833–1837, Church History Library.

the downtrodden members to take their case before the local circuit judge. If that course failed, he explained, then "my duty will require me to take such steps as will enforce a faithful execution" of the laws.[8]

Church leaders immediately hired four lawyers, which infuriated local residents who then renewed attacks on Church properties and drove members from their homes.[9] In early December 1833, Church leaders again petitioned Dunklin, asking him to help them secure assistance from "the militia of the State, if legal, or . . . a detachment of the United States Rangers."[10]

While Missouri members sent off another petition, news of the mob's renewed attacks arrived in Kirtland. The distraught Smith again instructed members to retain their lands and use every "lawful means to obtain redress."[11] Writing first descriptively and then prophetically, he noted, "When the Judge fails you, appeal unto the Executive, and when the Executive fails you, appeal unto the President, and when the President fails you . . . continue to weary" God, who "will not fail to exicute Judgment upon your enemies."[12] Smith was encouraging members to exhaust all legal means, but he was also reminding them to place their ultimate trust in God.

In less than a week, Smith's instruction gained the backing of a revelation. The Lord explained that his people "had been afflicted and persecuted" because of their "jar[r]ings and contentions."[13] Even still, he offered them mercy and promised vengeance.[14] The Lord explained that the members had a role to play in the divine calculus; they had to use the right of petition to secure the nation's condemnation. While giving this instruction, the Lord identified himself as the source of the Constitution. In urging members to "continue to importune for redress and redemption by the hand of those who are placed as rulers and are in authority over you," the Lord explained that he had "established the constitution . . . by the hands of wise men whom" he had "raised up unto this very purpose."[15] While an earlier revelation had commanded obedience to constitutional law, this revelation traced the origins of the Constitution to a divine source. This encouraged a shift among members from constitutional adherence to constitutional reverence.

However, the same revelation anticipated the failure of the members' petition efforts and signaled the limits of the Constitution. Comparing "the children of Zion" to the woman who petitioned the unjust judge, as recorded in Luke,[16] the Lord instructed the members to seek redress "at the feet of the judge if he heed them not let them impertune at the feet of the Govoner and if the Govoner heed them not let them importune at the feet of the President." As in Smith's letter, the revelation anticipated government inaction and promised godly retribution: "And if the President

Petition to President Andrew Jackson, 10 April 1834. W. W. Phelps Collection of Missouri Documents, 1833–1837, Church History Library.

heed them not then will the Lord arise and come forth out of his <hiding> place & in his fury vex the nation."[17] The very revelation that gave divine sanction to the members' constitutionalism reminded them that God was the supreme source of justice. It implied that they should not let inspired writings and rights take the place of the actual source of inspiration.

Smith's revelation proved prophetic. In February 1834, Dunklin responded to the Missouri members' new petition and again told them that he would "do every thing in [his] power, consistent with a legal exercise of them, to afford your society" redress. His qualification mattered more than what it qualified; as governor, Dunklin explained, he could not send a militia to protect them. While state laws allowed him to summon a militia in emergencies, he did not believe the members' situation met the legal requirements, and though the President of the United States could call upon him to send forth a militia, no such request had been made.[18] The governor's letter must have frustrated the Missouri members, but Smith's revelation had prepared them for the disappointment and instructed them about how to proceed.

A few months later, in April, "members of the Church of Christ" followed divine instruction by petitioning President Andrew Jackson. They explained that although they were "almost wholly native born Citizens," they had been deprived of "those sacred rights guaranteed to every religious sect." Borrowing and highlighting a term Governor Dunklin had used, they argued that the hostilities had created an "unprecedented emergency in the history of our Country." The petitioners then observed that "the powers vested in the Executive of this State appear to be inadequate," and asked the president to call on the governor to provide a protective force.[19]

The petitioners had reason to hope Jackson would help. In different ways, the Indian Removal Act of 1830 (which authorized the forced dislocation of American Indian tribes from their homelands in the southeast) and the Force Bill of 1833 (which empowered the president to ensure compliance with federal tariffs in South Carolina) had demonstrated Jackson's willingness to use federal power, including military might, to enforce federal legislation. But that overreach had been the result of political calculations and had come at a high political cost; although other Southern states

T. B. Welch engraving from drawing by J. B. Longacre, 1833 portrait of Lewis Cass, the secretary of war who responded to the members' petition on behalf of President Andrew Jackson. Library of Congress.

condemned South Carolina's confrontation with the federal government, many slaveholders began to view all federal interventions as a threat to slavery. In this context, lending national aid to a marginalized people in the slave state of Missouri promised little and risked much.

Church members could not have known the full scope of this background when Lewis Cass, Jackson's secretary of war, responded to their petition in May 1834.[20] Cass informed the members that "the offences . . . are violations of the laws of the State of Missouri" and that "the powers of the President . . . to direct the employment of a military force . . . extend only to proceedings under the laws of the United States." Cass noted that when a governor requests support to suppress an insurrection or execute state laws, the president can call forth a militia, but Cass did not believe these allowances applied to the petitioners' case. Dunklin had referred them to the president, and now Cass directed them back to the governor. It appeared that neither office was willing to assist the "Latter Day Saints."[21] The members continued to craft new petitions that aligned with their evolving grasp of the law, but political forces beyond their control undercut these efforts.

In particular, the anxious proslavery political response to the rise of radical abolitionism enervated the Saints' calls for redress. In the mid-1830s, abolitionists directed a mail campaign meant to flood the nation with antislavery literature and inundated Congress with petitions to abolish slavery in DC, suppress the domestic slave trade, and refuse to admit new slave states.[22] Southerners united in their condemnation of these

Letter from secretary of war Lewis Cass, 2 May 1834. W. W. Phelps Collection of Missouri Documents, 1833–1837, Church History Library.

efforts and, during the same period, anti-abolitionist violence spread in the North.[23] In light of these developments and their own experiences, Church leaders in both Missouri and Ohio tried to distance themselves from abolitionists.[24] And yet, their petition efforts were inextricable from the debate over slavery. In 1836 the Senate informally tabled all antislavery petitions and the House adopted a formal gag rule on the same, actions that threatened other petitions—including those submitted by the Saints.[25]

During the late 1830s, unwitting Church members broadened their petition efforts. In 1838, months after Smith had arrived in Missouri, new hostilities broke out, culminating in the Saints' removal from the state and Smith's own imprisonment. While languishing in jail in March 1839, he instructed members to document their "suffering and abuses."[26] He intended to present the resulting record "to the heads of the government in all there dark and hellish" hue in order to "claim that promise which shall call [God] forth from his hiding place and . . . the whole nation may be left without excuse."[27] In the revealed framework of petitioning, the Saints' continued efforts to obtain governmental remuneration further justified the nation's destruction.[28]

After Smith and his fellow prisoners were allowed to escape in April, he prepared to petition President Martin Van Buren.[29] During the next few months, members gathered affidavits and approved a delegation to travel to DC.[30] In October the delegation—comprised of Smith, Sidney Rigdon, and Elias Higbee—set off for the nation's capital. Along the way, Rigdon fell ill and rested while Smith and Higbee pushed on to DC, where they arrived on 28 November. The next day, they petitioned at "the feet of the President."[31] Records do not indicate what, exactly, they wanted the president to do, but whatever their request, he responded: "I can do nothing for you,— if I do any thing, I shall come in contact with the whole State of Missouri." As a renowned defender of states' rights, Van Buren needed no time to weigh the political costs of assisting the marginalized Saints for wrongs suffered in a slave state.

This meeting fulfilled a major requirement of the 1833 revelation, but the central purpose of the trip was to present the Saints' memorial to Congress. This, too, was part of the logic of divine retribution. Writing from DC to Church leaders in Commerce, IL, Smith noted, "we believe our case will be brought before the house, and we will leave the event with God— he is our Judge and the avenger of our wrongs."[32] Each petition was part of an apocalyptic equation that hastened God's calculated justice. With that

Senator Richard M. Young.

understanding in mind, the delegates met with Illinois congressmen to finalize the memorial.

The memorial outlined the Saints' losses in Missouri and laid claim to their constitutional "rights and immunities," including "religious freedom." The petitioners noted that if this "last appeal" failed, they would wait "until the Great Disposer of all human events shall in his own

Mr. YOUNG presented the memorial of Joseph Smith, jr. Sidney Rigdon, and Elias Higbee, in behalf of "The Latter Day Saints," commonly called Mormons, praying for a redress of grievances, inflicted on them by the people of the State of Missouri.

Mr. Y. moved that it be printed, and referred to the Committee on the Judiciary.

After some remarks from Mr. LINN,

Mr. NORVELL moved to lay the whole subject on the table,

HOUSE OF REPRESENTATIVES,
TUESDAY, January 28, 1840.

The first business in order was the proposition of Mr. THOMPSON of South Carolina to amend the rules, by the addition of the following:

Resolved, That, upon the presentation of any memorial or petition praying for the abolition of slavery or the slave trade in any District, Territory, or State of the Union, and upon the presentation of any resolution, or other paper touching that subject, the *reception* of such memorial, petition, resolution, or paper, shall be considered as objected to, and the *question of its reception* shall be laid on the table, without debate or further action thereon.

As recorded in the Congressional Globe, *Senator Richard Young introduced the Latter-day Saints' memorial. That same day, the House of Representatives made it even more difficult to consider abolition petitions.* Congressional Globe, *28 January 1840, 149, 150. Library of Congress.*

good time remove us from these persecutions to that promised land" of rest.[33]

While the Saints fulfilled their role in the divine drama, earthly factors shaped the more immediate outcome of their efforts. On 28 January 1840, the very day that Senator Richard M. Young presented the Saints' memorial, the House passed a rule prescribing that each abolition petition "shall be considered as objected to, and the *question of its reception* shall be laid on the table."[34] This created an extra barrier to the House's consideration of abolition petitions.

Meanwhile, Senator Young presented the Saints' memorial on the Senate floor and moved that it be referred to the Committee on the Judiciary. Missouri's Lewis F. Linn protested, "A sovereign State seemed about to be put on trial before the Senate . . . and he was entirely opposed to the juris-

---

149

Mr. YOUNG called for the reading of the memorial, and it was accordingly read.

After some further remarks from Messrs BENTON, PRESTON, and CLAY, of Kentucky, the motion to lay on the table was agreed to, with the understanding that it would be called up at an early day.

Mr. NORVELL said it appeared to him that Congress had no business with the subject at all, and that the memorial should go no further.

Mr. PRESTON said it was unusual on a preliminary question of this kind to authorize a committee to send for persons and papers, and he would suggest that it be sent to the committee, and if necessary they could ask for power to send for persons and papers.

Mr. LINN said he did not wish, as a representative from Missouri, to move to lay the subject on the table, but he would do so if no other person did.

Mr. NORVELL moved to lay it on the table.

Mr. YOUNG called for the reading of the memorial, which was read accordingly, giving a long and minute account the transactions in question.

Mr. BENTON asked with what view the motion had been made to lay this matter on the table?

Mr. NORVELL. That it may lie there forever.

150

ard, Spence, Sturgeon, Walker, Wall, Williams, and Young—25.

NAYS—Messrs. Allen, Benton, Betts, Brown, Calhoun, Clay, of Alabama, Clay, of Kentucky, Fulton, Henderson, Lumpkin, Mouton, Norvell, Ruggles, Sevier, Strange, and Tappan—16.

The Senate then adjourned.

HOUSE OF REPRESENTATIVES,
Tuesday, January 28, 1840.

The first business in order was the proposition of Mr. Thompson of South Carolina to amend the rules, by the addition of the following:

Resolved, That, upon the presentation of any memorial or petition praying for the abolition of slavery or the slave trade in any District, Territory, or State of the Union, and upon the presentation of any resolution, or other paper touching that subject, the *reception* of such memorial, petition, resolution, or paper, shall be considered as objected to, and the *question of its reception* shall be laid on the table, without debate or further action thereon.

Mr. Tallmadge presented two petitions from citizens of Oswego county, New York, praying the abolition of slavery and the slavetrade in the District of Columbia and Territories of the United States; and the petition of a number of citizens of Albany, in the State of New York, praying the abolition of slavery in the District of Columbia and Territories of the United States, the suppression of the slavetrade between the States, and that no State may be admitted into the Union whose constitution tolerates slavery.

A motion being made that the petitions be received, and the same being objected to;

Ordered, That the motion to receive the petitions lie on the table.

Mr. Tallmadge presented the petition of a number of citizens of Oneida county, in the State of New York, praying the prohibition of the use of intoxicating liquors in the army and navy, and among the Indians; that the sale of said liquors in the Capitol and public depots of the United States, be suppressed, and that an increase of duty be laid upon all importations of the same;

Ordered, That it lie on the table.

Mr. Young submitted additional documents in relation to the petition of the " Latter Day Saints," commonly called Mormons; which were referred to the Committee on the Judiciary.

Reports printed in the Congressional Globe, *the* Daily Intelligencer, *and the* Journal of the Senate *indicate that Senator Richard Young introduced the Latter-day Saints' memorial in the midst of a congressional debate about abolition petitions.*

diction." John Norvell of Michigan agreed, saying, "It appeared to him that Congress had no business with the subject at all." Proslavery politics had nurtured the federalism reflected in these statements. In other words, the forces supporting the right to slave property had developed the convincing constitutional argument that the status of slavery fell entirely outside federal jurisdiction—but completely inside state jurisdiction. Linn knew it would be awkward if he moved "to lay the subject on the table, but he would do so if no other person did." Norvell obliged him. But before the vote, Young succeeded in having the memorial read. After the reading, Missouri's Thomas Hart Benton asked about the intention to table the memorial, to which Norvell replied, "That it may lie there forever."[35] Norvell's proposal recalled the gag rule on antislavery petitions.

To be clear, those petitions and the Saints' memorial were different. The former seemed to threaten direct federal involvement in the Southern states, while the latter requested federal support for a people living in the North. And yet, while the decision to table antislavery petitions did not dictate Congress's determination regarding the Saints' memorial, debates over slavery demanded that politicians give constant consideration to state sovereignty and federal power. This is evident in a concluding suggestion made by the prominent senator from Kentucky, Henry Clay. He proposed that "inquiry should be made by the committee whether" the Saints' memorial "is a matter of grievance, and, if it is, whether Congress has any power of redress."[36] After Clay's proposal, the Senate agreed to lay the Saints' petition "on the table . . . with the understanding that it would be called up at an early day."[37]

A few weeks later, the Senate moved to refer the Saints' memorial to the Judiciary Committee.[38] The next day, the senators engaged in a protracted debate over abolition petitions and the right to petition itself. While Clay and Daniel Webster championed "the right," Calhoun demurred, insisting that "it was among the least important." Calhoun asserted that "there could be no local grievance but what could be reached by" suffrage and the right of instruction, by which a state legislature could direct their senator to vote a certain way.[39] New Hampshire's Henry Hubbard described the issue as one of jurisdiction, noting that "it seldom occurs (and perhaps has never occurred) that a petition is presented here which so mistakes its proper direction as to ask relief of this Government in matters respecting which the petitioner's State Government *alone* possessed the power to grant relief." Consequently, he explained, the "right of petition is the most limited of popular and political righ[t]s."[40] This discussion bore the marks of pro-slavery politics, which had placed severe restraints on the right to petition.

On 17 February, the Saints' petition again shared space with abolition petitions on the Senate floor. After the Senate tabled the latter, Young "submitted additional documents in relation" to the Saints' petition.[41] A few days later, the Judiciary Committee heard testimony from Elias Higbee, Senator Linn, and others; a few weeks later, on 4 March, the members of the committee issued their opinion.[42] They determined "that the case presented . . . is not such a one as will justify or authorize any interposition by this Government." They instructed the petitioners to "apply to the justice and magnanimity of . . . Missouri. . . . It can never be presumed," the committee continued, "that a State either wants the power, or lacks the disposition, to redress the wrongs of its own citizens."[43] These statements, which aligned perfectly with those made by Senator Hubbard, show that debates over slavery shaped the questions asked about the Saints' petition and furnished politicians with the language to argue that the Saints' case fell outside the realm of federal jurisdiction. Weeks later, the Senate approved the committee's resolution.[44]

When Higbee learned of the decision, he passed it on to Smith, who had returned to Illinois. "We have made our last appeal to all earthly tribunals," Higbee wrote, and we "have a right now which we could not heretofore so fully claim— That is of asking God for redress & redemption."[45] Days before Higbee's letter arrived, Smith publicly reported on his DC trip and warned of the justice that would befall the nation if it failed to offer redress.[46] News of the Senate's decision fueled his contempt.[47] During an April conference, the Saints agreed that in "turning a deaf ear," Congress called "down upon their heads, the righteous judgments of an offended God."[48] In a discourse given a few months later, Smith presented an apocalyptic vision in which God would "cast a vot[e] against van buren" and the nation.[49] When forces beyond his control mitigated efforts to obtain redress, Smith added them to the revealed reckoning of God's justice. The human effort to prepare the land for the Lord's harvest had neared completion.

During the 1840s, the Saints continued to petition for redress.[50] In November 1843 (the same month another doomed memorial was written to Congress), Smith wrote to five prospective presidential candidates, including Calhoun, asking whether they would provide redress if they were elected.[51] In his response, Calhoun wrote that the question "does not come within the Jurisdiction of the Federal Government."[52] A month later, Smith fired back. Mocking the champion of state sovereignty, he asked, "What think ye of *imperium in imperio*?" Showing little compunction at this stage, Smith warned that if the federal government lacked restorative power, "God will come out of his hiding place and vex this nation with a sore vexation."[53]

Most immediately, the Saints' failure to obtain redress generated Smith's 1844 presidential campaign, but the failed petitioning also shaped the simultaneous move to form a new government and a new constitution.[54] On 11 March, Smith organized the Council of Fifty, understood to be the political kingdom of God, and the council began discussing the creation of "a constitution."[55] Smith's faith in government had long since expired and his belief in the sacralized right to petition had been all but extinguished. Now his faith in the Founders' Constitution waned. The nature of the Saints' constitutionalism allowed for this development. The fact that their constitutional reverence rested on a revelation implied that their ultimate faith in law and justice went beyond the document produced by inspiration to the source of the inspiration itself. The Saints had adopted and advanced a view of the Constitution as a sacred text, but their understanding of inspiration and revelation as continual freed them from seeing the Constitution as a final legal arbiter. This version of constitutional reverence allowed Smith to set the Constitution aside when it proved insufficient.

On 18 April, Willard Richards presented the draft of a new constitution. The first line echoed the United States Constitution before making a quick departure: "We, the people of the Kingdom of God, knowing that all power emanates from God."[56] This reflected the council's belief that the time had come when "the supreme law of the land shall be the word of

Jehovah."[57] The new constitution also described the prophet as the Lord's mouthpiece. This emphasis anticipated Smith's instruction, given just a week later, to "let the constitution alone." In the voice of the Lord, Smith told the council, "yea are my constitution."[58] The same source that had encouraged constitutional reverence now interrupted the council's efforts to create a new constitution; all of these events indicated the Saints' ultimate allegiance to God.

On the surface, the developments during the spring of 1844 seemed to be a clear departure from the earlier emphasis on constitutional appeals. But the move to petition God himself had been commanded in the very revelation that sacralized that right. Indeed, the turn to God as ultimate legislator had been anticipated even before 1833. In a January 1831 revelation, the Lord had stated, "In time ye shall have no King nor Ruler for I will be your King . . . & ye shall be a free People & ye shall have no laws but my laws for I am your Law giver."[59] By March 1844, it seemed that the time had arrived for the Lord to fulfill this millennial promise.

NOTES

1. Revelation, 16–17 December 1833 [D&C 101], in Gerrit J. Dirkmaat, Brent M. Rogers, Grant Underwood, Robert J. Woodford, and William G. Hartley, eds., *Documents, Volume 3: February 1833–March 1834*, vol. 3 of the Documents series of *The Joseph Smith Papers (JSP)*, ed. Ronald K. Esplin and Matthew J. Grow (Salt Lake City: Church Historian's Press, 2014), 386–97.

2. *JSP*, D3:396.

3. Jonathan Gienapp, *The Second Creation: Fixing the American Constitution in the Founding Era* (Cambridge, MA: The Belknap Press of Harvard University Press, 2018).

4. See, for example, Revelation, 20 July 1831 [D&C 57], in Matthew C. Godfrey, Mark Ashurst-McGee, Grant Underwood, Robert J. Woodford, and William G. Hartley, eds., *Documents, Volume 2: July 1831–January 1833*, vol. 2 of the Documents series of *The Joseph Smith Papers*, ed. Dean C. Jessee, Ronald K. Esplin, and Richard Lyman Bushman (Salt Lake City: Church Historian's Press, 2013), 5–12.

5. Revelation, 6 August 1833 [D&C 98:5], in *JSP*, D3:224.

6. Joseph Smith to Church Leaders in Jackson County, Missouri, 18 August 1833, in *JSP*, D3:267.

7. "To His Excellency, Daniel Dunklin," *Evening and Morning Star* 2 (December 1833): 114–15.

8. Daniel Dunklin, Jefferson City, MO, to W. W. Phelps et al., Independence, MO, 19 October 1833, William W. Phelps, Collection of Missouri Documents, CHL.

9. See W. T. Wood et al., Independence, MO, to W. W. Phelps, et al., 28 October 1833, William W. Phelps, Collection of Missouri Documents, CHL; and W. W. Phelps, to Mssrs. Wood, Rees, Doniphan, and Atchison, 30 October 1833, William W. Phelps, Collection of Missouri Documents, CHL.

10. William W. Phelps et al., Clay Co., MO, to Daniel Dunklin, 6 December 1833, copy, William W. Phelps, Collection of Missouri Documents, CHL.

11. Joseph Smith to Edward Partridge, 10 December 1833, in *JSP*, D3:372.

12. Joseph Smith to Edward Partridge, 10 December 1833, in *JSP*, D3:379.

13. Revelation, 16–17 December 1833, in *JSP*, D3:389 [D&C 101:1–6].

14. Revelation, 16–17 December 1833, in *JSP*, D3:390 [D&C 101:1–6].

15. Revelation, 16–17 December 1833, in *JSP*, D3:395 [D&C 101:76–80].

16. See Luke 18:1–8.

17. Revelation, 16–17 December 1833, in *JSP*, D3:395–96, [D&C 101:81–89].

18. Daniel Dunklin, Jefferson City, MO, to W. W. Phelps et al., 4 February 1834, William W. Phelps, Collection of Missouri Documents, CHL.

19. Edward Partridge et al., Petition to Andrew Jackson, 10 April 1834, William W. Phelps, Collection of Missouri Documents, CHL. Phelps sent the same petition to Missouri Senator Thomas Hart Benton. W. W. Phelps to Thomas H. Benton, 10 April 1834, William W. Phelps, Collection of Missouri Documents, CHL.

20. Lewis Cass to A. S. Gilbert et al., 2 May 1834, William W. Phelps, Collection of Missouri Documents, CHL.

21. "Communicated," *The Evening and the Morning Star* 2 (May 1834), 160.

22. Bertram Wyatt-Brown, "The Abolitionists' Postal Campaign of 1835," *Journal of Negro History* 50 (October 1965): 227–38.

23. Susan Wyly-Jones, "The 1835 Anti-Abolition Meetings in the South: A New Look at the Controversy over the Abolition Postal Campaign," *Civil War History* 47, no. 4 (2001): 289–309. On the Southern response, see Stephen M. Feldman, *Free Expression and Democracy in America: A History* (Chicago: University of Chicago Press, 2008), 129–32.

24. See, for example, "The Outrage in Jackson County, Missouri," *Evening and Morning Star* 2 (January 1834), 241–44; Declaration on Government and Law, circa August 1835 [D&C 134:12], in Matthew C. Godfrey, Brenden W. Rensink, Alex D. Smith, Max H Parkin, and Alexander L. Baugh, eds.,

Documents, Volume 4: April 1834–September 1835, vol. 4 of the Documents series of *The Joseph Smith Papers*, ed. Ronald K. Esplin and Matthew J. Grow (Salt Lake City: Church Historian's Press, 2016), 484 [D&C 134:12]; [Oliver Cowdery,] "Abolition," *Northern Times*, 9 October 1835, 2; Joseph Smith to Oliver Cowdery, circa 9 April 1836, in Brent M. Rogers, Elizabeth A. Kuehn, Christian K. Heimburger, Max H Parkin, Alexander L. Baugh, and Steven C. Harper, eds., *Documents, Volume 5: October 1835–January 1838*, vol. 5 of the Documents series of *The Joseph Smith Papers*, ed. Ronald K. Esplin, Matthew J. Grow, and Matthew C. Godfrey (Salt Lake City: Church Historian's Press, 2017), 231–43; Warren Parrish, "For the Messenger and Advocate," *LDS Messenger and Advocate*, April 1836, 2:295–96; and "The Abolitionists," *Messenger and Advocate*, Apr. 1836, 2:299–301. On the broader context and racial implications of these publications, see W. Paul Reeve, *Religion of a Different Color: Race and the Mormon Struggle for Whiteness* (New York: Oxford University Press, 2015), 122–26. On Latter-day Saint antislavery and anti-abolitionism, see Newell G. Bringhurst, *Saints, Slaves, and Blacks: The Changing Place of Black People Within Mormonism* (Westport, CT: Greenwood Press, 1981), 15–22.

25. See William Lee Miller, *Arguing about Slavery: The Great Battle in the United States Congress* (New York: Knopf, 1995); and Stephen M. Feldman, *Free Expression and Democracy*, 133–39.

26. Joseph Smith to Edward Partridge and the Church, circa 22 March 1839, in Mark Ashurst-McGee, David W. Grua, Elizabeth Kuehn, Alexander L. Baugh, and Brenden W. Rensink, eds., *Documents, Volume 6: February 1838–August 1839*, vol. 6 of the Documents series of *The Joseph Smith Papers*, ed. Ronald K. Esplin, Matthew J. Grow, and Matthew C. Godfrey (Salt Lake City: Church Historian's Press, 2017), 343. See also Joseph Smith to Emma Smith, 21 March 1839, in *JSP*, D6:323.

27. Smith to Partridge and the Church, in *JSP*, D6:343.

28. Smith to Partridge and the Church, in *JSP*, D6:345.

29. See Historical Introduction to Promissory Note to John Brassfield, 16 April 1839, in *JSP*, D6:366–67.

30. See Minutes, 4–5 May 1839, in *JSP*, D6:383–88; and Joseph Smith, Bill of Damages, 4 June 1839, in *JSP*, D6:436.

31. For an overview of the trip, see Volume Introduction, in Matthew C. Godfrey, Spencer W. McBride, Alex D. Smith, and Christopher James Blythe, eds., *Documents, Volume 7: September 1839–January 1841*, vol. 7 of the Documents series of *The Joseph Smith Papers*, ed. Ronald K. Esplin, Matthew J. Grow, and Matthew C. Godfrey (Salt Lake City: Church Historian's Press, 2018), xxiv–xxviii.

32. Letter to Hyrum Smith and Nauvoo High Council, 5 December 1839, in *JSP*, D7:70.

33. Memorial to the United States Senate and House of Representatives, circa 30 October 1839–27 January 1840, in *JSP*, D7:138–74.

34. Cong. Globe, 26th Cong., 1st Sess. 150–51 (1840).

35. "Twenty-Sixth Congress," *Daily National Intelligencer*, 29 January 1840, 2.

36. "Twenty-Sixth Congress," 2.

37. Cong. Globe, 26th Cong., 1st Sess., 149.

38. Cong. Globe, 26th Cong., 1st Sess., 149, 185.

39. Cong. Globe, 26th Cong., 1st Sess., 149, 186–87.

40. Cong. Globe, 26th Cong., 1st Sess., 149, 195–96; emphasis in original.

41. Senate Journal, 26th Cong., 1st Sess., 179 (17 February 1840).

42. Cong. Globe, 26th Cong., 1st Sess., 232.

43. Appendix: Report of the United States Senate Committee on the Judiciary, 4 March 1840, in *JSP*, D7:543.

44. Senate Journal, 26th Cong., 1st Sess., 23 March 1840, 259–60.

45. Letter from Elias Higbee, 26 February 1840, in *JSP*, D7:199–200.

46. See Historical Introduction to Discourse, 1 March 1840, in *JSP*, D7:201.

47. Letter from Elias Higbee, 24 March 1840, in *JSP*, D7:232–34.

48. Minutes and Discourse, 6–8 April 1840, in *JSP*, D7:246–50.

49. Discourse, circa 19 July 1840, in *JSP*, D7:337.

50. The Saints sent three more redress petitions to Congress, one in 1840, another in 1842, and one more in 1844. All of these petitions failed. See Clark V. Johnson, ed., *Mormon Redress Petitions: Documents of the 1833–1838 Missouri Conflict* (Provo, UT: Religious Studies Center, Brigham Young University, 1992), 393–614.

51. Letter to Martin Van Buren, Henry Clay et al., 4 November 1843, Joseph Smith Collection, CHL. Smith also wrote Richard M. Johnson, who had served as Van Buren's vice president.

52. John C. Calhoun to Joseph Smith, 2 December 1843, Joseph Smith Collection, CHL. See also Lewis Cass to Joseph Smith, 9 December 1843, Joseph Smith Collection, CHL; and Henry Clay to Joseph Smith, 15 November 1843, Joseph Smith Collection, CHL.

53. Joseph Smith to John C. Calhoun, 2 January 1844, Joseph Smith Collection, CHL. On this interaction, see James B. Allen, "Joseph Smith vs. John C. Calhoun: The States' Right Dilemma and Early Mormon History," in *Joseph Smith Jr.: Reappraisals after Two Centuries*, ed. Reid L. Neilson and Terryl L. Givens (New York: Oxford University Press, 2009), 73–90. See also Brent M.

Rogers, *Unpopular Sovereignty: Mormons and the Federal Management of Early Utah Territory* (Lincoln: University of Nebraska Press, 2017), 25–28.

54. *General Smith's Views of the Powers and Policy of the Government of the United States* (Nauvoo, IL: John Taylor, printer, 1844).

55. Council of Fifty, "Record," 11 March 1844, in Matthew J. Grow, Ronald K. Esplin, Mark Ashurst-McGee, Gerrit J. Dirkmaat, and Jeffrey D. Mahas, eds., *Administrative Records, Volume 1: Council of Fifty Minutes, March 1844–January 1846*, vol. 1 of the Administrative Record series of *The Joseph Smith Papers*, ed. Roland K. Esplin, Matthew J. Grow, and Matthew C. Godfrey (Salt Lake City: Church Historian's Press, 2016), 40, 42.

56. Council of Fifty, "Record," 18 April 1844, in *JSP*, CFM:110.

57. Council of Fifty, "Record," 18 April 1844, in *JSP*, CFM:112.

58. Council of Fifty, "Record," 25 April 1844, in *JSP*, CFM:136, 137.

59. Revelation, 2 January 1831 [D&C 38], in Michael Hubbard MacKay, Gerrit J. Dirkmaat, Grant Underwood, Robert J. Woodford, and William G. Hartley, eds., *Documents, Volume 1: July 1828–June 1831*, vol. 1 of the Documents series of *The Joseph Smith Papers*, ed. Dean C. Jessee, Ronald K. Esplin, Richard Lyman Bushman, and Matthew J. Grow (Salt Lake City: Church Historian's Press, 2013), 231–32.

President James K. Polk (1795–1849). Library of Congress.

"OBLITERATED FROM THE FACE OF THE EARTH": LATTER-DAY SAINT FLIGHT AND EXPULSION

GERRIT DIRKMAAT

Gerrit Dirkmaat is an associate professor of Church history and doctrine at Brigham Young University.

As President James Polk waited for his next visitor on 3 June 1846, the White House was abuzz with activity. Only three weeks earlier, the United States had declared war on the vast, sprawling nation of Mexico, and Polk had held nearly constant meetings with his cabinet, generals, politicians, and office seekers. While many expansionists hailed the outbreak of the war, critics of the jingoistic decisions that led to the outbreak abounded. Nevertheless, a week earlier Polk had made the decision to make Northern Mexico the primary objective for the first stages of the war and was deep into planning the expedition that would invade the enormous territory. It was an audacious gamble, fraught with logistical and political difficulties. Thus, President Polk had determined to meet with his next visitor, although their obscure meeting has generally been lost to history.[1]

Polk was meeting with Jesse Little, an elder from The Church of Jesus Christ of Latter-day Saints who presided over the missionary work for the Church in the eastern United States. Stationed as he was in Washington, DC, Little was also the de facto liaison for the Church with the U.S. government. Brigham Young sent Little instructions to meet with federal officials over various matters and to secure some kind of aid for the suffering Saints, if possible. For his part, Little—like his predecessor Samuel Brannan—not only kept Young apprised of missionary and public sentiment efforts in the nation's capital and the East Coast generally, but also provided a watchful eye on the actions of the federal government and its officials in relation to the Latter-day Saints.

The actions of federal officials in Washington, including senators, cabinet members, members of the House of Representatives, and President James Polk himself, played a central role in the Latter-day Saint expulsion from the United States and in the creation of Latter-day Saint feelings of animosity toward the federal government for decades afterward. The federal government was often regarded as being apathetic and uninterested in the Latter-day Saint plight since mobs continued to commit acts of violence and local Illinois residents and newspapers demanded the "extermination" of the Saints from the state, even after the murders of Joseph and Hyrum Smith. Thus the federal story in the expulsion of the Saints—one of assumed inaction—is rarely considered, much less examined and told. It is often believed that the Saints were fleeing localized, though indefatigable and cruel, persecution. In reality, American foreign policy emanating from the nation's capital looms large over the actions of both the Latter-day Saints and the United States government.

Jesse Little's meeting with President Polk just after the outbreak of war could not have been more impactful on the relationship between the nation and the Saints. After assuring Little that he believed the Latter-day Saints now fleeing the United States were "true American citizens," President Polk asked if "500 or more of the Mormons now on their way to [Mexican] California would be willing" to volunteer to fight for the United States.[2]

For Little, the presidential request was a sweet vindication long in coming. After years of ignoring Latter-day Saint persecution and dismissing the Saints' petitions for redress for the personal and property crimes perpetrated against them in Missouri, after the lack of federal intervention in the decision to drive the Saints from Illinois, and after reports that the U.S. Army would in fact attempt to prevent them from leaving the nation

President James K. Polk in 1844. Library of Congress.

to Mexico, Little thought the president was now expressing regret for the wrongs committed against the Saints.

In actuality, President Polk's request for the Mormon Battalion was not an admission of past wrongdoing on the part of the nation but a culmination of the national political machinations that had driven the Saints from the country in the first place. While Little wrote an elated letter to Brigham Young explaining that the Latter-day Saints had finally received federal protection and acceptance, James Polk wrote his true feelings in his diary. He did not trust the Latter-day Saints at all. He had only met with Little and proposed the battalion to "prevent them from assuming a hostile attitude toward the U.S. after their arrival in [Mexican] California." Making the point more clear, Polk wrote, "It was with the view to prevent this singular sect from becoming hostile to the U.S. that I held the conference with Mr. Little, and with the same view I am to see him again tomorrow."[3]

Polk's duplicity, misrepresenting his purposes for calling hundreds of men into the war wholly apart from military necessity, did not occur in a vacuum. For the Latter-day Saints, years of persecution and political ineptitude culminated in their decision to abandon the United States.

For a few years after the establishment of Nauvoo, Joseph Smith continued to hope that Americans would come to at least tolerate the Latter-day Saints. The Nauvoo Charter granted liberal municipal powers, including a city militia, that helped the Saints to feel safer from the type of lawless abuses of power that had led to so much blood and terror in Missouri. Yet by late 1843, darkening clouds of antagonism in the press and the public portended a trajectory that could only end negatively. While political considerations fueled conflict from the external community, Joseph's revelations and teachings in Nauvoo also drove internal conflict that led some members to leave the faith. Foremost among those controversial doctrines was the secret practice of plural marriage by Joseph and many of his closest associates. Anathema as polygamy was to American Christianity and social tradition, even some previously devoted believers could not accept the radical new teaching and apostatized from the faith.

Before these controversies, however—even as early as 1841, when the Saints were enjoying relative quiet, peace, and even general political support in Illinois—Joseph Smith was already expressing the fear of a future violent attack on the Saints by their enemies, even using the massacre at Hawn's Mill to explain a revelation from the Lord that had called the Saints to move to communities in the immediate vicinity of Nauvoo to prevent such attacks on far-flung and isolated settlements.[4]

As the 1844 presidential election approached, Joseph Smith sent letters to all of the politicians thought most likely to stand for the presidency at their respective party conventions. The letters were direct:

As the Latter Day Saints . . . have been robbed of an immense amount of property, and endured nameless sufferings by the State of Missouri, and from her borders have been driven by force of arms, contrary to our National Covenants; and as in vain, we have sought redress by all Constitutional, legal and honorable means, in her Courts, her Executive councils, and her Legislative Halls; and as we have petitioned Congress to take cognizance of our sufferings without effect; we have judged it wisdom to address you this communication, and solicit an immediate, specific & candid reply To what will be your rule of action relative to us, as a people.[5]

Senators John C. Calhoun, Lewis Cass, and Henry Clay all replied that while they sympathized with the suffering the Latter-day Saints had experienced, they could not commit to help the Latter-day Saints if they were to become president. Henry Clay's letter stung Joseph most of all, as Joseph had already gone on record in an interview a few months earlier that he intended to vote for the Kentucky senator.[6] While Clay expressed regret for the Latter-day Saint difficulties, he flatly stated, "I can enter into no engagements, make no promises, give no pledges, to any particular portion of the people of the U. States."[7]

With most of the potential future presidents' on-record refusals to help the Saints in their decade-long quest for redress of grievances for stolen land, vicious assaults, and outright murders in Missouri, Joseph Smith made two fateful decisions. First, he declared his own presidential candidacy, adopting a platform that attempted to bridge the partisan chasm between Democrats and Whigs on several issues. While much of his platform was practical, moderate, and widely appealing, other positions were radical in the political world of the 1840s. Having had personal experience with the horrendous conditions of prisoners in the hellish purgatory of Liberty Jail, Joseph advocated for prison reform, urging Americans, "Petition your state legislatures to pardon every convict in their several penitentiaries: blessing them as they go, and saying to them in the name of the Lord, go thy way and sin no more."[8]

More radical still were the opening lines of his presidential platform. In a day and age when both major parties avoided the topic of slavery and its expansion as much as possible, Joseph Smith threw down the gauntlet.

He mocked the fact that the United States was supposedly a land patterned after the Declaration of Independence, in which "all men are created equal . . . but at the same time, some two or three millions of people are held as slaves for life, because the spirit in them is covered with a darker skin than ours." He proceeded to argue that the government should speedily purchase every slave from their masters so the dreadful institution would be defunct in six years.[9]

While Joseph Smith hoped his candidacy would bring attention to the Latter-day Saint cause and to the deficiencies of the federal government when it came to protecting minority rights, he had also begun to prepare for a much more practical and long-term solution to the incessant injustice they believed had been visited upon them by local, state, and federal politicians. By early 1844, Joseph had made the decision that the Latter-day Saints would need to abandon the United States.

Shortly after announcing his candidacy, Joseph Smith's diary recorded, "I instructed the 12 to send out a delegation & investigate the locations of California and Oregon to find a good location where we can remove after the Temple is completed & build a city in a day and have a government of our own." While publicly he was campaigning to become the chief executive of the United States, privately he was preparing to leave the United States altogether, convinced that the rights of his despised religious minority could not be protected in the face of overwhelming persecution and political pusillanimity and corruption.[10]

As his journal entry indicated, Joseph was strongly contemplating a move to the vast reaches of Mexican California, which in 1844 included all of the present states of California, Nevada, Utah, Arizona, and parts of Colorado and Wyoming. Some followers suggested that the Saints move to the Republic of Texas, which had won its independence from Mexico nearly a decade earlier. Texas had maintained a tenuous existence in the face of Mexican refusal to honor Texan independence, culminating in multiple invasions of Texas by Mexican forces in the early 1840s. While Texas president Sam Houston was fervently trying to secure American annexation of Texas to stave off an eventual Mexican reassertion of control, his efforts had thus far been met with marked political opposition, both from those who refused to expand the slaveholding territory of the United

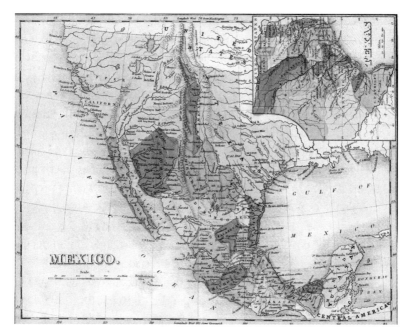

Map of Mexico and Texas, 1844. David Rumsey Map Collection.

States, and others who held no moral compunctions about slavery but understood that the annexation of Texas (which Mexico still claimed as part of its own nation) would surely lead to war.[11]

In March 1844, Joseph Smith formed a secretive council that would come to be known as the Council of Fifty. Its purpose was to seek out a place—in either Texas, Mexico, or the Oregon Territory—for the Saints to escape the persecuting sovereignty of the United States and establish their own nation where they were free to practice their religion. The council "agreed to look to some place where we can go and establish a Theocracy either in Texas or Oregon or somewhere in California."[12]

The council dispatched Lucian Woodworth to travel the nearly one thousand miles to the Republic of Texas to negotiate with President Sam Houston.[13] Surprisingly, though he was initially hesitant, Houston embraced the idea of Latter-day Saint settlement in the disputed territory between Texas and their archnemesis, Mexico. Indeed, he would write to prominent Latter-day Saint and former U.S. Army officer James Arlington

Bennet to persuade the Saints to move to Texas. Understanding both the tortured past of the Latter-day Saints in the United States and their resultant fears of unprincipled or ineffective sovereignty, Houston insisted that "if the Saints were in Texas then their religious & Civil rights should have the most ample protection." While antagonists decried the specter of Latter-day Saint military power embodied in the Nauvoo Legion, Houston explained that "he would receive the 'Mormon Legion' in Texas as armed Emigrants with open Arms." Determined to eliminate the fear of continued religious persecution and oppression, Houston flatly asserted, "I am no bigot."[14]

While the option of moving to the Republic of Texas was taken very seriously, the men in the Council of Fifty simultaneously discussed and prepared for the possibility of moving to the Mexican lands containing the Rocky Mountains. Part of their efforts were directed at drafting a new constitution to govern them in the kingdom they intended to set up wherever they eventually went. The daunting task of drafting a constitution for the kingdom of God weighed heavily on them, and Joseph Smith counseled them to "get knowledge, search the laws of nations and get all the information they can." They were indeed planning to set up a special type of theocracy, one in which the "people get the voice of God and then acknowledge it, and see it executed."[15]

Though it would be the kingdom of God, this theocracy would have religious freedom as a fundamental component—unlike the failed protections proffered by U.S. law. Joseph Smith told the men of the council, "We act upon the broad and liberal principal that all men have equal rights, and ought to be respected, and that every man has the privilege in this organization of choosing for himself voluntarily his God, and what he pleases for his religion." Joseph reaffirmed a belief that he had expressed on several occasions previously: he was not afraid of people being drawn away to another religious truth because the Church had the greatest light and "every man will embrace the greatest light." He continued, "God cannot save or damn a man only on the principle that every man acts, chooses and worships for himself; hence the importance of thrusting from us every spirit of bigotry and intollerance towards a mans religious sentiments, that spirit which has drenched the earth with blood." Indeed, Joseph asserted that it was "the inalienable fight of man" to think and worship as he pleases. Thoughtfully, he taught, "We must not despise a man on account of infirmity. We ought to love a man more for his infirmity."[16]

Joseph Smith wanted the Council of Fifty to understand that as they undertook the task of creating a new nation, their love for others was not to be constrained on the basis of whether or not someone embraced the Church and joined it. "Let us from henceforth drive from us every species of intollerance," Joseph declared, "When I have used every means in my power to exalt a mans mind, and have taught him righteous principles to no effect [and] he is still inclined in his darkness, yet the same principles of liberty and charity would ever be manifested by me as though he embraced [the gospel]." Joseph insisted that any man that will "stand by his friends, he is my friend." And with a dark allusion to his own rapidly approaching death, he added, "The only thing I am afraid of is, that I will not live long enough to enjoy the society of these my friends as long as I want to."[17]

Whatever Joseph Smith's detractors thought of him, on the point that his death was rapidly approaching, Joseph did indeed prove to be prophetic. As plans to leave the country continued to unfold, events rapidly spiraled out of control. Several opponents had rejected his more radical teachings on plural marriage and the idea that God had progressed to become God and aired their grievances, mincing no words, in the *Nauvoo Expositor*. Joseph Smith acted on an order from the Nauvoo city council to have the paper destroyed, declaring it a public nuisance. The Saints' brazen destruction of the *Expositor* caused long-simmering antagonisms directed at the Saints to explode violently into a public crisis.

As demands were made for Joseph and Hyrum Smith to surrender themselves to be tried outside of Nauvoo, Joseph Smith made one last appeal to the president of the United States, John Tyler. "Sir," Joseph appealed, "I am sorry to say that the State of Missouri, not contented with robbing, driving, and murdering many of the Latter day Saints, are now joining the mob of this state for the purpose of the 'utter extermination of the Mormons." Joseph implored of Tyler, "Will you render that protection which the constitution guarantees . . . and save the innocent and oppressed from such horrid persecution?"[18] What issued from Washington on this occasion, as with Joseph Smith's previous appeals, was a deafening silence.

Two days later, preparing to surrender himself to the governor's forces despite his premonitions that he and the others could not be protected by them, Joseph Smith reportedly gave his last public sermon, blessing the Nauvoo Legion and declaring, "You will gather many people into the fastness of the Rocky Mountains."[19]

The murder of the Smiths in the mob attack on Carthage Jail five days later devastated the Latter-day Saints. In their grief, and with even more evidence that neither the state of Illinois nor the U.S. government would or could intervene to protect them from the growing calls for mob violence and outright murder, Church leaders planned to bring Joseph Smith's intended abandonment of the United States to fruition. The new leader of the Church, Brigham Young, the President of the Quorum of the Twelve Apostles, responded indignantly to the continued persecution of the Saints, declaring, "The nation has severed us from them in every respect, and made us a distinct nation just as much as the Lamanites, and it is my prayer that we may soon find a place where we can have a home and live in peace according to the Law of God."[20] A few months later, as the Council of Fifty continued to prepare for an exodus from the United States, Young further explained, "The gentiles have rejected the gospel; they have killed the prophets, and those who have not taken an active part in the murder all rejoice in it and say amen to it, and that is saying that they are willing the blood of the prophets should be shed. The gentiles have rejected the gospel, and where shall we go to preach. We cannot go any where but to the house of Israel. We cant get salvation without it. We cant get salvation any where else."[21] In their view, the institutions of the United States had spectacularly failed the Saints, a conclusion that the increasing hostility and mob violence of 1845, combined with the repeal of the Nauvoo City Charter, further reinforced. The Saints, Young asserted, needed to "get out of the jurisdiction of the United States."[22]

Increasingly, the U.S. government was coming to be seen by the Saints as not just an incompetent steward, clumsily inept at protecting its citizens from lawlessness, but rather as an active participant in persecuting the Saints and driving them from the nation. By March 1845, Brigham Young concluded, "If we can get one hundred miles beyond the jurisdiction of the United States we are safe, for the present, and that is all we ask, . . . we want to get between some of those Mountains where we can fortify ourselves and erect the standard of liberty on one of the highest mountains we can find." Paradoxically for this native-born American, liberty could only be found outside of the "Land of the Free."[23]

Apostle John Taylor, his body permanently scarified by the mobocratic bullets that had nearly killed him in Carthage Jail as Joseph and Hyrum Smith were murdered, had no more patience with the supposedly just political institutions of the United States, "We know we have no more justice here . . . than we could get at the gates of hell." The Saints had been "excluded from all our rights as other citizens" and Taylor, like Young, wanted to leave the nation and find a place where they could "dwell in peace, and have our own laws."[24]

The annexation of the Republic of Texas to the United States in early 1845 ended Latter-day Saint contemplations of a possible removal there. The Saints had already learned by sad experience that their rights could not be protected inside the sovereignty of the United States. If they were to have freedom, they would need to leave the United States.

Throughout 1845, while Brigham Young was dealing with the realities of real or threatened mob violence in Illinois, he was also continually receiving reports from Washington that the federal government would intervene on the side of their enemies, prevent them from leaving the nation, and arrest the leaders of the Church for various purported crimes. One chilling report in particular from the president of the Eastern States Mission and Jesse Little's predecessor, Samuel Brannan, spurred this belief. Brannan had written to Young from Washington, DC, to explain that the "secretary of war and other members of the cabinet were laying plans" to stop the Latter-day Saints from moving to the Rocky Mountains of Mexican California. "They say," Brannan gravely wrote, "it will not do to let the Mormons go to California nor Oregon, neither will it do to let them tarry in the states, and they must be obliterated from the face of the earth."[25]

The Latter-day Saints demonstrated their displeasure at the apparently bigoted treatment they continued to receive in the Land of Liberty by boycotting the Fourth of July in 1845. Irene Haskell, a young married

Latter-day Saint in Nauvoo, bitterly reflected to her parents her personal protest, "The fourth of July is just past. I suppose there were balls, tea-parties and the like in the east, but here there were nothing of the kind. The Mormons think the liberty and independence of the Unites States has been too long trampled upon to be celebrated."[26] Such attempts to express frustration at the injustice inflicted upon them seemed to only bolster the negative opinions that antagonists already held against the Latter-day Saints. One Pennsylvania newspaper took this as proof of Latter-day Saint perfidy, writing that in Nauvoo, "that city of fanatics . . . no notice was taken" of the Fourth of July at all. The writer failed to inform his readers that the Latter-day Saints had boisterously celebrated the holiday in previous years in Nauvoo.[27]

By October 1845, violence was no longer threatened but had become reality. One journalist explained that the local mobs had been "out burning the Mormon houses, barns, stacks, etc. In this war of extermination, they include not only the Mormons, but all who are suspected of favoring the Mormon cause or harboring Mormons about them." Indeed, these American citizens had "determined to drive the Mormons out of the county" whether or not they were individually guilty of any crimes in a type of ethnic cleansing the Saints had already experienced in Missouri.[28] This renewed violence even resulted in the murder of Edmund Durfee, a Latter-day Saint living in the Yelrome (Morely) settlement. In 1831 Durfee had become one of the earliest converts to the Church and had persisted through the apostasies of Kirtland and the mobs and murders in Missouri only to be slaughtered in the Latter-day Saint settlement not far from Nauvoo, just months before the Saints had intended to leave. Durfee's story after joining the religion—persecution culminating in murder—seemed a fitting representation of the wider story arc of Latter-day Saints in the United States.

The end of the Saints' stay in Nauvoo came faster than Brigham Young had anticipated. They had agreed with local antagonists and state leaders to leave Nauvoo in the spring and to try to maintain a fragile and one-sided peace. But Governor Thomas Ford of Illinois, attempting to hasten the Latter-day Saint exodus, fabricated a lie so powerful in its implications that hundreds would indirectly die as a result. Ford indicated to Latter-day

Saint leaders that he had learned that U.S. government forces were headed for Nauvoo with the intent of preventing the Saints from leaving the United States for the Mexican territory that they had determined to settle in. An army was indeed en route, he claimed. It awaited only the breakup of the ice on the Mississippi River so that it could steam upstream from Saint Louis and intercept the Saints.[29] In his later book, Ford boasted about the duplicity that would send women and children streaming across a frozen river and into the Iowa wilderness, not wholly prepared, as all of the Latter-day Saints feared a repeat of the assaults, murders, and atrocities that had accompanied military intervention in Missouri. Thinking history would view him favorably for his sagacious plan, Ford claimed his blood-stained credit: "With a view to hasten their removal they were made to believe that the President would order the regular army to Nauvoo as soon as the navigation opened in the spring. This had the desired effect; the twelve, with about two thousand of their followers immediately crossed the Mississippi before the breaking up of the ice."[30]

Thus, as the Latter-day Saints struggled across Iowa while burying dozens along the way, they believed not only that their nation had refused to intervene on their behalf as Joseph Smith had so often begged but that their erstwhile nation was also actively taking a part in their attempted extermination. They believed that the halls of Washington were not just silent but were thundering with even greater threats of violence and persecution.

While President James K. Polk was not guilty of the actions Ford had dishonestly imputed to him, he did indeed see the Saints as less-than-American citizens and as a possible impediment to his planned invasion of Northern Mexico. His meetings with Jesse Little in early June 1846 and the subsequent enlistment of the Mormon Battalion were indeed part of wider duplicitous political machinations directed against the Latter-day Saints. Although the Saints would reach their new mountain home in the desert high places of Mexico, temporarily free of the corrupt political institutions that had driven them there, their respite was to be short-lived. American imperialism and sovereignty expanded faster than the Latter-day Saints could run from it. Throughout the remainder of the nineteenth century, clashes between the Latter-day Saints and the federal government over issues of individual liberty, voting rights, and religious freedom and sovereignty would characterize a difficult and painful inter-action.[31] The hoped-for kingdom of God—a popular Latter-day Saint the-ocracy—was not realized, and Saints had to look forward to a day when they believed political conflicts, like all other conflicts, would cease with the promised return of the Messiah.

NOTES

1. For an excellent historical investigation of the events and politics surround-ing the conflict, see Amy Greenberg, *A Wicked War: Polk, Clay, Lincoln, and the 1845 Invasion of Mexico* (New York: Knopf, 2012).
2. James K. Polk Papers, Diary, no. 4, 3 June 1846, Library of Congress; and Report of Jesse Carter Little to President Brigham Young and the Council of the Twelve Apostles, 6 July 1846, 22, Manuscript History of the Church (MHC), Church History Library (CHL).
3. Polk, Diary, 3 June 1846, Library of Congress.
4. Brent M. Rogers, Mason K. Allred, Gerrit J. Dirkmaat, and Brett D. Dowdle, eds., *Documents, Volume 8: February–November 1841*, vol. 8 of the Docu-ments series of *The Joseph Smith Papers*, ed. Ronald K. Esplin, Matthew J. Grow, Matthew C. Godfrey, and R. Eric Smith (Salt Lake City: Church His-torian's Press, 2019) 70.
5. Joseph Smith to Presidential Candidates, 4 November 1843, MS 155, CHL.
6. "The Prairies, Nauvoo, Joe Smith, the Temple, the Mormons &c.," *Pittsburgh Weekly Gazette*, 30 August 1845.
7. Henry Clay to Joseph Smith, 15 November 1843, CHL.
8. Joseph Smith, *General Smith's Views of the Powers and Policy of the Govern-ment of the United States* (Nauvoo: John Taylor, 1844), 6.
9. Smith, *General Smith's Views*, 1 and 7.
10. Joseph Smith, Journal, 20 February 1844, MS 155, CHL.
11. For a detailed examination of the events leading up to the annexation of the Republic of Texas, see Joel H. Sibley, *Storm Over Texas: The Annexation Controversy and the Road to the Civil War* (Oxford: Oxford University Press, 2005).
12. Council of Fifty record books 1844–1846 (COFRB), 11 March 1844, MS 30055, box 1, folder 1, CHL. These records have also been published in Mat-thew J., Grow, Ronald K. Esplin, Mark Ashurst-McGee, Gerrit J. Dirkmaat, and Jeffrey D. Mahas, eds., *Council of Fifty, Minutes, March 1844–January*

1846, vol. 1 of the Administrative Records series of *The Joseph Smith Papers*, ed. Ronald K. Esplin, Matthew J. Grow, and Matthew C. Godfrey (Salt Lake City: Church Historian's Press, 2016).

13. For more detail surrounding the Latter-day Saint negotiations with Texas and other areas debated by the Council of Fifty, see "Safely 'Beyond the Limits of the United States': The Mormon Expulsion and US Expansion," *Inventing Destiny: Cultural Explorations of US Expansion*, ed. Jimmy Bryan (Lawrence: University Press of Kansas, September 2019).

14. James Arlington Bennet to Willard Richards and Brigham Young, 4 June 1845, Willard Richards Papers, MS 1490, CHL.

15. COFRB, 11 April 1844.

16. COFRB, 11 April 1844.

17. COFRB, 11 April 1844.

18. Joseph Smith to John Tyler, 20 June 1844, CHL.

19. Joseph Smith, Discourse, 22 June 1844, reported by Alfred Bell and copied into the William Pace notebook, William Pace Papers, CHL.

20. William Clayton, Journal, 26 January 1845, as cited in *JSP*, CFM:258.

21. COFRB, 1 March 1845. Young's reference to the House of Israel is a reflection of his belief that American Indians were decedents of ancient Israelites.

22. COFRB, 11 March 1845.

23. COFRB, 18 March 1845.

24. COFRB, 1 March 1845.

25. Samuel Brannan to Brigham Young, 11 December 1845, MHC, CHL.

26. Irene Haskell, Letter to Parents, 6 July 1845, Irene Haskell Papers, Library of Congress.

27. "Fourth of July in Nauvoo," *Pittsburgh Weekly Gazette*, 16 July 1845.

28. "Mormon War," *Indiana Palladium* (Richmond), 4 October 1845.

29. Thomas Ford to Sheriff J. B. Backenstos, 29 December 1845, CR 1234 1, CHL.

30. Ford, *History of Illinois*, 291.

31. For an excellent historical work describing some of these interactions, see Brent M. Rogers, *Unpopular Sovereignty: Mormons and the Federal Management of Early Utah Territory* (Lincoln: University of Nebraska Press, 2017).

Brigham Young, photo by Charles W. Carter, ca. 1860, negative glass photo collection, Church History Library.

A MISSION TO WASHINGTON: ORSON PRATT'S PUBLISHING OF *THE SEER*

FRED E. WOODS

Fred E. Woods is a professor of Church history and doctrine at Brigham Young University.

The eloquent and systematic spokesperson designated to publicly announce the controversial Latter-day Saint doctrine of polygamy was carefully handpicked by Brigham Young.[1] The brilliant disciple selected, Orson Pratt, was certainly equipped for the job. Born in 1811 in Hartford, New York, Elder Pratt became one of the most influential Apostles in nineteenth-century Latter-day Saint history. What made Pratt an unlikely choice for this assignment was that he had previously fought against the principle, resulting in his Church discipline. However, the Apostle successfully wrestled for a testimony of its certainty, received and practiced the doctrine of plural marriage himself, and became an ardent lifetime defender of its truth.[2] Orson Pratt was multitalented and exceedingly bright, bringing a wealth of experience as a scientist, mathematician, philosopher, avid missionary, and bold Apostle. With Orson having been taught the restored gospel by his brother Parley, the two siblings became great defenders of the faith and prolific writers and pamphleteers.[3]

Following a three-year assignment as the president of the British Mission (1848–51), Pratt returned to Salt Lake City. He was well prepared

Orson Pratt (1811–81), photo by C. R. Savage. Ron Fox.

for the pronouncement and the opposition that would follow because he was proficient and experienced with the pen, having just published sixteen articles in defense of the faith in his role as the editor of the *Latter-day Saints' Millennial Star.*[4]

Pratt's polished announcement of plural marriage was made on 29 August 1852 via a special conference from the tabernacle. There was certainly a keen need to again take up the pen in defense of this controversial doctrine soon referred to in the public world as a relic of barbarism.[5] Young referred to the publication of this controversial practice as "cats and kittens . . . let out of the bag."[6] Soon after the announcement of plural marriage, indispensable polemical periodicals written by Latter-day Saint members and aimed at defending polygamy surfaced in the United States and as far as Sydney, Australia, where elders launched *Zion's Watchman.* The *St. Louis Luminary* emerged in 1854, *The Mormon* at New York City in 1855, and the following year, the *Western Standard* in San Francisco. Yet the first Church polemical publication following the announcement on plural marriage was *The Seer*, whose publisher and able editor was Orson Pratt. Pratt's editorial work was singular because he personally penned all the articles in both volumes of this monthly, sixteen-page, 6½″ x 9½″ periodical. Following the announcement of plural marriage, Pratt was quickly dispatched by President Young to Washington, DC, to defend Church doctrines at the federal city, particularly the Saints' practice of polygamy. Pratt's inauguration of *The Seer*

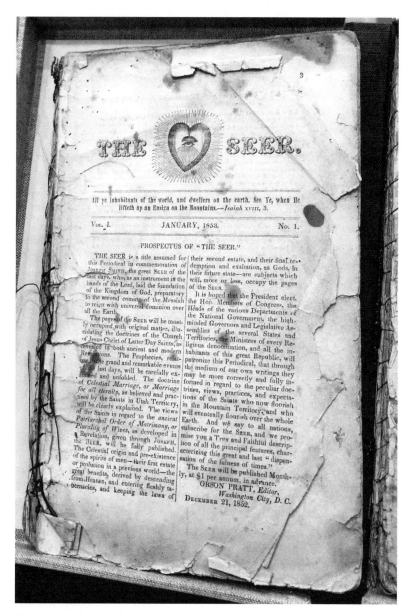

Prospectus, The Seer *1, no. 1 (January 1853). Reid Moon Rare Book Collection.*

at the dawn of 1853 would prove to be "the most detailed defense of the doctrine in LDS literature."[7]

Due to the expenses and lack of reception of this bold paper, there were only twenty issues published monthly between January 1853 and August 1854, and the entire first volume—twelve issues (1853)—dealt almost entirely with the subject of plural marriage, which Elder Pratt referred to as "Celestial Marriage." The prospectus explained the publication's title and outlined the purpose of the newly published *Seer*: "THE SEER is a title assumed for this Periodical in commemoration of Joseph Smith, the great SEER. . . . The pages of the Seer will be mostly occupied with original matter, illucidating [*sic*] the doctrine of the Church of Jesus Christ of Latter Day Saints."[8] Pratt boldly made it known that he was targeting U.S. government officials.

However, his exuberance coupled with the "peculiar doctrines" appear to have been too much for the U.S. officials to handle. Just weeks before, Dr. John M. Bernhisel,[9] Utah's territorial delegate to the House of Representatives, wrote from the capital with private concerns to Brigham Young about what might erupt if there was a work published on the topic of plural marriage: "Brother J. [Jedediah] M. Grant . . . intimated that he would ask Elder Orson Pratt to publish an exposition of the Peculiar Doctrine, but I would beg respectfully to suggest that, in my humble judgment, no such publication had better be made, for the public mind is exceedingly sensitive on that subject, not at all prepared to receive it, and its effect would be decidedly injurious."[10]

Bernhisel, a quiet, gentle man who continually sought to generate light instead of heat, was no doubt particularly concerned with how such a publication might be

John M. Bernhisel (1799–1881). Church History Library.

viewed by federal officials.[11] Notwithstanding, before the end of the month and just one day after Pratt announced the practice of polygamy, Brigham Young informed Bernhisel that there was already a plan to spread the word and that Orson Pratt would be coming to Washington.[12] About two weeks later, President Young again wrote to Bernhisel indicating that although he expected opposition, "truth is mighty and will prevail." Young further noted that he felt Pratt "will doubtless afford you much assistance as well as consolation in the things pertaining to our holy religion."[13]

Before September ended, President Young sent another letter to Bernhisel, who was concerned that the announcement concerning the Saints' public practice of polygamy was alienating the Congress from the Church even further. Young stated, "We are not dependent upon this generation for our position. . . . Let them howl and spend their fury, the Lord is our God and where he is, they cannot come. He is our defense and will sustain his cause against all opposition and . . . will hush every murmur. Therefore, do not let your heart be troubled. . . . God has spoken and his word shall not return unto him void."[14]

By November 1852, news had already reached Washington via the local newspaper, *The Republic*, that Pratt was coming to the nation's capital city.[15] The following month, the *Weekly National Intelligencer* also announced that Pratt, "one of the Twelve," was "destined for Washington where he is to commence the publication of a monthly paper devoted to the dissemination and defense of Mormonism."[16] By year's end, Pratt had arrived and soon he would be known by the local press as "the great expounder of . . . [Latter-day Saint] doctrines" who "boldly advocates this [polygamous] practice."[17] At the same time, public opinion was overwhelmingly negative against Pratt and his defense of plural marriage.

By the close of December, Young again wrote Bernhisel, "Remember me to Bro Orson Pratt, and be assured that we always remember you both, . . . praying my Father in Heaven to preserve and bless you always I remain as ever your friend and brother in Christ."[18] Prayers would certainly be needed. The following day, Pratt wrote President Young to give him an update regarding his reception in Washington as 1852 came to an end. He indicated that he had sent a copy of *The Seer* to major newspapers, as well as several local bookstores and repositories for periodicals, but mentioned that no copies had been sold due to the prejudice surrounding the Saints and publishers being ashamed to associate themselves with the Church and its doctrines. Pratt further noted, "I rented for three months a place for meetings in 'Temperance Hall' where I preach every Wednesday evening and three times every Sabbath. The meetings have been very well attended."[19] About that same time, he wrote, "The power of the Spirit has been upon me, and by the appearance of the people's countenances I should judge that many are convicted of the truth, whether they will ever muster courage enough to obey or not. . . . But do not think I am discouraged, for I do greatly rejoice in the mission you have given me." Pratt continued, "Bro Bernhisel is working in his mild way, and doing much good. . . . I have reasoned much with him & tried to show him that he had nothing to fear—that now was the time, and the best time, for declaring boldly our sentiments in regard to plurality."[20]

The following month, Pratt pushed hard to publish *The Seer*, knowing the Latter-day Saint practice he was defending was viewed widely as loathsome. In feeling the enormity of the task, Pratt meekly wrote President Young, "If you have any counsel for me, I can assure you that it will be gratefully received. I endeavor to live just as faithful as I can. And I call upon the Lord continually to direct me in all things. My heart is joyful in the Lord, though the people reject my testimony, for I feel as though I was doing that which is required at my hands."[21]

A week later, Bernhisel wrote to President Young regarding the stiff opposition Pratt was confronted with, which included a very influential cluster of federal politicians. Bernhisel noted, "Brother Pratt preached the 'doctrine' of celestial marriage &c fully and plainly, and in all its various ramifications, keeping nothing back. The discourse produced quite a sensation in the Hall, a number left, and when he had concluded his audience was reduced about one third." Further, "The promulgation of the doctrine from the pulpit, and the press, has greatly revived prejudice against us, not only in the city and throughout the country, but among the grave Senators and impulsive representatives of the people. Neither priests nor people, or members of any of the branches of the National Government, will condescend to hear or investigate."[22]

The boldness and reception of Pratt's preaching through word and pen are evident from the local Washington press. For example, the *Daily Evening Star* noted, "We learn from the *Seer*, a Mormon weekly oracle just established at Washington by Orson Pratt, an accredited saint from 'Deseret,' that there is a bad time coming for this sinful country—Elder Pratt paints the 'future of America,' as follows: 'The cup of the iniquity of this nation is nearly full; and woe unto them.'"[23]

Notwithstanding, the press circulated knowledge of *The Seer* and Washington's *Daily Union* and even published extracts of the second issue. Under the title "Mormon Matrimony," the *Union* noted, "We believe the public are already apprized of the fact that the disciples of Mormonism have established an 'organ' in this city. The second issue of this remarkable journal . . . makes some strange revelations concerning Mormon matrimony, we propose to submit to our readers a few extracts from the 'Seer' . . . under the supervision or rather inspiration of Elder Orson Pratt."[24]

The following month, Pratt again reported to Young of his tireless, diligent labors in Washington. He told of his good health and concerted efforts to move forward the Lord's work through his writing and preaching, though few responded to his message. Notwithstanding the lack of interest, Pratt said he "never enjoyed greater liberty of speech than I have in these lectures; the Spirit has rested upon me mightily, but the hearts of the people are sealed against the truth; and I marvel exceedingly at their unbelief & hardness of heart." Pratt then explained the demanding labor involved in producing *The Seer*, its intended results, and his belief that Washington was the best place for it to be published:

> Every item yet admitted into the Seer has been new matter of my own composition. It is no small task to write 112 pages of printed matter as large as the Seer. I am confident that I will have to rest my mind a little, and exercise my body more in order to preserve my health. My object has been to hurry out the whole twelve Nos. of the Seer as soon as possible in order that the evidences and arguments in relation to Plurality may be set before the minds of the people before other works shall appear in opposition, and also that they may be led to investigate while the subject is fresh before their minds. I am satisfied that Washington is the place above all others for us to publish

a Periodical. If I had commenced this paper in Philadelphia, or N. York, not one quarter of the notice would have been taken of it, that there is now. Almost every paper in the union now seems to notice us: the whole press is thundering down upon us; and this has been better than several million of advertisements.[25]

During the spring of 1853, Orson traveled to St. Louis to conduct business. During his time there, he also oversaw emigration in this region and carried out a variety of tasks, which included the printing and shipping of Church literature. By the end of May he had reached Liverpool to continue Church business. Writing from the British Isles, Pratt asked Young if Bernhisel had informed Young of Pratt's efforts to "wake up the people of Washington." Pratt continued, "I labored hard to raise an excitement but could not do it: the people would not turn out to hear and after preaching some 18 or 20 times to the bare walls and empty benches with here & there a half-frightened-to-death stragler [sic], I was obliged to give up my meetings for the want of hearers." He also noted, "The scattered saints throughout the U.S. and in the British Provinces are greatly revived up in their feelings, by reading the Seer. The subscription list, including St Louis & the Canadas, ~~are~~ is not far from 700." Notwithstanding, Pratt planned to return to the U.S. and "give Washington another thorough trial, after they have rested awhile; for I dislike very much to give up beat." He also told Young, "I shall be most happy to receive any counsel from you which you may have to impart to me. Shall I continue the Seer for another year? . . . I am somewhat at a loss whether to continue the Seer for another year or not."[26]

Two days later, Young wrote encouragingly to Pratt yet also gently raised some caution with regard to Pratt's doctrinal writings: "The news of your safe arrival at Washington, & of your proceedings there, was highly gratifying, evincing energy, zeal, perseverance, & the direction of the spirit of the Lord, though I must confess I was somewhat surprised to see the sealing ordinance in print at all, & especially in the prints of the Gentiles, however it may be all right." Young continued,

> We were not at all surprised, nor disappointed that you did not take
> Washington by storm, but on the contrary we can see the hand of

the Lord for our good in letting so prominent an item of our public doctrines strike the ears of the people at large with so little of bitter opposition; this affords us much pleasure, indicating that your main trial at present is simply to use patience, & exercise that perseverance, on your return from England, that you speak of in your letter, viz, to try them again, & continue so to do as long as the Spirit dictates, or until wisdom may otherwise direct.[27]

About this same time, Bernhisel returned home for a visit to Utah. On 19 June 1853, he spoke in the Tabernacle and talked about the fallout between the Saints in Utah Territory and the U.S. government. He also warned that the public press was against the Saints and that their enemies wanted to crush Church members. In addition, Bernhisel cautioned that Church leaders needed to avoid conflicts with the government. He also expressed his view that sending Pratt to Washington in defense of polygamy was a serious mistake and had caused more prejudice against the Saints.[28]

As noted, President Young quickly responded to Bernhisel's speech with a fiery sermon: "All the cats and kittens were let out of the bag when Brother Pratt . . . published the Revelation concerning the plurality of wives." Brigham further noted, "Do you suppose that this people will ever see the day that they will rest in perfect security? . . . They never will. Christ and Satan never can be friends." Young told the congregation, "Inasmuch as we send brother Bernhisel back to Washington, I say to him, 'Fear not their faces, nor their powder, for we are perfectly prepared to take all the nations of the earth on our back.'"[29]

After a three-and-a-half-month absence in Utah, Pratt once again returned to Washington, DC, which he referred to as "Gentile head-quarters." Upon arrival, he found several letters from President Young, including the one in which Young carefully raised the issue of Pratt's doctrinal teachings concerning temple sealings. Pratt responded, "In publishing the sealing ordinance, I was not aware that there was any thing in relation to it, that was to be kept any more secret, than the subject of Plurality of Wives; and being authorized to publish the latter, I supposed that the sealing ordinance was so closely connected with it, that it was right to publish it." Pratt further stated, "I am not aware that I have ever received any injunctions of secrecy in regard to the *method* of marriage . . . ; if you consider that I have erred in this thing, be assured that it was an error of ignorance, and I hope that I may be pardoned for this ignorance. I wish to do right, and often feel to mourn that I have not more of the Spirit to direct me." Pratt humbly continued to pen, "The article on *Celestial Marriage* will be closed in the 12th No. I have occupied about 8 pages of each . . . and have endeavored to set forth the arguments in clearness & simplicity; but being obliged to break up new ground without the assistance of previous Authors, I have not arranged the arguments as systematically as I should do were I to re-write upon the same subject."[30] About three weeks later, Pratt again wrote Young in a spirit of sincere repentance:

> One of your letters, you state that in some of the Seers, there are many points urged by me in my reasoning 'that are not *Sound* Doctrine, and will not be so received by the Saints.' This may be the case, for I am liable to err. . . . I desire that you & all the saints will forgive me for having published any thing which is in the least derogatory to your settled views: and had I been persuaded that you did in reality entertain permanent views contrary to what I have published, I should have kept my views away from the public, for it is not my prerogative to teach publicly that which I know the president considers to be unsound.[31]

With this correspondence, he enclosed a letter for the *Deseret News*, meekly stating,

> I have been informed by letter from our Beloved President Young, that in several of the Seers, 'there are many points' urged by me in my reasoning, 'that are not *Sound* Doctrine, and will not be so received by the Saints.' What those points are is not explained in the letter. This is, therefore, to acknowledge my weakness & liability to err, without the immediate inspiration of the Holy Ghost which leads into all truth. How great is the weakness of man! and how little can his teachings or writings be depended upon without revelation from the great fountain of truth! I do most earnestly hope that the Saints throughout the world will reject every unsound doctrine which they may discover in the 'Seer' or in any of my writings. Whatever may

come in contact with the *settled & Permanent* views of our president, should be laid aside as the emenations [*sic*] of erring human wisdom. God has appointed him as our president, and it is his province to correct us.[32]

Pratt had been particularly concerned about how President Young had viewed his doctrinal treatments on polygamy published in *The Seer*. In late January 1854, President Young wrote to Pratt to explain how he viewed such writings: "In alluding to certain Doctrine published in the [Millennial] Star, I did so with the best of feeling, & not with an idea that any harm had occurred therefrom, or would; and, as I wrote at the time, I *presumed* the 'Seer' might obtain a more extended circulation by treating more upon simpler subjects, & those doctrines that more immediately concerned unbelievers; hence there is no occasion for you to disquiet yourself on account of the item you commented upon."[33]

This same month, the first issue of the second volume of *The Seer* was published, and it did indeed have more of a focus on basic doctrines, following a full-year treatment of plural marriage in every issue of the first volume. The January 1854 issue was divided into three major segments. The first, five pages in length, was an article titled "The Treatment of the United States Towards the Saints"; the second, "Faith," was six pages long; and the third, nearly five pages, dealt with "Questions and Answers on Doctrine," written by the editor. The second issue of this volume again carried on a discussion of faith, "Faith is the gift of God," as well as a lengthy treatment on the topic of "repentance." Thus, Brigham's counsel to write "more upon simpler subjects" was certainly heeded.[34]

In mid-February, Pratt wrote to Young, first thanking him for the "privilege of returning home this season," to Utah, an option which Young had left for Pratt to choose. Yet Pratt added that he wanted to write "*ten* more Nos of the 'Seer'" before he returned. Concerning his work with the *Seer*, Pratt wrote,

> Many have been stirred up to investigate, and the Saints have begun to wake up out of their slumbers; and now and then one will keep awake, so that I greatly rejoice in the mission which you gave to me. . . . I have done the best with it that I could. I am happy to say that

no Gentile has, as yet, to my knowledge, been able to bring one argument against it [polygamy]. . . . In the second volume, I say nothing about that subject, but am treating upon Faith, Repentance, and other items of a more simple nature, according to your suggestion, and as I had intended to do, after having placed those other principles prominently before the public.[35]

The intense work of writing day after day as well as responding to attacks took its toll on Pratt: "As I have not extracted from other publications, but have taken pains to have all the contents of the Seer, so far, of my own composition, it has cost me an immense deal of labour. . . . My hair is getting somewhat grey, and considerably thinner by constant sitting and writing; I am crowded with letters of inquiry which take up a good portion of my time in answering.[36]

Nearly two months later, Pratt, still frustrated with the hard-heartedness of DC, or "Gentile head-quarters," wrote, "the selling of L.D. Saint's publications to the Gentiles in this country is altogether out of the question. There is not, I suppose, one out of a hundred that would take them as a gift, unless, they took them to burn."[37] Such a poor reception would soon influence Pratt's return to Utah, yet there was much more for Pratt to do in the remaining decades of his life.

Soon Young penned another letter to Pratt, stating, "I was pleased to learn of your faithful perseverance. . . . You will learn from the Deseret News . . . Bros Orson Pratt & Orson Spencer were appointed on missions . . . more immediately in the neighborhood of Cincinnatti [sic] though it is presumed you will start for home soon . . . & spend the coming winter with us & your family."[38]

By August 1854 the final issue of The Seer (vol. 2, no. 8) was published. The entire sixteen-page issue treated a topic titled "Preparations for the Second Advent." On the final page of The Seer, Pratt described the future glory of the Lord when he again appears: "Reader, contemplate for a moment this grand and magnificent scenery. Contemplate a great and extended city, with a dazzling and glorious light, enveloping every habitation. . . . Such a scene as this the earth has never realized." He concluded with the thought that at the time when the Savior appears, "then shall the glorious reign of peace commence, and the earth shall be full of the knowledge of the Lord, as the waters cover the sea."[39] Although Pratt knew this day would come, neither the nation's capital city, nor the world at large was ready for such a flood, or even a trickle. Even the Saints sometimes struggled with his profound intellectual capacity.

Orson's explorative understanding of some doctrines he wrote about in *The Seer* sometimes came into conflict with Church leaders, particularly with Brigham Young. This resulted in occasional reproof from President Young, to which Orson was willing to submit. However, one historian noted, when Elder Pratt was criticized by "exceptionally orthodox" Church members, Brigham Young "dismissed the remarks with a tribute: 'If Brother Orson were chopped up in inch pieces, each piece would cry out Mormonism was true.'"[40]

Orson's mission to Washington and publication of *The Seer* was but one of his many missions for a season. Elder Pratt would continue to serve vigorously and faithfully the remainder of his days. Leonard J. Arrington paid this tribute to Pratt: "He was the best-known Mormon besides Joseph Smith and Brigham Young. He was the foremost intellectual in the Church. . . . He was at the time of his death in 1881, the oldest most experienced general authority of the Church. He was one of the first missionaries, one of the original group of the Twelve Apostles, the official Church Historian, and leading Mormon scripturist. He was the first Mormon in the Salt Lake Valley, the leading exponent of Mormon doctrines, and for seven terms served as speaker of the territory's House of Representatives."[41]

When Pratt was approaching seventy, his last mission was to the British Isles. One author noted, "The strain of working eighteen hours a day . . . sapped his vigor, broke his health, and brought about his death in 1881." Summarizing his impressive life, the *Deseret News* noted, "Orson Pratt was truly an Apostle of the Lord. Full of integrity, firm as a rock to his convictions, true to his brethren and to his God, earnest and zealous in defense and proclamation of the truth, ever ready to bear testimony to the latter-day work . . . [he] was an eloquent speaker, a powerful minister."[42] Orson's publication of *The Seer* represents but one parcel of his life, a life devoted to a declaration of the faith that he defended with all his heart, might, mind, and strength.

NOTES

1. For coverage of this landmark address to a crowd of about three thousand, see *Deseret News*, Extra, 14 September 1852.

2. David J. Whittaker, "Pratt, Orson," in *Encyclopedia of Mormonism*, ed. Daniel H. Ludlow (New York: Macmillan, 1992), 3:1114–15 notes that Pratt was excommunicated in August 1842 for his negative reaction to the practice of polygamy and struggled to obtain a witness of the doctrine. Pratt eventually did and had seven wives and forty-five children.

3. Donald Q. Cannon, "Pratt, Orson," and Peter Crawley, "Pratt, Parley, P.," in *Encyclopedia of Latter-day Saint History*, ed. Arnold Garr, Donald Q. Cannon and Richard Cowan (Salt Lake City: Deseret Book, 2000), 939–41. See also David J. Whittaker, "Orson Pratt: Prolific Pamphleteer," *Dialogue* 15 (Autumn 1982): 27, who notes that Pratt was "the most prolific and perhaps most influential early Mormon pamphleteer. . . . He authored over thirty works on both religious and scientific topics. Influential during his own lifetime, he wielded even more influence after his death."

4. David J. Whittaker, "Pratt, Orson," in *Encyclopedia of Mormonism*, 3:1114–15.

5. The 1856 republican platform designated slavery and polygamy as "the twin relics of barbarism." For more on this issue, see Richard D. Poll, "The Twin Relic: A Study of Mormon Polygamy and the Campaign by the Government of the United States for its Abolition, 1852-1890" (master's thesis, Texas Christian University, 1939).

6. Brigham Young, "Where the Wicked Go—Continual Opposition to and Prejudice Against the Truth—The Judges and the Delegate of Utah—The Spirit of God and the Spirit of the World—Potency of the Gospel" (discourse given 19 June 1853), *Journal of Discourses* (London: Latter-day Saints' Book Depot, 1854–86), 1:188.

7. David J. Whittaker, "Pratt, Orson," in *Encyclopedia of Mormonism*, 3:1115. With regards to the timing for the public announcement of the revelation, David J. Whittaker, "The Bone in the Throat: Orson Pratt and the Public Announcement of Plural Marriage," *Western Historical Quarterly* 18, no. 3 (July 1987): 295 explained three major reasons why the Saints decided to go public in 1852, although there is evidence it had been privately practiced as early as 1831. First, because there had been charges made against the Saints by federal agents in 1851. Second, the Saints were approaching the end of their isolation in Deseret and third, because of what Whittaker calls, "Mormon millennialism," a belief that the Second Coming of the Lord and the ushering of the millennial era was nigh at hand.<?> Orson Pratt, ed., "Prospectus of 'The Seer,'" *The Seer* 1, no. 1 (January 1853): 1. At this time, the

U.S. president elect was Franklin Pierce, who served in his presidential office from 1853 to 1857.

8. Orson Pratt, ed., "Prospectus of 'The Seer,'" *The Seer* 1, no. 1 (January 1853): 1.

9. John M. Bernhisel graduated with his doctoral degree in medicine in 1827. He was a personal physician to Joseph Smith Jr. Dr. Bernhisel was also an able politician. He was a Utah Territorial delegate, appointed by Governor Brigham Young from 1851 to 1859 and was again appointed as delegate from 1861 to 1863. He was instrumental in helping to reconcile the strained relationship between Utah Territory and the federal government on several occasions. See Lynn M. Hilton and Hope A. Hilton, "John Milton Bernhisel," in *Utah History Encyclopedia*, ed. Allan Kent Powell (Salt Lake City: University of Utah Press, 1994), 41–42.

10. John M. Bernhisel to Brigham Young, 12 August 1852, Brigham Young Correspondence, CR 1234/1 Church History Library, Salt Lake City; hereafter cited as BYC.

11. For a complete treatment on Bernhisel's political service, see Gwynn Barrett, "John Bernhisel: Mormon Elder in Congress" (PhD diss., Brigham Young University, 1968).

12. Brigham Young to John Bernhisel, 28 August 1852, BYC; note that he was still writing on 30 August.

13. Brigham Young to John Bernhisel, 14 September 1852, BYC.

14. Brigham Young to John Bernhisel, 29 September 1852, BYC.

15. "The Mormons," *The Republic*, 23 November 1852, 3.

16. *Weekly National Intelligencer*, 4 December 1852, 2.

17. "The Mormons," *The Republic*, 1 April 1853, 2.

18. Brigham Young to John M. Bernhisel, 30 December 1852, BYC.

19. "Doctrines of Mormonism," *Weekly National Intelligencer*, 1 January 1853, 7, confirming Pratt's letter to Young, noted that in the nation's capital, "One of the twelve Apostles of the church of the 'Latter-day Saints,' is preaching thrice on Sunday and once on Wednesday evening of each week, at Temperance Hall, on the subject of Mormonism. . . . There appears no disposition to deny the *polygamistic* principles and habits that prevail amongst them." In addition, the *Daily Evening Star*, 10 January 1853, 2, noted, "There has heretofore been some doubt as to the practice of polygamy among these Saints, . . . but all doubt is now removed by the explicit declaration of Elder Pratt."

20. Orson Pratt to Brigham Young, 31 December 1852, BYC.

21. Orson Pratt to Brigham Young, 30 January 1853, BYC.

22. John M. Bernhisel to Brigham Young, 5 February 1853, BYC.

23. "Stand from Under," *Daily Evening Star*, 2 February 1853, 4.

24. "Mormon Matrimony," *Daily Union*, 23 January 1853, 2.

25. Orson Pratt to Brigham Young, 4 March 1853, BYC.

26. Orson Pratt to Brigham Young, 30 May 1853, BYC.

27. Brigham Young to Orson Pratt, 1 June 1853, BYC.

28. John M. Bernhisel, 19 June 1853, box 4, disk 9, images 167–83, Papers of George D. Watt, Church History Library, as cited in Bruce W. Worthen, "Out of the West: John M. Bernhisel, Washington, and the Mormon Frontier" (PhD diss., University of Utah, 2018), 238–39. The author thanks Bruce Worthen for this information.

29. Brigham Young Discourse, 19 June 1853, box 2, folder 11, CR 100/317, CHL, as cited in Bruce W. Worthen, "Out of the West," 240–41.

30. Orson Pratt to Brigham Young, 10 September 1853, BYC.

31. Orson Pratt to Brigham Young, 4 November 1853, BYC. See also Gary James Bergera, "The Orson Pratt–Brigham Young Controversies: Conflict within the Quorums, 1853–1868," *Dialogue* 13, no. 2 (Summer 1980): 42, who explains that notwithstanding the occasional dissimilar doctrinal opinions between Pratt and Young, "both Orson Pratt and Brigham Young found themselves inextricably united in a common cause—Mormonism and its expansion. Each man, however, pursued this goal from subtly different points of view—which, as a direct consequence, were to produce seemingly different views. Young, as President and Prophet, saw his fundamental responsibilities as overseeing official church doctrine and maintaining unity within the Church as a whole." For a more detailed treatment of the quorum conflict, see Gary James Bergera, *Conflict in the Quorum: Orson Pratt, Brigham Young, Joseph Smith* (Salt Lake City: Signature Books, 2002).

32. Orson Pratt to Brigham Young, 4 November 1853, BYC.

33. Brigham Young to Orson Pratt, 31 January 1854, BYC.

34. Orson Pratt, "Faith Is the Gift of God," *The Seer* 2, no. 2 (February 1854): 209.

35. Orson Pratt to Brigham Young, 14 February 1854, BYC.

36. Orson Pratt to Brigham Young, 14 February 1854, BYC.

37. Orson Pratt from Baltimore to Brigham Young, 3 April 1853, BYC.

38. Brigham Young to Orson Pratt, 29 April 1854, BYC.

39. Orson Pratt, "Preparations for the Second Advent," *The Seer* 2, no. 8 (August 1854): 320. These scriptural words are taken from either Isaiah 11:9 or Habakkuk 2:14.

40. Breck England, *The Life and Thought of Orson Pratt* (Salt Lake City: University of Utah Press, 1985), 217.

41. Leonard J. Arrington, foreword to England, *Life and Thought of Orson Pratt*, ix.

42. "Death of Apostle Orson Pratt," *Deseret Evening News*, 3 October 1881, 2, as cited in Flake, *Prophets and Apostles*, 373. The following day another Salt Lake newspaper article titled "Orson Pratt," *Salt Lake Herald*, 4 October 1881, 4, paid tribute to the faithful Apostle: "There is mourning again today from one end of Utah to the other, and in fact wherever there are Mormons who have heard of the death of Orson Pratt. His brave heart has ceased to beat, his noble brain is no longer active, his voice is hushed, and his pure soul has gone. . . . The mourning of this mighty dead is of that character which commands respect."

William Weeks's architectural drawing of the west wall of the original Nauvoo Temple. Church History Library.

THE SMITHSONIAN SUNSTONE: AN ICONIC NAUVOO TEMPLE RELIC

ALEXANDER L. BAUGH

Alexander L. Baugh is a professor of Church history and doctrine at Brigham Young University.

Visitors to the Smithsonian National Museum of American History in Washington, DC, will find thousands of artifacts of every type and description on display, each of which is associated with a variety of historical themes—pop culture, business, politics, exploration, transportation, innovation, and religion, among many others. It's America's premier historical museum and draws millions of visitors each year. On the main floor in the "American Stories" exhibition is a rather unusual artifact—a capital sunstone from the original Latter-day Saint temple in Nauvoo, Illinois, constructed between 1841 and 1846—one of only two complete sunstones in existence.

Richard Kurin, a cultural anthropologist and at one time the Smithsonian's Distinguished Scholar and Ambassador-at-Large, included a feature story about the sunstone and the Latter-day Saints in his book *The Smithsonian's History of America in 101 Objects*. Concerning this unique symbolic historical object, Kurin wrote, "It is among the most important relics to survive from the Mormon Temple, a site that played an important role in the religion of the Latter-day Saints."[1] Every historical artifact has a unique story and a history all its own, and the Smithsonian Nauvoo Temple sunstone is no exception.

NAUVOO TEMPLE ARCHITECTURAL DRAWINGS AND DESCRIPTIONS

In late August or early September 1840, a year after the Latter-day Saints had first begun to settle Commerce (later Nauvoo), Illinois, Joseph Smith formally announced to the Saints that they were to move forward with plans to construct a temple.[2] About this same time, William Weeks, an experienced builder who had some knowledge and architectural training in the Greek Revival style, was selected to be the architect and general superintendent for the building.[3]

A revelation received by Joseph Smith in January 1841 indicated that he would receive revelatory knowledge regarding "all things that pertain to this house."[4] This not only included an understanding of the sacred ordinances that would make up the temple's rituals but also encompassed an understanding of the temple's overall appearance and ornamental design, which Smith said he had received from a heavenly vision. For example, on 5 February 1844, Weeks met with the Prophet to discuss the type of windows that he was proposing be used in the half-story "office space" floor that separated the lower hall from the upper hall of the temple. Smith proposed having circular exterior windows, but Weeks objected, saying that a circular window went against the known rules of architecture for a building of that size and height. Smith replied, "I wish you to carry out my designs. I have seen in vision the splendid appearance of that building illuminated and will have it built according to the pattern shewn [shown] me."[5]

Unfortunately, only a small portion of Weeks's Nauvoo Temple architectural drawings have survived. These include two different full depictions of the temple's west (front) exterior wall—an earlier rendition and the final one—along with fourteen fragments of various sizes containing a number of preliminary sketches. An examination of these drawings, along with several early photographic images (daguerreotypes and tintypes) and some of the remnant ornamental stones of the completed temple, illustrates that Weeks made changes and modifications in the temple's design during the construction. Architectural drawings of the capital sunstones are a good example. One of Weeks's early detailed drawings of a capital stone shows a singular sunburst with a human-like face that is almost completely obscured by acanthus leaves (figure 1).[6] In contrast, Weeks's final architectural rendering of the temple's front facade (i.e., west wall) includes a less detailed illustration of six capital stones, each depicted with a full-facial sunburst figure rising from a representation of clouds. Also included above each sunburst are two hands, each holding a trumpet (see figure 2).[7] Brigham Young's description of the finished capitals aligns closely with Weeks's final drawings as well as with close-up photographic images of the completed temple. Young wrote that each capital consisted of "one base stone, one large stone representing the sun rising just about the clouds, the lower part obscured; the third stone represents two hands each holding a trumpet, and the last two stones form a cap over the trumpet stone, and these all form the capital."[8] No full-scale architectural drawings

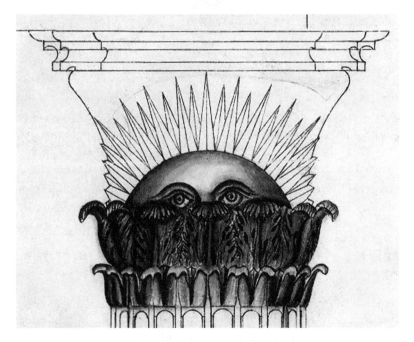

Figure 1. *Portion of an early drawing by William Weeks of a Nauvoo capital sunstone, circa 1841–46. Church History Library.*

Figure 2. *Portion of what was likely the final architectural drawing by William Weeks of the front of the Nauvoo Temple showing two "full-faced" sunstone capitals on the pilaster, circa 1841–46. Church History Library.*

of the temple's east wall exist; however, it featured six sunstones, just like the west-facing front wall. Photographic images of the south wall of the completed temple show nine sunstones; the north wall had the same number. In total, there would have been thirty sunstones—six each on the front and back walls, and nine each on the north and south walls (see figure 3).

TEMPLE CONSTRUCTION—CARVING THE SUNSTONE CAPITALS

Groundbreaking ceremonies for the temple took place on 6 April 1841. Thereafter construction on the main structure proceeded as funds and labor (both paid and donated labor) became available and as weather permitted. Because of winter conditions, most actual construction on the temple walls ceased in December and resumed in March, although

Figure 3. *Louis Rice Chaffin daguerreotype copy of an earlier daguerreotype of the original Nauvoo Temple, circa 1847. The image shows a full view of the south wall of the temple and an obscured view of the front west wall. Church History Library.*

Figure 4. Original moonstone from the Nauvoo Temple located for many years on the home property of Blake T. Roney, Provo, Utah. The stone is one of only two complete original moonstones. The stone is currently in the possession of The Church of Jesus Christ of Latter-day Saints. Photograph by author, 1998.

stonecutters worked during the winter months by quarrying the limestone and rough-cutting the blocks.

By late 1842, some eighteen months after construction began, the temple's foundation walls had been completed, and the outside walls reached to the bottom of where the windowsills would be.[9] This would indicate that at least some of the thirty moonstones, which formed the base of each capital pilaster, would also have been set in place (see figure 4).[10] At the time of the April 1843 general conference, the outside walls were between four and twelve feet high.[11] Five months later (in August 1843), David Nye White, a Philadelphia newspaper reporter, visited Nauvoo and reported that the walls of the temple were between fifteen and eighteen feet in height.[12] However, it would take another thirteen months before the temple walls were high enough that the capital sunstones could be set in place.

Beginning in March 1844, the more experienced and skilled stone-cutters began the more detailed, intricate work of shaping the capital sunstones. That same month, Charles Lambert, a Latter-day Saint convert from Yorkshire, England, and a highly skilled stone carver, arrived in Nauvoo. It did not take long for the temple foremen to recognize his proficiency and mastery of the craft and set him to work carving the capitals. "I worked and finished the first capital," he wrote. He also assisted in sculpting eleven others, the most of any of those who are known to have worked on the temple sunstones.[13] Benjamin T. Mitchell, another highly skilled stone carver, is also credited with sculpting the first sunstone, in addition to three other capitals.[14] Given the nature of the craft, both Lambert and Mitchell may have collaborated or assisted each other in fashioning the first capital.

An entry in a Nauvoo Temple committee account book gives the names of four other highly skilled stone carvers who sculpted all or some portion of a number of sunstones—namely, Harvey Stanley, John Harper, James Sharp, and Rufus Allen. The account ledger indicates that each of these carvers were compensated proportionate to the work they did on a particular stone, which amount could be used to purchase food, commodities, and merchandise that had been donated or appropriated to the temple fund from tithing contributions, or other types of donations given to the fund by Church members. For example, Harvey Stanley was credited $300 for carving an entire sunstone, $150 for carving part of another, $75 for assisting Rufus Allen, and another $5 for assisting James Sharp with their carvings. Sharp assisted Lambert and Stanley on a sunstone and received $10 credit, and then received an additional $5 credit for moving a sunstone from the south side of the temple to the north side and resetting the stone.[15] Another carver whose name does not appear in the account book is James Henry Rollins, who learned to cut stone as an apprentice under Harvey Stanley. Eventually, Rollins was able to work on his own and cut stones for the pilasters and archways. Later, Mitchell, Lambert, and another stone carver asked Rollins to "rough out" three capital stones, which he did. Finally, William Weeks, the temple architect, and William Player, the chief "stone setter" who mortared the stones in place, requested that Rollins dress one of the capital stones. "I told them I didn't think I was

Figure 5. *Individuals who are known to have worked as stone carvers on the Nauvoo Temple capital sunstones. Left to right: Charles Lambert, Benjamin T. Mitchell, Rufus Allen, and James Henry Rollins. Church History Library.*

capable of cutting one of those stones," Rollins said, "but they persuaded me to try it and they would help me out." He then added, "I did so with reluctance, but accomplished this task." Rollins further noted that his sunstone was placed on the northeast corner of the north wall (figure 5).[16]

On 15 May 1844, Josiah Quincy and Charles Francis Adams, prominent residents of Boston who were sightseeing in the West, spent much of the day visiting with Joseph Smith in Nauvoo, part of which included an afternoon visit to the temple grounds. At the construction site, they passed one of the stone carvers working on the face of a sunstone. At the time, it had only been about two months since the carvers had begun sculpting the capitals, so this was likely one of the first to be fashioned. Upon seeing the Prophet and his guests, the worker stopped chiseling, looked up, and asked, "Is this like the face you saw in vision?" Smith replied, "Very near it, . . . except that the nose is just a thought too broad." Quincy was impressed with the yet uncompleted building, calling it "striking" and a "wonderful structure," but considered the sunstones and moonstones "queer carvings."[17]

SETTING THE CAPITAL SUNSTONES

By late September 1844, the outside temple walls—including the capital pilasters—were approximately forty-four feet from the ground and high enough to begin setting the actual capitals.[18] As noted, each capital sunstone consisted of four parts: (1) the base stone; (2) the lower portion of the sunstone, which included the clouds, the sun's face, and the side portion of the sunburst; (3) the top portion of the sunburst and the trumpet stones; and (4) the abacus stone, or the block or "cap" that was set over the trumpet stone (see figure 6).

Both the upper and lower sections of each sunstone appear to have been carved as separate stones, although it is possible that the entire sunstone was shaped from one complete block of stone and then cut. Regardless, the likely reason the sunstone was in two separate pieces was to facilitate hoisting lighter, less cumbersome stones to their positions on the pilasters, rather than trying to lift entire stones that would have been much larger and heavier. Using a crane and pulley system, workers winched the base stone to the top of the pilaster, where it was mortared into place and left to fully cure. With that process completed, the sunstone could be hoisted and cemented onto the base stone. First, the lower section (the clouds and the sun's face) was fixed to the base stone, then the smaller top section (upper portion of the sunburst and the trumpets) was mortared or "attached" to the lower section, and finally, the abacus stone (the top block or cap) was added, thus completing the setting.

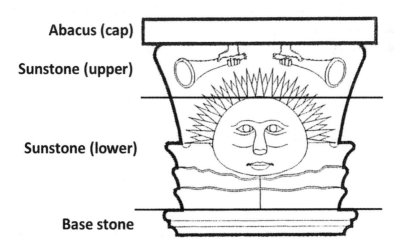

Figure 6. *Diagram showing the sections that composed the sunstone capital.*

Workers installed the first capital sunstone on 23 September 1844, but it was not without incident. The crew working the crane from the top succeeded in raising the stone to where it was to be set, but while attempting to draw it to the wall, a portion of the crane gave way due to the stone's weight. It was only by "great care," William Clayton wrote, that "the stone was safely landed and set without further accident."[19] Two days later, as the workers attempted to raise the second capital, the entire crane fell from the top of the wall, falling within a foot of one of the workers on the ground. It was several days before the crane was repaired and work could proceed again.[20] By 1 October, six additional capitals had been raised and set into place, bringing the total to seven.[21] During the next two months, the work of setting the capitals progressed slowly because of bad weather and because the carvers had not completed their cuttings on the remainder of the capitals. On 6 December, the last capital was set in place, although Clayton indicated that twelve of the capitals did not include the trumpet stones. He then noted that they would be set in place the following spring.[22] Nonetheless, the "near-completion" of the placement of the capitals marked a milestone in the temple's construction.

It took crews another eighteen months to finish the top portion of the upper hall, the attic, the clock and bell tower, and the interior. By this time, Brigham Young and most of the members of the Twelve had permanently left Nauvoo and were making their way across southern Iowa. Young left the formal public dedication of the temple, held on 1 May 1846, to Elder Orson Hyde—a member of the Twelve still in Nauvoo—whose dedication marked the building's official completion.

NAUVOO TEMPLE SYMBOLISM

Situated a few feet above each of the thirty capital sunstones was an inverted star stone, which completed the three major exterior symbolic carvings—the moonstone at the base of the pilaster, the sunstone capital, and the star stone above the capital. Some have assumed that the sun, moon, and star motifs of the Nauvoo Temple represented the three degrees of eternal glory as given in section 76 of the Doctrine and Covenants—the sun (celestial kingdom), moon (terrestrial kingdom), and the stars (telestial kingdom). But this was not the case. Reflecting on his labors as a construction foreman on the temple, Wandle Mace provided the following symbolic representation for the stone pieces: "The architecture of the temple was purely original and unlike anything in existence, being a representation of the Church, the Bride, the Lambs wife—John the revelator says in Rev. 12 ch. 1st verse 'And there appeared a great wonder in heaven; a woman clothed with the sun, and the moon under her feet, and upon her head a crown of twelve stars.' This is portrayed in the beautiful cut stone of this grand temple."[23]

Thus the sun-moon-star design represents the glory of the latter-day church or kingdom, further symbolized by the sun rising through the clouds, with the trumpets heralding the restoration of the gospel and the glory of the latter-day Church of Jesus Christ (see figure 7).

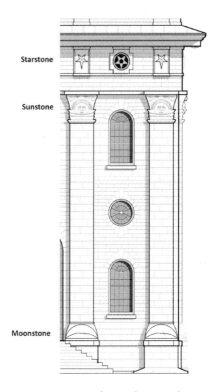

Figure 7. Portion of an architectural drawing of the Nauvoo Temple showing the position of the decorative sun, moon, and starstones. The stones were meant to represent the imagery in Revelation 12:1. "And there appeared a great wonder in heaven; a woman clothed with the sun, and the moon under her feet, and upon her head a crown of twelve stars." Roger P. Jackson, FFKR Architects, Salt Lake City.

NAUVOO TEMPLE RUINS

On 9 October 1848, just two and a half years after the main body of Latter-day Saints left Nauvoo to settle in the West, arsonists set fire to the abandoned temple, destroying the temple's interior structure, the attic story, and the bell and clock tower, leaving a blackened facade and three unsupported sixty-foot walls.[24] In March 1849, David T. LeBaron, who had been appointed caretaker of the temple, sold the burned-out structure for two thousand dollars to the Icarians, a French-based utopian socialist group led by Étienne Cabet. The Icarians planned to refurbish and restore the temple, but as if destined by fate, on 27 May 1850, a tornado struck the temple shell, collapsing the north wall and severely damaging the west and south walls. Only the front of the temple withstood the blast, but it was structurally unsafe. During the next few years, the Icarians used stone from the rubble and what remained of the temple's walls to build a school, a dining hall, and a few smaller structures. However, in 1856, the group splintered, and Cabet and his followers left Nauvoo.[25]

By 1865 only a portion of the southwest corner of the original temple remained. As a safety measure, an explosive was used to bring it down. A newspaper reporter wrote that following the demolition, some of the ornamental stonework (with probable reference to the sun, moon, and star stones) had been saved by the current owner of the property, a Mr. Dornseiff (first name not known), and were sold or given to "curiosity seekers in all parts of the country."[26]

TWO ORIGINAL SUNSTONES SURVIVED

At that time (1865) George W. Gray, president of the Methodist English and German College, in Quincy, Illinois (often referred to as the Methodist College), went to Nauvoo, where he acquired two sunstones from what remained of the Nauvoo Temple. The sunstones were intact, but the base stones and the top abacus stones were missing. Given the circumstances surrounding the temple's destruction, first by fire, then by windstorm, and then by detonation, it is remarkable that the two sunstones remained unbroken and sustained only minor damage. Gray transported the capital stones by steamboat to Quincy, where they were placed on opposite sides of the main entrance of the school grounds of the college, which at the time was located at Third and Spring Streets (figures 8 and 9).[27] In time, these two stones would find different twentieth century

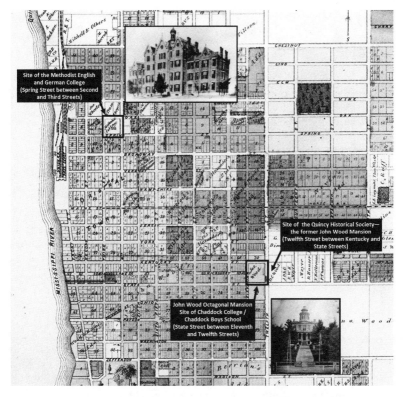

Figure 8. Map of Quincy, Illinois, showing the location of the Methodist English and German College/Jefferson School, the Chaddock College/Chaddock Boys School, and the Quincy Historical Society (now the Historical Society of Quincy and Adams County) in the Atlas of Adams County, Illinois *(Davenport, IA: Andreas, Lyter, and Company, 1872), 148.*

homes; one would return to the Church, and the other would end up in the Smithsonian.

NAUVOO LATTER-DAY SAINT VISITORS' CENTER SUNSTONE—THE "SISTER SUNSTONE"

In 1870 one of the sunstones from the Methodist English and German College was donated to or acquired by the State of Illinois and taken to Springfield, where it was placed on the old statehouse

Figure 9. *The Methodist English and German College, Quincy, Illinois, 1884. The building housed the college from 1847 to 1875, after which it was sold to the Quincy School Board and renamed the Jefferson School. At one time, two Nauvoo Temple capital sunstones were displayed on the school property. Quincy Area Historic Photograph Collection, Quincy Public Library, Quincy, IL.*

grounds (the former state capitol building made famous by Abraham Lincoln). In 1876 the sunstone was moved southwest four blocks to the new state capitol grounds, where samples of native Illinois stones were being brought for the new capitol building (the current state capitol), which was then under construction. The stone remained there until 1894, when it was moved to the entrance of the Illinois State Fairgrounds in Springfield and placed in the middle of a decorative lily pond, where it remained until 1955. It was then moved again, this time to the Nauvoo State Park.[28] It remained there until 1992, when The Church of Jesus Christ of Latter-day Saints was made custodian of the sunstone. In June 1994, it was relocated to the original temple block on the bluff and placed in a sealed display case to protect it from vandalism and the elements.[29] In 1999 the stone and the sealed display case were moved just outside the north entrance to the Nauvoo Latter-day Saint Visitors' Center. Finally, in November 2012, the stone was placed in an open display case inside the visitors' center (figure 10).[30]

Figure 10. Sunstone from the original Nauvoo Temple. Following the destruction of the temple, this sunstone was one of two sunstones procured by George W. Gray in 1865 and taken to Quincy, Illinois, where it was displayed on the grounds of the Methodist College. It was later moved to the state capital in Springfield, Illinois, and displayed on the capitol grounds of the old and current state capitol buildings and on the Illinois State Fairgrounds. In 1955 it was moved to the Nauvoo State Park. The Church of Jesus Christ of Latter-day Saints became the custodian of the stone in 1992. Photograph by author, 2013.

THE QUINCY-SMITHSONIAN SUNSTONE

The second sunstone remained on the property of the Methodist English and German College on Spring Street for several years. In 1872 the college merged with Johnson College. Three years later, in December 1875, the college officials sold the property and the building to the Quincy Board of Education for $30,000, and it became the Jefferson School (an elementary school). Following the sale, the college relocated in 1876 to the John Wood Octagonal Mansion located on State Street, between Eleventh and Twelfth Streets (figure 8). At the same time, Charles C. Chaddock gave the college $24,000, and the name of the school was changed to Chaddock College.[31]

In 1890 the college became a private school for boys ages six to sixteen and was renamed Chaddock Boys School.[32]

How long the sunstone remained on the Jefferson School property is unknown, but D. L. Musselman Sr., an assistant administrator at the elementary school, remembered that the stone was in the schoolyard for years and that the children attending the school were known to crack nuts and sharpen their pencils on the nose of the stone's face. Recognizing the historical significance of the stone, Musselman made arrangements with Chaddock College officials to have the stone moved from the Jefferson School property to the grounds of the college. It is not known exactly when the sunstone was moved to the Chaddock College/Chaddock Boys School, but it was sometime before 1900.[33]

Several photographs of the sunstone on the Chaddock College/Chaddock Boys School campus are extant. One shows the sunstone on the east side of the sidewalk leading to the John Wood Octagonal Mansion (partially obscured by trees), which was the main building of the school

Figure 11. The John Wood Octagonal Mansion, on the main campus building of Chaddock College/Chaddock Boys School, date unknown. The sunstone is pictured in the lower right corner. Historical Society of Quincy and Adams County, Quincy, Illinois.

Figure 12. Nauvoo sunstone on Chaddock College/Chaddock Boys School campus, date unknown. Historical Society of Quincy and Adams County.

campus (figure 11). Another image is a close-up view of a nearly full frontal image of the sunstone, the right side of the face partially obscured by a shadow. The brickwork of the sidewalk to the John Wood Octagonal Mansion can also be seen (figure 12). A final photograph shows a complete frontal view of the sunstone. The location where the photo was taken cannot be determined precisely, but it is assumed that it was somewhere on the

Figure 13. Nauvoo sunstone on the Chaddock College/Chaddock Boys School campus, date unknown. Note the coloration of the sun's pupils. Historical Society of Quincy and Adams County.

Chaddock College/Chaddock Boys School property and shows that some person or persons painted the pupils in the sun's eyes (figure 13). Given that the sunstone was on the school grounds of the Methodist College/Jefferson School for a number of years and the Chaddock College/Chaddock Boys School for several years as well, it would be easy to assume that some precocious youngsters or students painted the pupils.

HISTORICAL SOCIETY OF QUINCY AND ADAMS COUNTY ACQUISITION

In December 1912, officials and administrators of the Chaddock Boys School made arrangements to purchase a new location for the school at Twenty-fourth and Jersey Street in Quincy. (The current Chaddock School in Quincy still occupies this property.) Rather than move the sunstone to the school's new location, the school trustees made inquiries to the Quincy Historical Society—housed in the former John Wood Mansion (not to be confused with the John Wood Octagonal Mansion) located across the street to the east of the Chaddock School property—to see if the society would be interested in acquiring the sunstone at no cost. Given the stone's historical significance, and the fact that the school was not asking for any money, the society accepted the offer.[34] On 11 January 1913, the sunstone was moved to a location on the south side of the society's building in a partially covered area. Sometime later it was moved to a spot on the northeast side of the main lot.[35]

THE SMITHSONIAN'S NATIONAL MUSEUM OF AMERICAN HISTORY ACQUISITION

For much of the twentieth century, the Nauvoo Temple sunstone remained on display on the property of the Historical Society of Quincy and Adams County, where, unfortunately, it continued to be exposed to the elements. This exposure resulted in noticeable signs of deterioration over the years. Eventually, the society's officials realized that the sunstone's deteriorating condition would necessitate investing in costly conservation and restoration work if it were to be preserved. They further reasoned that the sunstone had little connection to Quincy and questioned whether or not to continue to retain ownership of the relic, given its lack of relevance to the area's local history. After all, it was a Latter-day Saint artifact from Nauvoo, not Quincy. For these and other reasons, in the late 1970s, the society officers decided to try to find a buyer. Discussions with officials from The Church of Jesus Christ of Latter-day Saints took place on and off for ten years but without success. Finally, in early 1988, negotiations ended when the Church formally rejected the idea of purchasing the sunstone. When these talks ended, the directors of the society hired an agent who was given an asking price and charged to "seek a good home for the sunstone." The directors also decided to reject the idea of selling the stone to a private collector, so that that sunstone would find "a place in a public repository where it would receive the largest 'public exposure.'" The agent had discussions with officials from the Reorganized Church of Jesus Christ of Latter Day Saints (now the Community of Christ), but they also rejected the society's offer. It was at this time that the agent approached administrators from the Smithsonian's National Museum of American History, and the negotiations were successful. The museum sent two representatives to Quincy, one to confirm the authenticity of the stone, and the other to take photos and examine the stone's condition. In October 1988, the Smithsonian's directors agreed to the asking price—$100,000.[36] "It was one of the largest expenditures the museum ever made," said Richard Ahlborn, curator in the museum's division of community life. "That's because we're a history museum and artifacts usually don't cost that much. . . . In fact, the board of regents of the Smithsonian had to approve it."[37] On 9 December, Joel W. Scarborough, president of the Historical Society of Quincy and Adams County, announced the sale by letter to the organization's members:

> The Society's Board of Directors authorized the acquisition by the Smithsonian Institute for several reasons. The sunstone has primarily a Nauvoo historical connection. It has little meaningful historical association with Quincy. . . .
>
> At its outdoor location . . . the soft limestone sculpture is subject to weathering and deterioration and vandalism. The location in the Smithsonian's National Museum of American History will enable

Figure 14. *Richard E. Ahlborn, Community Life curator for the Smithsonian's National Museum of American History, by the Nauvoo Temple sunstone exhibit. Ahlborn played a leading role in securing the sunstone for the museum. Photo by Rick Vargas. National Museum of American History, 1990.*

conservation experts to preserve and protect this interesting monument.

Over six million people visit the Smithsonian each year. Far more people will have a chance to view the sunstone in "America's Museum" than would ever see it in Quincy. . . .

The sunstone will be welcomed and preserved in its new location in America's most prestigious museum, sheltered from the ravages of time and elements of man and nature.[38]

Within a week after the announcement, a three-man crew, headed by Wayne Field, supervisor of the Smithsonian's rigging shop, arrived in Quincy to transport the sunstone to the Museum of American History in Washington, DC.[39]

Before the stone could be displayed, the Smithsonian's professional conservators first needed to perform an extensive cleaning. Most noticeable were patches of green algae and a black sulfate-like crust, both of which were chemically removed. The blue-colored paint on the sunstone's pupils proved to be more difficult. Martin Burke, one of the museum's conservators said that the stone was so porous that they were unable to remove all the paint from the eyes. "We tried an arsenal of solvents," he said, but finally "settle[ed] for a little watercolor 'make up' to cover up the traces."[40]

Museum staffers also had to design and create the exhibit to provide information to patrons. This included background information about Latter-day Saints and a history of the Nauvoo Temple, as well as architectural drawings and photographs. The final procedure involved the actual construction of the exhibit—no small task, considering that the designers had to figure out how to construct a platform for the two-and-a-half-ton stone. All of these processes took considerable time.

In early January 1990, a little over a year after the Smithsonian acquired the sunstone, the reconditioned artifact was displayed for the first time.[41] The exhibit was located in the main floor gallery, immediately to the west of the museum's most prominent exhibition—the Star-Spangled Banner, the historic flag that flew over Fort McHenry during the British bombardment of Baltimore during the War of 1812. Curator Richard Ahlborn noted the significance of the sunstone's location. "Except for the Star Spangled Banner," he said, "you couldn't ask for a more central location."[42] The sunstone rested on an eight-foot pedestal so visitors would look up, similar to how they would have looked up to see it on the original temple (see figures 14 and 15). It remained in this location in the museum for twenty-two years.

In April 2012, a new exhibition opened in the National Museum of American History called "American

Figure 15. Location of the Nauvoo Temple sunstone exhibit in the Smithsonian's National Museum of American History from 1990 to 2012. Photo by author, 1998.

Figure 16. *"American Stories" exhibition, Smithsonian National Museum of American History. The Nauvoo Temple sunstone is a major feature of the exhibit. Photo by author, 2018.*

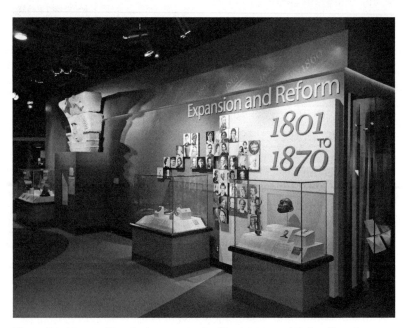

Figure 17. *Nauvoo Temple sunstone in the "Expansion and Reform" section of the "American Stories" exhibition in the Smithsonian National Museum of American History. Photo by author, 2018.*

Figure 18. *Side view of the Nauvoo Temple sunstone in the "American Stories" exhibition in the Smithsonian National Museum of American History. Photo by author, 2018.*

Stories" and was located in the northeast section on the main floor of the museum. The exhibition included objects that examined or represented "the manner in which culture . . . [has] shaped life in the U.S. and how the peopling of America has contributed to the rich distinctiveness of a country influenced by diverse cultural communities."[43] Recognizing the unique influence the Church has had on the religious culture and landscape of American history, the Smithsonian's administrators and staffers relocated the Nauvoo Temple sunstone to the new exhibit, where it currently remains (see figures 16–19).

Figure 19. Front view of the Nauvoo Temple sunstone in the "American Stories" exhibition in the Smithsonian National Museum of American History. Photo by author, 2018.

CONCLUSION

What makes the Nauvoo sunstone such an important and significant artifact that it has found a place in the Smithsonian's collection? Curator Richard Ahlborn noted, "Few religions have their beginnings in America. That alone is quite a phenomenon, not to mention the strength and growth the Mormon Church has shown. The stone is symbolic of the most persistent religious movement in American history."[44] Journalist and author Elizabeth Schleichert observed that the sunstone symbolized "the tumult and tragedy of the early Mormons."[45] True indeed! The sunstone symbolizes the early beginnings of the Church, the determination of its leaders and members to prevail against their antagonists, and the tragedies and setbacks that accompanied the Church during the first two decades of its existence. But the Nauvoo sunstone is representative of something more— much more. Ultimately, this rare artifact represents the commitment and sacrifice of a people to build a temple wherein they could worship God, make covenants, and receive the ordinances that they believed were necessary to bring about their salvation and ultimate exaltation in the kingdom of God. A fitting epitaph to that purpose was inscribed above the pulpits on the east wall of the abandoned temple's main hall by someone before leaving Nauvoo for the journey to the west: "The Lord has beheld our sacrifice: come after us."[46]

NOTES

1. Richard Kurin, *The Smithsonian's History of America in 100 Objects* (New York: Penguin Press, 2013), 153, 156.

2. See Joseph Smith, "Epistle to the Saints," JS History, vol. C-1, 1092–93, Church History Library, Salt Lake City, Utah, hereafter cited as CHL.

3. See J. Earl Arrington, "William Weeks, Architect of the Nauvoo Temple," *BYU Studies* 19, no. 3 (Spring 1979): 340.

4. Revelation, 19 January 1841, in Matthew C. Godfrey, Spencer W. McBride, Alex D. Smith, and Christopher James Blythe, eds., *Documents Volume 7: September 1839–January 1841*, vol. 7 of the Document series of *The Joseph Smith Papers*, ed. Ronald K. Esplin, Matthew J. Grow, and Matthew C. Godfrey (Salt Lake City: Church Historian's Press, 2018), 518; see Doctrine and Covenants 124:42.

5. JS History, vol. E–1, 1875–1876, CHL.

6. William Weeks, Nauvoo Temple architectural drawings, drawing 5, MS 11500, William Weeks Papers, CHL. While the sunburst motif appears in various forms in architectural patterns and ornamentations, the inclusion of a face in the sun generally does not. However, an exception to this is the sunburst engraving on the top of the chair that George Washington occupied during the Constitutional Convention held in Independence Hall in Philadelphia in 1787, known as the speaker's chair. One of the chair's most noticeable features is the sunburst on the top of the chair that shows a partial human-like face in the sun. Weeks may have been familiar with the famous chair and adapted the sunburst design for his initial design for the sunstone, but the more likely conclusion is that Weeks took the often-used architectural sunburst motif and adapted it to suit Joseph Smith's visionary understanding.

7. Weeks, Nauvoo Temple architectural drawings, drawing 2, CHL.

8. Brigham Young, "The Placing of the Last Capital on the Temple," in Joseph Smith Jr., *History of the Church of Jesus Christ of Latter-day Saints*, ed. B. H. Roberts, 2nd ed., rev., 7 vols. (Salt Lake City: Deseret Book, 1971), 7:323. It is important to note that although Young indicated each capital included "five

stones," it was actually only four. Situated above the top of the sunstone was an abacus stone or what Young called "the cap." But above the abacus stone was another abacus layer of stone that went all the way around the temple, which explains why Young indicated the capitals consisted of five stones. The additional abacus layer can be seen in several of the photographic images of the original Nauvoo Temple.

9. George D. Smith, ed., *An Intimate Chronicle: The Journals of William Clayton* (Salt Lake City: Signature Books, 1991), 533.

10. It is not known who crafted the moonstones. The moonstones are not nearly as ornate as the sunstones and would require less skill by the stone carver to fashion. Two moonstones are known to exist. One is on display in the Joseph Smith Historic Site, owned by the Community of Christ (formerly RLDS). Blake M. Roney, cofounder and former chair of Nu Skin, procured an original moonstone and later donated it to the LDS Church in the late 1990s. According to Roney, the moonstone is being stored in Nauvoo, Illinois.

11. Andrew H. Hedges, Alex D. Smith, and Richard Lloyd Anderson, eds., *Journals Volume 2: December 1841–April 1843*, vol. 2 of the Journal series of *The Joseph Smith Papers*, ed. Dean C. Jesse, Ronald K. Esplin, and Richard Lyman Bushman (Salt Lake City: Church Historian's Press, 2011), 329.

12. David Nye White, "The Prairies, Nauvoo, Joe Smith, the Temple, the Mormons, etc.," *Pittsburgh Weekly Gazette*, 15 September1843, 3.

13. Charles Lambert, Autobiography, circa 1885, 13, typescript, MS 1130, CHL.

14. William Clayton, History of the Nauvoo Temple, 96, MS 3365, CHL. Clayton's history is also cited in the Journal History of the Church of Jesus Christ of Latter-day Saints, 31 December 1843, 96, CHL; see also Benjamin Mitchell, Autobiography, in Autobiographies of Early Seventies, typescript, 53, CHL.

15. See Nauvoo Temple Committee Daybook E, 6 December 1844, 58, CR 342 9, CHL.

16. James Henry Rollins, Reminiscences, 23–24, typescript, MS 2393, CHL.

17. Josiah Quincy, *Figures from the Past from the Leaves of Old Journals* (Boston: Roberts Brothers, 1883), 389–90. See also Jed W. Woodworth, "Josiah Quincy's 1844 Visit to Joseph Smith," *BYU Studies* 39, no. 4 (2000): 71–87.

18. Roger P. Jackson to Alexander L. Baugh, 24 October 2019, in author's possession. Jackson is president of FFKR Architects in Salt Lake City and the architect of the reconstructed Nauvoo Illinois Temple, completed in 2002.

19. See Clayton, History of the Nauvoo Temple, 59–60; see also Smith, *History of the Church*, 7:274, 323–24.

20. Clayton, History of the Nauvoo Temple, 60; see also Smith, *History of the Church*, 7:323–24.

21. Brigham Young, "An Epistle of the Twelve," *Times and Seasons* 5, no. 18 (1 October 1844): 668.

22. Clayton, History of the Nauvoo Temple, 62–63. Clayton also noted that the last capital was carved by Harvey Stanley.

23. Wandle Mace, Autobiography, manuscript, 120, MSS 921, L. Tom Perry Special Collections, Harold B. Lee Library, Brigham Young University, Provo, UT, copy in author's possession.

24. Joseph Earl Arrington, "Destruction of the Mormon Temple at Nauvoo," *Journal of the Illinois State Historical Society* 40, no. 4 (December 1947): 418–19.

25. See Matthew S. McBride, *A House for the Most High: The Story of the Original Nauvoo Temple* (Salt Lake City: Greg Kofford Books, 2007), 360–63; and Glen M. Leonard, *Nauvoo: A Place of Peace, A People of Promise* (Salt Lake City: Deseret Book; Provo, UT: Brigham Young University Press, 2005), 627–30.

26. *Carthage Republican*, 2 February 1865, as cited in Virginia S. Harrington and J. C. Harrington, *Rediscovery of the Nauvoo Temple: Report on Archaeological Excavations* (Salt Lake City: Nauvoo Restoration, Inc., 1971), 6.

27. D. L. Musselman Sr., to Mr. E. G. Thompson, 9 November 1903, Historical Society of Quincy and Adams County, Quincy, Illinois (hereafter cited as HSQAC), copy in author's possession. See also Joel W. Scarborough to Dear Historical Society Member, 9 December 1988, HSQAC, copy in author's possession.

28. "Nauvoo Sunstone a Century Later," *Journal of the Illinois State Historical Society* 50, no. 1 (Spring 1957): 100; see also Carl Landrum, "Sun stones go back to Mormons," *Quincy Herald-Whig*, 7 August 1983, 4E.

29. See "Sunstone is unveiled at the temple site," *Church News*, 2 July 1994, 7; also *Nauvoo Temple Sunstone Commemoration Program*, 26 June 1994, M282.1 N314scp 1994, CHL.

30. Benjamin C. Pykles to Alexander L. Baugh, November 26, 2019, copy in author's possession. Pykles is the historic sites curator for The Church of Jesus Christ of Latter-day Saints.

31. See Carl and Shirley Landrum, *Images of America: Quincy, Illinois* (Charleston, SC: Arcadia Publishing, 1999); and Carl and Shirley Landrum, *Landrum's Quincy*, vol. 4 (Quincy: Justice Publications, 1997), 146.

32. See "Chaddock College," Wikipedia.

33. D. L. Musselman Jr., to the Historical Society of Quincy and Adams County, Illinois, 14 October 1953, MS 361, HSQAC, copy in author's possession. Musselman also said that before the sunstone was moved from the Jefferson School ground to the Chaddock College campus, it was placed for a short time on the grounds of Washington Park in downtown Quincy, but there is no existing documentation to support this. A short newspaper article published in the *Quincy Herald-Whig* states that after the stone was moved from the Jefferson School property to the Chaddock College campus, the local school board challenged the acquisition of the Mormon relic by the college. See "From the Mormon Temple," undated *Quincy Herald-Whig* newspaper clipping, MS 361, HSQAC.

34. J. H. Grafton to J. W. Emery, 4 December 1912; J. W. Emery to J. H. Grafton, 5 December 1912 (the letter was incorrectly dated 1913); J. H. Grafton to J. W. Emery, 12 December 1912; and J. H. Crafton to J. W. Emery, 12 December 1912, HSQAC, copies in author's possession. J. H. Grafton represented the trustees of the Chaddock Boys School, and J. W. Emery was the president of the Quincy Historical Society.

35. Joel W. Scarborough to Dear Historical Society Member, 9 December 1988.

36. See Eric Johnson, "Historical Society sells Mormon Temple 'sunstone' to Smithsonian Institution," *Quincy Herald-Whig*, undated newspaper clipping, HSQAC, circa 9 December 1988, copy in author's possession.

37. Richard E. Ahlborn, as quoted in Lee Davidson, "Smithsonian pays $100,000 for sunstone from Nauvoo Temple," *Church News*, 2 December 1989, 5.

38. Joel W. Scarborough to Dear Historical Society Member, 9 December 1988. See also Eric Johnson, "Smithsonian pays $100,000 for Mormon Temple sunstone," *Quincy Herald-Whig*, 13 December 1988, 10–B, HSQAC, copy in author's possession.

39. Johnson, "Smithsonian pays $100,000," 10–B; and "Crew begins removing sunstone," *Quincy Herald-Whig*, 15 December 1988, newspaper clipping, HSQAC, copy in author's possession.

40. "Around and About SI," *The Torch*, July 1990, 2. The periodical is the Smithsonian employee newsletter.

41. See Joel W. Scarborough to Dear Historical Society Member, January 1990, HSQAC, copy in author's possession.

42. Richard E. Ahlborn, as cited in Davidson, "Smithsonian Pays $100,000," 5.

43. See "'American Stories' Exhibition Opens at National Museum of American History," https://americanhistory.si.edu/press/releases/%E2%80%9Camer

ican-stories%E2%80%9D-exhibition-opens-national-museum-american
-history.

44. Richard E. Ahlborn, as cited in Davidson, "Smithsonian pays $100,000," 5.

45. Elizabeth Schleichert, "The object at hand," *Smithsonian Magazine*, August 1994, 14.

46. Charles Lanman, *Summer in the Wilderness; Embracing a Canoe Voyage up the Mississippi and around Lake Superior* (New York: D. Appleton and Company, 1847), 32. In July 1847, while on his river excursion, Lanman stopped at Nauvoo, where he spent several hours in the community during which time he was given a personal tour of the Nauvoo Temple by an unnamed Latter-day Saint, possibly Joseph L. Heywood, John S. Fullmer, or Almon W. Babbitt, who had been appointed trustees of the Church's properties and had remained in Nauvoo. Lanman's narrative about Nauvoo comprises four printed pages.

Richard L. Evans at Music and the Spoken Word. © *Intellectual Reserve, Inc.*

"MAKE THE AIR WITH MUSIC RING": A PERSONAL PERSPECTIVE ON THE TABERNACLE CHOIR AT TEMPLE SQUARE

LLOYD D. NEWELL

Lloyd D. Newell is a professor of Church history and doctrine at Brigham Young University who has served for three decades as the announcer and writer of Music and the Spoken Word.

> *The Mormon Tabernacle Choir has become so much a part of America. I think of it as being like the Grand Canyon or Mount Rushmore.*[1]
>
> —Charles Osgood

My involvement with the Tabernacle Choir at Temple Square spans more than three decades. *Music and the Spoken Word*, the choir's weekly broadcast, began its ninetieth year in July of 2019. But to really tell the story of this remarkable choir, you have to go back to at least the summer of 1847.

That was when trail-weary pioneers began planting crops in their new home, the wilderness of the Salt Lake Valley. A lot depended on the success of those crops. But the pioneers seemed to sense that they were doing more than just establishing an agricultural community; they were creating a religious haven. They were building the kingdom of God. So every Sunday, they set aside the plow and gathered for worship services under a crude bowery of brush and branches.[2] From the beginning, their worship included songs of praise, and a favorite was "Come, Come, Ye Saints," an anthem by William Clayton with lines that describe well their singing in the desert:

We'll make the air with music ring,
Shout praises to our God and King. . . .
Oh, how we'll make this chorus swell—
All is well! All is well![3]

Needless to say, there were not many choirs like this one making the dry western air ring with praise in 1847. These were not your typical fur trappers, prospectors, explorers, or homesteaders seeking a grubstake in the West. No, these were humble religious folk who had been converted to The Church of Jesus Christ of Latter-day Saints, primarily from western Europe and the northeastern United States. Most of them would just as soon have remained in their comfortable settlements in Nauvoo, Illinois, and the surrounding areas. But religious persecution drove them away, and their prophetic leader, Brigham Young, led them west in search of peace and religious freedom. It was love of God, not love of adventure or open spaces, that brought them to "the place which God for us prepared, far away in the West."[4] They took with them what they could carry in a

The Tabernacle Choir has provided more than ninety years of continuous network broadcasting. Church History Library.

wagon and in their hearts—courage, tenacity, faith in God, and, of course, a love of singing.

And so it was that just months after the first wagons rolled into the barren Salt Lake Valley, Brigham Young asked John Parry (from Wales) to prepare a choir for the Church's first general conference in the Great Basin.[5] Prophetic though he was, could Brother Brigham have known that he had just founded what would become arguably the most widely recognized choir in the world?

The choir rehearsed twice weekly and sang at all kinds of Church functions and community celebrations. The choir first made its home on Temple Square in an outdoor bowery, but the Saints quickly outgrew it and the small building that replaced it. In April 1863, Church leaders announced plans to build a massive tabernacle to accommodate its quarterly general conferences, along with other religious and community events. The intent was to seat as many as ten thousand—ambitious plans for a group that only sixteen years earlier was clattering down Emigration Canyon in covered wagons.

The staggering cost of three hundred thousand dollars was amassed in donations from the people, much of it in the form of building materials, bread, vegetables, jewelry, clothing, and labor. The building was usable by 6 October 1867 and formally finished and dedicated in October 1875. The choir has been singing in the Salt Lake Tabernacle ever since.[6]

Besides its iconic pipe organ, the Tabernacle is known for its spectacular acoustics and vibrant sound, making it the perfect home for a choir. The Tabernacle has carried the distinctive sounds of the choir clearly and faithfully for more than 150 years, so it is fitting that the Tabernacle Choir would carry the Tabernacle's name.

Before long, the choir set out to share its gifts outside the Salt Lake Valley. This included participating in an eisteddfod, a renowned choral competition, at the Columbian Exposition at the 1893 World's Fair. Four hundred choir members and support personnel traveled to Chicago on a ten-car train for the event. It had been less than fifty years since their wagon trains had made their trek in the opposite direction, and some of those pioneers were now among the singers returning to Illinois.

The music at the competition was not for the fainthearted: "Worthy Is the Lamb," from Handel's *Messiah*; "Blessed Is the Man Who Fears Him," from Mendelssohn's *Elijah*; and "Now the Impetuous Torrents Rise," from the oratorio *David and Saul*. The choir took second place to a combined choir from Scranton, Pennsylvania, although the judges admitted, "It was in reality very difficult to determine who were the victors, the Scranton or the Tabernacle singers, the contestants being so nearly equal, and the degree of excellence with each on all points being of such a high standard." The runners-up were not disheartened, feeling "that in a contest of such magnitude, to be almost if not equal to the best talent the country could produce, was something for the West to be proud of."[7]

Over the next few years, the choir performed in Denver (1896), the San Francisco World's Fair (1902), the Yukon Exposition in Seattle (1909), New York (1911), and Washington, DC (1911). But nationwide exposure was about to reach a major turning point because of a new communication technology that would change the world.

MUSIC AND THE SPOKEN WORD

In the 1920s, radio fascinated the public. All across the country, people began to recognize its tremendous possibilities. In Utah, a tiny radio station called KZN—later known as KSL—was launched by The Church of Jesus Christ of Latter-day Saints in 1922 as an offshoot of the Church-owned newspaper, the *Deseret News*. An NBC radio affiliate, KZN broadcast from the roof of a building in downtown Salt Lake City. Its first broadcast, on 6 May 1922, was a message from Church President Heber J. Grant. Within a few years, Latter-day Saints listened to the first radio broadcast of general conference, and listeners in Salt Lake City could tune in to Tabernacle choir rehearsals every Thursday evening.

Soon afterward, station manager Earl J. Glade had a brilliant idea: a nationwide, weekly broadcast of the Tabernacle Choir. He convinced both the choir and NBC management that it could be done. So on 15 July 1929 they gave it a try. By today's standards, it was a low-tech production: a young announcer, Ted Kimball, climbed a fifteen-foot ladder and spoke into a single microphone (borrowed from the radio station); a technician

Tabernacle Choir in 1991, photo by Christina Smith. © Intellectual Reserve, Inc.

stood on the basement stairs so he could communicate with headquarters in New York by telegraph; and *Music and the Spoken Word* was born. Thirty radio stations received that first transmission.[8]

It was an immediate success. The *New York City Telegraph* gave this praise: "Somewhere in the world there may be more than one brilliant choral organization other than the Mormon Tabernacle Choir, but there is no broadcasting in America today to equal the one that comes from the air over the National Broadcasting System."[9] NBC president M. H. Aylsworth wired congratulations: "Your wonderful Tabernacle program is making great impression in New York. Have heard from leading ministers. All impressed by the program. Eagerly awaiting your next."[10]

Well, what came next is more than ninety years of continuous network broadcasting—the longest run in history. Today, *Music and the Spoken Word* is carried to the world on radio, television, cable, and YouTube, in addition to a live stream each Sunday morning at 9:30 a.m. mountain standard time. These platforms can be accessed from anyplace in the world, and they reach a weekly audience of millions.

Among those audience members from the past were my grandparents. They tuned in on an old upright Philco radio from the Idaho family farm during the 1930s. My mother has since handed that radio down to me, and it is a cherished family heirloom. It still works, even with antique tubes and wiring. Though it embodies so much history, its wooden frame is smooth and mostly unmarked. For me, it is a visual and auditory link to the early years of *Music and the Spoken Word*.

In my mind's eye, I can see my forebears gathered around the radio on a Sunday morning, tuning in to hear the choir's weekly broadcast. Their tiny farm town was hundreds of miles away from Salt Lake City, so it must have seemed like a miracle that they could hear the Tabernacle Choir in their own living room! Week after week, they looked forward to the program's uplifting music and familiar refrains: "From the Crossroads of the West, we welcome you to a program of inspirational music and spoken word."

Literally every week since 15 July 1929, *Music and the Spoken Word* has seen its audience through war and depression, peace and prosperity. Its inspirational programming has steadied troubled hearts, brought peace, added upon joys, and led one generation after another to God. And while the times and technology have certainly changed, the essence of this broadcast has remained the same week after week, encouraging, comforting, and guiding its audience to greater good. In a world of increasing negativism, this timeless treasure of music and message is a beacon of hope and harmony that calms troubled hearts. In a world of loud noises and confusing voices, the choir's broadcast is a secure and steady anchor of timeless truth and reassuring joy. The broadcast has endured through the pages of history, always there—steady, reliable, and strong in uncertain times.

In 1954, *Life* magazine commemorated the twenty-fifth year of *Music and the Spoken Word* with these words: "Those who know this program need no arguments for listening to it. . . . Millions have heard [the choir], and more millions, we hope, will hear them in years to come. It is a national institution to be proud of, but what matters more is that Americans can be linked from ocean to ocean and year to year by the same brief respite from the world's week, and by a great chord of common thoughts on God and love and the everlasting things."[11]

Among all of the praise and awards *Music and the Spoken Word* has gathered over the years, and they are many, this may be its most important achievement: the way it has connected with generation after generation over the decades. Somehow, the choir and its music has found a way to touch hearts, consistently, for more than ninety years and counting.

Music and the Spoken Word was inducted into the National Association of Broadcasters Hall of Fame in 2004, joining such legends as Bob Hope, Edward R. Murrow, Bing Crosby, Paul Harvey, and Oprah Winfrey. The broadcast was inducted into the National Radio Hall of Fame in 2010. Other awards and honors given to the choir include a Grammy for its rendition of "Battle Hymn of the Republic" (1959), the Peabody Award (1944, 1962), the Freedoms Foundation's George Washington Honor Medal (1981), two Emmy Awards (1987, 2013), the National Medal of Arts (2003), the Mother Teresa Award (2006), and the Library of Congress's National Recording Registry (2004) for the choir's 1958 recording of *Messiah*. The choir's recordings regularly top the Billboard charts and include multiple gold and platinum records.

As its worldwide reach expanded through weekly broadcasts, the choir continued to tour nationally and internationally, allowing more people to hear the choir in person. Their first international tour, in 1955, included performances in Scotland, London, Copenhagen, Amsterdam, Berlin, and Paris. Subsequent tours have taken the choir (along with orchestra members and support staff—a small army of more than five hundred) to the finest music halls in the world, from Jerusalem to Sydney, Mexico City to Budapest, Moscow to São Paulo, and Vienna to Tokyo. They have been on stage at the Boston Esplanade, the Hollywood Bowl, Carnegie Hall, Wolf Trap, Red Rocks, Chautauqua, Tanglewood, and Mount Rushmore, to name just a few. The choir's largest audience for a single performance came during the opening ceremonies of the 2002 Winter Olympics, when 3.5 billion people watched as highly acclaimed conductor and composer John Williams directed the choir in a composition written specifically for them. Williams commented later, "I think the Mormon Tabernacle Choir has a glow about it, an inspirational glow.

They enjoy making music that is not commercially driven in any way. These are people who are there for the joy of music. It's not a job with them; it's a mission."[12]

CHANGING HEARTS AND PERCEPTIONS

And it's not just about beautiful music, although the choir, of course, excels at that. It's also about changing hearts and perceptions about the Church. Several years ago, choir officials conducted a survey of listeners; commenting on the results of that survey, music historian Michael Hicks noted "that the onetime emblem of the Mormon menace had become an American institution. Even a cursory examination of the country's mass culture suggests how thoroughly it has embraced and absorbed the . . . Tabernacle Choir." According to Hicks, the Tabernacle Choir has "come to symbolize what seem to many non-Mormons the church's most admirable and even most 'American' traits: cooperation, conservatism, ceremoniousness, and the pursuit of recognition."[13] Another historian, Reid Neilson, added, "The choral group that traces its musical roots to a hobbled-together pioneer choir is now part of America's popular culture. The church was mainstreamed into America in large measure by its Tabernacle Choir."[14]

Good feelings toward the choir don't always equate to good feelings toward the Church, but they're definitely a good start. Historian Gerald A. Petersen put it this way: "It is not unusual for a minister or layman of another religion to vigorously attack the Mormons' beliefs while anxiously awaiting his newest recording of the Mormon Tabernacle Choir—and thereafter to use the recording as an example for his own choir to emulate."[15]

THE NATION'S CAPITAL AND THE CHOIR

One key to the choir's nationwide respect has been its many high-profile performances in the nation's capital. The Washington, DC, area is the choir's most-visited location outside Utah with seventeen visits since 1911.[16] Those visits include seven presidential inaugurations and sold-out concerts where U.S. presidents, dignitaries, politicians, and other civic and business leaders—along with countless residents from all walks of life—were their honored guests. It's an appropriate setting for "America's Choir," which is the unofficial title given by President Ronald Reagan, who said, "At my first inauguration as president of the United States, I wanted very much to reignite the fires of liberty and re-inspire the American spirit. And no one sings the anthems of America quite like the Mormon Tabernacle Choir." Reagan continued, "The Choir's singing was a highlight of our inauguration, as we knew it would be. I'm sure I speak for all Americans when I say thank you for saying so well what all of us feel about this land of the free and home of the brave. There is no more inspirational moment for any American—and that includes Ronald Reagan—than to hear the Mormon Tabernacle Choir sing 'Glory, glory, hallelujah, His truth is marching on.'"[17]

The first time the choir traveled to Washington, DC (and the first time they performed for a U.S. president) was in November 1911—sixty-four years after the pioneers arrived in the Salt Lake Valley, fifteen

The Tabernacle Choir at President Ronald Reagan's inaugural parade, 20 January 1981. Ronald Reagan Presidential Library.

The Tabernacle Choir float during President Reagan's inaugural parade. Ronald Reagan Presidential Library.

years after Utah became a state, and eighteen years before the choir launched its nationwide broadcast. It was part of a fifty-five-hundred-mile, twenty-three-city public relations tour across the country and to major cities along the East Coast.[18] And it came at a critical time for the Church's public relations. Popular bias against the Church was strong, and many people across the nation still viewed Latter-day Saints with suspicion. This sentiment was particularly evident just a few years earlier during the nationwide controversy over the seating of Latter-day Saint Apostle Reed Smoot in the U.S. Senate. The Smoot hearings, as they came to be known, drew national attention and revealed that many Americans, including leaders in Washington, held strong prejudices and misconceptions about the Church.

It was in this climate that the choir arrived in the nation's capital for a command performance in the East Room of the White House to sing for President and Mrs. Taft and about fifty other guests, including a group of senators and ambassadors. This would begin a tradition of singing for presidents that would reach into the twenty-first century.[19]

The Tabernacle Choir float at President Reagan's inaugural parade. Ronald Reagan Presidential Library.

Favorable comments by music critics along the way boosted the image of the Latter-day Saints, yet reception during the tour varied widely as recurrent antagonistic feelings in some areas of the country were present. In several cities, hall managers refused to book the choir, and campaigns were organized to discourage people from attending choir concerts. In Philadelphia, local clergy circulated a petition decrying the appearance of the choir, saying that it was "Mormon propaganda" and calling for a boycott of the performance. The effort failed.[20] In Richmond, Virginia, protests erupted and the local newspaper opined that the choir's tour was a plot to "propitiate favor for Mormonism with the uninformed and thoughtless."[21] And the Union Theological Seminary asked people to "give up fine music rather than lead your fellowman toward [the] standards of Joseph Smith."[22] Yet performing at the White House and for the president was a signal to the nation of the acceptance of religious diversity and the acknowledgment that members of the restored Church of Jesus Christ were part of America. As one historian noted, "The president's invitation was a clarion call that religious prejudice would not be tolerated in the United States."[23]

The choir did not perform in the nation's capital again for forty-seven years, returning in 1958 to perform for President Dwight D. Eisenhower at the White House. This tour included three performances and a recording of *Messiah* with the Philadelphia Orchestra and Eugene Ormandy, who once called the choir "the greatest choir in the world."[24]

After that, visits to Washington, DC, became much more frequent as the choir became more embedded in Americana and its cultural and musical landscape. In February 1964, U.S. president Lyndon B. Johnson [LBJ] asked President David O. McKay if the choir could come to sing at the White House that summer. President McKay was thrilled with the opportunity; a date was agreed upon and a tour arranged. On 23 July, while on their New York World's Fair Tour,[25] the choir sang at the White House under the direction of Richard P. Condie.

Before the year was up, and upon the presidential election of LBJ in the fall of 1964, the choir was invited to return to Washington, DC, to perform at President Johnson's inaugural ceremonies. The choir sang "This Is My Country" at the U.S. Capitol in the official swearing-in ceremony; LBJ had the stand at the capitol rebuilt to accommodate the choir. He remarked that the choir was "the best thing connected with the inaugural ceremonies." It was the first of seven performances at presidential inaugurations, a tradition that has earned the choir nicknames like "the state choir of the republic" or "the anointed voice of America's civil religion."[26] President David O. McKay called this performance for President Johnson "the greatest single honor that has come to the Tabernacle Choir."[27] It lifted the reputation and visibility of the choir and the Church across the country.

Since then, the choir has performed for U.S. presidents of both parties in many settings, including swearing-in ceremonies, inaugural parades, inaugural opening ceremonies, and devotional programs. The choir is nonpartisan, and its participation in these events is not an implied support of party affiliations or politics but rather a demonstration of its support for freedom, civility, and the peaceful transition of power.[28]

One national publication reflected, "The Tabernacle Choir has performed for royalty and heads of state from the world over, but never has it lost the common touch, the ability to stir the hearts of all mankind as it lifts its collective voices in singing of the values we all cherish and in praising the God who created us all."[29]

PERSONAL EXPERIENCE WITH THE CHOIR

I have been involved with the choir long enough to get a sense of its enduring legacy. For me, as the program's announcer, that legacy begins with nineteen-year-old Ted Kimball. The son of Tabernacle organist Edward P. Kimball, Ted served as the first announcer, filling this role for several months before leaving to serve a full-time Church mission. Then, in June 1930, a twenty-four-year-old announcer from KSL Radio, Richard L. Evans, was chosen to replace him. In time, he would begin to add short thoughts, called sermonettes, to the weekly program. Just four years later, he received a national award as the best radio announcer in the country. He subsequently served as an Apostle for the Church, a nationally syndicated newspaper columnist, and the president of Rotary International. Perhaps no one has had a greater impact on *Music and the Spoken Word* than Richard L. Evans. He was the broadcast's announcer and writer for forty-one years; he produced the program each week and toured with the choir, all while serving as a General Authority for The Church of Jesus Christ for more than thirty years.

After Elder Evans, J. Spencer Kinard spent eighteen years as the announcer of *Music and the Spoken Word*, and then I was asked by Church President Gordon B. Hinckley to serve in this assignment. "This calling will change your life," he told me. My first broadcast was on 25 November 1990, the Sunday before Thanksgiving. Now, more than three decades later, I deeply understand the truth of President Hinckley's words—this calling has changed my life. It has been a marvelous blessing, a weighty responsibility, and a sacred trust and honor. My life and my family's lives are undeniably better because of it.

President Hinckley said something else that still rings in my ears all these years later. He said with great earnestness, "Each week, your Spoken

Word should be an inspirational gem." Every time I prepare one of these weekly messages, I ponder his charge. I ask myself: Is this message inspirational? Does it enlighten and uplift? Does it add an insight and perspective that is wise and interesting and encouraging? I can sincerely say that each message is carefully considered and lovingly written, and each is motivated by a genuine desire to share some timeless wisdom, an eternal truth, or a principle that will teach and lift and inspire.

I have been blessed to travel the world with the choir—from Jerusalem to Berlin to Paris to Toronto to Washington, DC, to Dallas to Los Angeles and many points in between—announcing and emceeing countless concerts and performances, as well as presenting more than sixteen hundred Spoken Word messages. I may be biased, but I believe the Tabernacle Choir at Temple Square is the greatest choir of all time, and it truly just keeps getting better. I cannot express the joy, blessing, comfort, and strengthening influence it has been for me to begin every Sunday morning since 1990 with these dedicated, talented singers and musicians at my side. There's nothing like this remarkable broadcast with this remarkable choir and orchestra anywhere in the world.

In 1974 Richard Condie concluded his seventeen-year tenure as conductor of the Tabernacle Choir with a simple gesture. At the end of his final *Music and the Spoken Word* broadcast, he gave the choir the downbeat for the final song and then, with no fanfare, simply set down his baton and stepped down from the podium as the choir went on singing. Since that day, the director at the conclusion of every performance has set down his baton, turned to the audience, and joined the choir in singing those poignant words, "God be with you till we meet again."[30]

This song, which continues to be the choir's signature signoff, is a fitting expression of our mission: "We hope we have helped you feel a little closer to God today, and we hope that feeling can continue in your heart until we have a chance to be with you again."

Beyond the tours and recordings, the awards and the accolades, no matter how well known the choir may become around the world, it will always be composed of individuals—thousands of them over the years—who still "make the air with music ring." All who associate with the choir—and most who hear the choir perform—know full well that its mission is about far more than beautiful music or exemplary expression and tonality. These singers see themselves as musical ambassadors of Jesus Christ. Their mission is to share his love, his truths, and his Spirit with all who listen.

That has always been the focus of the Tabernacle Choir—to bless the people who gather to be uplifted, to be filled, and to find what they are missing inside themselves. Listeners who tune in to the broadcast and come to the Tabernacle, the Conference Center, and concert halls around the world speak not only of what they hear but also of what they feel. The heart of the choir's message is simple: "God lives. Jesus is the Christ. Life is worth living. There is hope and healing ahead." They don't sing words, they sing feelings. As former organist John Longhurst said, "The choir members come to this work with a high sense of purpose, a very strong unifying sense of mission, and when they perform you can sense this spirituality, this deep inner commitment musically and spiritually to what they are doing."[31]

As one of the least of those who have been part of the choir's longstanding legacy, I leave you with the same words with which I have concluded the broadcast each week for more than thirty years: "Until we meet again, may peace be with you . . . this day and always."

APPENDIX

TABERNACLE CHOIR TRIPS TO THE WASHINGTON, DC AREA

YEAR	TRIP PURPOSE	LOCATION
1911	American Land & Irrigation Congress Tour; Concert for President and Mrs. Taft	Washington, DC, White House
1958	Grand American Tour	Washington, DC, White House
1964	New York World's Fair Tour	Washington, DC, White House
1965	Inauguration of President Lyndon B. Johnson	Washington, DC
1969	Inaugural concert for President Richard Nixon	Washington, DC
1970	National Christmas Tree Lighting Ceremonies	Washington, DC
1973	Inauguration of President Richard Nixon	Washington, DC
1974	Washington, DC, Temple Tour	Washington, DC
1976	U.S. Bicentennial Tour	Washington, DC
1981	Inauguration President Ronald Reagan	Washington, DC
1989	Inauguration of President George H. W. Bush	Washington, DC
1995	American Requiem Tour	Washington, DC, Kennedy Center
2001	Inauguration parade for President George W. Bush	Washington, DC
2003	Northeast United States Tour	Wolf Trap, Fairfax County, Virginia
2011	Eastern States Tour	Wolf Trap, Fairfax County, Virginia
2015	Atlantic Coast Tour	Bethesda, Maryland
2017	Inauguration of President Donald Trump	Washington, DC

NOTES

1. Heidi Swinton, *America's Choir: A Commemorative Portrait of the Mormon Tabernacle Choir* (Salt Lake City: Deseret Book, 2004), 99. In October 2018 the Mormon Tabernacle Choir changed its name to the Tabernacle Choir at Temple Square.

2. For additional information, and a previous work on portions of this content, see Lloyd Newell and Heidi Swinton, *Pioneer Magazine* 64, no. 2 (2017): 2–16.

3. William Clayton, "Come, Come, Ye Saints," *Hymns* (Salt Lake City: The Church of Jesus Christ of Latter-day Saints, 1985), no. 30.

4. Clayton, "Come, Come, Ye Saints."

5. Other conductors in the early days included Stephen Goddard (choir leader from Nauvoo), James Smithies, Charles John Thomas, Robert Sands, Ebenezer Beesley (choir conductor from 1860–89), Evan Stephens (1889–1916), Anthony C. Lund (1916–35), J. Spencer Cornwall (1935–57), Richard P. Condie (1957–74), Jay E. Welch (1974), Jerold D. Ottley (1975–98), Craig Jessop (1999–2008), and Mack Wilberg (2008–present). Compositions by several of these conductors are included in the Church's current hymnal.

6. When necessary to accommodate larger audiences, the choir also performs in the Conference Center, a nearly twenty-two-thousand-seat facility north of Temple Square, dedicated in 2000. For example, the choir's annual Christmas concerts and its weekly *Music and the Spoken Word* broadcasts during the summer months originate from the Conference Center.

7. E. A. McDaniel, *Utah at the World's Columbian Exposition* (n.p., self-pub., 1894), 14; digitized by David O. McKay Library, Brigham Young University–Idaho.

8. At the enticement of CBS founder and broadcast pioneer William S. Paley, in 1932 the broadcast switched to the CBS Radio Network, where it remains today.

9. Swinton, *America's Choir*, 102. "The Choir's 300 members practiced for a month before the first live broadcast, holding a final 'radio dress rehearsal' the week before. The chief divisional engineer of NBC called it an 'epic' event, with 10,000 radio fans eagerly awaiting the program. In the early broadcasts, the announcer would aim the one microphone in the direction of whichever section was singing at the moment."

10. Swinton, *America's Choir*, 104.

11. Richard L. Evans, *From the Crossroads* (New York: Harper and Brothers, 1955), 14.

12. Swinton, *America's Choir*, 3.

13. Michael Hicks, *Mormonism and Music: A History* (Urbana: University of Illinois Press, 1989), 166.

14. Reid Neilson, *Exhibiting Mormonism: The Latter-day Saints and the 1893 Chicago World's Fair* (New York: Oxford, 2011), 109.

15. Gerald A. Petersen, *More Than Music: The Mormon Tabernacle Choir* (Provo, UT: Brigham Young University Press, 1979), 36.

16. See appendix.

17. The Tabernacle Choir at Temple Square, "Where Does the Title America's Choir Come From?" *The Tabernacle Choir Blog*, 15 January 2014.

18. Several of the stops took choir members back to significant sites in Church history—Omaha (near Winter Quarters, Nebraska); Toledo (near Kirtland, Ohio); Rochester (Palmyra, New York). The choir performed three times a day for ten days in Madison Square Garden in New York City for the opening of the American Land and Irrigation Exposition.

19. See Charles Jeffrey Calman, *The Mormon Tabernacle Choir* (New York: Harper and Row, 1979), 76–77.

20. See Swinton, *America's Choir*, 73.

21. See *Mormon Studies Review* 2 (2015): 134–39; "East Fights West at the Land Show," *New York Times*, 4 November 1911, 7; Hicks, *Mormonism and Music*, 156–57.

22. Hicks, *Mormonism and Music*, 156–57.

23. Calman, *Mormon Tabernacle Choir*, 77.

24. Calman, *Mormon Tabernacle Choir*, 178.

25. The choir was part of the "Mormon Pavilion" at the New York World's Fair. The pavilion also included a replica of the Salt Lake Temple, murals depicting the history of the Church, and the film *Man's Search for Happiness*. The purpose was to introduce what many then considered an obscure religion to a national audience. Familiar with the popular *Music and the Spoken Word*, which by that time had an immense following, the fair leadership pressed for the choir to perform. On Sunday, 26 July, the choir performed in the Texas Pavilion Music Hall, filling nearly all twenty-four-hundred seats. They also performed the following day in front of record numbers. The fair was the choir's first stop on a 1964 nationwide tour that included stops at the White House in Washington, DC, as well as Rochester, Atlanta, Cleveland, Milwaukee, New Orleans, and Houston. The choir had a long history of performing at World's Fairs, beginning at the World's Columbian Exposition in 1893–94 in Chicago. The choir went on to sing in the 1934 Century of Progress Exposition in Chicago, the California-Pacific International Exposition in San Diego in 1935, and the Seattle World's Fair in 1962.

26. Michael Hicks, *The Mormon Tabernacle Choir: A Biography* (Urbana: University of Illinois Press, 2015), ix.

27. Hicks, *Mormon Tabernacle Choir*, 124.

28. Another noteworthy choir that should be mentioned is the Mormon Choir of Washington, DC, now known as the Washington DC Temple Choir. This respected choir was formed under the direction of Dr. Eugene Morlan in the fall of 1980. The choir is composed of singers and musicians selected by audition, with a current membership of eighty to one hundred from approximately fifty congregations in the Maryland and Virginia regions. The choir performs twelve to eighteen concerts each year and continues to include the traditional opening night of the Festival of Lights each Christmas at the Washington D.C. Temple Visitors' Center. The choir has also performed in the priesthood room on the seventh floor of the Washington D.C. Temple; the East Room of the White House; Brucker Hall on Fort Myer in Arlington, Virginia; the Kennedy Center for the Performing Arts; and the Maryland Statehouse at Annapolis. See dctemplechoir.org; see also Florian H. Thayn and Julian C. Lowe, *History of the Mormons in the Greater Washington Area: Members of the Church of Jesus Christ of Latter-Day Saints in the Washington, D.C. Area, 1839–1991* (Washington, DC: Community Printing Service, 1991).

29. "The Salt Lake Mormon Tabernacle Choir," *American Organist*, December 1988, 62.

30. Jeremiah E. Rankin, "God Be with You Till We Meet Again," *Hymns*, no. 152.

31. Swinton, *America's Choir*, 10.

THE FAMILY

A PROCLAMATION TO THE WORLD

THE FIRST PRESIDENCY AND COUNCIL OF THE TWELVE APOSTLES
OF THE CHURCH OF JESUS CHRIST OF LATTER-DAY SAINTS

WE, THE FIRST PRESIDENCY and the Council of the Twelve Apostles of The Church of Jesus Christ of Latter-day Saints, solemnly proclaim that marriage between a man and a woman is ordained of God and that the family is central to the Creator's plan for the eternal destiny of His children.

ALL HUMAN BEINGS—male and female—are created in the image of God. Each is a beloved spirit son or daughter of heavenly parents, and, as such, each has a divine nature and destiny. Gender is an essential characteristic of individual premortal, mortal, and eternal identity and purpose.

IN THE PREMORTAL REALM, spirit sons and daughters knew and worshipped God as their Eternal Father and accepted His plan by which His children could obtain a physical body and gain earthly experience to progress toward perfection and ultimately realize their divine destiny as heirs of eternal life. The divine plan of happiness enables family relationships to be perpetuated beyond the grave. Sacred ordinances and covenants available in holy temples make it possible for individuals to return to the presence of God and for families to be united eternally.

THE FIRST COMMANDMENT that God gave to Adam and Eve pertained to their potential for parenthood as husband and wife. We declare that God's commandment for His children to multiply and replenish the earth remains in force. We further declare that God has commanded that the sacred powers of procreation are to be employed only between man and woman, lawfully wedded as husband and wife.

WE DECLARE the means by which mortal life is created to be divinely appointed. We affirm the sanctity of life and of its importance in God's eternal plan.

HUSBAND AND WIFE have a solemn responsibility to love and care for each other and for their children. "Children are an heritage of the Lord" (Psalm 127:3). Parents have a sacred duty to rear their children in love and righteousness, to provide for their physical and spiritual needs, and to teach them to love and serve one another, observe the commandments of God, and be law-abiding citizens wherever they live. Husbands and wives—mothers and fathers—will be held accountable before God for the discharge of these obligations.

THE FAMILY is ordained of God. Marriage between man and woman is essential to His eternal plan. Children are entitled to birth within the bonds of matrimony, and to be reared by a father and a mother who honor marital vows with complete fidelity. Happiness in family life is most likely to be achieved when founded upon the teachings of the Lord Jesus Christ. Successful marriages and families are established and maintained on principles of faith, prayer, repentance, forgiveness, respect, love, compassion, work, and wholesome recreational activities. By divine design, fathers are to preside over their families in love and righteousness and are responsible to provide the necessities of life and protection for their families. Mothers are primarily responsible for the nurture of their children. In these sacred responsibilities, fathers and mothers are obligated to help one another as equal partners. Disability, death, or other circumstances may necessitate individual adaptation. Extended families should lend support when needed.

WE WARN that individuals who violate covenants of chastity, who abuse spouse or offspring, or who fail to fulfill family responsibilities will one day stand accountable before God. Further, we warn that the disintegration of the family will bring upon individuals, communities, and nations the calamities foretold by ancient and modern prophets.

WE CALL UPON responsible citizens and officers of government everywhere to promote those measures designed to maintain and strengthen the family as the fundamental unit of society.

This proclamation was read by President Gordon B. Hinckley as part of his message at the General Relief Society Meeting held September 23, 1995, in Salt Lake City, Utah.

The Family: A Proclamation to the World. © *Intellectual Reserve, Inc.*

THE PROPHETIC NATURE OF THE FAMILY PROCLAMATION

W. JUSTIN DYER AND MICHAEL A. GOODMAN

W. Justin Dyer and Michael A. Goodman are associate professors of Church history and doctrine at Brigham Young University.

Within the restored gospel of Jesus Christ, "The Family: A Proclamation to the World" is arguably one of the most influential documents produced in the past hundred years. Since its inception twenty-four years ago, it has been cited more than 230 times in general conference, hung on the walls of Latter-day Saint homes throughout the world, and presented to leaders around the globe. Indeed, in the first ever meeting between a pope and a prophet of The Church of Jesus Christ of Latter-day Saints, President Russell M. Nelson presented the pope with two items—a *Christus* statue and a copy of the family proclamation. Despite its central location within the teachings of the restored gospel of Jesus Christ, the purpose and place of the proclamation has been debated in many circles. Our purpose here is to provide clarity on both the cultural and political context and the prophetic nature of the family proclamation of The Church of Jesus Christ of Latter-day Saints.

The debates regarding the proclamation are particularly pointed in regard to the proclamation's political implications and uses. Indeed, although "The Family: A Proclamation to the World" was given to help individuals

President Russell M. Nelson and Elder M. Russell Ballard visit with Pope Francis at the Vatican in Rome, Italy, 2019. Deseret News.

avoid "deception concerning standards and values," it was also explicitly designed to encourage "officers of government" to promote "measures designed to maintain and strengthen family as the fundamental unit of society."[1] And while the personal application of the proclamation by individuals may be its most prominent feature, its public policy applications were immediate and are continuing. Indeed, Washington, DC, became a location central in efforts to promote the proclamation's principles.

On 13 November 1995, less than two months after presenting "The Family: A Proclamation to the World" in the general Relief Society meeting, President Gordon B. Hinckley traveled to Washington, DC, where the proclamation would be central in his visits with leaders in the nation's capital. President Hinckley gave a copy of the proclamation to U.S. president Bill Clinton in a meeting at the White House.[2] A prominent theme of the meeting was the "importance of promoting measures that maintain and strengthen the family as the fundamental unit of society."[3] The night before this White House meeting, President Hinckley hosted an informal reception with several Latter-day Saint members of Congress, providing each with a copy of the proclamation.[4] Four days after this meeting, Utah Congressman James Hansen read the proclamation into the congressional record of the House of Representatives. On December 15 of that same year, Utah senator Orrin Hatch read the proclamation on the floor of the Senate, stating, "I believe President Hinckley's words have relevance for all Americans and will help each of us reaffirm our commitment to the primacy of the family as the basis for strong communities and to the sanctity of marriage as the foundation for healthy families."[5] Before the year was out, the proclamation had gone from members of the Church to both houses of Congress and to the president of the United States. Later it would be included in an amicus brief to the U.S. Supreme Court, completing the proclamation's formal presentation to all three branches of the U.S. federal government.

As these events unfolded and as the proclamation became a prominent feature of Church teachings and its public activism, individuals became divided on several of the proclamation's statements. This generated some division on how the proclamation should be categorized within the theology of The Church of Jesus Christ of Latter-day Saints: Is it mainly political or religious in nature? Is the proclamation scripture? And does

President Gordon B. Hinckley and Sister Marjorie Hinckley. Photo by Jeffrey D. Allred, Deseret News.

the proclamation declare changeable policies or immutable principles? This chapter will seek to bring greater clarity to these important questions.

THE CONTEXT OF THE FAMILY PROCLAMATION'S ORIGINS

Although family norms have shifted considerably over time, the past half century has seen the most rapid and fundamental changes to marriage law in U.S. history. During the 1960s and 1970s, an emphasis on the individual grew into "expressive individualism,"[6] which asserts that an individual's desires are of primary moral concern. That is, within expressive individualism the highest "good" is the expression of oneself, however one chooses to define that self. Marriage laws and norms began to reflect these morals, and "individualistic marriages" began to rise in prominence in the 1960s, continuing to the present. Within an individualistic marriage, love is necessary to initiate the marriage, but the marriage was only seen as successful if it met "each partner's innermost psychological needs."[7] The rationale became "whatever an individual wants in a marriage is what they should be able to have, independent of any other considerations." In other words, the most noble responsibility one had was to oneself.

These changes have been recognized as creating increased fragility in family relationships by both conservative and liberal scholars. Progressive scholar Stephanie Coontz concludes, "Everywhere marriage is becoming more optional and more fragile. Everywhere the once-predictable link between marriage and child rearing is fraying. And everywhere relations between men and women are undergoing rapid and at times traumatic transformation."[8] Within this transformation the most fundamental shift of marriage law in U.S. history occurred: same-sex marriage. With individualistic marriage, societies began to view limits on the definition of marriage as nonsensical—despite the uniqueness of the male-female relationship that led virtually every society to define marriage as between a man and a woman. With the new moral groundwork of the individualistic marriage laid, in May 1970, the first same-sex couple in the U.S. applied for a marriage license.[9] The cultural tide that led to this attempt was not simply about same-sex marriage but a wholesale rethinking of

President Gordon B. Hinckley. Photo by Chuck Wing, Deseret News.

family relationships. This tide coincided with other rapid changes including higher rates of divorce, cohabitation, and out-of-wedlock child-
bearing. These and other family-related issues were not simply cultural
phenomena. Several of these family issues were featured in important Supreme Court rulings.[10] Within this background, we study the key cultural

events, social trends, and Church responses in the two decades preceding the proclamation.

The Stonewall riots of 1969 led to national attention of homosexuality, and calls for protections and rights for homosexuals emerged. For instance, in the 1970s, three same-sex couples applied for, but were denied, marriage licenses.[11] Man-woman family arrangements were also undergoing substantial change. Compared to the 1960s, the 1970s showed a 50 percent increase in the divorce rate and a doubling of the rate of out-of-wedlock childbirths. From 1970 to 1980, the number of cohabitating couples more than tripled, the percentage of children born to unmarried women nearly doubled, the marriage rate dropped 15 percent, and the divorce rate increased by 52 percent.[12] Legislation and policies recognizing same-sex partnerships and marriages began to increase, and the Unitarian Universalist Association was the first major Protestant denomination to approve same-sex marriages.[13] During this time of substantial family change, the Church's emphasis on the family appeared to grow. According to the LDS General Conference Corpus,[14] the use of the word "family" in general conference doubled from the 1960s to the 1970s, with its usage increasing in nearly every decade since. The October 1970 general conference was the first time "family" was said to be under "attack."[15] In 1970, the Church designated Monday nights as a night reserved for family home evening.[16] The Church began producing materials regarding homosexuality for ecclesiastical leaders and members alike. For example, in 1971 the Church produced a pamphlet authored by Spencer W. Kimball entitled *New Horizons for Homosexuals.*

While divorce rates tapered off from the 1980s to the 1990s (though still remaining high), the rate of out-of-wedlock births, cohabitation, and single-parent families continued to increase.[17] The 1990s were also a turning point in same-sex marriage. In December 1990, three same-sex couples applied for marriage licenses at the Hawaii Department of Health but were denied. A lawsuit ensued but was dismissed in October of 1991. The next month, the First Presidency issued a letter to all Church members that focused on standards of sexual purity, declaring—among other things—homosexual behavior as sinful and making a distinction between homosexual thoughts, feelings, and behaviors.[18] The 1991 Hawaii lawsuit was appealed to the Hawaii Supreme Court, which ruled in 1993 that limiting marriage to the male-female couple was discrimination based on sex. The case went to lower courts, where the burden of proof was on the state to show a compelling interest for denying same-sex couples the right to marry. This was the first time in the U.S. that a court of last resort employed a constitutional principle as the basis for same-sex marriage.[19]

Spurred by these and other events, lawmakers in Washington, DC were also active in the same-sex marriage debate, passing the Federal Defense of Marriage Act (DOMA) in 1996, an act that allowed states not to recognize same-sex marriages performed in other states. Even though Hawaii was one of the first states to seriously grapple with same-sex marriage legislation, the issue was spreading throughout the country. Eight of the first ten states or districts to legalize same sex marriage were on the east coast—Washington, DC, being one of them.[20]

During 1994, as the Hawaii case made its way through the courts, the Church was active on various fronts in supporting traditional marriage in Hawaii. This included a First Presidency letter sent to Church leaders throughout the world titled "Same Gender Marriages." The letter stated that "the principles of the gospel and the sacred responsibilities given us request that The Church of Jesus Christ of Latter-day Saints oppose any efforts to give legal authorization to marriages between persons of the same gender" and that "we encourage members to appeal to legislators, judges, and other government officials to preserve the purposes and sanctity of marriage between a man and a woman."[21]

This same year was the UN's International Year of the Family, which became pivotal in the creation of the proclamation. The Church sent representatives to a conference in Beijing, and Elder Boyd K. Packer asserted, "It was not pleasant what they [the representatives] heard." Although not elaborating on this statement, Elder Packer noted that he read the proceedings of a subsequent UN family conference in Cairo (5–13 September 1994) in which "the word *marriage* was not mentioned. It was at a conference on the family, but marriage was not even mentioned."[22] In New York, the UN Secretary General acknowledged initial conflict over even having a year of the family, stating, "At the time, there was no consensus. Some did not see the point of an International Year of the Family. . . . Some people argued that support for the family discriminates against those who prefer to live outside family units."[23]

It was later announced that a conference on the family would occur in Salt Lake City. Referring to a recommendation by his fellow Apostles, Elder Packer said, "Some of us made the recommendation: 'They are coming here. We had better proclaim our position.'" Elder Ballard similarly described the conference: "Various world conferences were held dealing either directly or indirectly with the family. In the midst of all that was stirring on this subject in the world, the First Presidency and the Quorum of the Twelve Apostles could see the importance of declaring to the world the revealed, true role of the family in the eternal plan of God."[24]

The proclamation became the Church's central document in defining its tenets on the family. Although primarily designed to aid individuals in their own family lives, it also called on government officials to "promote those measures designed to maintain and strengthen the family" and was given to government leaders in the U.S. and abroad. In June 2006, Elder Russell M. Nelson quoted from the proclamation at the U.S. Capitol Building in support of a constitutional amendment protecting marriage. As he later recounted, "Over the years, I've given copies of the proclamation to many governmental leaders not of our faith who've been grateful, telling them they were free to use it any way they might care to."[25]

The Church again brought the proclamation to Washington, DC, with eighteen religious groups in an amicus brief to the U.S. Supreme Court regarding same-sex marriage. A portion of the brief reads, "Marriage is also fundamental to the doctrine of The Church of Jesus Christ of Latter-day Saints. A formal doctrinal proclamation declares that 'marriage between a man and a woman is ordained of God.'" Whether coincidental or not, several dissenting opinions about the brief reflect principles within the proclamation. For instance, Justice John Roberts notes that marriage is fundamentally about establishing a family pattern that involves (1) those who conceive children caring for them and (2) the promotion of a lifelong, sexually faithful union between a man and a woman.[26]

Three days after the Supreme Court's decision legalizing same-sex marriage, the First Presidency (Thomas S. Monson, Henry B. Eyring, and Dieter F. Uchtdorf) referenced the proclamation and said, "Changes in the

The First Presidency: Thomas S. Monson, Henry B. Eyring, and Dieter F. Uchtdorf, 2008. © Intellectual Reserve, Inc.

civil law do not, indeed cannot, change the moral law that God has established. . . . We invite all to review and understand the doctrine contained in 'The Family: A Proclamation to the World.'"[27] The First Presidency directed local leaders to "meet with all adults, young men, and young women on either July 5 or July 12 in a setting other than sacrament meeting and read to them the entire statement."[28] The Church continued using the proclamation in court cases around the world. For example, in 2016 a letter from the Church was read in all congregations in Mexico, citing the proclamation as reasoning for members to oppose same-sex marriage.

THE PROPHETIC NATURE OF THE FAMILY PROCLAMATION

On learning of the political and public context behind the family proclamation, some have questioned what role God and revelation played in its inception. How members view the family proclamation can have profound consequences on their testimony of the restored gospel, the role of prophets and apostles, and doctrines related to gender, sexuality, and the family. Though a clear majority of members express confidence in Church teachings overall,[29] on issues regarding gender, sexuality and the family, that confidence appears to be lessoning for a minority of members. Questions related to many of the teachings in the proclamation appear to be strongest among the younger generations.[30]

CURRENT MEMBER UNDERSTANDING REGARDING GENDER, SEXUALITY, AND THE FAMILY

In her 2016 Next Mormons Survey (NMS), Jana Reiss asked a representative panel of Latter-day Saints about their views on issues related to gender, sexuality, and the family. The results indicate a moderate generational divide. Younger members appear to be less confident in Church teachings in general, especially teachings contained in the family proclamation. Figure 1 illustrates some of the NMS findings. The bars represent the percentage of members who consider each action to be morally wrong.

Similarly, when a PEW Research Center study asked whether homosexuality should be accepted by society, the number of Church members who agreed has risen from 24 percent in 2007 to 36 percent in 2014.[31] In the NMS study, that number was 48 percent in 2016. Between 50 and 60 percent of Latter-day Saint millennials agreed with the statement. When asked whether married or unmarried homosexual sex was morally wrong,

60 percent of millennials agreed that unmarried homosexual sex was immoral, while 50 percent agreed that married homosexual sex was immoral.

For some millennials, there appears to be a cultural disconnect from the teachings of the family proclamation, which state that the "powers of procreation are to be employed only between man and woman, lawfully wedded as husband and wife." Such a disconnect fits with a popular narrative that the family proclamation is largely a statement of policy rather than a prophetic doctrinal pronouncement. However, that narrative is contrary to how the First Presidency and Quorum of Twelve have described and defined the document for over two decades.

PROPHETIC DEFINITIONS AND DESCRIPTIONS OF THE FAMILY PROCLAMATION

To get a more complete view of how the family proclamation has been defined and described by Church leaders, we studied every reference to the family proclamation in general conference since it was given on 23 September 1995. There have been more than 230 references to the family proclamation in general conference alone, with many more in the Church periodicals and curricular material. All members of the First Presidency

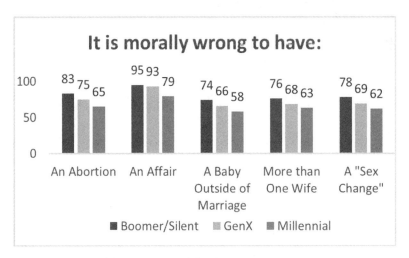

Figure 1. Reprinted from Jana Riess, The Next Mormons, 179.

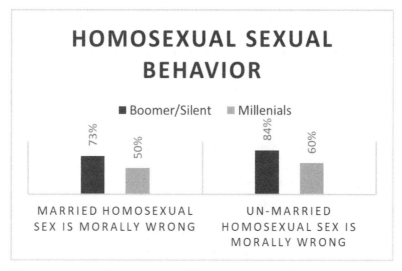

Figure 2. Reprinted from Jana Riess, The Next Mormons, *182.*

and Quorum of Twelve who were coauthors of the document referred to it in general conference, most multiple times. This pattern continues today with almost all of the current First Presidency and Quorum of Twelve having referred to it numerous times in general conference.

An analysis of these statements reveals several repeated themes. When describing or defining the family proclamation, the most frequent themes were that the family proclamation was (1) inspired, (2) revealed, (3) eternal truth, (4) principles/doctrine, or (5) prophecy. Representative statements from the general leadership of the Church will be used to illustrate each theme below. Though many more statements could be included for each theme, no attempt will be made to include every reference within each theme.

INSPIRED

Elder L. Tom Perry explained, "The inspired document 'The Family: A Proclamation to the World' states: 'Husband and wife have a solemn responsibility to love and care for each other and for their children.'"[32] Similarly, Elder Richard G. Scott taught, "Carefully study and use the proclamation of the First Presidency and the Twelve on the family. *It was inspired of the Lord.*"[33] Three years later Elder M. Russell Ballard warned that "to justify their rejection of God's immutable laws that protect the family, . . . false prophets and false teachers *even attack the inspired proclamation on the family.*"[34]

REVEALED/REVELATION/REVELATORS

Similarly, President Gordon B. Hinckley stressed that the teachings contained in the document come from prophets, seers, and revelators: "We of the First Presidency and the Council of the Twelve Apostles now issue a proclamation to the Church and to the world."[35] Elder W. Eugene Hansen stated, "I leave you my witness that the proclamation on the family, which I referred to earlier, is modern-day revelation provided to us by the Lord through His latter-day prophets."[36] Similarly, President Dallin H. Oaks bore his witness of the revelatory nature of the document when he proclaimed, "I testify of the truth and eternal importance of the family proclamation, revealed by the Lord Jesus Christ to His Apostles for the exaltation of the children of God."[37]

ETERNAL TRUTH

Sister Bonnie Oscarson testified, "The proclamation on the family has become our benchmark for judging the philosophies of the world, and I testify that the principles set forth within this statement are as true today as they were when they were given to us by a prophet of God nearly 20 years ago."[38] In a different conference, Elder Neil L. Andersen testified that "these are eternal truths."[39] President Oaks also taught, "Modern revelation defines truth as a "knowledge of things as they are, and as they were, and as they are to come" (Doctrine and Covenants 93:24). That is a perfect definition for the plan of salvation and 'The Family: A Proclamation to the World.'"[40]

PRINCIPLES/DOCTRINES

President Dieter F. Uchtdorf explained, "Procedures, programs, policies, and patterns of organization are helpful for our spiritual progress here on earth, but let's not forget that they are subject to change. In contrast, the core of the gospel—the doctrine and the principles—will never change."[41] When describing the teachings within the family proclamation, the general leadership of the Church almost always refers to those teachings as doctrines or principles. In 1996, Elder Robert D. Hales explained that [the family proclamation] "summarizes eternal gospel principles that have been taught since the beginning of recorded history and even before the earth was created."[42] Elder L. Tom Perry exclaimed, "The doctrine of the family and the home was recently reiterated with great clarity and forcefulness in 'The Family: A Proclamation to the World.'"[43] Elder David B. Haight explained, "That marvelous document brings together the scriptural direction that we have received that has guided the lives of God's children from the time of Adam and Eve and will continue to guide us until the final winding-up scene."[44]

PROPHETS/PROPHECY

Since the proclamation was introduced, more than 30 of the 230 references in general conference have mentioned or emphasized the prophetic source and nature of the document, several of which have already been quoted. Elder Robert D. Hales explained that we should "watch, hear, read, study, and share the words of prophets to be forewarned and protected. For example, 'The Family: A Proclamation to the World' was given long before we experienced the challenges now facing the family."[45] Elder M. Russell Ballard simply taught, "The proclamation is a prophetic document, not only because it was issued by prophets but because it was ahead of its time."[46]

It is important to realize that even though the First Presidency and Quorum of Twelve have consistently spoken of the prophetic and revelatory basis of the family proclamation, it shouldn't be thought that this means the doctrines contained therein are new. President Hinckley explicitly stated that the family proclamation is "a declaration and reaffirmation of standards, doctrines, and practices relative to the family which the prophets, seers, and revelators of this church have repeatedly stated throughout its history."[47] This reality has been restated by several members of the First Presidency and Quorum of Twelve. Several sources have compiled lists that enumerate each doctrine contained in the family proclamation and when those doctrines were taught throughout the Church's history.[48]

PROPHETIC PROCESS

Until 2017 there were few statements from authoritative sources on the circumstances and processes which led to the family proclamation. That changed when President Dallin H. Oaks delivered his October 2017 general conference address "The Plan and the Proclamation." Another important source became available in 2019 when Sheri Dew published her memoir of President Russell M. Nelson: *Insights from a Prophet's Life: Russell M. Nelson.* Combining both sources provides the best picture currently available of the circumstances and processes that led to the creation and publication of the family proclamation.

President Oaks explained that "the inspiration identifying the need for a proclamation on the family came to the leadership of the Church over 23 years ago."[49] The decision was made to prepare a document, "perhaps even a proclamation," and to present that document to the First Presidency for their consideration.[50] A committee consisting of Elders James E. Faust, Neal A. Maxwell, and Russell M. Nelson was appointed to create the first draft of the proposed document. The combined document was submitted to each member of the Quorum of the Twelve for review and revision.[51] President Oaks explained, "Subjects were identified and discussed by members of the Quorum of the Twelve for nearly a year."[52] Further, he explained that "language was proposed, reviewed, and revised. Prayerfully we continually pleaded with the Lord for His inspiration on what we should say and how we should say it. . . . During this revelatory process, a proposed text was presented to the First Presidency, who oversee and promulgate Church teachings and doctrine."[53] The First Presidency made further changes before the united First Presidency and Quorum of Twelve formally ratified the final document under President Howard W. Hunter's leadership just before he passed away in March 1995.[54]

CONCLUSION

The family proclamation was created in the context of secular and cultural realities that caused grave concerns among Church leaders regarding the family. These realities led the First Presidency and Quorum of Twelve to action. The overwhelming consensus of all statements by Church leaders since its inception is that the family proclamation is a prophetic document based on revealed eternal truth. Perhaps the most concise statement of this reality was given in the October 2017 general conference by President Oaks: "I testify that the proclamation on the family is a statement of eternal truth, the will of the Lord for His children who seek eternal life. It has been the basis of Church teaching and practice for the last 22 years and will continue so for the future. Consider it as such, teach it, live by it, and you will be blessed as you press forward toward eternal life. . . . I testify of the truth and eternal importance of the family proclamation, revealed by the Lord Jesus Christ to His Apostles for the exaltation of the children of God (see Doctrine and Covenants 131:1–4)."[55]

It is important to recognize that the Lord and his leaders love and care about all individuals, independent of how their lives may be progressing relative to the patterns within the family proclamation. As President Nelson recently stated, "Because we feel the depth of God's love for His children, we care deeply about every child of God, regardless of age, personal circumstances, gender, sexual orientation, or other unique challenges."[56]

A more accurate understanding of the cultural and political context that created the original need and the prophetic process by which the family proclamation was created can help members as they seek to gain their own testimony of this important proclamation to help us all understand the challenges inherent in our time and stand firm in that test.

NOTES

1. Gordon B Hinckley, "Stand Strong against the Wiles of the World," *Ensign*, November 1995, 100.
2. Jocelyn Mann Denyer and Michael R. Leonard, "President Hinckley Visits U.S. President, Others during Busy Period," *Ensign*, February 1996.
3. United States Congress, "Congressional Record—Extensions of Remarks," 17 November 1995.

4. Denyer and Leonard, "President Hinckley Visits U.S. President."

5. United States Congress, "Congressional Record—Senate," 15 December 1995. S18674.

6. Robert N. Bellah et al., *Habits of the Heart: Individualism and Commitment in American Life* (Berkeley: University of California Press, 1985).

7. Paul R. Amato, "Institutional, Companionate, and Individualistic Marriages," in *Marriage at the Crossroads: Law, Policy, and the Brave New World of Twenty-First-Century Families*, ed. Marsha Garrison and Elizabeth S. Scott (New York: Cambridge University Press, 2012), 110.

8. Stephanie Coontz, *Marriage, a History: How Love Conquered Marriage* (New York: Penguin, 2006), 4.

9. Daniel R. Pinello, *America's Struggle for Same-Sex Marriage* (New York: Cambridge University Press, 2006).

10. For example, *Grisold v. Connecticut (1965)* and *Eisenstadt v. Baird* (1972) legalizing contraceptives; *Phillips v. Martin Marietta Corp* (1971) on mothers' employment; and, of course, *Roe v. Wade (1973)*, legalizing abortion.

11. Pinello, *America's Struggle*, 22.

12. The National Marriage Project, *The State of Our Unions* (Provo, UT: The Wheatley Institution and the School of Family Life, Brigham Young University, 2019) 15-30.

13. Pew Research Center, "Religious Groups' Official Positions on Same-Sex Marriage," 7 December 2012.

14. Mark Davies, LDS General Conference Corpus (website).

15. Boyd K. Packer, in Conference Report, October 1970, 118.

16. Michael A. Goodman, "Correlation: The Turning Point (1960s)," in *Salt Lake City: The Place Which God Prepared*, ed. Scott C. Esplin and Kenneth L. Alford (Provo, UT: Religious Studies Center, Brigham Young University; Provo, UT: Deseret Book, 2011), 259–84.

17. The National Marriage Project, *The State of Our Unions*, 15–30.

18. See pertinent text in Dallin H. Oaks, "Same-Gender Attraction," *Ensign*, October 1995, 8.

19. Pinello, *America's Struggle*, 25.

20. See "A Timeline of the Legalization of Same-Sex Marriage in the U.S.," A Brief History of Civil Rights in the United States, Georgetown Law Library (website).

21. See Douglas Palmer, "3 LDS Officials Seek to Join Hawaii Suite," *Church News*, 14 April 1995.

22. Boyd K. Packer, "The Instrument of Your Mind and the Foundation of Your Character," (Church Educational System Fireside for Young Adults, 2 February 2003).

23. United Nations General Assembly Forty-ninth Session, 35th Meeting, 18 October 1994.

24. M. Russell Ballard, "The Sacred Responsibilities of Parenthood" (address at Brigham Young University, 19 August 2003).

25. Sheri L. Dew, *Insights from a Prophet's Life: Russell M. Nelson* (Salt Lake City: Deseret Book, 2019), 211–12.

26. See also Justice Alito's dissent in United States Supreme Court, *Obergefell v. Hodges, No. 576* (United States Supreme Court October 2015).

27. "Church Leaders Counsel Members after Supreme Court Same-Sex Marriage Decision," 1 July 2015, Newsroom.org.

28. "Church Leaders Counsel Members after Supreme Court Same-Sex Marriage Decision," 1.

29. Pew Research Center: Religion and Public Life. "Mormons in America— Certain in Their Beliefs, Uncertain of Their Place in Society," 12 January 2012.

30. Jana Riess, *The Next Mormons: How Millennials Are Changing the LDS Church* (Oxford: Oxford University Press, 2019), 15–18.

31. Pew Research Center, "Most U.S. Christian Groups Grow More Accepting of Homosexuality," 18 December 2015.

32. L. Tom Perry, "Mothers Teaching Children in the Home," *Ensign*, May 2010, 31.

33. Richard G. Scott, "The Joy of Living the Great Plan of Happiness," *Ensign*, November 1996, 75.

34. M. Russell Ballard, "Beware of False Prophets and False Teachers," *Ensign*, November 1999, 64.

35. Hinckley, "Stand Strong," 100.

36. W. Eugene Hansen, "Children and the Family," *Ensign*, May 1998, 63.

37. Dallin H. Oaks, "The Plan and the Proclamation," *Ensign*, November 2017, 31.

38. Bonnie L. Oscarson, "Defenders of the Family Proclamation," *Ensign*, November 2015, 14–15.

39. Neil L. Andersen, "The Eye of Faith," *Ensign*, May 2019, 34.

40. Dallin H. Oaks, "Truth and the Plan," *Ensign*, November 2018, 25.

41. Dieter F. Uchtdorf, "Christlike Attributes—the Wind beneath Our Wings," *Ensign* November 2005, 100.

42. Robert D. Hales, "The Eternal Family," *Ensign*, November 1996, 64.

43. L. Tom Perry, "Obedience to Law Is Liberty," *Ensign*, May 2013,88.

44. David B. Haight, "Be a Strong Link," *Ensign*, November 2000, 20.

45. Robert D. Hales, "General Conference: Strengthening Faith and Testimony," *Ensign*, November 2013, 7.

46. M. Russell Ballard, "What Matters Most Is What Lasts Longest," *Ensign*, November 2005, 41.

47. Hinckley, "Stand Strong," 100.

48. For example, see "Question: Have the Doctrines in the Mormon Document 'The Family: A Proclamation to the World' Long Been Taught in the Church?," FairMormon (website).

49. Oaks, "The Plan and the Proclamation," 30.

50. Dew, *Insights from a Prophet's Life*, 208.

51. Dew, *Insights from a Prophet's Life*, 209.

52. Oaks, "The Plan and the Proclamation," 30.

53. Oaks, "The Plan and the Proclamation," 30.

54. Dew, *Insights from a Prophet's Life*, 209.

55. Oaks, "The Plan and the Proclamation," 30–31.

56. Russell M. Nelson, "The Love and Laws of God" (address at Brigham Young University, 17 September 2019).

Salt Lake City's Olympic Flame, 2002. More than three dozen articles in the Washington Post *dealt with some aspect of "Mormons" and the "Olympics" in the years between 2000 and 2002.* Washington Post *report Hank Steuver summarized his coverage of the games by noting that the Mormons "looked golden" in 2002. Photo by Preston Keres.*

ON THE PAGES OF THE *POST*: LATTER-DAY SAINTS AND WASHINGTON'S NEWSPAPER OF RECORD

J. B. HAWS

J. B. Haws is an associate professor of Church history and doctrine at Brigham Young University.

Let's imagine a strangely specific hypothetical situation as a way of setting this up. Imagine a man waking up in a Washington, DC, hospital in the 1970s after suffering from amnesia. He has no memory of ever encountering "Mormons" before—and because he needs the constant scrutiny of interested doctors, and because, luckily, he is especially fond of hospital Jell-O, the decision is made to keep our imaginary patient in the hospital for the remainder of his life. His only contact with the outside world is a daily subscription to the *Washington Post*. The question at hand is this: What would our confined but comfortable and contented reader think about Latter-day Saints if his only source of information were the *Washington Post*?

The sheer absurdity of this scenario underscores just how impossible it is to focus exclusively on only one source of information when we think about the influences that shape our perceptions and opinions. Still, if we imagine the public image of The Church of Jesus Christ of Latter-day Saints as something like a mosaic made up of numerous overlapping pieces, even examining one piece can be instructive in discerning how the entire image was (and still is) created. The argument here is that the *Washington Post's* reporting on Latter-day Saints is just such a piece of the mosaic—and a significant one at that—for two broad reasons: the amount (and type) of coverage devoted to Latter-day Saints by the paper; and the prominent place that the paper itself occupies in the public arena—a position that is perhaps more prominent than ever, thanks to the vision of Jeff Bezos.[1]

Bezos, the billionaire founder of Amazon, purchased the *Post* in 2013. He told *CBS This Morning* two years later that "we're working on becoming the new paper of record."[2] Considering all that was happening in the newspaper world, thinking *bigger* was unexpected, to say the least. Despite hitting several journalistic homeruns in the 1970s (the Vietnam Papers, Watergate), the *Washington Post*—like all newspapers—faced new electronic curveballs in the 1990s. The internet changed everything. Newspaper circulation numbers fell across the nation, from 62.5 million paying daily newspaper subscribers in 1968 to 34.7 million in 2016; in the case of the *Washington Post*, the statistics were just as stark: its weekday circulation was 832,000 in 1993, but down to 432,000 in 2015. The bulk of newspapers' advertising revenue stayed with print editions, but those print runs were shrinking. Newsroom staffs were gutted as newspapers across the country closed or merged with competitors. The question that was consistently asked as a digital world dawned was this: do newspapers even still matter?[3] In the midst of this floundering, Bezos infused new capital and focus into the *Post*, and it worked.[4]

A strong case can be made that the *Washington Post* matters as a source of public information now more than ever. Research shows that the *Post's* attention to its online platforms was paying off: in February 2016, for example, the *Washington Post* had more online hits (890.1 million page views) than did any other newspaper—even outpacing the *New York Times* that month (721.3 million)—landing second only to CNN.com among all news sites. (This itself was big news, since the *Post's* rivalry with the *New York Times* has been a running theme in the paper's existence almost since the day the *Post* was founded in 1877.)[5] If all of this, taken together, makes the case for the cultural prominence of the *Washington Post*, what case does the *Washington Post* make for the public standing of Latter-day

Saints, as we try to put ourselves in the minds of readers who encounter this coverage?

Thanks to the comprehensiveness of search databases like LexisNexis and ProQuest, we can get a quick handle on the level of coverage the *Post* has devoted to Latter-day Saints. Between 1977 and early 2020, about 4,200 *Washington Post* articles included the word "Mormon."[6] Importantly, that coverage has not come at a constant rate. Database graphs show a remarkable spike around the "Mormon Moment," starting about 2007. And, of course, there is a wide range in that coverage, from one-line mentions of local Latter-day Saints in obituaries or wedding notices, to two-thousand-word features on local Latter-day Saint welfare farms or that "Mysterious Citadel on the Beltway"—the Church's Washington D.C. Temple.[7] One gets the impression very quickly just how visible Latter-day Saints are in the local news scene in Washington, DC, and just how integrated they are in community affairs. That speaks, as other researchers have noted, to the way Latter-day Saints seek to be something of the leaven in the lump.[8] Here are two telling examples: In June 1981, a story appeared in which Catholic leaders encouraged their parishioners to follow the Latter-day Saints' example of having a weekly family night.[9] And in November 1980 (in a time of rising suspicion against Muslims because of anti-Iranian sentiment), a Muslim community spokesman made the case for Muslims' place in American society by saying "we would not be isolationists, but we would be like the Mormons."[10] It says something that in looking to reassure the public, he saw in the Latter-day Saints the kind of comparison he wanted to make.

Yet the Latter-day Saint image in the American mind has always been a contested one. There always have appeared counterbalancing articles, like one in the *Post* in February 1978 that noted (as if it were common knowledge) that "Wahhabis,"—followers of a very conservative movement in Islam, prominent in Saudi Arabia—"it is often said, are the Mormons of the Middle East."[11] Or take this unexpected account: a brief October 1977 police beat article noted that a man was found with 42 fishhooks stuck in his skin. Vincent Pervel claimed he had been abducted and assaulted. "Police said they are unsure whether the wounds were self-inflicted or whether they were inflicted by 'three mysterious men' who Pervel said perpetrated the crime. According to police, Pervel said three men snagged each hook into his body after asking the question 'Are you a Mormon?'" Police dropped the case when Pervel "refused to cooperate in the investigation," [12] but the article itself is a subtle reminder that in many minds, a bit of weirdness will always be associated with the Latter-day Saints. (No one really wondered at the fact that President Gordon B. Hinckley felt compelled to say to *60 Minutes'* Mike Wallace in 1996, "We're not a weird people"!)[13]

With this sampling of *Washington Post* snapshots in mind, this essay proposes to do two things: discuss a handful of key case studies in which stories about the Church figured prominently on the pages of the *Washington Post*; and then ask what the history and nature of those stories— when taken together—can say about the place of Latter-day Saints on the public opinion landscape of the the United States, especially in the years since the "Mormon Moment" of the 2008 and 2012 presidential campaign seasons.

BEFORE THE MORMON MOMENT: THE 1970s TO THE EARLY 2000s

One way to come at this is to consider that the golden age of the *Washington Post*—the 1970s and 1980s—came about one decade after "the golden era of Mormonism," which is the felicitous phrase that a retired director of Church public affairs used to describe President David O. McKay's tenure.[14] The two decades (roughly) of the 1950s through the early 1970s were a time when, as a number of observers have noted, American Latter-day Saints found themselves in lockstep with the general spirit of the times perhaps more so than at any other time before or since.[15]

But then the trend line tracing American public perception of Latter-day Saints changed. For one thing, American cultural norms began to diverge from the conservative family-centeredness that Latter-day Saints espoused. This divergence manifested itself in both politics and pop culture. A number of influential groups, both on the political left and the political right, grew more and more suspicious of Latter-day Saint prosperity and potential power.

Three episodes stand out as the one-two-three punches that left the Latter-day Saint image bruised in the late 1970s and early 1980s.[16] First, the Church came out in opposition to the Equal Rights Amendment (ERA) in the late 1970s and 1980s. Then the *God Makers* movie highlighted a resurgence of "anti-Mormon" polemics, especially in evangelical Christian circles. Finally, the tragedies surrounding forger-turned-murderer Mark Hofmann raised all kinds of questions about intrigue and secrecy in The Church of Jesus Christ of Latter-day Saints. All three episodes found their way onto the pages of the *Post*.

In 1978, 1979, and 1980, the Equal Rights Amendment and the "Mormons for ERA" leader Sonia Johnson were the Latter-day Saint–related topics that generated the greatest number of articles in the *Washington Post*. There were six ERA articles in 1978 that mentioned the Church, sixteen in 1979—including page one coverage of Sonia Johnson's excommunication—and twenty-two in 1980, which represented fully 33 percent of that year's mentions of Mormons (sixty-five articles) in the newspaper. Because Sonia Johnson was a northern Virginia local—and because ERA protests and counterdemonstrations so often took place in Washington— this level of coverage is not surprising; but it also reflected national attention to this issue and the persons involved. This is a complex story that deserves the extensive analysis it has received in other places, but one April 1980 headline in the *Washington Post* can serve to encapsulate the public perception impact of the ERA coverage: "Mormon Anti-ERA Money."[17]

This headline—and other related coverage—introduced a new motif in reporting about the church: fear. In national stories about the Mormons and the ERA, there flowed an undercurrent of suspicion that the Latter-day Saint potential for political influence had gone underappreciated. The nineteenth-century bugaboo of theocratic aspirations still lurked.

This kind of suspicion, but on religious more than political grounds, drove the second of the aforementioned one-two-three punches: the rise of a new (and successful) brand of polemical, religiously focused materials (like the *God Makers* film) aimed at stemming the Latter-day Saints' unsettling growth. Critics in the *God Makers* vein deemed the Latter-day Saints too close to what was, in these critics' minds, authentic Christianity—and for these concerned critics, that's what made the

JACK ANDERSON

No discussion involving journalism, Latter-day Saints, and Washington, DC, would be complete without including Jack Anderson. He was a pioneering figure in twentieth-century investigative reporting. In his sixty years of reporting, he broke story after story—the CIA and the Mafia conspiring to kill Fidel Castro, the Iran-Contra affair, and a story about U.S. support for Pakistan over India that won Anderson the Pulitzer Prize in 1972, among many, many other scoops. When he died in late 2005, he was remembered for holding the distinction "for years . . . [of being] America's most widely read columnist."[1]

From his home base in Washington, he not only worked on the "Washington Merry-Go-Round" column for almost a half century, a column that eventually appeared in an astounding one thousand newspapers and had forty-five million readers every week, but he also hosted radio and television shows. He took over the column from Drew Pearson in 1969, who had hired a young Anderson twenty years earlier after Anderson had stints as a reporter in Utah for the *Deseret News* (first when he was twelve on the "Boy Scout" page), the *Salt Lake Tribune*, and as an army news reporter in China. Between reporting jobs, he served a two-year mission for the Church.

Religion mattered to Anderson, and colleagues knew he was a devout Latter-day Saint. Critics and supporters alike saw his strong sense of morality as deriving from his faith. Anderson also noted, in a darkly humorous way, that his large family—he and his wife, Olivia, had nine children—likely saved his life. So frustrated with Anderson's dogged reporting did Richard Nixon and his inner circle become that several Nixon staffers bandied about some ideas on how they might get rid of him, including the possibility of slipping poison into Anderson's aspirin bottle. However, Anderson noted, they were deterred by a worry that in a household with that many children, the chances of an inadvertent victim were just too high.[2]

Such was the life of one who felt called—and he did see his journalism profession as a "calling"—to "afflict the comfortable and comfort the afflicted."[3]

NOTES

1. Patricia Sullivan, "Investigative Columnist Jack Anderson Dies," *Washington Post*, 18 December 2005, C08.

2. See Douglas Martin, "Jack Anderson, Investigative Journalist Who Angered the Powerful, Dies at 83," *New York Times*, National Edition, 18 December 2005, section 1, p. 58. See also Jack Anderson's retelling of the exploratory conversations between the potential perpetrators, in his book (with Daryl Gibson), *Peace, War, and Politics: An Eyewitness Account* (New York: Forge, 1999), 228–30. *Washington Post* reporter Bob Woodward broke the initial story of the plot in "Hunt Told Associates of Orders to Kill Jack Anderson," *Washington Post*, 21 September 1975, A1. For one author's analysis that this episode represented a turning point in the relationship between powerful politicians and the media, see Mark Feldstein, *Poisoning the Press: Richard Nixon, Jack Anderson, and the Rise of Washington's Scandal Culture* (New York: Farrar, Straus and Giroux, 2010).

3. Leigh Dethman and the Associated Press, "Jack Anderson, Columnist and Ex-Utahn, Dies," *Deseret News*, 18 December 2005, A01.

Mormons-as-counterfeit-Christians so dangerous. A September 1981 *Washington Post* article carried this headline: "Pastors Act to 'Save' Flock from Mormons." The article detailed how "five local ministers of various denominations sent out some forty-three hundred letters warning residents not to be misled by the doctrine of the Church of Jesus Christ of Latter-day Saints." One of the ministers said, "In common with many other cults, they use the same words as Christianity but attach different meaning to them."[18] Any time the word *cult* appeared in the late 1970s and 80s, the descriptor carried a particularly negative potency because of the 1978 Jonestown mass suicide of over nine hundred individuals that was still very much in the national consciousness.

Hence, for some people, their distrust of Latter-day Saints turned into an apparent case of suspicions confirmed when violence and fanaticism seemed to manifest themselves in the breaking news of two bombing murders in Salt Lake City in October 1985. For the five years previous to that, Mark Hofmann, a covertly disaffected Latter-day Saint, had generated growing attention for a series of remarkable "finds" of important historical documents related to the Church's founding. Those documents grew increasingly controversial, as they painted foundational events in new hues, often strange ones. After five years of grabbing headlines, Mark Hofmann perpetrated two heinous murders via package bombs. Investigators discerned that Hofmann was a master forger who had resorted to murder to cover his double-crossing tracks. However, what national media outlet after national media outlet reported was that the business of historical documents that threatened the Church's standard narrative was serious enough that some people died because of their involvement. Words like "shadowy" and "secretive" became standard media descriptors of the Church and its leadership. The *Post* ran thirteen stories—some extensive—on Mark Hofmann. One headline from five days after the bombings can convey the feeling of the time: "Utah's Mormon Community Transfixed by Bombing Incidents; Focus on Documents Heightens Sensitivity about Church Origins."[19]

Trying to trace the trend lines of public opinion on Latter-day Saints is more impressionistic than precise—more like the pain scale at the doctor's office. A lot is eye-of-the-beholder-type evaluation and assessment. Still, some broad trends do seem discernible. In 1977 a Gallup poll found that

54 percent of Americans surveyed responded that they viewed Mormons "very favorably" or "somewhat favorably." In 1991 a Barna poll with a slightly different wording and metric approach found that only 27 percent of respondents rated Mormons favorably.[20] The one-two-three punches of the long 1980s had taken a toll.

Latter-day Saints would see the picture painted here as pretty bleak, yet another detectable trend over the past four decades has been what might be thought of as a public perception split: esteem for Latter-day Saint *individuals* in spite of distrust of the Latter-day Saint *institution*.[21] This individual-versus-institution divergence allowed for positive publicity for a number of prominent Latter-day Saints—and the spotlight they were under seemed to dispel some of the shadows surrounding the more suspect institution to which they belonged. It was this kind of coverage that signaled something of a new day in the mid-1990s, supported by the energetic leadership of President Gordon B. Hinckley. When he appeared for an extensive, unscripted interview on *60 Minutes* with Mike Wallace, something seemed to change. The *Washington Post* quoted Apostle Dallin H. Oaks: "If he [President Hinckley] can stand up to Mike Wallace, he can stand up to anybody," Oaks said. Of the broadcast itself, the *Post* noted that Wallace "complimented and joked with Hinckley more than [Wallace] attacked."[22]

Something *had* seemed to change. Charges of secretiveness and defensiveness waned. This changing of the winds of public perception coincided with two moments that brought unprecedented attention to the Church and its people: the 1997 sesquicentennial wagon train and the 2002 Winter Olympics. In June 1997 a two-thousand-word front-page feature came under this headline in the *Post*: "Latter-day Trek Honors Pilgrims." The article noted that "this once-persecuted sect is one of the world's fastest growing faiths."[23] Apostle M. Russell Ballard captured the sense of Latter-day Saint wonder at the amount of media attention that came in 1997 when he said, in August of that year, "When we can finally assess the number of newspaper articles and the extent of the television and radio coverage of the sesquicentennial, we will likely find that the Church has had more media exposure this year than in all the other years of our history combined."[24]

Even more coverage was soon to come. The *Washington Post* featured forty-four articles from 2000 to 2002 that dealt with some combination of "the Mormons" and the Olympics. The *Post*'s Hank Steuver summarized his impressions this way: "The only religious shenanigans and Bible-thumping at the Winter Games came courtesy of angry other denominations, whose members circled Temple Square with anti-Mormon signs and pamphlets and posters." The irony for Steuver was that in the end, "everyone looked nutty except the Mormons, who looked golden."[25]

THE MORMON MOMENT: PRESIDENTIAL CAMPAIGN SEASONS OF 2008 AND 2012

With this apparent upswing in positive attention, it is little wonder that many Latter-day Saints were taken by surprise by the way Mitt Romney's first run for the U.S. presidency seemed to be something of a rehash of the controversies of the 1980s. This is not to say that Latter-day Saints had found nothing controversial in recent *Post* reporting; after all, the Hank Steuver column just quoted about the 2002 Olympics was titled "Unmentionable No Longer: What Do Mormons Wear? A Polite Smile, If Asked about 'the Garment.'" His article was a front-page feature in the "Style" section of the newspaper, and it included photographs of the Latter-day Saints' temple garments taken from Church ordering catalogues. Steuver used his interest in the undergarment worn by temple-initiated Latter-day Saint adults as the springboard for a larger discussion about Latter-day Saint beliefs and practices, including the Saints' Olympic hospitality during the Salt Lake Games. Steuver's piece drew a swift and articulate letter to the editor written by two prominent DC-area Latter-day Saints. J. Willard Marriott Jr. and Ralph Hardy Jr. pointedly asked, "Would the *Post* be so bold to publish an equally invasive and derisive piece on the religious clothing worn by the faithful of any other religion or faith group . . . ? We think not. . . . Why, therefore, is there a double standard in the case of the Church of Jesus Christ of Latter-day Saints?" It was an important question—and a prescient one.[26]

It is hard to know how readers took the overall tone of a piece like Steuver's, which was at turns complimentary and at other turns quizzical.

What was easier to ascertain, a few years later, was the level of public dis-comfort with the idea of a U.S. presidential candidate who was a Latter-day Saint. A December 2006 *Washington Post*–ABC News poll showed that 35 percent of respondents "said they would be less likely" to "vote for a can-didate who is Mormon."[27] The evidence of public consternation over Mitt Romney's faith was everywhere during that 2008 campaign season.

Thankfully, for those interested in Latter-day Saint media trends and coverage, Mitt Romney ran for president again, a boon for comparative purposes. (A whopping six hundred articles in the *Washington Post*, since 2000, have included the words "Romney" and "Mormon" in the same ar-ticle.) So much could be said here about the differences between the 2008 election cycle coverage and the 2012 election cycle coverage, but one *Wash-ington Post* story in particular—a February 2012 article that made instant waves—can stand in as a multilayered case study. In the article, journalist Jason Horowitz quoted a Latter-day Saint interviewee who promulgated some outdated and paternalistic explanations for the Church's pre-1978 priesthood and temple restrictions on Black members of the Church. So prominent *and* out-of-step were the comments that the Church took the unusually strong step of disavowing both the comments and the commen-tator, by name, and condemning (using that very word) racism, past and present. But for a time, it appeared that this controversy would overshadow all else, as the first Latter-day Saint national party candidate for president was about to square off against the nation's first Black president.[28]

But that is what made 2012 so interesting. In the weeks that followed, *Sports Illustrated* and ABC News had extensive features (and a *Sports Illustrated* cover) of the nation's best high school basketball player, Jabari Parker, a Black Latter-day Saint from Chicago.[29] All of this suggested in the press that common assumptions about Latter-day Saints needed reex-amination. Latter-day Saints could not be so easily painted as the mono-lith that they had long been assumed to be; displaying the diversity of the church's membership was one of the key themes of the church's "I'm a Mormon" campaign that ran in those very years. And for this reason, an Associated Press headline that appeared the day after the election trum-peted, "And the Winner Is . . . the Mormon Church."[30]

On election day 2012, before the results were in, the *Washington Post* ran "Relishing the Mormon Moment." This 1,400-word feature quoted Senator Orrin Hatch calling "the monolithic view of Mormons . . . 'really unfair.'" Relatedly, church public affairs director Michael Otterson said that "while the church had studiously maintained its political neutrality," still the "election had been an important opportunity for the church to 'really depict who we are.'"[31] Two days after the election, this telling headline in the *Post* showed how much the world had turned in just four years: "Mormonism Not an Issue with White Evangelical Voters."[32]

AFTER THE "MORMON MOMENT"

With all of this in mind, what can be said of the post–"Mormon Moment" coverage in the *Washington Post*? What stands out?

In a word, complexity—and for many, *unexpected* complexity.

A survey of "Mormon"-related articles in the *Post* over the past half-dozen years, from 2013 to early 2020, suggests that no single issue or event has dominated recent coverage in the way that some past events have—with the exception, perhaps, of reviews and notices for various runs of the *Book of Mormon* musical, of which there have been more than three hundred in the newspaper since 2011 (including a March 2013 article with the headline "Book of Mormon Ticket Sales Crash Kennedy Center Site Again").[33] But there are some themes that do show up with regularity. And what is striking is how that regularity in the *Washington Post's* coverage can work to signal to readers that the contemporary Latter-day Saint community cannot be painted (or dismissed) with the broad brushstrokes of standard stereotypes or tropes.

Take two examples of this type of complexity that have appeared with consistency since 2013: first, the Church's position on LGBTQ issues and its relationship with its LGBTQ members; and second, Latter-day Saints' unexpected coolness toward a Republican president.

It is never easy to assess with confidence the impact of an individual story or even a series of stories, or to know how a broad and diverse readership might perceive the nuances of those stories. Still, what can be asked is, What do readers encounter when they come to a story? What elements are highlighted? What is prominent?

In that vein, and in terms of Latter-day Saint and LGBTQ-related stories, the *Post's* reporters have depicted a church trying to navigate a path less traveled. In the first half of 2013, two dozen stories in the *Washington Post* gave attention to deliberations by Boy Scouts of America administrators over the question of admitting gay young men as Scouts—and the surprise for many was that Latter-day Saint Church officials signaled their support for this change in BSA admission policy. Two front-page stories in May and June 2013 noted Latter-day Saint support for the change.[34] In May, the *Post* hosted a blog entry from Michael Otterson, the Church's managing director of Public Affairs: "Why Mormons Back the New Scouting Policy."[35] The year had started with a January article in the *Washington Post* from a Utah reporter, Peggy Fletcher Stack, with the headline "Tolerance on the March in Utah." The article pointed to church efforts, including the newly launched website mormonsandgays.org, to "[acknowledge] that homosexuality is neither a choice nor a sin . . . to soften the rhetoric about homosexuality and to allow gay Mormons to tell their stories."[36]

In March 2015, the *Post* online had trumpeted this headline about compromise legislation that passed the Utah legislature: "Utah, Yes Utah, Passes Landmark LGBT Rights Bill." The story opened with this sentence: "Utah lawmakers and Mormon Church leaders celebrated a landmark moment Wednesday night, when a bill banning discrimination against lesbian, gay, bisexual and transgender people passed the state's Republican-controlled legislature." In thinking of the bill's impact, the story continued, "the move has been seen by some as a model in compromise as the Church of Jesus Christ of Latter-day Saints endorsed the legislation last week. The partnership helped accelerate the bill's passage through Utah's legislature. It was proposed only last week. The church, while standing by its views, has been a voice of tolerance on issues of gender equality in a manner that has surprised some of its traditional critics."[37]

This acknowledgment of surprise drew attention to what many saw as unexpected: a church, widely recognized for its conservative stand on marriage, seeking to find ways to advocate for LGBTQ rights while preserving protection for religious freedom. But the road less traveled can also be a bumpy one. While the paper included voices of praise for this kind of leadership on compromise and bridge building, the tone was different in the coverage of the announcement of a new church policy in November 2015 that affected the Church status of same-sex married couples and their children. *Post* reporters noted that while the Church had been sending signals of tolerance and cooperation with the LGBTQ community, the new policy was interpreted by observers as a "line in the sand," and disquieted some members who questioned whether they would stay in the Church.[38] The policy's rescission in April 2019 also drew the *Post*'s attention. An article from that month demonstrated well the impressive nuance that *Post* writers have given this issue. The article quoted a woman who had left the Church in 2016, "cranky and annoyed" that her planned marriage to a woman would be seen as "a 'serious transgression' by the church." "You're constantly made to think there's something broken about you," she said. But the article also noted that "before the policy was announced in 2015, Mormon leaders were becoming known for trying to find a balance between advocating for their religious freedom and allowing for LGBT rights by working out a political compromise with LGBT leaders in Utah earlier that year." The same article quoted this line from Church leaders' April 2019 statement: "We want to reduce the hate and contention so common today."[39]

The church's relationship with national political parties became another recurring theme in post–"Mormon Moment" America. Partisan politics are admittedly charged in any context, but perhaps never more so than in the years since the 2016 presidential election. On the pages of the *Post*, Latter-day Saints—including some of their most prominent political figures—came to represent (and surprisingly so) opposition voices in the Republican Party against policies and practices, and especially a president, that seemed to run counter to Latter-day Saint ideals—and they were lauded for their courage in doing so.

For example, in the lead-up to the 2016 election, a number of articles noted that Utah's Latter-day Saint population was not lining up behind the Republican candidate for president, Donald Trump, as that population had for the previous three decades—and, more importantly, as they had come to be *expected* to do. The headline of a late October 2016 article

United States Senators Jeff Flake (Arizona) and Mitt Romney (Utah), both Latter-day Saints, came to represent for a number of Washington Post *reporters those lawmakers within the Republican Party who opposed President Donald Trump's approach to several key issues, including immigration policy.*

summed up this surprise: "Unlikeliest of Battlegrounds: Utah, where Antipathy to Donald Trump Is High." This was issue-based, too. In March 2016, a headline noted, "Trump's Immigration Stance Expected to Help in Arizona, but Hurt in Utah," and the article cited Church reactions against a proposed Muslim immigration ban.[40] Nearly two dozen articles in the fall of 2016 noted that a third-party candidate, Evan McMullin (a Latter-day Saint), was polling in significant numbers in Utah because of dissatisfaction with the candidates from the two major parties. In 2017, Senator Jeff Flake was the subject of an editorial under the headline, "The Bravest Political Act of This Era," and the commentator celebrated the Latter-day Saint and Republican politician from Arizona for a willingness to sacrifice his political career, if that was the cost, to openly criticize President Trump's policies.[41] Then, in the midst of growing rumbles of impeachment in the fall of 2019, a front-page, 2,600-word story in the *Washington Post* called Utah senator Mitt Romney "one of the most outspoken critics in the Senate of Trump's telephone call with Ukrainian President Volodymyr Zelensky and the president's decision to withdraw troops from Syria. The senator was praised by Democrats for showing spine, and, on cue, he was attacked by Trump on Twitter."[42] It had become standard fare in the paper to note Latter-day Saints' "skepticism of Trump," or to describe Utah as a place "where Trump is less popular (largely due to strong opposition among Mormons)."[43] That trend continued when Mitt Romney made history in February 2020 as the first U.S. senator to vote against a president from his or her own party in an impeachment trial, and in June 2020, when Mitt Romney joined protesters marching for racial justice after the death of George Floyd.[44]

Regardless of one's political leanings, the contention here is that Latter-day Saints who are interested in accurate representations of their community should see this kind of reporting as a good thing. If the accepted wisdom is that American Latter-day Saints are in lockstep with the Republican Party (and recent polling suggests that the strong majority of American Latter-day Saints still align themselves with the GOP), the *Post*'s reporting offered additional impressions: that Latter-day Saints are not unquestioningly loyal to one party, that they come in all political varieties, that the Church's statements about nonpartisanship really are sincere; and that The Church of Jesus Christ of Latter-day Saints can comfortably accommodate members who approach political issues differently.[45] It is likely that another reason behind this repeated attention to Latter-day Saint political views is the contrast with evangelical Protestants. That two conservative religious groups seemed to be trending in opposite directions in their support of President Trump only reinforced the sense of unexpected complexity in the story of Latter-day Saints in twenty-first century America.[46]

CONCLUSION

Let's return to our opening hypothetical. What impressions would our *Washington Post* reader who had no previous knowledge of "the Mormons" come away with? He would learn that the Tabernacle Choir is a go-to literary device: so many creative comparisons have centered on the Tabernacle Choir, as if it is a cultural shorthand that needs no explanation. A classic usage came in a February 1978 article that stated that an old-school basketball coach at the University of Maryland and his freelancing junior college transfer players were about as "compatible as [the rock band] Kiss and the Mormon Tabernacle Choir."[47] On the pages of the *Post*, the Tabernacle Choir is America's choir, making repeated appearances at presidential inaugurations. Our reader would learn that the grounds of the Washington D.C. Temple garner nearly annual notice as a must-see location for Christmas lights. There have also been instances when the *Post* gives unexpected notice to internal Church matters such as President Spencer W. Kimball's hospitalizations, or Helvecio Martins's call as the first Latter-day Saint of black African descent to be named a member of a stake presidency (in Brazil in January 1979).[48] Our hypothetical hospital reader would have read that former Washington Nationals baseball star Bryce Harper eschewed alcohol because of his faith,[49] and that the Marriotts bucked national trends by continuing to place copies of the Bible *and* the Book of Mormon in three hundred thousand newly acquired hotel rooms as they brought the Starwood Hotels into their company.[50] This reader would learn something of a Latter-day Saint lifestyle, something of growing Latter-day Saint diversity.

Some religionists will understandably find the whole premise of an essay like this problematic, since the worry might be that preoccupation with public perception can lead to pandering. After all, Christians readily remember that Jesus told his followers that they would be hated by the world. Leading Latter-day Saint thinker Terryl Givens told filmmaker Helen Whitney, "Brigham Young once said that he feared the day [when] Mormons would no longer be the object of the pointing finger of scorn." But Givens recognized that this is "one of those paradoxes," especially for a church that has a message it wants to share: "You want to be mainstream enough that people will give your message a fair hearing."[51]

In 2015, Latter-day Saint political scientist and University of Notre Dame professor David Campbell noted from his research on religion in America that Americans have the warmest feelings for Jews and Catholics. Professor Campbell's takeaway was that these are the religious groups that are best at building bridges.[52] What can the *Washington Post* offer in a review of Latter-day Saints on this score? While repeating one more time that snapshots only capture pieces of a much more textured whole, it still seems telling that in a November 1978 article, a local Latter-day Saint said, "It is unusual for us to go in on these [interfaith] things," when DC-area

Church leaders led out on an interfaith statement in support of "family week." The reason for the exception, the Church spokesperson explained, was that "we felt so strongly the importance of anything to strengthen the family ties that we decided to do it."[53] Four decades later, it would seem that the exception has become the rule. A March 2019 headline reporting on the meeting between Church President Russell M. Nelson and Pope Francis reads, "After Decades of Behind-the-scenes Diplomacy, Leaders of Catholic, Mormon Churches Meet in Rome." This line from the article stands out: "The two groups work together on relief efforts in 43 countries."[54]

If you thought you knew the Latter-day Saints, the *Washington Post* seems to say, keep reading.

NOTES

1. Special thanks to Annie Mangus and Liel Maala for their research assistance and insights on this project. For a succinct history of the *Washington Post* and its owners, see Dan Kennedy, *The Return of the Moguls: How Jeff Bezos and John Henry Are Remaking Newspapers for the Twenty-First Century* (Lebanon, New Hampshire: 2018), 19. See also chapter 7 of Aurora Wallace, *Newspapers and the Making of Modern America: A History* (Westport, CT: Greenwood Press, 2005). New ownership at the *Post* in the 1930s started the paper on its current trajectory. The paper was purchased by Eugene Meyer in 1933, whose investment in the paper paid off in editorial weight. Articles in the *Post* had significant bearing on contests over increasing the size of the Supreme Court—and importantly, that editorial charge against President Roosevelt's plan to expand the court was led by a Latter-day Saint, Merlo Pusey. He was a fixture on the pages of the *Post* for forty-three years, and a Pulitzer Prize winner for his biography of Supreme Court Justice Charles Evans Hughes. See Merlo J. Pusey, "My Fifty Years in Journalism," *Dialogue: A Journal of Mormon Thought* 10, no. 3 (Spring 1977): 70–81.

2. Kennedy, *Return of the Moguls*, 14.

3. The argument that "newspapers matter" is a driving thesis in Kennedy, *Return of the Moguls*. These statistics come from pages 7–8, 16. Kennedy also notes that "media scholar Alex Jones . . . [estimates] at least 85 percent of original, professionally reported accountability journalism is produced by newspapers"—and then often repeated or disseminated by television and radio and other online outlets. *Return of the Moguls*, 4.

4. See, for example, Jen Wieczner, "How Jeff Bezos Reacts to 'Negative' Amazon Articles in Washington Post," *Fortune*, 27 October 2017, https://fortune .com/2017/10/27/amazon-jeff-bezos-washington-post/, for observations about Bezos's involvement at the *Washington Post*, as well as the fact that the *Post* had become profitable in 2016, "after 'many years' of losing money, thanks in large part to new online-only subscribers."

5. For statistics about online hits in 2016 and 2017, see Kennedy, *Return of the Moguls*, 16.

6. This number comes from a keyword search of "Mormon" in the LexisNexis database of the *Washington Post*—1977 to 2019.

7. "Mysterious Citadel on the Beltway," *Washington Post*, 1981, A1.

8. See G. Wesley Johnson and Marian Ashby Johnson, "On the Trail of the Twentieth-Century Mormon Outmigration," *BYU Studies* 46, no. 1 (2007): 41–83.

9. Marjorie Hyer, "Archbishop Urges Catholic Families to Hold Family Nights on Mondays," *Washington Post*, 27 June 1981, C10.

10. Elsa L. Walsh, "American Muslims: Area's Muslims Find Discrimination, Lack of Understanding by Americans: Searching for a Place in the Melting Pot," *Washington Post*, 20 November 1980, "Virginia Weekly" section, Va. 1, Va. 5.

11. Richard Harwood, "Change is Slow for Saudi Women: Arabia's Tradition-Bound Women; But Prosperity and Modernism Are about to Pierce the Veils Dividing the Sexes," *Washington Post*, 12 February 1978, C1. The previous sentence described Wahhabism as "flaming, puritanical evangelism."

12. "42 Seahooks Stuck in Seaman," *Washington Post*, 23 October 1977, B3.

13. Gordon B. Hinckley said this to Mike Wallace during a *60 Minutes* piece that aired on 7 April 1996.

14. Bruce L. Olsen, former managing director of the Church's Public Affairs Department, interview with Jonice Hubbard, 8 September 2006, transcript included in "Pioneers in Twentieth Century Mormon Media: Oral Histories of Latter-day Saint Electronic and Public Relations Professionals" (master's thesis, Brigham Young University, 2007), 121.

15. See, for example, Jan Shipps, *Sojourner in the Promised Land: Forty Years Among the Mormons* (Urbana: University of Illinois Press, 2000), 100: "I am convinced that it was the dramatic discrepancy between clean-cut Mormons and scruffy hippies that completed the transformation of the Mormon image from the quasi-foreign, somewhat alien likeness that it had in the nineteenth century to the more than 100 percent super-American portrait of the late sixties and early seventies."

16. This is the principal argument of chapters 4, 5, and 6 of J. B. Haws, *The Mormon Image in the American Mind: Fifty Years of Public Perception* (New York: Oxford University Press, 2013).

17. "Mormon Anti-ERA Money," *Washington Post*, 22 April 1980, A9. For important accounts on both sides of the ERA debate, see Martha Sonntag Bradley, *Pedestals and Podiums: Utah Women, Religious Authority and Equal Rights* (Salt Lake City: Signature Books, 2005); D. Michael Quinn, "A National Force, 1970s–1990s," chapter 10 of *Mormon Hierarchy: Extensions of Power* (Salt Lake City: Signature Books, 1997); "Not All Alike" and "Bullying the Saints," chapters 6 and 7 of Colleen McDannell, *Sister Saints: Mormon Women since the End of Polygamy* (New York: Oxford University Press, 2019); William P. Connors, "Missionaries *to* the Mormons: NOW's ERA Missionary Project," *Journal of Mormon History* 45, no. 4 (October 2019): 105–32; and "The Politics of Family Values: 1972–1981," chapter 4 of Haws, *The Mormon Image in the American Mind.*

18. Ronald D. White, "Pastors Act to 'Save' Flocks from Mormons," *Washington Post*, 5 September 1981, B1.

19. T. R. Reid, "Utah's Mormon Community Transfixed by Bombing Incidents; Focus on Documents Heightens Sensitivity about Church Origins," *Washington Post*, 20 October 1985, A12; see also T. R. Reid, "Police Peruse Documents in 2 Murders: Fatal Bombings Stun Salt Lake City," *Washington Post*, 18 October 1985, A3.

20. See Question qn19k, The Gallup Poll #978, 14 June 1977, accessed at Gallup Brain database. The 1977 poll used a numerical scale to gauge opinion, from +5 (for a very favorable opinion) to -5 (for a very unfavorable opinion); 9.88 percent answered "+5," and 7.92 percent "+4," and 36 percent of respondents gave Mormons a "+1, +2, or +3" rating, meaning that 54 percent of those surveyed ranked Mormons on the positive side of the scale. Compare Barna Research Group, "Americans' Impressions of Various Church Denominations," 18 September 1991, copy in author's possession, 1: "How favorably do you consider the Mormon denomination? Very favorably—6 percent"; only 21 percent felt "somewhat favorable" about Latter-day Saints, meaning that 27 percent chose a "very" or "somewhat" favorable response in 1991.

21. For more exploration of this "individual-institutional" split in the 1980s and 1990s, see chapters 6 and 7 of *The Mormon Image in the American Mind.*

22. Bill Broadway, "10 Million Strong, Mormons Move Toward Mainstream," *Washington Post*, 3 May 1997, B06. The occasion of the report was a visit by Gordon B. Hinckley to the University of Maryland's basketball arena.

23. Laurie Goodstein, "Latter-day Trek Honors Pilgrims: Wagon Train Retracing Mormon Exodus of 1846-47," *Washington Post*, 22 June 1997, A1.

24. M. Russell Ballard, "Sharing the Gospel Message through the Media," in *Out of Obscurity: Public Affairs and the Worldwide Church: The 8th Annual Conference of the International Society, 17–18 August 1997* (Provo, UT: Brigham Young University, 1998), 5.

25. Hank Stuever, "Unmentionable No Longer: What Do Mormons Wear? A Polite Smile, If Asked about 'the Garment,'" *Washington Post*, 26 February 2002, C1.

26. J. Willard Marriott Jr. and Ralph W. Hardy Jr., "Intolerant and Insensitive," *Washington Post*, 6 March 2002, A18.

27. Dan Balz and Jon Cohen, "Clinton and Giuliani Have the Early Edge for '08, Poll Shows," *Washington Post*, 14 December 2006, A03.

28. See Jason Horowitz, "A Genesis: Equality in Mormonism," *Washington Post*, 29 February 2012, C03. For the Church's response, see "Church Statement Regarding Washington Post Article on Race and the Church," newsroom.churchofjesuschrist.org of Latter-day Saints, 29 February 2012, https://newsroom.churchofjesuschrist.org/article/racial-remarks-in-washington-post-article.

29. Jeff Benedict, "Jabari Parker Is . . .," *Sports Illustrated*, 21 May 2012, accessed at http://sportsillustrated.cnn.com/vault/article/magazine/MAG1198498/index.htm.; the cover read, "The best high school basketball player since LeBron James is Jabari Parker, but there's something more important to him than NBA stardom: his faith." Jabari Parker's conversation with Katie Couric was aired on ABC's *Good Morning America*, 14 June 2012.

30. Rachel Zoll, "And the Winner Is . . . the Mormon Church," Associated Press, 15 November 2012.

31. Jason Horowitz, "Relishing the 'Mormon Moment,'" *Washington Post*, 6 November 2012, C01.

32. Michelle Boorstein and Scott Clement, "Mormonism Not an Issue with White Evangelical Voters," *Washington Post*, 8 November 2012, A23.

33. The count represents search results based on a keyword search using ProQuest Global Newsstream database. The counts listed here and throughout should be taken as broad estimates, especially in the years since the early 2000s, since the ProQuest database aggregates both print and online articles, such that there is some repetition involved if an online article appeared with a different headline from the print version.

34. See Marc Fisher and Michelle Boorstein, "Long Road to Scouts' Change in Gay Policy," *Washington Post*, 2 June 2013, A1; see also Michelle Boorstein, "Scouts Say Yes to Gay Youths, No to Adults," *Washington Post*, 24 May 2013, A1.

35. Michael Otterson, "Why Mormons Back the New Scouting Policy," blog post in "On Faith," *Washington Post*, 31 May 2013.

36. Peggy Fletcher Stack, "Tolerance on the March in Utah," *Washington Post*, 5 January 2013, B2.

37. Lindsey Bever, "Utah—Yes, Utah—Passes Landmark LGBT Rights Bill," *Washington Post*, posted online on 12 March 2015, https://www.washington post.com/news/morning-mix/wp/2015/03/12/utah-legislature-passes -landmark-lgbt-anti-discrimination-bill-backed-by-Mormon-church/. See also this page-one feature in print: Niraj Chokshi, "Gay Rights, Religious Rights and a Compromise in Utah," *Washington Post*, 13 April 2015, A1; see also Michelle Boortsein, "LGBT, Mormon Groups Unveil Anti-Bias Measure," *Washington Post*, 7 March 2015, B2.

38. Sarah Pulliam Bailey, "Mormons Issue Policy on Gay Households," *Washington Post*, 7 November 2015, A2. See also Michelle Boorstein, "Mormon Church: Same-sex Baptism Ban Protects 'Harmony,'" *Washington Post*, 14 November 2015, B2.

39. Sarah Pulliam Bailey, "Mormons Reverse Policy on Children of LGBT Parents," *Washington Post*, 5 April 2019, A3. In a *Washington Post* article in 2018, Orrin Hatch stood in as a Latter-day Saint representative of a change in approach and tone in relation to LGBTQ issues and individuals. The newspaper noted that the retiring senator, one characterized as a "socially conservative 84-year-old Mormon, . . . long one of the most outspoken critics of gay people in Congress . . . took to the Senate floor" during Pride Month "to send 'a message of love' to 'my LGBT brothers and sisters. . . . They deserve to know that they belong and that our society is stronger because of them.'" James Hohmann, "Hatch Sends 'Message of Love' in Pride Month Speech," *Washington Post*, 15 June 2018, A16. The article also highlighted Hatch's approach as contrasting with that of a number of fellow conservatives.

40. For recent data and analysis about how American Latter-day Saints diverge from other Christian conservatives in voting patterns and attitudes about immigration reform (and other contemporary issues), see "A Politically Peculiar People," chapter 5 of David E. Campbell, John C. Green, and J. Quin Monson's detailed study, *Seeking the Promised Land: Mormons and American Politics* (New York: Cambridge University Press, 2014).

41. Michael Gerson, "The Bravest Political Act of this Era," *Washington Post*, 4 August 2017, A15. The author was specifically referring to the publication of Flake's book, *Conscience of a Conservative*. Gerson wrote, "Flake is a member of the Church of Jesus Christ of Latter-day Saints, and one explanation for the skepticism many of his fellow Mormons share about Trump is surely their focus on personal character and rectitude. But another is their own history as victims of persecution." Gerson quoted Flake as saying, "When we say 'No Muslims' or 'No Mexicans,' we may as well say 'No Mormons.' Because it is no different."

42. Michael Kranish, "Trump-Romney Bond Turns Cold in a Blizzard of Bitter Words," *Washington Post*, 27 October 2019, A1. The online version of the article carried this headline: "They bonded over football years ago. Now President Trump sees Mitt Romney as his harshest GOP foe"; https://www.washingtonpost.com/politics/they-bonded-over-football-years-ago-now-president-trump-sees-mitt-romney-as-his-harshest-gop-foe/2019/10/26/d1083370-f682-11e9-829d-87b12c2f85dd_story.html.

43. John Hudson and John Wagner, "Trump Realigns National Security Staff," *Washington Post*, 18 September 2019, A6. The article dealt with the appointment of Robert C. O'Brien as the president's "new national security adviser," which made O'Brien "the highest-ranking Mormon in the U.S. government, an important development for a religious community that has shown some skepticism of Trump and will be a closely watched voting demographic in states such as Arizona." The line about "strong opposition" came in Jennifer Rubin, "As Orrin Hatch Retires, Here Are Six Things to Watch," *Washington Post*, 3 January 2018, A15.

44. See, for example, "History Will Remember This," a piece written by the editorial board of the *Washington Post*, 6 February 2020, A20 (online on 5 February 2020 as "History Will Remember Mitt Romney," https://www.washingtonpost.com/opinions/history-will-remember-mitt-romney/2020/02/05/b5945e22-4856-11ea-8124-0ca81effcdfb_story.html; Michael Gerson, "Thank You, Mitt Romney," *Washington Post*, 6 February 2020, https://www.washingtonpost.com/opinions/mitt-romney-is-not-alone/2020/02/06/7668c2ea-4916-11ea-9164-d3154ad8a5cd_story.html; Michelle Boorstein and Hannah Natanson, "Mitt Romney, Marching with Evangelicals, Becomes First GOP Senator to Join George Floyd Protests in D.C.," *Washington Post*, 8 June 2020, https://www.washingtonpost.com/dc-md-va/2020/06/07/romney-protest-black-lives-matter/; and Aaron Blake, "Why Mitt Romney Stands Apart among Republicans in Criticizing Trump," *Washington Post*, 8 June 2020, https://www.washingtonpost.com/opinions/history-will-remember-mitt-romney/2020/02/05/b5945e22-4856-11ea-8124-0ca81effcdfb_story.html.

45. See Michael Lipka, "U.S. Religious Groups and Their Political Leanings," Pew Research Fact Tank, 23 February 2016, https://www.pewresearch.org/fact-tank/2016/02/23/u-s-religious-groups-and-their-political-leanings/: "Mormons are the most heavily Republican-leaning religious group in the U.S., while a pair of major historically black Protestant denominations—the African Methodist Episcopal (AME) Church and the National Baptist Convention—are two of the most reliably Democratic groups, according to data from Pew Research Center's 2014 Religious Landscape Study." For Latter-day Saint voting patterns in 2018, see Hannah Fingerhut and Brady McCombs, "Most Mormons Voted Republican in the Midterms—But Their

Trump Approval Rating Continues to Decline, Study Finds," *Salt Lake Tribune*, 29 November 2018, https://www.sltrib.com/religion/2018/11/29/most-Mormons-voted/: "About two-thirds of Mormon voters nationwide favored Republicans in the midterm elections, but President Donald Trump's approval rating among members of the faith lagged behind, according to a nationwide survey of midterm voters." See also "Mormon Political Views: Cohesive, Conservative, and Republican," chapter 4 in Campbell, Green, and Monson, *Seeking the Promised Land: Mormons and American Politics*.

46. For recent examples, see Steven Waldman, "What Happened to U.S. Evangelical Leaders? In Early America, They Were Our Freedom Fighters," *Washington Post*, 8 May 2019, https://www.washingtonpost.com/religion/2019/05/08/what-happened-us-evangelicals-early-america-they-were-our-freedom-fighters/: "Most important, they [Franklin Graham and Jerry Falwell] have been fervent supporters of Trump, even after he took the historic step of proposing a ban on Muslim immigrants. While Jewish and Mormon groups opposed the plan, 61 percent of white evangelicals supported it." See also Sarah Pulliam Bailey, "Did the Election Damage Christianity in the U.S.?" *Washington Post*, 12 November 2016, B2; see also Fingerhut and McCombs, "Most Mormons Voted Republican in the Midterms—But Their Trump Approval Rating Continues to Decline, Study Finds": "The new data reaffirms Trump's struggle to gain widespread acceptance among Mormons despite the faith's deep-rooted conservative leanings. Voters of other religious faiths such as evangelical Christians and Catholics are more consistent in their ratings of the president and vote choice. Across most other religious affiliations, about the same share voted for Republican candidates as said they approve of the president. That's not the case with Mormons: 67 percent voted for Republicans, but 56 percent said they approve of the way Trump is handling his job as president. That's according to an analysis of 1,528 Mormon voters based on data from VoteCast, a survey of more than 115,000 voters nationwide conducted for The Associated Press by NORC at the University of Chicago. The data offers an unusual level of detail about the voting decisions of a sometimes misunderstood religion. Among Mormon voters in Utah, 76 percent preferred Republican congressional candidates, but only 56 percent said they approved of Trump. By comparison, 8 in 10 white evangelical Christians nationwide voted for Republican candidates, and nearly as many (79 percent) said they approve of Trump. Among Catholics, nearly half voted for Republican candidates and said they approve of Trump (49 percent each)."

47. Ken Denlinger, "Poor Chemistry," *Washington Post*, 3 February 1978, B1.

48. These notices appeared in the *Washington Post* in several articles in 1981.

49. See, for example, two recent examples: Scott Allen, "Bye, Bryce: Harper Leaves Memes and Memories," *Washington Post*, 1 March 2019, D6; Scott

Allen, "Harper Goes Dark as Intrigue Intensifies," *Washington Post*, 8 November 2018, D2. Both articles call Harper a "devout Mormon." The first article highlighted his abstaining from alcohol; the second his response to Church president Russell M. Nelson's call for a 10-day "social media fast."

50. See Rachel Siegel, "Going against the Trend, Marriott Will Add Bibles to 300,000 Hotel Rooms," *Washington Post*, 28 August 2018, A13.

51. Terryl Givens in part 2 of the documentary *The Mormons*, ; transcript accessible at http://www.pbs.org/ Mormons/interviews/givens.html.

52. David Masci, "Q&A [with David Campbell]: A Look at What's Driving the Changes Seen in Our Religious Landscape Study," Fact Tank, Pew Research Center, 27 May 2015, https://www.pewresearch.org/fact-tank/2015/05/27 /qa-a-look-at-whats-driving-the-changes-seen-in-our-religious-landscape -study/. See also David E. Campbell and Robert D. Putnam, "Islam and American Tolerance: What the Experience of Jews and Catholics Suggests about the Future of Muslims," *Wall Street Journal*, 12 August 2011, https:// www.wsj.com/articles/SB10001424053111903918104576500813668126384.

53. "Church Leaders Boost National Family Week," *Washington Post*, 25 November 1978, A22: "Initiative for the statement came from [Washington Stake president Ralph] Mecham, who cleared the proposal with international Mormon headquarters in Salt Lake City."

54. Michelle Boorstein, "After Decades of Behind-the-scenes Diplomacy, Leaders of Catholic, Mormon Churches Meet in Rome," *Washington Post*, 9 March 2019, https://www.washingtonpost.com/religion/2019/03/09/after-decades -behind-the-scenes-diplomacy-leaders-catholic-Mormon-churches -meet-rome/.

★ PEOPLE ★

Senator Reed Smoot. Reed Smoot Papers, L. Tom Perry Special Collections, Harold B. Lee Library, Brigham Young University.

LATTER-DAY SAINTS IN THE NATIONAL CONSCIOUSNESS: THE SEATING OF SENATOR REED SMOOT

CASEY PAUL GRIFFITHS

Casey Paul Griffiths is an assistant teaching professor of Church history and doctrine at Brigham Young University.

Reed Smoot burst onto the national scene in the middle of a crucial transformation for the Latter-day Saints.[1] The Manifesto of 1890 had begun the gradual end of plural marriage in the Church, moving the Saints closer to mainstream American life. The 1896 entry of Utah into the Union further pushed the Saints into the national spotlight. Following the inauguration of statehood for Utah, Latter-day Saint soldiers fought alongside compatriots in the Spanish-American War.[2] In the early 1900s, the Saints' isolation seemed to have ended, and Latter-day Saints occupied positions in local and state governments throughout the West. However, a crucial question remained: Could a believing Latter-day Saint occupy a position in the federal government of the United States?

Reed Smoot sought to answer this question with his candidacy for a seat in the U.S. Senate. His eventual election led to national uproar and a series of hearings during which Smoot's involvement with the Church was questioned. The heated nature of the Smoot hearings cast the Church into an intense crucible of public examination. Plural marriage, Church finance, and even the sacred ordinances of the temple were thrust into the

Reed Smoot around the time of the Senate hearings. Reed Smoot Papers, L. Tom Perry Special Collections, Harold B. Lee Library, Brigham Young University.

public spotlight. Church leaders responded to the controversy by working to clarify Church teachings and by bringing Church membership into line with official Church positions. As a result, the transformation in the Church started by the 1890 Manifesto intensified, and, in the end, the Church found greater acceptance in the eyes of many Americans. Though the Saints' isolation from mainstream America effectively started to diminish with the dissolution of plural marriage, the Smoot hearings accelerated the process by intensely involving the public eye in the internal processes of the Church.

The hearings, spread out over four years, created a 3,500-page record of the testimonies of one hundred witnesses on every facet of the Latter-day Saints' lives, practices, and beliefs. At the peak of the hearings, some senators received a thousand letters a day from outraged citizens. The record of these public petitions today fills eleven feet of shelf space in the National Archives, the largest collection of its kind.[3] The hearings were also well documented by Reed Smoot himself, who kept a detailed scrapbook of many of the public articles supporting, opposing, and documenting his seating in the U.S. Senate. A full review of all the material related to the hearings is not possible in this format. Despite the overwhelming amount of material, a brief review of the events of the Smoot hearings is vital in understanding this important episode in the development of the national identity of the Latter-day Saints.

LATTER-DAY SAINTS AND THE
UNITED STATES GOVERNMENT

Reed Smoot was not the first active Latter-day Saint elected to a position in the federal government. Frank J. Cannon,[4] who later became a Church antagonist, was an active Church member at the time of his election to the U.S. Senate (1896). He was seated in the Senate without much controversy. W. H. King, another active Latter-day Saint, served one term and part of another in the U.S. House of Representatives from 1896 to 1898.[5] However, trouble began brewing with the election of B. H. Roberts to the House of Representatives in 1898. Roberts was denied his seat because he was married to three women, one of whom he married after the 1890 Manifesto. A petition bearing seven million signatures was delivered to Congress—the greatest number of Americans to ever seek congressional action—demanding the denial of Roberts's place in the House. Roberts eloquently defended his place in the government; visiting British writer H. G. Wells even noted, "Mr. Roberts stood like a giant and defended himself and his Church. I never heard a more eloquent or cogent speaker in all my travels."[6] Unfortunately, the public's pressure was too much, and congressional leaders barred him from serving.[7] The controversy surrounding Roberts was linked to his identity as a polygamist and his place in Church hierarchy, where he served as a member of the First Council of the Seventy. Roberts also did not seek the approval of Church leadership before he ran for office, a move that led Church leaders to provide him with only lukewarm support.[8] When he fought the might of the U.S. government, he fought alone.

When Reed Smoot announced his candidacy in 1902, questions swirled around his chance of taking a seat in the Senate. Like Roberts, Smoot was a leader in the Church. He was called to serve in the Quorum of the Twelve in April 1900. Unlike Roberts, however, Smoot was a monogamist, married to Alpha Mae Eldredge in 1884. Smoot also went to great lengths to secure the approval and support of Church President Joseph F. Smith in Smoot's run for office. President Smith felt strongly that Smoot's senatorial service would serve to further the purposes of the Church. At the height of the Smoot controversy, Charles W. Nibley, a close friend of President Smith, attempted to persuade the Church President to

Senator Smoot (left) in front of the United States Capitol. Reed Smoot Papers, L. Tom Perry Special Collections, Harold B. Lee Library, Brigham Young University.

withdraw his support. Nibley recalled that President Smith brought down his fist and declared, "If I have ever had the inspiration of the spirit of the Lord given to me forcefully and clearly it has been on this one point concerning Reed Smoot, and that is that instead of his being retired, he should be continued in the United States Senate."[9] Reed Smoot would serve in the Senate with the full support of Church leadership, which was certainly needed. Almost immediately after his election in 1902, the battle began.

EARLY ATTACKS ON SENATOR SMOOT

The campaign against Smoot began with a meeting of the Salt Lake Ministerial Association, held on 24 November 1902. At the meeting, fifteen ministers representing several Protestant churches in Salt Lake City passed a resolution opposing Smoot's election. A few weeks later, the Reverend J. L. Leilich, head of Methodist missions in Utah, accused Smoot of secretly being a polygamist. Leilich refused to provide the name of Smoot's supposed plural wife but publicly accused the Church of performing the plural marriage and holding a "secret record [that] is in exclusive custody and control of the First Presidency and the quorum of the Twelve Apostles."[10] Joseph F. Smith quickly responded "that there is not one word of truth in the assertion that Reed Smoot is or has been a polygamist, or that he has married a plural wife either since or before Utah became a state."[11]

Leilich's charge was a blatant untruth, but it raised the specter of polygamy and brought up a significant number of charges in the Senate. Smoot was quick to recognize the stakes of the protest. In a letter to the president of the Eastern States Mission, he wrote,

> The Ministers will have to show their hand to get anywhere and then the people of the United States will know and realize that it is not a fight against Reed Smoot, but that it is a fight against the authority of God on earth and against the Church of Jesus Christ of Latter-day Saints. . . . If this gang wins in this fight you can depend upon it that it will be only a stepping stone to disbar every Mormon from the halls of Congress. If they can expel me from the Senate of the United States they can expel any man who claims to be a Mormon.[12]

Within a year, more than thirty-one hundred petitions had arrived in Washington, DC, requesting Reed Smoot's removal from the Senate. During the summer of 1903, articles and editorials appeared throughout the country making similar calls for Smoot's ouster. The *New York Sun* declared a "War on Senator Smoot" and quoted the leader of an interdenominational women's club who said, "We will fight Apostle Smoot and defeat him. It is remarkable how easy it is to touch public feeling on the subject. . . . An Eastern audience today is like a bundle of combustible material, and the question of polygamy is like a lighted match."[13]

Young Reed Smoot. The Smoot trials included an extensive airing of the Latter-day Saint temple rituals. Reed Smoot Papers, L. Tom Perry Special Collections, Harold B. Lee Library, Brigham Young University.

The *Pittsburgh Gazette* declared "Smoot's Toga is in Danger" and painted Smoot's senatorial service as part of a conspiracy to reinstitute plural marriage. An editorial in the paper charged, "The reason for the contest is that the Mormon church is using its tremendous power and influence to gain political control, not only in Utah, but in all the Western States where it has a following. . . . Christian people firmly believe that the Mormons are only waiting until they are strongly in power to again preach the doctrine of plural marriages."[14]

The revival of sentiment against the Church eventually led to the launch of a series of Senate hearings lasting from 1904 to 1907 that called into question nearly every practice and teaching of the Church. Historian Harvard S. Heath summarized the aim of the hearings: "The prosecution focused on two issues: Smoot's alleged polygamy and his expected allegiance to the Church and its ruling hierarchy, which, it was claimed, would make it impossible for him to execute his oath as a United States senator. Though the proceedings focused on senator-elect Smoot, it soon became apparent that it was the Church that was on trial."[15] Historians and even Smoot himself have agreed that the hearings were aimed at the Church and not at Smoot; Smoot was told this directly. In a letter to a friend, Smoot wrote, "Chairman [Julius C.] Burrows today very frankly told me, and has done so on several occasions, that I was not on trial, but that they were going to investigate the Mormon Church."[16]

INVESTIGATING PLURAL MARRIAGE

Because the hearings seemed to probe Latter-day Saints broadly instead of just Smoot himself, it makes sense that the first witness called to the stand during the hearings, and the one who created the greatest sensation in the national media, was Joseph F. Smith, the President of the Church. Over the course of six days, President Smith was interrogated about the finances, doctrines, and practices of the Church. A memorable exchange took place when Massachusetts senator Joseph Hoar questioned President Smith about the scriptural basis for plural marriage:

> Senator Hoar: Now I will illustrate what I mean by the injunction of our scripture—what we call the New Testament.
>
> Mr. Smith: Which is our scripture also.
>
> Senator Hoar: Which is your scripture also?
>
> Mr. Smith: Yes sir.
>
> Senator Hoar: The apostle says that a bishop must be sober and be the husband of one wife.
>
> Mr. Smith: At least.[17]

More than a decade after the Manifesto was issued, the Reed Smoot trials sensationalized the practice of plural marriage. Reed Smoot Papers, L. Tom Perry Special Collections, Harold B. Lee Library, Brigham Young University.

Putting humor aside, President Smith staunchly defended the sincerity of the Manifesto, telling the prosecutors, "It has been the continuous and conscientious practice and rule of the church ever since the manifesto to observe that manifesto with plural marriages."[18]

The most dramatic moment of Smith's testimony—and perhaps of the entire hearings—took place when President Smith was asked about his own families. He told the audience that he still lived with and took care of his polygamous wives and the children from their unions. President Smith felt that marriages carried out before the Manifesto were still legitimate, and therefore he acted in opposition to the law. He told the prosecutors, "I simply took my chances preferring to meet the consequences of the law rather than to abandon my children and their mothers; and I have cohabited with my wives, not . . . in a manner that I thought would be offensive to my neighbors—but I have acknowledged them; I have visited them. They have borne me [eleven] children since 1890, and I have done it, knowing the responsibility and knowing that I was amenable to the law."[19] In other testimonies given in the hearings, other Church leaders, including Francis M. Lyman, Clara M. B. Kennedy, and Charles E. Merrill, admitted to continued cohabitation after the Manifesto.[20]

The admissions caused a firestorm of controversy throughout the country. President Smith was caricatured in the national media as a sinister manipulator of Smoot and the locus of all negative charges fixed on the Church. In a cartoon appearing in *Collier's Weekly*, President Smith was depicted in a striped prison outfit with a ball and chain attached to his foot, portraying him as "a dissipated and convicted criminal."[21] Even Smoot acknowledged how devastating President Smith's testimony was to the public image of the Church. "The testimony of Joseph F. Smith has startled the nation," he wrote to a friend, "and the papers are having a great deal to say about the lack of faith on the part of the Mormon people with the government of the United States."[22]

The hearings highlighted the difficulty in ending the practice of plural marriage within the Church. The ambiguity of the 1890 Manifesto caused confusion on the part of some Church members. It did not address the subject of continued cohabitation of pre-Manifesto marriages or the provision of emotional and financial support for plural families. In a closed-door meeting after the Manifesto was given, President Wilford Woodruff advised, "I did not, could not, and would not promise that you would desert your wives and children. This you cannot do in honor."[23] While concern for the care of pre-Manifesto plural families was understandable, church members also struggled to give up the concept of polygamy after the Manifesto. There is significant evidence that a number of post-Manifesto plural marriages took place. A ledger of "marriages and sealings performed outside the temple" lists 315 marriages performed between 17 October 1890, and 8 September 1903. Of the 315 marriages recorded, 25 (7.9 percent) were plural marriages and 290 were monogamous (92.1 percent). Eighteen of the plural marriages from this time took place in Mexico, though there were also three in Arizona, two in Utah, and one in Colorado, along with one on a boat in the Pacific Ocean.[24] These marriages exhibit the struggle for individual Latter-day Saints at this time to conform to the teachings within the Manifesto.

The furor caused by the discussions of plural marriage in the Smoot hearings led to direct action in the Church. Realizing their approach to the end of plural marriage needed a more forceful method of enforcement, President Smith issued the "Second Manifesto," making new plural marriages an excommunicable offense. In a general conference address, President Smith declared, "I hereby announce that all such [plural] marriages are prohibited, and if any officer or member of the Church shall assume to solemnize or enter into any such marriage, he will be deemed in transgression against the Church, and will be liable to be dealt with according to the rules and regulations thereof and excommunicated therefrom."[25] This exchange eventually led to the removal of two members of the Quorum of the Twelve, John W. Taylor and Matthias Cowley, who admitted they had performed post-Manifesto plural marriages.[26]

While the Church tried to bring membership into accordance with the Manifesto's teachings, the hearings continued. Reed Smoot never practiced plural marriage and, because of this, was somewhat insulated against the charges regarding plural marriage. During one exchange in the hearings, Senator Boies Penrose of Pennsylvania glared at some of his philandering colleagues impugning Smoot's integrity and then quipped, "As for me, I would rather have seated beside me in this chamber a polygamist who doesn't polyg than a monogamist who doesn't monog."[27] Senator Albert Hopkins of Illinois brought up questions about the dangerous precedent that might be set by denying an elected representative based on his religion. He declared, "Never before in the history of the government has the previous life or career of a Senator been called into question to determine whether or not he should remain in the Senate. . . . If members of any Christian Church were to be charged with all of the crimes that have been committed in its name where is the Christian gentleman who would be safe in his seat?"[28] In another essay written in Smoot's defense, Senator Hopkins added, "The people of Utah have the same right to elect their Senator from the Mormon faith that the people of another State have to elect their Senator who is a member of the Methodist, Presbyterian, or Catholic Church."[29]

TEMPLE CEREMONIES AND ALLEGIANCE TO THE CHURCH HIERARCHY

Despite Smoot's innocence on the charge of polygamy, his Church membership alone was reason enough to bar him from the Senate according to some people. In January 1905 the *New York Press* listed eight senators who deserved to have their place in the legislature removed. A picture of each of the accused lawmakers was shown with their crime listed below. Three

SEEN IN THEIR TRUE RELATION.
"SPEAK FOR YOURSELF, REED."

In this cartoon appearing in the Salt Lake Tribune, *12 February 1905, Smoot is depicted as a puppet being manipulated by the Church hierarchy, caricatured here as President Joseph F. Smith. Utah Digital Papers.*

of the senators were listed as "indicted." Other charges included "accused of fraud," "expulsion asked for," and "financially embarrassed through trying to elect notorious addicks [*sic*] to the Senate." The charge below Reed Smoot simply read "Mormon."[30]

Perhaps knowing the practice of plural marriage was on the decline, Smoot's opponents also centered on a more universal charge with
far-reaching consequences. They began to make accusations that a Latter-
day Saint who entered into the covenants of the temple was automatically
guilty of sedition against the U.S. government. One article charged, "It is
generally admitted in Utah that the priesthood, and all the leading spirits of
the Mormon church are members of a secret oath-bound fraternity, whose
chief meeting place is in the Temple at Salt Lake City. This massive stone
edifice, sacred in the eyes of the followers of the 'Prophet' Joseph Smith,
and it is the one building in Utah within which no Gentile may enter."[31]
An editorial appearing in the *Salt Lake Tribune* demanded Smoot answer
a number of questions, including, "Have you taken an oath to avenge the
blood of Joseph Smith upon this nation? Have you taken the endowment
in the temple of the Mormon church or elsewhere? Have you taken the
obligations which are given all who go through the endowment house?"[32]
The implications of this line of questioning came with a more sinister mo-
tive. Where earlier attacks questioned the endurance of plural marriage,
now the opposition was unmistakably implying that no temple-endowed
Latter-day Saint could loyally serve the U.S. government.

The exploitation of temple liturgy in the Smoot hearings and the national media produced great discomfort among the Saints. A New York
newspaper blared sensational headlines about "Death Penalties in Mormon Oath" and "Dead Married to Living" without attempting to explain
or contextualize the temple ordinances.[33] In two major newspapers in
California, photographs depicting temple clothing, oaths, and rites were
splashed across whole pages.[34] A particularly difficult moment for Church
supporters came late in the hearings when Walter W. Wolfe, a former
teacher at Brigham Young College in Logan who left the Church in 1906,
was called to the stand. Only two years earlier, Wolfe wrote a defense of
Reed Smoot's right to serve in the Senate, which appeared in the Church
periodical the *Millennial Star*. But now Wolfe took the opportunity to
speak out on temple covenants. Though Wolfe called the endowment "a
very impressive ceremony," he also declared his feelings that "in [the] covenant the seed of treason is planted."[35]

During the hearings when Smoot was asked about the endowment oath, he downplayed his involvement in it. He mentioned receiving his endowment when he was eighteen, stating, "My father was going to visit the Sandwich [Hawaiian] Islands for his health, and he asked me to go with him." He continued, "I of course was very pleased, indeed to accept the invitation, and before going my father asked me if I would go to the endowment house and take my endowments. I did not particularly care about it. He stated to me that it certainly would not hurt me if it did not do me any good, and that, as my father, he would like very much to have me take the endowments before I crossed the water or went away from the United States."[36] When Smoot was asked directly what he would do if the laws of God conflicted with the laws of the land, he replied, "If the revelation were given to me, and I knew it was from God, that; that law of God would be more binding upon me, possibly than a law of the land, and I would do what God told me, if I were a Christian. . . . And I would further state this, that if it conflicted with the law of my country in which I live, I would go to some other country where it would not conflict."[37]

When the hearings wrapped up in the spring of 1906, many news outlets crowed over the harsh exposure given to the Saints, their history, and their doctrine. The *Baltimore Herald* declared, "Morman Church Flayed; Smoot Report Goes In."[38] The *Salt Lake Tribune* reveled in the scourging of the Church in the national scene, gleefully adding, "Reed Smoot's ambition has brought more suffering to his people than the work of every opponent of the church in the land, . . . the destructive force of which, was never equaled by the ambition of any man in the history of the Republic."[39] Smoot himself wondered if his ambition had wrought too heavy a price for the Church to pay. In a pleading letter written at the height of the hearings, Smoot wrote to Joseph F. Smith, "I would also like to suggest that the General Authorities of the church; meaning the Presidency, Apostles, First Presidents of Seventy, Patriarch, and Bishopric meet a day in the near future for fasting and prayer. I am sure it can do no harm and I fully believe it will do some good." He expressed remorse over the role he played in the controversy, continuing, "If they think it is my ambition that has brought this trouble upon the church, I think they ought to have charity enough to ask God to forgive me." At the same time, he added, "But I would like to impress upon them the fact that it is not me that is in danger, but the church." He also asked Church leaders to pray to "prevent another crusade against her people; to save the liberties of our people."[40]

While Smoot worried about the impact of his trial on the Church, he was not without defenders in the Senate. Illinois senator Albert Hopkins gave an impassioned defense of Smoot during the hearing. "It is conceded by the chairman of the committee on privileges and elections that Senator Smoot possesses all of the qualifications spoke of in the Constitution itself," he argued. "It also conceded that he has never married a plural wife, and has never practiced polygamy. . . . Why then, should he be dispelled from this body, disgraced and dishonored for life, a stigma placed upon his children, his own life wrecked, and the happiness of his wife destroyed?" He concluded, "He is a Christian gentleman, and his religious belief has taken him into the Mormon church."[41]

OUTCOME AND IMPACT OF THE SMOOT HEARINGS

The day of reckoning came at last on 20 February 1907. Final arguments were made in the Senate and a vote taken around four o'clock in the afternoon. When the votes were tallied, Smoot was allowed to retain his seat since his opponents failed to reach the necessary two-thirds majority to remove him from the Senate. In the end, thirty-nine Republican and three Democratic senators voted for Smoot to retain his seat.[42] Though a number of political factors affected the outcome, one of the most important elements in Smoot's victory was his personal character. The hearings, drawn out over nearly three years, took place concurrent to Smoot's service in the Senate. During that time, Smoot developed important relationships with party leaders, fellow senators, and President Theodore Roosevelt. Even Michigan senator Julius Burrows, one of Smoot's primary antagonists, conceded that "the Senator [Smoot] stands before the Senate in personal character and bearing above criticism and beyond reproach."[43] Senator Albert Hopkins, a Smoot advocate, stated, "Reed Smoot himself has never had but one wife. He is a model husband and father, an honest and upright citizen in every respect, and has made an honest, painstaking

Senator Smoot (right) with President Calvin Coolidge (center). After a rocky start in his senatorial career, Reed Smoot became one of the most influential senators in Washington, DC. Reed Smoot Papers, L. Tom Perry Special Collections, Harold B. Lee Library, Brigham Young University.

and conscientious official as a representative from his State in the Senate of the United States."[44]

The crucible of the Smoot hearings brought pain and embarrassment to Church leaders and the general membership, but it also hastened the transformation of the Latter-day Saints started by the 1890 Manifesto and the entry of Utah into the Union in 1896. The Smoot hearings publicly purged Church leadership of outspoken proponents of plural marriage. The Second Manifesto, issued in 1904, gave Church leaders a method to enforce the end of plural marriage and hasten its demise in the Church.[45] A watershed moment came at the April 1906 general conference when three strong proponents of plural marriage in the Quorum of the Twelve—Marriner W. Merrill, John W. Taylor, and Matthias F. Cowley—were replaced by three new Apostles: George F. Richards, Orson F. Whitney, and David O. McKay. Merrill had passed away two months before in February, while Taylor and Cowley had both resigned from the Quorum of the Twelve a year earlier because of their involvement in post-Manifesto plural marriages.[46] Five years later, Taylor was excommunicated from the Church, and Cowley was disfellowshipped two months after Taylor's excommunication.[47] Their replacements—Richards, Whitney, and McKay—were all monogamists and influential leaders later in the Church.[48]

Smoot went on to serve five more terms in the Senate until his eventual defeat in the Democratic wave of 1933, which was caused by the Great Depression. Along the way, he worked closely with presidents such as William Howard Taft, Calvin Coolidge, and Herbert Hoover. Was his service worth the sacrifice? Even though the Church had to deal with extremely negative press and address internal membership issues during the Smoot Hearings, Smoot's affiliation with the Church provided valuable exposure. Jan Shipps, a Methodist historian, conducted a study on Smoot's identification with the image of the Church and found that in the early period of Smoot's service, his identification with the Church was almost overwhelming. During his first Senate term, 94 percent of the articles about Smoot mentioned his Church membership. While these numbers declined to around 20 percent in the 1920s, it is indisputable that Smoot's senatorial tenure brought visibility to the Church and hastened its integration into the fabric of American culture.[49] "No person did more, during the first third of the twentieth century, to promote a positive image for the state of Utah than Reed Smoot," one team of historians concluded. They continued, "Reed Smoot led Utah's march into the national mainstream, both he and the state found rapid acceptance. This was a class moment in Utah history; the right personality and the right circumstance interacting to consummate a great change."[50]

Even after the hearings ended, Smoot continued to be an ambassador for the Church. While his hesitance in his senatorial testimony may have caused some to question the sincerity of his connection to his faith, his actions throughout his time in Washington, DC, told a different story. The Smoot home became a hub of activity for Latter-day Saints in the DC area. Sacrament meetings were held biweekly in the Smoot home, with his family putting up enough folding chairs to accommodate the entire Latter-day Saint community in the area. When his senatorial duties allowed, Smoot was also diligent in carrying out his apostolic duties. A quick review of his journals lists his attendance at dozens of meetings and prayer circles in the Salt Lake Temple and with the First Presidency and Quorum of the Twelve.[51] When Smoot's senatorial duties forced him to miss the April 1918 general conference, President Smith wrote to Smoot, "While you were missed, we all felt that the work you are engaged in was in the line of your duty and in harmony with this great work in which we are engaged."[52]

Given the heavy weight of his senatorial duties, his record of Church service becomes even more outstanding. At times the two roles overlapped, providing Senator Smoot with opportunities to not only preach but demonstrate the power of his religion. On one occasion, President Warren G. Harding telephoned Smoot late at night. The first lady, Florence Harding, was very ill. President Harding recalled Smoot's description of a priesthood blessing and asked the senator to come to the White House and perform the rite for his sick wife. Smoot immediately went to the executive mansion carrying a vial of consecrated oil and gave a priesthood blessing to Mrs. Harding.[53] This was only one of dozens of unique opportunities given to Senator Smoot because of his closeness to the leaders of the nation. During his time in Washington he worked with nearly every prominent politician of the age. Due to his prominence in the Republican Party, he was particularly close to presidents William Howard Taft, Warren G. Harding, Calvin Coolidge, and Herbert Hoover.

One historian commenting on Smoot's record wrote, "There was little political glamor surrounding Reed Smoot. He was no orator. He shunned peccadilloes of his fellows; he staged no rebellions; he coined no phrases; he offered no intriguing new ideas. He merely worked without stint or respite and continued to win elections."[54] Another major impact of Smoot's lengthy senatorial career was borne out in the number of fellow Westerners he helped bring to the nation's capital. Materials from one of his senate campaigns noted, "Not only has Senator Smoot become a household figure throughout the nation, but he has become successful in placing many Utahans in positions of national prominence where they, too, have brought honor and credit to the state of Utah."[55]

But his primary benefit to the Church during his time in Washington, DC, came in his role of breaking down barriers of misunderstanding and prejudice toward the Saints. Though he was not the first Latter-day Saint to serve in Congress, Smoot's trials opened the door for many of the Latter-day Saints who also served in the Senate, including William H. King (1917–41), and Elbert D. Thomas, who defeated Smoot in 1933 and then served until 1951. In the latter half of the twentieth century, the Senate included such notable Latter-day Saints as Frank Moss (1959–77), Jake Garn (1973–93), Paula Hawkins (1981–87), Harry Reid (1987–2017), and Orrin Hatch (1977–2019), to name only a sampling.[56] Recently the *Washington Post* has noted the unusually high number of Latter-day Saints in Congress, noting that Latter-day Saints "represent 1.6 percent of the country's population, but the [Latter-day Saint] Church has long had a disproportionately large number of high profile leaders in Washington, both in Congress and in the federal government, which some attribute to the faith's emphasis on public service. [Latter-day Saints] make up 6 percent of the Senate and 2 percent of the House."[57] Every Latter-day Saint serving in government today is a part of the legacy of Senator Smoot.

When Smoot left the Senate in 1933, the *Deseret News* editorialized that he had "added more luster to the name of Utah than any man . . . since the days of its founder."[58] A more personal tribute came from President Joseph F. Smith, who remained one of Smoot's greatest advocates. Only a few months before President Smith's death, he wrote to Senator Smoot, "I cannot understand how anyone, not even your bitterest opponents, can fail to see the handwriting of an overruling providence in the success and honor you have won and achieved at the seat of government. Surely the Lord has magnified his servant."[59]

NOTES

1. Major sources for this study include the Reed Smoot Papers, found in the L. Tom Perry Special Collections of the Harold B. Lee Library at Brigham Young University, Utah. Smoot kept a detailed scrapbook of newspaper articles written about the controversy, which are found in boxes 111–12 of the Smoot Papers. Many of these articles are also found in the Jour-

nal History of the Church, available online. The most thorough treatment of Smoot's life and accomplishments is found in Milton R. Merrill, *Reed Smoot: Apostle in Politics* (Logan: Utah State University Press, 1990). Studies of the Smoot hearings are numerous, but among the most useful is Kathleen Flake, *The Politics of American Religious Identity: The Seating of Senator Reed Smoot, Mormon Apostle* (Chapel Hill: University of North Carolina Press, 2004). Other significant studies include Harvard S. Heath, "The Reed Smoot Hearings: A Quest for Legitimacy," *Journal of Mormon History* 33, no. 2 (2007): 1–80 and Konden R. Smith, "The Reed Smoot Hearings and the Theology of Politics: Perceiving an 'American' Identity," *Journal of Mormon History* 35, no. 3 (2009): 118–62. To access the text of the hearings, see Michael Harold Paolos, ed., *The Mormon Church on Trial: Transcripts of the Reed Smoot Hearings* (Salt Lake City: Signature Books, 2008). The diaries of Reed Smoot are available and have been published but unfortunately do not cover the period of the Smoot hearings. See Harvard S. Heath, ed., *In the World: The Diaries of Reed Smoot*, ed. (Salt Lake City: Signature Books, 1997).

2. See James I. Mangum, "The Spanish-American and Philippine Wars," in *Nineteenth-Century Saints at War*, ed. Robert C. Freeman (Provo, UT: Religious Studies Center, Brigham Young University, 2006), 151–92.

3. Flake, *The Politics of American Religious Identity*, 5.

4. Frank Cannon was one of the more colorful figures in Latter-day Saint political history. The eldest son of George Q. Cannon, he was elected as a Republican in 1896 as Utah's first U.S. senator and served in the Senate from 1896 to 1899. He lost his reelection bid in part because of his determined support of free silver and a loss of institutional support from the Church. He later became head of the Utah Democratic Party and an ardent critic of the Church. At one point President Joseph F. Smith branded him a "furious Judas." See Kenneth Godfrey, "Frank J. Cannon," *Utah History Encyclopedia,* ed. Allen Kent Powell (Salt Lake City: University of Utah Press, 1994), 70. See also Richard S. Van Wagoner and Steven C. Walker, eds., *A Book of Mormons* (Salt Lake City: Signature Books, 1982), 44–48.

5. Merrill, *Reed Smoot*, 31.

6. Truman G. Madsen, *Defender of the Faith: The B. H. Roberts Story* (Salt Lake City: Bookcraft, 1980), 261.

7. See Davis Bitton, "The Exclusion of B. H. Roberts from Congress," in *The Ritualization of Mormon History and Other Essays* (Urbana: University of Illinois Press, 1994), 150–70; Madsen, *Defender of the Faith*, 245. See also "The Manifesto and the End of Plural Marriage," Gospel Topics Essay.

8. Madsen, *Defender of the Faith*, 245–246.

9. Charles W. Nibley, "Reminiscences of Charles W. Nibley," MS, Church History Library, Salt Lake City; see Merrill, *Reed Smoot*, 25.

10. "Smoot Charged with Polygamy," *Deseret News*, 26 February 1903, copy in Smoot Newspaper Scrapbooks, Smoot Papers.

11. "President Smith Makes Unqualified Denial; Smoot Is Not and Never Was a Polygamist," *Deseret News*, 26 February 1903, Smoot Papers.

12. Reed Smoot to John G. McQuarrie, 16 December 1902, Smoot Papers, box 27a; see Merrill, *Reed Smoot*, 31.

13. "War on Senator Smoot," *New York Sun*, 13 May 1901, Smoot Papers.

14. "Smoot's Toga is in Danger," *Pittsburgh Gazette*, 15 May 1903, Smoot Papers.

15. Harvard S. Heath, "Smoot Hearings," in *Encyclopedia of Mormonism*, ed. Daniel H. Ludlow (New York: Macmillan, 1992), 3:1363.

16. Reed Smoot to C. E. Loose, 26 January 1904, Smoot Papers, box 27a.

17. Paolos, *Mormon Church on Trial*, 95.

18. Paolos, *Mormon Church on Trial*, 51–52.

19. Committee on Privileges and Elections, S. Rep. No. 486-1 at 129–31; see also Paolos, *Mormon Church on Trial*, 52–53.

20. Merrill, *Reed Smoot*, 48.

21. Flake, *Politics of American Religious Identity*, 69.

22. Reed Smoot to James H. Anderson, 18 March 1904, Smoot Papers, box 27; cited in Heath, "Reed Smoot Hearings," 29.

23. Abraham H. Cannon, Diary, 7 October 1890 and 12 November 1891; see "Manifesto and the End of Plural Marriage," 2019.

24. "Manifesto and the End of Plural Marriage," 2019.

25. Joseph F. Smith, in Conference Report, April 1904, 75.

26. "Manifesto and the End of Plural Marriage," 2019.

27. Paul B. Beers, *Pennsylvania Politics Today and Yesterday: The Tolerable Accommodation* (University Park: Pennsylvania State University Press, 1980), 51.

28. "Hopkins Lauds Smoot," *Chicago Record Journal*, 12 January 1907, Smoot Papers.

29. Albert J. Hopkins, "The Case of Senator Smoot," *Independent* 62 (24 January 1907): 207.

30. "If There Should Be a House Cleaning in the Senate," *New York Press*, 19 February 1905, Smoot Papers.

31. "Mul's Letter," *Citizen* (Brooklyn), 8 March 1903, Smoot Papers. The author fails to mention the St. George, Logan, and Manti Temples as other places in Utah where those of other faiths were not allowed to enter.

32. A. F. Phillips, "Smoot Must Answer Specific Questions for His Church or His Country," *Salt Lake Tribune*, December 16, 1904, Smoot Papers.

33. "Death Penalties in Mormon Oath," *Herald* (New York), December 14, 1904, Smoot Papers.

34. *Express* (Los Angeles), 20 December 1904, Smoot Papers; *Enquirer* (Oakland), 19 December 1904, Smoot Papers.

35. Paolos, *Mormon Church on Trial*, 640–41n63; see Harvard S. Heath, "Reed Smoot: First Modern Mormon" (PhD diss., Brigham Young University, 1990), 174.

36. Paolos, *Mormon Church on Trial*, 526–27.

37. Paolos, *Mormon Church on Trial*, 526–27.

38. "Morman Church Flayed; Smoot Report Goes In," *Baltimore Herald*, 11 June 1906; spelling in original.

39. "Remarkable Career of Reed Smoot," *Salt Lake Tribune*, 18 December 1904, 7, Smoot Papers; spelling kept as shown in the original.

40. Reed Smoot to Joseph F. Smith, 21 January 21, 1906, Smoot Papers, box 50, folder 5.

41. "Hopkins Lauds Smoot," *Chicago Record Herald*, 12 January 1907, Smoot Papers.

42. Merrill, *Reed Smoot*, 80.

43. Flake, *Politics of American Religious Identity*, 138.

44. Albert J. Hopkins, "The Case of Senator Smoot," *Independent* 62 (24 January 1907): 204–6.

45. See Brian C. Hales, *Modern Polygamy and Mormon Fundamentalism: The Generations after the Manifesto* (Salt Lake City: Greg Kofford Books, 2006), 102–4.

46. The resignation letters of John W. Taylor and Matthias F. Cowley are both found in the Smoot Papers, box 50.

47. Thomas G. Alexander, *Mormonism in Transition* (Urbana: University of Illinois Press, 1986), 70.

48. Calling three new Apostles simultaneously would not happen again until over a century later, when in October 2015 Elders Ronald A. Rasband, Gary E. Stevenson, and Dale G. Renlund were called to fill the vacancies left by Boyd K. Packer, L. Tom Perry, and Richard G. Scott. "The Sustaining of Church Officers," October 2015, churchofjesuschrist.org.

49. Jan Shipps, "The Public Image of Reed Smoot, 1902–32," *Utah Historical Quarterly* 45, no. 4 (Fall 1977): 382.

50. "In This Issue," *Utah Historical Quarterly* 45, no. 4 (Fall 1977): 324.

51. See Heath, *In the World.*

52. Joseph F. Smith to Reed Smoot, 7 May 1918, cited in Merrill, *Reed Smoot,* 129.

53. Merrill, *Reed Smoot,* 155.

54. Milton R. Merrill, *Reed Smoot: Utah Politician* (Logan: Utah State Agricultural College Monograph Series, 1953), 5.

55. Campaign document, *What Has Senator Smoot Done for Utah?* (Salt Lake City, Smoot Campaign, 1932), quoted in Merrill, *Reed Smoot: Utah Politician,* 53.

56. Latter-day Saints who have served in the U.S. Senate and their terms of service include Reed Smoot (R-Utah, 1903–33), William H. King (R-Utah, 1917–41), Elbert Thomas (D-Utah, 1933–51), Berkeley L. Bunker (D-Nevada, 1940–42), Orrice Abraham Murdock (D-Utah, 1941–47), Arthur V. Watkins (R-Utah, 1947–59), Wallace F. Bennett (R-Utah, 1951–74), Howard W. Cannon (D-Nevada, 1959–83), Frank E. Moss (D-Utah, 1959–77), Edwin Jacob "Jake" Garn (R-Utah, 1974–93), Orrin G. Hatch (R-Utah, 1977–2019), Paula F. Hawkins (R-Florida, 1981–87), Harry M. Reid (D-Nevada, 1987–2017), Robert F. Bennett (R-Utah, 1993–2011), Gordon Smith (R-Oregon, 1997–2009), Michael Crapo (R-Idaho, 1998–present), Thomas S. Udall (D-New Mexico, 2008–present), Michael S. Lee (R-Utah, 2011–present), Jeffrey L. Flake (R-Arizona, 2013–19), Willard Mitt Romney (R-Utah, 2019–present). This list takes into account politicians who openly identified as Latter-day Saints when they served in the Senate. There are a number of senators such as Frank J. Cannon (R-Utah, 1896–99) and Kyrsten Sinema (D-Arizona, 2019–present) who came from Latter-day Saint backgrounds. See Robert R. King and Kay Atkinson King, "Mormons in Congress, 1851–2000," *Journal of Mormon History* 26, no. 2 (Fall 2000): 11, 13. See also Manuel Roig-Franzia, "Congress' First Openly Bisexual Member Grew Up Mormon, Graduated from BYU," *Standard Examiner,* 3 January 2013; Jason Swensen, "U.S. Congress Includes 10 Latter-day Saints—the Fewest Number in a Decade," *Church News,* 28 January 2019.

57. Sarah Pulliam Bailey, "Romney Is Running for Senate. Even If He Wins, the Mormon Church Has Already Lost Powerful Status in D.C.," *Washington Post,* 16 February 2018.

58. *Deseret News,* 13 March 1933, quoted in Shipps, "Public Image of Reed Smoot," 382.

59. Joseph F. Smith to Reed Smoot, 5 January 1918, in Harvard S. Heath, "The Reed Smoot Hearings: A Quest for Legitimacy," *Journal of Mormon History* 33, no. 2 (2007): 77.

Theodore Roosevelt, 15 August 1913. Pach Brothers.

THEODORE ROOSEVELT, REED SMOOT, THE CHURCH, AND RELIGIOUS TOLERANCE

CARTER CHARLES

Carter Charles is an assistant professor of Church history and doctrine at Brigham Young University.

The assertion that America is a land of religious freedom is accurate only to a certain extent. Indeed, some of those who founded the nation did so to escape religious tyranny in Europe. In 1620, the Pilgrims, one of such persecuted groups, boarded the *Mayflower* with travelers who had different motivations and viewpoints. Their differences, or diversity, soon became one of the greatest threats to the future of their community and to their experiment. The Mayflower Compact is evidence that they agreed to turn diversity into a strength: they combined "into a civil body politick."[1] However, Roger Williams's 1644 *Bloody Tenet of Persecution* shows that one of the historical ironies is that some of the believers also transplanted to the land of refuge the same kind of territorial religious hegemony that often informed the religious intolerance they had fled. For settlers like Nathaniel Ward, religious freedom meant the opposite of the spirit of the Mayflower Compact. It meant freedom *from* sharing the sociopolitical realm with those who believed differently: they "shall have free Liberty to keepe away from us, and such as will come to be gone as fast as they can, the sooner the better." Ward further asserted that "God doth no where in his word tolerate Christian States, to give Tolerations to such adversaries of his Truth [i.e., those who believe differently], if they have power in their hands to suppresse them."[2]

Drawing on John Locke's theory of a "body politic"[3] and theories of other philosophers, the nation's founders sought to ensure that religious intolerance did not become the norm. Yet several cases in the nineteenth and twentieth centuries show that the spirit of intolerance continued, that some Americans had yet to rise to America's founding ideals when it came to Catholics and—as will be illustrated here—to Latter-day Saints,[4] who were often depicted as scoundrels and predators who did not belong in Washington, DC, or anywhere else in the country. But history shows there have also been times when honorable men have stood for the ideals of justice, social cohesion, and religious freedom. This paper highlights how one such honorable man, President Theodore Roosevelt, embodied those ideals in 1911. It will be argued that by so doing, he made a case for a return to the best tradition of religious plurality in the country. For contextual clarity, this paper surveys the historical trend leading to Elder Reed Smoot's election in 1902 to the U.S. Senate and his subsequent trial in that chamber before considering Roosevelt's arguments on behalf of Smoot and his fellow Church members, and the meaning of those arguments for social cohesion.

BRIEF HISTORICAL BACKGROUND

The history of the Latter-day Saint movement has been, on the one hand, one of marginalization and self-isolation from its inception down to the seating of Apostle Reed Smoot in the U.S. Senate and, on the other hand, one of struggle for national acceptance and belonging. Persecutions in Missouri, for instance, led Joseph Smith to petition President Martin Van Buren for redress in November 1839. Smith reported that Van Buren sympathized with the Saints and acknowledged their sufferings, but he would not act: "I can do nothing for you," Van Buren declared, "if I do any thing, I shall come in contact with the whole State of Missouri."[5]

Van Buren's reply was surely politically motivated. He was, after all, a Jacksonian Democrat; he believed in states' rights. But as I have written elsewhere,[6] while all of that can explain his refusal to opt for a federally mandated reparation, the possibility that he may also have been genuinely constrained should not be excluded. His rhetorical "what can I do?" hints at real constitutional limitations. While those limitations were ignored, of course, when federal intervention in local matters meant dispossessing the Native Americans of their lands, they continued to inform Van Buren's belief that he could not act on behalf of the unpopular Saints without coming "in contact [i.e., constitutional conflict] with the whole State of Missouri." This means that while Smith was also a man of the Jacksonian age, he was probably ahead of his time in asking the federal government to order a state to honor the First Amendment.[7] Smith would denounce this constitutional discontinuity in his presidential platform, lamenting that because of states' rights, the Constitution was "not broad enough to cover the whole ground."[8]

Despite this lack of broad territorial continuity raised by Smith, one still wonders why it was possible, long after Nathaniel Ward, to dispossess and drive away a religious group that had originated within the United States. A simple answer is that the movement was also a radical departure from and a challenge to anything that existed on the religious market. Jan Shipps suggests that Smith was a Lutheran figure in that he "not only proscribed Roman Catholicism," but he also "went on to reject all the institutional outgrowths of the Protestant Reformation," to the extent that "The Church of Jesus Christ of Latter-day Saints was *a protest against Protestantism*."[9]

Protestants did not sit by to be protested against. They took matters into their own hands, in a Wardian fashion, to drive the Church away from the sociopolitical realm. The first step in that effort consisted in admitting that while the roots of the Church went deep into the religious and social history of the country, it was also foreign, so much so that it was not fit to belong in the land of its emergence. This paradoxical belief became commonplace in the second half of the nineteenth century. Terryl Givens, whose *Viper on the Hearth*[10] captures well the tension between the undesirability of the Church and its quest to belong, refers—for instance—to journalist John Hanson Beadle, who wrote that "the only native American Church has lost every trace of Americanism and become an essentially foreign theocracy."[11] For Beadle, there were two explanations to this "anomaly": it was either because "the Americans [were] not really a tolerant people, and that what is called toleration is only such toward our common Protestantism, or more common Christianity"—a sure observation that again echoes Ward's—or because there was "something peculiar to Mormonism [that] takes it out of the sphere of religion and necessarily brings it into conflict with a republican people and their institutions."[12] Kathleen Flake shows that some ten years later, Congregationalist minister A. S. Bailey not only concurred with Beadle but also enlivened the fire of an ontological anti-patriotism among the Saints.[13] Bailey wrote, "A traveler visiting Utah would find in the habits and customs of the people . . . *more that is European than that is American. But besides these foreign customs,* is *a spirit foreign to the spirit of Americans,* from which has sprung *a system, indigenous indeed, but hostile to American ideas.* The root of these anti-American influences is an organization known as the Mormon Church. . . . It possesses none of the characteristics of a Church, save a few counterfeit religious elements."[14] Bailey argued further that because the Church was not a church, nor a religion, "according to the American idea and the United States Constitution," it could not qualify for First Amendment protection.[15] The Wardian spirit is implicit: an organization that was not a church and that was alien did not qualify for First Amendment protection and could logically be driven away from or rooted out of the land.

The view that Latter-day Saints were so foreign that they had forfeited their constitutional rights to believe and belong as any other group of citizens was embraced by all three branches of government, including the Supreme Court in *Reynolds v. United States* (1879). In that ruling, the court declared that the practice of polygamy made the movement foreign, that polygamy belonged "almost exclusively" with the Asiatic and African peoples.[16]

Polygamy was not the only aspect that made the movement foreign in the eyes of its detractors. It was, however, easier to rally the nation against it in a crusade of mass disenfranchisement on account not only of religious practice—as evidenced in *Reynolds,* followed by the 1882 Edmunds Act—but also of belief, as evidenced in the infamous "Idaho Test Oath" (1884), a law upheld by the Supreme Court in *Davis v. Beason* (1890) that made it unconstitutional to even *believe* in the doctrine of the Church.

This attempt to legislate belief can be seen as the ultimate Wardian way to "suppresse" an undesirable religion.

Beyond Idaho, the disenfranchisement of Latter-day Saints on account of both religious belief and practice led to the expulsion of Elder Brigham H. Roberts from the lower chamber of Congress in January 1900. Two years later, another attempt was made to prevent the seating of Elder Reed Smoot in the United States Senate. Again, passions ran high, and public opinion about the Saints was at a low point. Being associated with the Saints, therefore, was not without political risks. But as will be shown, that did not deter Theodore Roosevelt from standing up for Smoot and religious tolerance.

REED SMOOT, THE CHURCH, AND NATIONAL POLITICS

Reed Owen Smoot was born on 10 January 1862, in Salt Lake City. He was concurrently an apostle and a United States senator for over thirty years. His father, Abraham Owen Smoot, is a more familiar name in Latter-day Saint circles, especially in Utah: the Abraham O. Smoot Building is the administrative heart of Brigham Young University in Provo, Utah. Yet the younger Smoot's contribution, under prophetic guidance, in bringing the Church out of obscurity and darkness cannot be overstated.

In his early years, Smoot walked closely in his father's footsteps when it came to business and politics. He struggled, however, to emulate his parents' devotion. Records show that he was a Saint by tradition but not by faith. Harvard Heath notes that Smoot's mother admonished him at the age of twenty to read the Book of Mormon, probably hoping that he would thus gain a testimony, but Smoot confessed later, "I suppose many people of Utah and particularly my neighbors knew that I had up to that time not taken much interest in Church work. I was wrapped, body and soul, in commercial affairs. I had no testimony that this was God's work."[17]

Smoot's testimony was long in coming, even after his mother's challenge. He recalled, for instance, that he "did not particularly care about [the endowment],"[18] which he eventually obtained because his father offered him a leisure trip to the Sandwich Islands (Hawaii). He was indeed so wrapped up in the things of the world that he declined twice the call to go on a mission. Smoot eventually accepted a third call in November 1890 to serve in Great Britain but returned in October 1891, in part because his father's health was declining.[19]

Smoot struggled in the mission field. Writing to Ern Eldredge, his brother-in-law, he confessed, "If I am going to be anything in a religious way it will be a Mormon or at least until I find something better and I have not done that as yet, but I am afraid I shall never be very religious."[20] Smoot's devotion had not increased one bit by 1895 when, against all odds, he was called as a counselor in a stake presidency. Not surprisingly, he voted against himself, insisting that he still needed to sit in the pews to "grow up with the people in spiritual things."[21] Wilford Woodruff, who had extended the call, concurred: he was not spiritually of age; but the call was not withdrawn. Smoot must have felt even less spiritually mature—and probably as if the earth were retreating from under his feet—when Lorenzo Snow called him to be a member of the Quorum of the Twelve Apostles five years later, in April 1900. Even his father, a committed pioneer since Nauvoo, who had always put God first, had not received such an honor. Aside from spiritual maturity, timing was also a major obstacle for Smoot to accept the call. He intended to run for the United States Senate; so becoming an Apostle the year B. H. Roberts was expelled from the House of Representatives could thwart his plans. But in this instance, Smoot chose to serve God. Little did he know that his worldly talents would help fulfill otherworldly purposes. Indeed, his plans in 1900 were only delayed. With the blessing of Joseph F. Smith, who had become president of the Church in October 1901, Smoot ran for the Senate in 1902 and won the vote of the Utah legislature.[22] Seating, however, was a different story. Because Smoot was a member of the Church's second-highest governing body, critics viewed him as the political face of the Church. The Salt Lake Ministerial Association, a Protestant umbrella organization set up during the campaign to denounce the election of a member of "the Mormon Apostolate," took a resolution—phrased in Wardian terms—accusing the Church of fomenting "a political *invasion* of Congress." The Ministerial Alliance called for a "vigorous and rigorous execution of a law like the [1887] Edmunds-Lucker [sic] law" to "*drive the Mormon Church and the majority of its apostles into exile* or throw them in prison."[23] The Ministerial

Association orchestrated a national drive that yielded 3,482 petitions, with about three million signatures, mainly from the northeastern states (2,476 of them), including 1,045 from Pennsylvania,[24] but less than 100 from the southern states.[25] Their efforts culminated in one of the most important religious persecution trials in the history of the country since settlement.[26]

As the records show, Smoot and the Church were on trial for treason, the highest crime against the nation. Smoot and other Church leaders had to account for the Church's nonconformity in regard to American Protestantism before two tribunals—that of the *vox populi* and that of legislators whose committee room had become a pillory.[27] Siding with Smoot and the Church then meant exposing oneself to popular outrage. Yet some did both during and after his confirmation. Chief among them was President Theodore Roosevelt.

THEODORE ROOSEVELT'S DEFENSE OF THE SAINTS

Theodore Roosevelt is mentioned early in connection to Reed Smoot. Members of the Salt Lake Ministerial Association indicated in their *New York Times* op-ed that they would appeal to him in their strategy to oppose Smoot. During the campaign, Thomas Kearns, owner of the *Salt Lake Tribune*, told the Utah press that Roosevelt had commissioned him to declare that the president discouraged the election of any Apostle to the U.S. Senate.[28] Roosevelt may have told Kearns something about how the people of the United States would not want a "Mormon" senator, but the president's cordial correspondence with Smoot and his public position indicates that Kearns probably twisted the president's words to serve his own political interest.

For example, to the question "Who was the greatest statesman whom you met in your thirty-year career as Utah's Senator?" Milton R. Merrill quotes Smoot's unequivocal response: "Theodore Roosevelt."[29] Merrill concludes that Smoot's four years of investigation and scrutiny came to a positive end thanks to the continued efforts of Theodore Roosevelt. He held Smoot in high regard simply because during their first interview, Smoot gave the president his word that he was a loyal citizen and was not

James S. King, Theodore Roosevelt, *head-and-shoulders portrait, ca. 1912.*

a polygamist. Upon hearing that, the president reportedly replied, "Senator Smoot, that is enough for me."[30]

On 8 January 1904, less than a year later, with the investigation still underway, Smoot reported to Joseph F. Smith that Roosevelt confirmed he would be an indefatigable supporter. Roosevelt, Smoot said, "would assist me in this matter in every way in his power." He promised to strategize with Smoot, considering "the supposed [negative] attitude toward me of each of the members of the Committee, and he promised me that he would see the greatest number of them. . . . He told me also that he would see that Senator [Albert J.] Beveridge was put right on this subject."[31] And Beveridge, a Methodist, saw to it that Smoot was confirmed. Before the vote, he declared with passion, "Obedience to law, tolerance of opinion, loyalty to country—these are the principles which make the flag a sacred thing and this Republic immortal. These are the principles that make all Americans brothers and constitute this Nation God's highest method of human enlightenment and living liberty. By these principles let us live and vote and die, so that 'this Government of the people, for the people, and by the people may not perish from the earth' [Applause in the galleries]."[32]

Years after the hearings and Smoot's confirmation, Roosevelt was attacked in the media for rubbing shoulders with the "Mormon devils" in return for the votes of Utah and the surrounding states. Frank J. Cannon (a son of George Q. Cannon) publicly blamed Roosevelt for helping the Saints into national politics and for condoning the supposed resurgence of polygamy. Cannon accused him further, saying, "President Theodore Roosevelt, representing the majesty of the Republic, stayed us when we might have won our own liberties. He seduced senators from their convictions. He certified the ambassador from the Kingdom of God as a qualified senator of the United States. He gave the hand of fellowship to Joseph [F. Smith], the tyrant of the Kingdom."[33]

In January 1904, *McClure's Magazine* ran a special issue that illustrated the public's hostile views about the Church. The issue's cover showed the Church's iconic Salt Lake Temple enveloped in red and dark colors and announced that the intention of the magazine was to uncover the deep, hidden secret the image conveyed: the practice of polygamy was thriving in Utah.[34] The cover's flame-red color also announced the intent of the magazine to use polygamy, once again, to light a fire. The introductory paragraph of the article read in part, "Extensive investigations recently made by *McClure's Magazine* . . . show that polygamy is still practiced in the Mormon States on a considerable scale. Burton J. Hendrick . . . has

Theodore Roosevelt riding in an early automobile. American Press Association (1910).

gone thoroughly over the ground—he has traveled through the Mormon towns in Utah, talked with scores of people, and derived his information largely from Mormon sources."[35]

In their February issue, *McClure's* published the portraits and names of seven Apostles[36] who had claimed to have received revelations from God to ignore the Manifesto and take plural wives.[37] Fact-checking was not as widespread then, but it was not unusual for journalists to "double-check" sources. And that is what Isaac Russell, a Church member and journalist, did.[38] Russell wrote to Roosevelt, asking him to address accusations of collusion regarding the seating of Reed Smoot. Roosevelt sent Russell a lengthy letter whose content will soon be considered. Russell's second approach was to debunk *McClure's* February claims in *Collier's Weekly*. Russell shows in the article that the assertation that *McClure's* Burton J. Hendrick "ha[d] gone thoroughly over the ground" was at best superficial: five of the seven apostles who had supposedly unearthed the practice of polygamy were probably doing that from beyond the grave because they were all dead,[39] and the remaining two polygamists (Cowley and Taylor) were apostles in name only because they were disfellowshipped in 1904 during Smoot's Senate trial.

Russell also published Roosevelt's response to the accusations leveled at him. Instead of backing down, Roosevelt doubled on his defense of the probity of Church members and of their rights:

> The Mormon has the same right to his religious belief that the Jew and the Christian have to theirs but like the Jew and the Christian, he must not practice conduct which is in contravention of the law of the land. I have known monogamous Mormons whose standard of domestic life and morality and whose attitude toward the relations of men and women was as high as that of the best citizens of any other creed; indeed, among these Mormons the standard of sexual morality was unusually high. There [*sic*] children were numerous, healthy, and well brought up; their young men were less apt than their neighbors to indulge in that course of vicious sexual dissipation so degrading to manhood and so brutal in the degradation it inflicts on women; and they were free from that vice more destructive to civilization than any other can possibly be[:] the artificial restriction of families, the

practise of sterile marriage; and which ultimately means destruction of the nation.[40]

Establishing further connections between family, citizenship, and the future of the nation, Roosevelt wrote,

> If the average man is not most anxious to be a good father, performing his full duty to his wife and children; if the average woman is not most anxious to be a good and happy wife and mother, the mother of plenty of healthy and happy and well trained children then not only have the average man and the average woman missed what is infinitely the highest happiness of life but they are bad citizens of the worst type and the nation in which they represent the average type of citizen is doomed to undergo the hopeless disaster which it deserves. In so far as the Mormons will stand against all hideous and degrading tendencies of this kind, they will set a good example of citizenship. . . . The Mormons who realize this fact and stand as you [Isaac Russell] do, and as I have every reason to believe Senator Smoot does, on these matters, are not only fighting for the best interests of the Mormon Church, but are performing well the highest duties of American citizenship.[41]

Times have changed since Roosevelt, of course. But the general tone of his statements suggests he was most interested in a virtuous cycle of family life that included not only the number of children raised and taught at home but also good matrimonial relations, as well as high moral and sexual standards. The Saints were to be exemplified because they were "performing well the highest duties of American citizenship."[42] Latter-day Saints, in his view, belonged in the country as much as "the best citizens of any other creed."[43]

Ultimately, Roosevelt's defense of the Saints was a departure from the spirit of intolerance and of suppression of those who believe differently. It was a stand for social cohesion and for the sharing of the sociopolitical realm. Roosevelt took a higher ground, one consistent with the spirit of the Mayflower Compact, creating strength out of differences by uniting different groups into a "civil body politick." Sociologist Robert Bellah later called this approach a "civil religion,"[44] a notion he borrowed from Rousseau's *Social Contract*.[45]

Rousseau's "civil religion" was supported by four pillars: the existence of (1) God, (2) of an afterlife, (3) reward for virtue and punishment for vice, and (4) religious tolerance. Still, Rousseau saw the need for a "civil religion" because Christianity, as he had experienced it, was no longer that of "the Gospel."[46] He did see something sublime in Christianity, especially the belief that humans are one family in God, that does not dissolve at death.[47] Conversely, Rousseau considered that one of Christianity's weaknesses was that "instead of attaching the hearts of the citizens to the State, it detaches them as it does for all other earthly things."[48] Rousseau's remedy to the patriotic apathy and disconnect with the non-Christian part of a nation was a secular, "purely civil religion" for which the sovereign had the right "to decide the articles—not exactly as religious dogmas but as feelings of sociability—without which it is impossible to be a good citizen."[49] It is tempting to interpret the term *secular* in light of its modern-day understanding. There is in Rousseau's theory a thread that runs through "secularization," "secularism," and "separation of church and state," with the state having its own *nonreligious religion*. But he would have rejected any appropriation of the theory to force religion out of the public square. His intent, in proposing a "civil religion" was to ensure that people of all creeds—and noncreeds—could find a reason and a space where they could belong together.

Applied to Roosevelt, Rousseau's articles of a secular religion need to be understood as the Constitution and other laws that the "sovereign"—that is, Roosevelt, previous presidents, or magistrates—had approved to determine the conditions of social acceptance and participation in national life. By those articles, the Saints were both "fighting for the best interests of the Mormon Church" and "performing well the highest duties of American citizenship."[50] In making that observation, Roosevelt not only broke from Ward; he also disavowed James Buchanan, who had marched American troops against the supposedly "treasonous Mormons" in Utah. Roosevelt had a clear understanding of how the Saints navigated religion and country. Latter-day Saints could declare, as Smoot did in his final remarks before his confirmation as a senator, "I owe no allegiance to any church or other organization which in any way interferes with my supreme allegiance *in civil affairs* to my country—an allegiance which I freely, fully, gladly give."[51] Rousseau would also have praised the way the religion of the Saints allowed for a balance between devotion to God in otherworldly, or spiritual, matters and devotion to country in this-worldly, or civil, ones.[52]

CONCLUSION

Roosevelt's defense of Smoot and the Church sounds somewhat like a precursor to the prophetic invitation issued in 1995: "We call upon responsible citizens and officers of government everywhere to promote those measures designed to maintain and strengthen the family as the fundamental unit of society."[53] The way the family is defined today is different compared to Roosevelt's time, but the overall principles are timeless: family provides balance to our lives. It is the very essence of and gives meaning to our

Theodore Roosevelt on horseback. © 1907 by B. M. Clinedinst.

existence as social beings; and it is what sustains nations and guarantees their continuity. Roosevelt understood the close interconnections between family and country and saw, in spite of bigotry, how the Saints were upholding it. He did not have to step into the fray to defend a group of believers who were not popular. But Roosevelt did so because he understood how cohesion was in the country's best interest. His courage in consistently supporting a despised religious group is probably among the reasons Smoot felt he was "the greatest statesman" he associated with during his thirty-three years as a U.S. senator.[54]

NOTES

1. William Bradford, "The Mayflower Compact."
2. Nathaniel Ward, *The Simple Cobler of Aggawam in America* (Boston, MA: James Munroe & Company, 1647).
3. See John Locke's 1668 *Two Treaties of Civil Government*, more specifically the chapter "Of the Beginning of Political Societies."
4. Mark W. Cannon, "The Crusades Against the Masons, Catholics, and Mormons: Separate Waves of a Common Current," *BYU Studies* 3, no. 2 (1961): 23–40.
5. "Letter to Hyrum Smith and Nauvoo, Illinois, High Council, 5 December 1839," 85, The Joseph Smith Papers.
6. Carter Charles, "Review: In the Whirlpool: The Pre-Manifesto Letters of President Wilford Woodruff to the William Atkin Family, 1885–1890," *International Journal of Mormon Studies* 4 (2011): 107.
7. The First Amendment was generally construed as applying only to Congress before *Cantwell v. Connecticut* (310 U.S. 296, 1940). Despite that decision, the Constitution of Maryland contained, until *Torcaso v. Watkins* (1961), a provision that required prospective office holders to declare a "belief in the existence of God." This decision does not eradicate God from public life; it removes obstacles that excluded from the public square people who believed differently.
8. "Discourse, 15 October 1843, as Reported by Willard Richards," 128, The Joseph Smith Papers. Smith must have used the phrase "the whole ground" in the same sense that Van Buren did in "The Whole State of Missouri," meaning that they were not referring to population and constituents but to the legal and administrative entities of "country" (for Smith) and "State" (for Van Buren).

9. Jan Shipps, "The Mormons in Politics: The First Hundred Years" (PhD diss., University of Colorado, 1965), 38.

10. Terryl L. Givens, *The Viper on the Hearth: Mormons, Myths, and the Construction of Heresy* (New York: Oxford University Press, 1997). Givens's title came from a series of two articles published by *Cosmopolitan Magazine* in 1911.

11. John H. Beadle, "The Mormon Theocracy," *Scribner's Monthly*, July 1877.

12. Beadle, "Mormon Theocracy," 392.

13. Kathleen Flake, *The Politics of American Religious Identity: The Seating of Senator Reed Smoot, Mormon Apostle* (Chapel Hill, NC: University of North Carolina Press, 2004), 22.

14. Rev. A. S. Bailey, "The Anti-American Influences in Utah," in *The Situation in Utah: The Discussions of the Christian Convention, Held in Salt Lake City, Utah, April, 1888* (Salt Lake City: Parsons, Kendall & Company), 17–18; emphasis added.

15. Bailey, "Anti-American Influences in Utah," 18.

16. *Reynolds v. United States*—98 U.S. 145 (1879).

17. Harvard S. Heath, "Reed Smoot: The First Modern Mormon" (PhD diss., Brigham Young University, 1990), 30.

18. Proceedings Before the Committee on Privileges and Elections of the U.S. Senate in the Matter of the Protests Against the Right of Hon. Reed Smoot, a Senator from the State of Utah, to Hold His Seat, vol. 3 (Washington, DC: Government Printing Office, 1906), referenced hereafter as "Proceedings."

19. Flake, Politics of American Religious Identity, 40.

20. Correspondence to Ern Eldredge, 28 January 1891. See Harvard S. Heath, ed., *In the World: The Diaries of Reed Smoot* (Salt Lake City: Signature Books, 1997), xxxi.

21. David John Journal, April 21, 1895. Quoted in Heath, "Reed Smoot," 65.

22. Direct suffrage for Senators came with 17th Amendment in 1913.

23. "Oppose Mormon Candidate," *New York Times*, 25 November 1902; emphasis added.

24. Heath, "Reed Smoot," 97, plausibly explains why so many petitions came from Pennsylvania.

25. Heath, "Reed Smoot," 95–96.

26. Carter Charles, "L'intégration Politique des Mormons aux États-Unis, de Reed Smoot à Mitt Romney" (PhD diss., Université Bordeaux Montaigne, 2013), 157–250.

27. Carter Charles, "Mormonism in America: Itinerary to Allegiance from Joseph Smith to Mitt Romney," in *Handbook of Contemporary Christianity:*

Movements, Institutions & Allegiance, ed. Stephen Hunt (Leiden, NL: Brill, 2006), 441–60; Charles, "Mormonism in America," 168–73.

28. Flake, Politics of American Religious Identity, 12–13.

29. Milton R. Merrill, "Theodore Roosevelt and Reed Smoot," *Western Political Quarterly* 4, no. 3 (September 1951): 440–53.

30. "Reed Smoot to Joseph F. Smith, March 5, 1903," quoted by Merrill, "Theodore Roosevelt and Reed Smoot," 441.

31. Merrill, "Theodore Roosevelt and Reed Smoot," 441.

32. Albert Jeremiah Beveridge, *The Reed Smoot Case: Speech of Hon. Albert J. Beveridge of Indiana, in the Senate of the United States, in Support of the Minority Report . . .* (Washington, DC: Government Printing Office, 1907), 15.

33. Frank J. Cannon and Harvey J. O'Higgins, *Under the Prophet in Utah: The National Menace of a Political Priestcraft* (Boston, MA: C. M. Clark, 1911), 399–400.

34. Burton J. Hendrick, "The Mormon Revival of Polygamy," *McClure's Magazine*, February 1911; Burton J. Hendrick, "Mormon Theological Doctrine," *McClure's Magazine*, January 1911.

35. *McClure's*, January 1911, 243.

36. George Teasdale, John W. Taylor, Brigham Young Jr., Matthias F. Cowley, Abraham H. Cannon, Marriner W. Merrill, and Abraham Owen Woodruff.

37. Hendrick, "The Mormon Revival of Polygamy," 451, 453.

38. See Isaac Russell Papers, Special Collections M444, Stanford University. Russell was also a Philippine-American War veteran with the Utah Volunteer Battalion, serving under Richard W. Young, the distinguished West Point graduate and grandson of Brigham Young, who commanded the battalion and returned to the Philippines as president of the criminal branch of the American Supreme Court there. See *Proceedings*, vol. 2:950–51; and Louis Paul Murray, "Life of Brigadier General Richard W. Young" (master's thesis, University of Utah, 1959).

39. Russell republished the picture page, titling it "Dead Apostles Pictured as Alive." Isaac Russell, "Mr. Roosevelt to the Mormons: A Letter with an Explanatory Note by Isaac Russell," *Collier's Weekly*, April 1911, 28.

40. Russell, "Mr. Roosevelt to the Mormons," 28.

41. Russell, "Mr. Roosevelt to the Mormons," 28.

42. Russell, "Mr. Roosevelt to the Mormons," 28.

43. Russell, "Mr. Roosevelt to the Mormons," 28.

44. Robert N. Bellah, "Civil Religion in America," *Daedalus* 96, no. 1 (1967): 1–21.

45. *Du Contrat Social ou Principe du Droit Politique* (On the Social Contract or Principles of Political Rights) (Amsterdam, Netherlands, 1762). All translations are mine.

46. Du Contrat Social, 237.

47. Du Contrat Social, 237.

48. Du Contrat Social, 238.

49. Du Contrat Social, 244.

50. Russell, "Mr. Roosevelt to the Mormons," 28.

51. See Senate Congressional Record, 1907, 3270; emphasis mine.

52. For Rousseau, "The citizens report of the opinions to the Sovereign only insofar as these opinions have to do with the commonwealth" *Du Contrat Social*, 242-243.

53. See "The Family: A Proclamation to the World," *Ensign*, November 2020, 129.

54. Milton R. Merrill, "Theodore Roosevelt and Reed Smoot," *Western Political Quarterly* 4, no. 3 (September 1951): 440.

Senator Elbert Thomas, a former missionary to Japan, working on the translation of a script for a shortwave radio broadcast in Japanese beamed from the Pacific Coast to Japan, 11 January 1942. Before him on the desk is an English-Japanese dictionary and other reference books. AP Wire Photo.

SENATOR ELBERT D. THOMAS: ADVOCATE FOR THE WORLD

R. DEVAN JENSEN AND PETRA JAVADI-EVANS

R. Devan Jensen is the executive editor at the Religious Studies Center at Brigham Young University. Petra Javadi-Evans is an assistant editor at the Joseph Smith Papers Project.

Utah governor Jon M. Huntsman Jr. designated 8 April 2005 as Elbert Thomas Day to honor the late senator's role in Washington, DC, during a crucial time in U.S. history.[1] Thomas, a three-term U.S. senator (1933–51), served through much of the Great Depression and through World War II, but by 2005 he was a surprisingly forgotten figure. In addition to his many contributions for U.S. citizens, particularly during World War II, Senator Thomas was an advocate for Jewish refugees, Japanese nationals, and American GIs.[2] His service to his country and to the world should be remembered and honored. This chapter tells the important but overlooked story of Elbert D. Thomas, a Democratic senator who served as a statesman and an effective advocate for world citizens.

SEEDS OF ADVOCACY

Elbert Thomas's advocacy emerged from his membership in The Church of Jesus Christ of Latter-day Saints. He grew up in Salt Lake City in the late 1800s, a time of intense persecution and prosecution toward those of his faith because of the Church's practice of plural marriage. Elbert wrote, "I saw the confiscation of Mormon property and the Mormon leaders disfranchised by the Federal Government."[3] These experiences spurred him to spend much of his life as a labor advocate and mediator, ensuring that individuals received just and humane treatment from corporations and the federal government.

Elbert was the fifth of twelve children born to Richard and Caroline Thomas, British converts who moved to the United States in 1863.[4] His parents loved the arts, especially the theater. They built a barn and children's playhouse combination that they called the Barnacle. Elbert was involved in many plays held for the public there. His father hosted conventions and political rallies in the Barnacle as well. Elbert wrote, "My father was always a leading businessman. He was a 'Sagebrush' Democrat in that he became a Democrat when the state divided on party lines."[5] In that era, Democrats and Republicans were both fairly evenly represented in Utah, and Elbert adopted his parents' party, believing that the federal government could become a powerful force for good to promote the rights and well-being of its citizens.

In 1906 Elbert was commissioned as a second lieutenant in the Utah National Guard. That year his parents moved to a large, beautiful home at 137 North West Temple Street.[6] (That home still stands just west of today's Conference Center and is on the National Historical Landmark Registry.)

While attending the University of Utah, Elbert helped found the Amici Fidissimi Society, an organization later affiliated with the Phi Delta Theta fraternity. He participated in the Utah Dramatic Club and began dating Edna Harker, daughter of Benjamin E. and Harriet Bennion Harker. Edna was a popular actress who performed at the Salt Lake Theatre.[7] Later, after graduation, she taught physical education.[8]

Elbert and Edna courted and became engaged, and the two were called on a five-year mission to Japan. After marrying on 25 June 1907, Elbert was set apart by Latter-day Saint Apostles Heber J. Grant and George Albert Smith. Elbert first served as mission secretary, and then in 1910 he began serving as mission president.[9] As he and Edna served, each became fluent in the Japanese language, grew to love the people of Japan, and developed a fascination with international affairs, particularly regarding

Senator Thomas, who succeeded the veteran U.S. senator Reed Smoot, with his wife, Edna, and daughter, Esther, 13 March 1933. Harris & Ewing Photographic News Service.

Asian cultures.[10] There Edna gave birth to their first daughter, Chiyo, who was well-loved by the new parents and fellow missionaries. After returning to the States, Edna gave birth to two more daughters.

The Thomases returned to Utah in 1912. On their way home, they traveled through Europe and visited Turkish-occupied Palestine. There Elbert and Edna pondered the plight of the Jews and the loss of their temple, feeling a spiritual connection with them. Elbert wrote this of their experience:

> The evening that Palestine impressed me most was when Mrs. Thomas and I sat on the Mount of Olives and looked across the valley to the place of the temple and the Mosque of Omar. While our baby gathered pebbles, we read the dedicatorial prayer offered by Orson Hyde on October 21, 1841, when the land of Palestine was dedicated by a Mormon elder sent by the Prophet Joseph Smith to dedicate Palestine for the return of the Jews. Here again deep, meaningful, long range spiritual understanding entered my soul. At the time I read

the prayer, just twenty years after the dedication of our own temple, a few Jews were returning to Palestine to be buried near Jerusalem. Tel-Aviv was a doubtful venture, for in all there were only sixty or seventy thousand Jews in the Holy Land. Belief in the restoration of Jerusalem is part of my religion.[11]

Back in Utah, Elbert became an instructor of Greek and Latin at the University of Utah and simultaneously worked as the school's secretary and registrar.[12] He took a leave of absence to attend UCLA, where he earned a PhD in government. Returning to work as a professor at the University of Utah, he taught political science, history, and Asian languages.[13] In 1926 Dr. Thomas, along with other professors, traveled to Europe to study international law and relations at the seat of the World Court in The Hague, Geneva, and Paris. There he delivered a speech titled "World Unity through the Study of History," arguing that conflicting national interests gave rise to wars, revolts, disease, and famine. He argued that whenever trade is free, peace is inevitable. Biographer Linda Zabriskie noted that, while Dr. Thomas continued to teach at the University of Utah, his "thesis was published as a monograph by the Carnegie Institute and he was accepted as an advanced theorist by academics in international law. Four times the Carnegie Endowment for International Peace recognized Dr. Thomas's ability and conferred on him the responsibility of teaching courses related to the Far East and Latin America."[14] His reputation as an international scholar continued to grow when he published his book *Chinese Political Thought* in 1927.

Having witnessed the start of the Great Depression in 1929, Dr. Thomas argued for greater cooperation between state and federal interests.[15] At that time, Apostle Reed Smoot was serving as a powerful, high-profile Republican U.S. senator from Utah, and he was popular among Church members. In 1930 Senator Smoot cosponsored the Smoot-Hawley Tariff Act, increasing duties on almost nine hundred imports. That act triggered retaliatory tariffs from other nations, which unfortunately exacerbated the effects of the Great Depression. Dr. Thomas disagreed with the tariff act and promised his political science students that Senator Smoot could "be defeated."[16] Dr. Thomas made good on his promise by running for office and defeating Senator Smoot in 1932.

EARLY CONTRIBUTIONS

Elected at the same time as President Franklin D. Roosevelt, during the Great Depression when millions were deprived of work, Senator Thomas moved to Washington, DC. There his family worshipped with fellow Saints at the Washington Chapel on Sixteenth Street. In his spiritual autobiography, he mentioned being inspired by its statue of the angel Moroni as a symbol for taking the gospel of Jesus Christ to the world (after the building was sold, the statue was removed).

Senator Thomas became immersed in New Deal advocacy for U.S. citizens. As chair of the Senate Committee on Education and Labor, he worked to establish the Civilian Conservation Corps (CCC), a Depression-era work relief program employing millions of young men in environmental projects and national parks.[17] Utah had 116 CCC camps with about two hundred men each, including three camps in Zion National Park that "built and improved many of the Zion Canyon's trails, created parking areas, fought fires, helped build campgrounds, built park buildings and reduced flooding of the Virgin River."[18] He coauthored the Fair Labor Standards Act in 1938, which established maximum hours of labor per week, overtime pay, and a minimum wage. He moderated negotiations that resolved a nationwide strike led by the mining industry. And he "helped create the Department of Education and Social Services, the National Science Foundation, and other agencies."[19] Though his goals often aligned with Roosevelt's, Thomas sometimes found himself in disagreement with the president.

ADVOCATE FOR JEWISH REFUGEES

After Adolf Hitler was appointed chancellor of Germany on 30 January 1933, he began oppressing religious minorities in Germany, including Jews and Christians from smaller sects. Early in 1934 President Roosevelt asked Senator Thomas, "Elbert, won't you tell me what to do in these cases?"[20] In a major address titled "World Unity as Recorded in History" and given in February 1934, Thomas argued for world peace and recognized that Hitler's hatred of the Jews might threaten that peace: "Hitler and his attack on the Jews is viewed by most as a purely local or national problem. Is it only that? Hitlerism may be classified . . . as a new religion, contesting with the old order. . . . Hitlerism, viewed as a spiritual movement, must of necessity be anti-Jewish."[21] Within a year, Senator Thomas traveled to Germany with funds from the Oberlander Award in German-American relations.[22] There he met Rudolf Hess, Hitler's Deputy Führer,[23] and concluded "that the Nazis intended to rule the world."[24] Returning to Washington, he at first argued for neutrality. In a 1935 National Radio Forum address about the ongoing aggression in Europe, Senator Thomas argued that America "must stay out of war."[25] However, he transitioned from neutrality to intervention when he learned how the State Department had minimized the gravity of the refugees' plight. Following the leadership of assistant secretary of state Breckinridge Long, the State Department staunched the flow of European refugees and expressed concerns about spies entering the United States. Because of these concerns, the State Department chose not to fill immigration quotas and tried to stop intelligence about mass murders in Europe from reaching the public.[26] When news about human rights violations finally trickled out in February 1939, Senator Thomas decided to intervene for European refugees by introducing Senate Joint Resolution 67, which would have aided "victims of aggression, sending a clear message to allies while giving aggressors reasons to reconsider their ambitions for territorial conquest."[27] That resolution failed because of American reluctance to trigger retaliation.

U.S. citizens initially disbelieved accounts of Nazi atrocities toward the Jews, only later coming to understand the seriousness of the situation. "Between June 1941 and May 1945, five to six million Jews perished at the hands of the Nazis and their collaborators," wrote David S. Wyman. "Germany's control over much of Europe meant that even a determined Allied rescue campaign probably could not have saved as many as a third of those who died. But a substantial commitment to rescue almost certainly could have saved several hundred thousand of them, and done so without compromising the war effort."[28] Unfortunately, the U.S. State Department and British Foreign Office chose not to rescue large numbers of European Jews or open Palestine for further Jewish immigration.[29]

Senator Thomas was an avid Zionist and argued throughout his life for the establishment of Palestine as a gathering place for the Jews.[30] On

1 November 1942, on the twenty-fifth anniversary of the Balfour Declaration, Thomas spoke in Carnegie Hall, urging the United States to establish "a Jewish commonwealth in Palestine as one of our war aims and peace aims."[31]

During the war, Senator Thomas became one of the nation's most vocal advocates to save Jewish refugees from Nazi-controlled Europe. He found himself in disagreement with President Roosevelt, who wanted to focus on the war effort rather than intervene on behalf of refugees. Dr. Rafael Medoff, founding director of the David Wyman Institute for Holocaust Studies, wrote that Thomas worked closely with "a lobbying group led by Jewish activist Peter Bergson [Hillel Kook]. Thomas signed on to its full-page newspaper ads criticizing the Allies for abandoning European Jewry. He also cochaired Bergson's 1943 conference on the rescue of Jews, which challenged President Roosevelt's claim that nothing could be done to help except win the war."[32]

Senator Thomas then helped advance the Gillette-Rogers congressional resolution by calling for the creation of a government agency to rescue Jews from the Nazis. Senator Tom Connally, the aging chair of the Senate Foreign Relations Committee, initially blocked the resolution, and Senator Thomas said, "Wait, one day I'll preside and it will pass unanimously."[33] When Connally became ill, Thomas introduced the measure, and it did pass unanimously. Bergson noted that Thomas "was a very much admired man in the Senate. . . . He was a very religious man, he was a real Mormon—a real practicing religious man. . . . And the fact that he stood, and Johnson stood, and Gillette, made a small but very strong core."[34]

That effort snowballed into success. In January 1944, after Treasury secretary Henry Morgenthau Jr. learned that State Department officials had hindered chances to rescue Jewish refugees, Morgenthau and his staff approached President Roosevelt with a report that the State Department had concealed news of the European refugee crisis. Morgenthau told the president, "You have either got to move very fast, or the Congress of the United States will do it for you."[35] With just days to go before the full Senate would act on the resolution, Roosevelt used executive authority to form the agency they had demanded—the War Refugee Board.

Dr. Medoff later summed up the contributions of this board: "Although understaffed and underfunded, the board agents persuaded a young Swede, Raoul Wallenberg, to go to German-occupied Budapest in 1944, playing a major role in saving more than 200,000 Jews during the final fifteen months of the war."[36] Dr. Medoff wrote of Thomas, "At a time when too many people and governments turned their backs on Hitler's Jewish victims, Senator Elbert D. Thomas was a voice of courage and humanitarianism on Capitol Hill. He played a major role in the campaign leading to the creation of the War Refugee Board, a U.S. government agency that helped rescue over 200,000 Jews from the Holocaust. Every resident of Utah can take special pride in the knowledge that their Senator spoke out when others were silent."[37]

ADVOCATE FOR THE WAR EFFORT IN UTAH

U.S. indifference toward the war transformed into anger and retribution when Japan attacked U.S. forces at Hawaii's Pearl Harbor on 7 December 1941. Based on his visit to Germany and firsthand witness of German aggressions, Senator Thomas had already begun war preparations and had continued those efforts. In 1935, with Thomas's support, Congress had passed the Wilcox-Wilson Bill authorizing a permanent air corps station in the Rocky Mountains.[38] Thomas promoted a Works Progress Administration project to rebuild the Ogden Arsenal in Sunset, Utah, expanding it to include several new structures. By the time the United States entered the war in 1941, the arsenal had grown to be a vital storage site for military vehicles and ammunition.[39] With Thomas's support, the military built or enhanced more installations in Utah such as the Hill Field Air Depot in Davis County, Utah General Depot in Ogden, Wendover Army Air Base, Kearns Army Air Base, Dugway Proving Ground, Tooele Army Depot, Deseret Chemical Depot near Tooele, Bushnell General Military Hospital in Brigham City, and Clearfield Naval Supply Depot.[40] Geneva Steel Mill in Utah County was also part of the war effort, and Thomas persuaded administrators to complete the project.[41] These military installations boosted the war effort and Utah's booming wartime economy.

ADVOCATE FOR JAPANESE NATIONALS

Japan's attack on Pearl Harbor had launched a wave of anger and fear toward people of Japanese heritage. Because of Thomas's fluency in Japanese and his extensive knowledge of Japanese politics and culture, the Office of War Information invited him to broadcast monthly radio addresses across the United States and to Japan.[42] On the seventh of each month, from December 1941 until the end of the war, Thomas broadcast messages to Japan urging citizens to overthrow their imperialist leaders. Of those messages, he said,

> I had but one theme, and that was that Japan was ruining herself, because she had turned apostate to the best ideals that Japanese civilization had developed. I knew how the Japanese constitution worked. I knew that the generals in the field were absolute. They could not be controlled by the home government. I knew, therefore, that we had to have a constitutional surrender under the auspices of the Emperor. . . . The opposition to my ideas by those who wanted to destroy and bring anarchy in Japan, hurt me in much the same way all prejudicial opposition has hurt me. But in this activity, as in my religious activity, I was sustained by a sense of knowing that I was right.[43]

Senator Thomas appealed to Japanese nationals with clear, logical, and passionate arguments, urging them to overthrow their tyrannical military. His monthly messages prompted Japanese wartime leaders to identify Senator Thomas as a public enemy, but today's Japanese scholars honor his role in promoting peace and understanding.[44]

In his messages to U.S. citizens, Senator Thomas sought to promote understanding of Japanese culture and politics,[45] but fear and mistrust of the Japanese continued to grow until February 1942, when President Roosevelt issued Executive Order 9066, which forced 110,000 people of Japanese ancestry to relocate to ten internment camps based on their race, not on an accusation of a crime.[46] In this area, Roosevelt overruled Thomas's objections. Historian Nancy J. Taniguchi described this troubling time in Utah:

Voluntary exclusion from the West Coast remained open until March 30, 1942, allowing Oakland resident Fred Isamu Wada, whose wife Masako was from Ogden, to negotiate a lease of almost 4,000 acres near Keetley, Wasatch County. Soon ninety relocated American Japanese grew food there for the war effort. Another group of forty families leased 1,500 acres to raise sugar beets near Green River despite anti-Japanese protests by Emery County residents.

Some businesses welcomed American Japanese employees; others were fired and some had radios, cameras, and hunting rifles confiscated by municipal authorities. Senator Thomas, a mentor to Mike Masaoka [national secretary of the Japanese Americans Citizens League], tried to mitigate the effects of wartime hysteria.[47]

The U.S. created a relocation center near Delta, Utah, called the Topaz War Relocation Center, also known as the Central Utah Relocation Center (Topaz). Living conditions there were difficult, with both extreme hot and cold temperatures in the uninsulated barracks. Contrary to the overall U.S. position, Senator Thomas argued for more humane treatment and understanding of Japanese people at home and overseas, but the tide of popular opinion had turned, and Thomas was largely powerless in this area.[48]

ADVOCATE FOR THE END OF THE WAR

As a member of the Senate Foreign Relations Committee, Thomas was aware of the development of the atomic bomb. He wrote about this project in his autobiography: "I could never rid myself of the idea that ultimate victory can only come through a change in men's hearts and ideas. More with that zeal than the idea to destroy I supported the experimentation which resulted in the atom bomb."[49] President Roosevelt died while U.S. troops were advancing on Japan, and President Harry S. Truman authorized the use of atomic bombs on Hiroshima and Nagasaki. Senator Thomas was horrified with the devastation. Historian Haruo Iguchi summarized Thomas's efforts during this crucial period:

> Thomas made 44 monthly broadcasts to Japan during wartime, in addition to his weekly commentaries shortly before Japan's surrender.

Informal photo of Elbert D. Thomas at Washington, DC, 7 June 1940.
Harris Ewing Photographic News Service.

His senatorial colleagues, impressed by his activities, urged him to insert some of his messages in the *Congressional Record*. . . . In his August 7 [1945] broadcast Thomas urged the Japanese to overcome the resistance of the Japanese militarists to accept the Potsdam Declaration or face another destruction such as that which befell Hiroshima;

Thomas cited some potential cities that could suffer from future nuclear destruction if Japan did not immediately surrender. Thomas
urged Japanese listeners to stay away from the cities cited as well as
others that produced military goods and served as military installations, including Nagasaki. Thomas argued the U.S. had three "huge
plants" capable of producing many atomic bombs that unleashed the
same destructive energy as that emitted by the sun. Thomas emphasized that both the U.S. and the U.K. had no intention of enslaving
the Japanese population and only the militarists stood in the way of
Japan's accepting the terms expressed in the Potsdam Declaration.[50]

Only days after the bomb was dropped on Nagasaki on 9 August, Em-
peror Hirohito announced Japan's surrender on 15 August.

ADVOCATE FOR AMERICAN GIs

As a ranking member of the Senate's Military Affairs Committee, Senator
Thomas amended the Selective Service Act so that the jobs GIs had had
before entering the armed forces would be kept open in anticipation of the
GIs' eventual return. He promoted the role of women in the U.S. Army by
making the Women's Army Corps an integral part of the army rather than
an auxiliary. Toward the end of the war, he coauthored the Servicemen's Re-
adjustment Act, which commonly became known as the GI Bill. He wrote
the education portion that helped thousands of soldiers attend colleges and
universities after the war.[51] The bill offered veterans government-financed
education, government-guaranteed loans, job-finding assistance, hospital
benefits, and a year of unemployment compensation.[52] Many benefits secured by this bill continue to this day, assisting veterans to transition to civilian life—a lasting tribute to his advocacy for veterans.

SENATOR TO HIGH COMMISSIONER

Ironically, Senator Thomas's advocacy for world citizens led to his defeat.
In 1944 Senator Thomas published a book titled *The Four Fears* that ar-
gued for global peace and against fear-based nationalism. In 1945 Senator
Thomas became "a leader in bringing into being the United Nations."[53]

He advocated policies that favored global interests over purely national interests. These views made him unpopular with some during the "Red Scare" era of the 1950s. "In the early months of 1950," wrote Richard Swanson, "Senator Joseph McCarthy of Wisconsin embarked on what may be recorded as a most energetic attempt to rid the United States of persons linked, even remotely, with Communist sympathies or associations." He added, "Capitalizing on the prevalent mood of disgust with foreign policy failures, the junior senator offered the oversimplified explanation that Communists had infiltrated high-level State and Defense Department positions."[54] Swanson wrote that "the use of slanderous insinuations to give the impression that a politician was pro-Communist was widespread and effective in Utah," and "the first victim of this deluge of McCarthyism was the state's senior senator, Democrat Elbert Thomas."[55]

During the 1950 senatorial campaign, attack ads "accused [Thomas] of presiding at Communist meetings and of sponsoring leftist organizations. He was cartooned as a puppet of the Communists and the radical unionists," and "the Republican candidate, Wallace Bennett, did nothing to deter the attacks," wrote historian Richard D. Poll.[56] Fellow Utah senator Arthur Watkins also joined the attacks; ironically, he later chaired the Senate committee censuring McCarthy.[57] Even though Senator Thomas was not a Communist, his critics "publicized enough implicative insinuations and accusations" that Thomas was defeated in the election cycle of 1950.[58]

The following year, Elbert Thomas was appointed high commissioner of the Trust Territory of the Pacific Islands, the highest civilian authority that presides over a vast stretch of the Pacific Ocean. While serving in that position, he supervised humanitarian aid and rebuilding efforts in Micronesia.[59] On 11 February 1953, he passed away in Honolulu, Hawaii, serving his country until the very end. His family received hundreds of letters of condolence from global leaders, including the U.S. president and members of Congress. They appropriately remembered and honored Elbert D. Thomas, an effective Washington statesman and advocate for world citizens.

NOTES

1. David S. Wyman Institute for Holocaust Studies, "Utah Senator Honored for Holocaust Rescue Efforts" (press release), 5 April 2005, Wyman Institute (website).

2. Where did the term GI come from? In the early twentieth century, GI—meaning galvanized iron—was stamped on military trash cans and buckets often made from that material. During World War I, the term began to refer to all things Army related. GI was then reinterpreted as "government issue" or "general issue." World War II soldiers began referring to themselves as GIs. Patricia T. O'Conner and Stewart Kellerman, *Origins of the Specious: Myths and Misconceptions of the English Language* (New York: Random House, 2009), 72.

3. "Elbert D. Thomas," in *Thirteen Americans: Their Spiritual Autobiographies*, ed. Louis Finkelstein (New York: Harper and Brothers, 1953), 144.

4. Joyce S. Goldberg, "FDR, Elbert D. Thomas, and American Neutrality," *Mid-America* 68 (January 1986): 35.

5. Elbert D. Thomas to Frank Jonas, 13 September 1943, Elbert D. Thomas Papers, 1933–1950, MSS 129, box 1, 1, Utah State Historical Society. The *Salt Lake Tribune* coined the derisive term "Sagebrush Democracy" to refer to Utah's efforts in the late 1880s to join with the national Democratic movement.

6. Linda Muriel Zabriskie, "Resting in the Highest Good: The Conscience of a Utah Liberal" (PhD diss., University of Utah, 2014), 18.

7. "Miss Edna Harker of the Washington," *Salt Lake Tribune*, 18 January 1903; "Dramatic Club University of Utah," *Salt Lake Tribune*, 14 February 1904; "The University Dramatic Club Is Booked for 'Niobe,'" *Truth* (Salt Lake City), 24 March 1906, 6.

8. "Mrs. Thomas' Funeral Set for Tomorrow," *Washington Post*, 1 May 1942.

9. Zabriskie, "Resting in the Highest Good," 19.

10. Goldberg, "FDR, Elbert Thomas, and American Neutrality," 36.

11. "Elbert D. Thomas," 138.

12. Goldberg, "FDR, Elbert Thomas, and American Neutrality," 36.

13. Sharon Kay Smith, "Elbert D. Thomas and America's Response to the Holocaust" (PhD diss., Brigham Young University, 1992), 72.

14. Zabriskie, "Resting in the Highest Good," 55–56.

15. Thomas to Jonas, 23 September 1943, 1.

16. Elbert D. Thomas, as quoted in Ralph Hann, *Tomorrow and Thomas* (pamphlet, n.d., reprinted from *Reader's Scope* magazine), 1.

17. John A. Salmond, "The Fight for Permanence," chap. 9 of *The Civilian Conservation Corps, 1933–1942: A New Deal Case Study* (Durham, NC: Duke University Press, 1967).

18. "Civilian Conservation Corps in Utah," Mountain West Digital Library; "Civilian Conservation Corps," National Park Service (website).

19. "Helping Common People: Elbert Thomas (1883–1953)," Utah State History (website).

20. "Elbert D. Thomas," in *Thirteen Americans*, 151.

21. Elbert D. Thomas, "World Unity as Recorded in History," *International Conciliation*, no. 297 (February 1934): 40, 50.

22. Zabriskie, "Resting in the Highest Good," 56.

23. Hann, *Tomorrow and Thomas*, 3.

24. Smith, "Elbert D. Thomas," 76.

25. "Neutrality Plea Made by Thomas," *Evening Star* (Washington, DC), 13 September 1935, A-6.

26. "Breckinridge Long," *Holocaust Encyclopedia*, https://encyclopedia.ushmm.org/content/en/article/breckinridge-long.

27. Goldberg, "FDR, Elbert D. Thomas, and American Neutrality," 35.

28. David S. Wyman, *The Abandonment of the Jews: America and the Holocaust, 1941–1945* (New York: Pantheon Books, 1984), ix.

29. Wyman, *Abandonment of the Jews*, x.

30. Rafael Medoff, "Senator Elbert D. Thomas: A Courageous Voice against the Holocaust" (Washington, DC: David S. Wyman Institute for Holocaust Studies, 2004), Wyman Institute (website). For more about the War Refugee Board, see Rebecca Erbelding, *Rescue Board: The Untold Story of America's Efforts to Save the Jews of Europe* (New York: Anchor Books, 2018).

31. Elbert D. Thomas, "The Hillsides and Valleys of Palestine Bloom Again," *Congressional Record: Proceedings and Debates of the 77th Congress, Second Session* (1942), 1.

32. Rafael Medoff, "A Mormon in the Holy Land," *Los Angeles Times*, 29 July 2012.

33. Rafael Medoff, *Blowing the Whistle on Genocide: Joseph E. DuBois, Jr., and the Struggle for a U.S. Response to the Holocaust* (West Lafayette, IN: Purdue University Press, 2009), 62.

34. David S. Wyman, "The Bergson Group, America, and the Holocaust: A Previously Unpublished Interview with Hillel Kook/Peter Bergson," *American Jewish History* 89, no. 1 (March 2001): 28.

35. Medoff, *Blowing the Whistle on Genocide*, 63.

36. Medoff, "Mormon in the Holy Land."

37. David S. Wyman Institute for Holocaust Studies, "Utah Senator Honored for Holocaust Rescue Efforts."

38. Thomas G. Alexander and Bob Folkman, "Utah's Legacy of U.S. Military In-stallations," *Pioneer* 65, no. 3 (2018): 50.

39. Alexander and Folkman, "Utah's Legacy of U.S. Military Installations," 47–48.

40. Alexander and Folkman, "Utah's Legacy of U.S. Military Installations," 50–55; "Legislative Record of Senator Elbert D. Thomas of Utah with Spe-cial Relation to America's Position in the World Today," Legislative Record, 1907–1912, 1932–1950, Elbert D. Thomas Papers, 1933–1950, MSS B 129, box 1, folder 1, Utah State Historical Society.

41. "Industry and Utah," Legislative Record, 1907–1912, 1932–1950, Elbert D. Thomas Papers, 1933–1950, MSS B 129, box 1, folder 1, Utah State Historical Society.

42. Elbert D. Thomas to Frank H. Jonas, 13 September 1943, Elbert D. Thomas Papers, Utah State Historical Society.

43. "Elbert D. Thomas," in *Thirteen Americans*, 135–36.

44. See, for example, Haruo Iguchi, "Elbert D. Thomas: Forgotten Internation-alist Missionary, Scholar, New Deal Senator, Japanophile, and Visionary," *Nanzan Review of American Studies* 29 (2007): 115–23; Haruo Iguchi, "Sen-ator Elbert D. Thomas and Japan," *Journal of American & Canadian Stud-ies* 25 (March 2007): 75–104, http://dept.sophia.ac.jp/is/amecana/J2/PDF/25-04SenetaorElbertD.ThomasandJapan.final.pdf.

45. "Ex-Senator Elbert D. Thomas, Pacific Commissioner, Dies," *Evening Star* (Washington, DC), 12 February 1953, A-26, Elbert D. Thomas Papers, 1933–1950, MSS B 129, box 225, obits, 1953, Utah State Historical Society.

46. Helen Z. Papanikolas and Alice Kasai, "Japanese Life in Utah," in *The Peo-ples of Utah*, ed. Helen Z. Papanikolas (Salt Lake City: Utah State Historical Society, 1976), 352–53.

47. Nancy J. Taniguchi, *Discover Nikkei*, 27 February 2008.

48. Papanikolas and Kasai, "Japanese Life in Utah," 358.

49. Elbert D. Thomas, "Spiritual Autobiography of Elbert D. Thomas" (draft pre-pared for Rabbi Louis Finkelstein, Institute for Religious and Social Studies), spiritual autobiography and correspondence, 1949–1950, Elbert D. Thomas Papers, 1933–1950, MSS B 129, box 1, folder 2, Utah State Historical Society.

50. Iguchi, "Senator Elbert D. Thomas and Japan," 82–83.

51. Smith, "Elbert D. Thomas," 176.

52. "Thomas and the Veterans," in *Elbert D. Thomas: Your United States Senator* (pamphlet, 1944).

53. "Memorial Addresses on the Floor of the United States Senate," 13 February 1953, in H. L. Marshall, comp., *A Memorial to Elbert Duncan Thomas: United States Senator from Utah, High Commissioner, Trust Territory of the Pacific Islands* (Salt Lake City: n.p., 1956), 71, Church History Library.

54. Richard Swanson, "McCarthyism in Utah" (master's thesis, Brigham Young University, 1977), 1.

55. Swanson, "McCarthyism in Utah," 99.

56. Richard D. Poll, David E. Miller, Eugene E. Campbell, and Thomas G. Alexander, eds., *Utah's History* (Provo, UT: Brigham Young University Press, 1978), 518.

57. Swanson, "McCarthyism in Utah," 111.

58. Swanson, "McCarthyism in Utah," 101.

59. R. Devan Jensen, "Micronesia's Coming of Age: The Mormon Role in Returning Micronesia to Self-Rule," *Pacific Asia Inquiry* 7, no. 1 (Fall 2016): 46.

Ezra Taft Benson, February 1953, newly appointed secretary of agriculture. Utah State Historical Society.

EZRA TAFT BENSON'S INFLUENCE ON WASHINGTON

MARK D. OGLETREE

Mark D. Ogletree is an associate professor of Church history and doctrine at Brigham Young University.

> *The family is the rock foundation, the cornerstone, of civilization.*
> *The Church will never be stronger than its families,*
> *and this nation will never rise above its home and families.*
> —Elder Ezra Taft Benson[1]

Ezra Taft Benson and his wife, Flora, were devoted to raising a righteous posterity. They spent many hours with their children by teaching them the gospel, working side by side with them, and recreating with them. Both Ezra and Flora Benson were raised in strong families. Consequently, family life was the core of their existence, and that practice continued through their lives. When President Benson spoke in Seattle, Washington, in 1976 at a National Family Night program, he stated, "Some of the sweetest, most soul-satisfying impressions and experiences of our lives are those associated with home, family, children, brothers, and sisters."[2] President Benson went on to explain that he and his wife had hoped to have twelve children—they had six instead. Flora quipped, "If we could have just had twins each time we would have made it."[3]

THE PREPARATORY YEARS:
BOISE AND WASHINGTON, DC (1930-43)

In the fall of 1930, Ezra was appointed to the Idaho State University Extension Service, headquartered in Boise. By 1931, he became the executive secretary of the Idaho Cooperative Council for farmers. During the 1930s, Ezra began a climb to prominence, becoming notable in the agriculture industry not just locally but also nationally. Many leaders in national organizations viewed him as a man with great leadership potential.

While living in Idaho and serving in the stake presidency, Ezra took a short leave of absence to work on a doctorate at the University of California, Berkeley.[4] He and his family lived in California for nine months while Ezra worked feverishly on his graduate work. Although he never finished his degree, studying at Berkeley raised his visibility within the agricultural

Secretary Ezra Taft Benson, September 1960, taking time to catch up on the news. Utah State Historical Society.

field.[5] In 1938 Ezra spoke at the annual National Council of Farmer Co-operatives conference in Washington, DC.[6] When the National Council looked for a new executive secretary, Ezra's name rose to the top. The National Council of Farmer Cooperatives was a large federation, comprising 4,600 farmers market organizations.[7] Although Ezra had little interest in the job, the National Council remained interested in him. Still needing persuading, Ezra counseled with President David O. McKay, who helped him understand that the Church needed people in key positions in the nation's capital.[8] Ezra accepted the position in March of 1939 and soon moved his family to Washington, DC.

The Bensons immersed themselves in the Church and the community. The family frequently hosted dances, parlor games, ping-pong, and other activities in their home.[9] Holidays became a special time to gather—especially for those who did not have family nearby. Reminiscing on those early days in Washington, President Benson explained, "Almost every year we held a Christmas fireside in our home. Sometimes over a hundred young people crowded inside and sat on the floor, steps, anywhere they could find a place. My wife and our daughters prepared wonderful refreshments for everyone, and I was honored to talk about the Savior and His mission. It was some of these simple occasions that brought greatest satisfaction."[10]

MR. BENSON GOES TO WASHINGTON—AGAIN (1953-61)

The Bensons left Washington in 1943 when Ezra was called to serve in the Quorum of the Twelve Apostles, and from 1943 to 1952 he was fully engaged in apostolic duties. After World War II, he spent a substantial amount of time in Europe, where he served as mission president and helped distribute welfare supplies to many in need. For the Bensons, life changed significantly after 4 November 1952 when Dwight D. Eisenhower won the presidency and appointed Ezra Taft Benson as secretary of agriculture. Ezra had no desire to serve in the president's cabinet.[11] However, with President McKay's support and encouragement,[12] Ezra finally accepted the appointment, and the Benson family returned to Washington, DC. Elder Benson became the first member of a clergy to serve in the cabinet in over a century.[13]

Secretary Ezra Taft Benson, his wife, Flora, and their youngest daughter, Flora Beth, traveling together in the spring of 1955. Library of Congress.

Many agricultural leaders cheered his appointment. Victor Emanuel, an industrial leader, said, "I have known Ezra Taft Benson for many years, and I cannot think of a wiser selection for the post of Secretary of Agriculture. Ezra Benson combines the practical outlook of farmers and agriculture with spiritual qualities of the highest degree. . . . I predict that Ezra Taft Benson . . . will be one of the great secretaries of all time."[14] Edward R. Eastman, editor of the *American Agriculturist*, declared Ezra's appointment was "the best news farmers of America have had in years."[15] J. A. McConnell, executive vice president of the Grange Lee Federation (one of America's largest farming cooperatives), predicted that "Benson's high character will make him one of the great, if not the greatest, agricultural secretaries since the establishment of an agricultural department in the executive branch of our government. He will be completely fair, will listen to the proponents of ideas from every section of the country and from every segment of agriculture, and will make his decisions based on an honest and intelligent appraisal of the facts."[16]

Ezra did not waste time making his presence known as he urged President Eisenhower to begin cabinet meetings with prayer. President Eisenhower accepted the invitation, and the practice was instituted—with Ezra offering the first prayer.[17] A *Time* magazine story titled "Apostle at Work" mentioned that department meetings commenced with prayer,[18] and coworkers were never surprised when they walked in on the secretary to find him praying. One colleague quipped, "'He spends as much time on his knees as he does on his feet.' For the tireless Benson machine, prayer is the basic fuel."[19]

WALKING INTO A MINEFIELD

Although many Church members—including President David O. McKay—were excited for his appointment, Ezra understood he was walking into a minefield. On 1 December 1952, a month prior to Eisenhower's inauguration, he told students at Brigham Young University, "I didn't want to be Secretary of Agriculture. I can't imagine anyone in his right mind wanting it."[20] He further explained, "Because I know something of what it entails, I know something of the crossfires, the pressures, the problems, the difficulties."[21]

A 1954 Herblock Cartoon, © The Herb Block Foundation.

"Ezra, I Don't Know What We'd Do Without You"

A 1957 Herblock Cartoon, © The Herb Block Foundation.

Ezra's concerns about becoming secretary were well founded. One month into the new administration, *Barron's National Business and Financial Weekly* reported, "Because of the current decline in farm prices—down 11% from a year ago—Mr. Benson finds himself sitting on the hottest of seats as boss of one of Washington's largest Cabinet empires."[22] He quickly became a favorite target of the press, politicians, and farmers. There was no honeymoon period. Many pundits predicted he would be the first cabinet member to resign.[23] Historian Francis M. Gibbons observed that the press, hostile opponents, and even the farming community were quick to attack. "This controversy," Gibbons wrote, "at the threshold of his administration robbed Secretary Benson of the usual period of grace accorded to new officeholders in Washington. His opponents lost no time in attacking him in Congress and in the media. He was put on the defensive immediately. His opponents scrutinized his statements intently, looking for hooks on which to hang their criticisms."[24] The *Farm Journal* reported, "Ezra Benson is going to shock Washington. He's in the habit of deciding everything on principle."[25] Many felt he was too outspoken and passionate about his beliefs. He believed that "to sit in silence when the truth should be told makes cowards of men."[26]

Ezra did not waste any time clearing, purging, and reorganizing the Department of Agriculture. He felt the department was a bureaucracy draining taxpayer money. He reorganized the department's twenty agencies into four divisions. "Some agencies were combined; some transferred to other departments; and some eliminated."[27] Heated criticism was directed toward Secretary Benson as he shuffled the department in seemingly partisan ways by ousting Democrats M. L. Wilson, Louis Bean, and Claude Wickard. Some claimed the "purge constituted an example of pure ideological zealotry."[28]

One of his first department memorandums outlined his expectations. "The people of this country," he wrote, "have a right to expect that every one of us will give a full day's work for a day's pay."[29] Many employees took offense, feeling the remark implied that "all bureaucrats were inherently lazy, especially those hired by Democrats."[30] The press had a heyday with the memorandum.

Ezra's first speech as secretary—addressing the Central Livestock Association in St. Paul, Minnesota, in February 1953—landed like a lead balloon as he pleaded with cattle ranchers to shut government beef bounties, condemned price supports, and urged a "return to the fundamental virtues which have made this nation great."[31] He was widely criticized for the speech. During the next eight years, the scrutiny and criticism only intensified. His critics were relentless. However, by the time the Eisenhower administration completed their tenure in 1961, Ezra would be one of only two cabinet members who served the entire eight years. Secretary Benson would be in the spotlight during the entire administration, being viewed "as one of the most active and controversial figures of the administration and the national

Republican party. Fierce critiques and frequent calls for his resignation were matched by an equal outpouring of accolades and genuine respect."[32]

While serving in the cabinet, Secretary Benson developed into a strong and opinionated leader. Historian Patrick Q. Mason argued that Ezra Taft Benson "took clear and often controversially conservative positions on the many of the 'historic conflicts of our time,' including anticommunism, the proper role of government, civil rights, church and state, the women's movement, international and domestic conflicts, and the culture wars. Due to his prominence both internally and externally, Benson thus [became] a prism through which the American public and the media perceived Latter-day Saints and their religion."[33]

Perhaps at the heart of all controversy was Secretary Benson's strong views against socialism and communism. He believed our nation was at war with international communism.[34] He viewed communism as a significant threat to American freedoms. Communism "is a total philosophy of life, atheistic and utterly opposed to all we hold dear," he said.[35] On other occasions he remarked, "I'd rather be dead than lose my liberty"[36] and observed that communism offered "the death knell of freedom and all we hold dear."[37] He felt that American agriculture was drifting toward socialism—evidenced by government bailouts, subsidies, and federal meddling.

Ezra supported government-funded agricultural research and marketing but held that government assistance should come only in times of emergency.[38] It was Ezra's position that stored food and commodities were a drain on taxpayers and "a threat to the farmer's opportunity to obtain a fair portion of the prosperity being enjoyed all around him."[39] Shortly after taking office, he crafted a 1,200-word "General Statement" on farming, which declared, "It is impossible to help people permanently by doing for them what they could and should do for themselves. It is a philosophy that believes in the supreme worth of the individual as a free man, as a child of God, that believes in the dignity of labor and the conviction that you cannot build character by taking away man's initiative and independence."[40]

Ezra believed strongly that the government should never do for individuals what they could do for themselves. He worried too many American farmers were becoming dependent on the federal government. He likened the situation to "a political fairy that will wave a wand and all vexations and anxieties will disappear."[41] He stated, "It is doubtful if any man can be politically free who depends upon the state for sustenance. A completely planned and subsidized economy weakens initiative, discourages industry, destroys character, and demoralizes the people."[42]

President Eisenhower was in favor of agricultural price support—at least initially, which Ezra believed to be misguided.[43] Ezra agreed, though, to abide by the president's pledge to farmers to continue price supports for a short time.[44] Nevertheless, Secretary Benson became the most criticized member of Eisenhower's cabinet. *Time* magazine reported, "Of all the storms that rage about the heads of Washington officials, none matches in intensity and duration the high, fine gale that whistles about Secretary of Agriculture Ezra Taft Benson."[45]

Eisenhower was "constantly urged by others to drop the Secretary from his Cabinet."[46] Walter Judd and Arthur Miller, members of congress from Minnesota and Nebraska respectively, met with Secretary Benson and urged him to resign. They predicted that if he did not step down, their party would lose 20–25 seats in the next election. Secretary Benson replied that he would not quit but would "continue to pursue a course which

I believe is best for our farmers."[47] South Dakota senator Karl Mundt cautioned, "I am writing to tell you candidly . . . we cannot come close to electing a Republican House of Representatives or a Republican Senate in 1958 unless Secretary of Agriculture Benson is replaced by somebody who is personally acceptable to the farmers of this country."[48]

Eisenhower was reelected in November 1956; however, during the mid-term elections in 1958, Republicans lost forty-seven seats in the House

Secretary Ezra Taft Benson, March 1955, on his way to another meeting. Utah State Historical Society.

of Representatives and thirteen seats in the Senate. The Midwestern farm belt experienced the greatest losses. Catholic University political scientist Norman Ornstein called Ezra Taft Benson the "Achilles heel" of the Eisenhower administration, placing the Republican losses squarely on his shoulders.[49] Yet Secretary Benson remained unflappable. "Resign? I am resigned to one thing—to do my duty as I see it, to continue my flight for a prosperous, expanding, and free agriculture."[50] He told Senator Kenneth B. Keating, "I'm not in the habit of running away from a fight—a tough job . . . I didn't ask for this job and I'm very busy trying to do it the best way I can."[51]

Importantly, Eisenhower remained loyal to his agriculture secretary. "The only way 'you can get Ezra discharged from the Cabinet . . . is to ask for my resignation as President. If you want that, then you can get Ezra. It's just that simple.'"[52] Ezra initially pledged he would serve two years because he longed to return to Utah. Informing the president that he considered resigning, Eisenhower retorted, "If you quit, I quit."[53]

Despite the criticism and ridicule Secretary Benson received, he conducted himself as a disciple of Jesus Christ. A *U.S. News & World Report* article observed, "As secretary of agriculture, Mr. Benson has encountered little but frustration and criticism. . . . [He] has taken the criticisms and frustrations placidly. No one has seen him angered. His manner is warm and friendly, his smile habitual. He speaks quickly, but earnestly."[54] Historian Francis M. Gibbons believed poise and self-control were two of Ezra's most salient characteristics. He wrote, "In more than twenty years of personal association with him, in conversations with others who knew him well, and in reviewing voluminous documents about his life while writing his biography, I found or learned of no instance when he allowed his temper or anger to dominate his conduct. I know of many instances when he was heavily provoked, but in no case did he ever lose his temper. He was always in control of himself. His feelings were kept in check.[55]

THE BENSON FAMILY'S INFLUENCE

With all of the opposition Ezra faced, his family became his refuge, and his home was his sanctuary. Many individuals in Washington, DC, admired the Benson family. They were inclusive, always inviting others to become

Newly appointed secretary of agriculture Ezra Taft Benson with his wife, Flora, and their four daughters, spending time together as a family, February 1953. Utah State Historical Society.

part of what made them happy—the gospel of Jesus Christ. No matter how strongly the pressure intensified, the Bensons did not compromise their standards. "As the embodiment of family, home, and the American way, the Bensons were the focus of perhaps the most positive attention the Church had ever received throughout the country."[56]

Consequently, many people grew to respect their morals and religious principles. For instance, at the annual convention of the World Food and Agriculture Organization in Rome, Italy, "The customary cocktail hour was replaced with a soft drink and fruit juice reception in honor of Elder Benson's Word of Wisdom standards."[57] Patrick Q. Mason summarized the Benson's influence this way: "The entire Benson family came to represent Mormon normality by way of exemplifying the ideals of postwar American domestic life. *Time* [magazine] gave its readers a peek into the Benson household, which showed the family praying, reading scriptures, doing chores, dancing around the jukebox, and together deciding curfews and how much television the kids could watch. . . . Together the family plans the week's meals and shopping. . . . In the late 1950s, *Leave it to Beaver* could have been set in the Benson home—with troublemaking Eddie Haskell nowhere to be found."[58]

FLORA'S INFLUENCE

During the Eisenhower administration, Ezra and Flora enjoyed their relationship with members of the cabinet and their spouses. The wives of cabinet members often gathered for luncheons and other social activities. Sometimes they would gather at the White House; sometimes in their homes. Ezra wrote, "Another family joy was to have guests in our home. At such times we always tried to arrange to have the children at the table also, to participate in the delightful conversation of the evening."[59]

In May 1954 the Bensons hosted a luncheon. Attendees included Mamie Eisenhower, Pat Nixon, Rachel Adams, the cabinet wives, and Oveta Hobby (the first secretary of Health, Education, and Welfare). Flora and her children catered the entire event themselves, spending weeks "carefully planning a menu, cleaning their home, preparing entertainment, and brushing up on etiquette and protocol. As was common practice in the Benson household, no outside help was hired for the affair."[60] When Ezra saw how much work Flora was putting into the party, he expressed his concern. Flora countered, "This isn't just a luncheon to me. It's something more than that. I want to show that it's possible to uphold the standards of the Church and have a wonderful time, too."[61]

The day of the luncheon, Flora greeted her guests by saying, "'You'll find things a bit different in our home. We don't serve cocktails, or play cards, there is no smoking and no tea or coffee—but we'll try to make it up to you in our own way, and we hope you enjoy our home."[62] Instead of cocktails, the Bensons served ginger ale and home-bottled apricot juice—which was a big hit.[63] They served a delicious meal and provided a wonderful family program of music, poetry, and ballet. The BYU Madrigal singers also performed, and their daughter Barbara was one of the soloists. Their son Reed delivered Wordsworth's poem "Happy Warrior," dedicating it to President Eisenhower. Mamie Eisenhower was so impressed that she invited all twenty-eight Madrigal singers for a White House tour. Flora said, "The most exciting part was the beautiful letters we received afterward from women telling us what a thrill it was to experience a touch of 'Mormonism' and family cooperation and what wonderful youth the BYU singers were."[64]

Throughout the Eisenhower administration, the Bensons continued to have a positive effect on the cabinet and their families. After Ezra shared passages from the Book of Mormon with the president, he received a personal note thanking him "for drawing on your wide knowledge of the Book of Mormon to send me certain prophecies and revelations. The quotations I have read with great interest."[65] On another occasion, the Bensons invited the Eisenhower's for family home evening in their home.[66] The President and First Lady remained friends with Ezra and Flora after Eisenhower's presidency.

THE EDWARD R. MURROW EXPERIENCE

Edward R. Murrow hosted the popular television program *Person to Person* from 1953 to 1961—interviewing professional athletes, politicians, and celebrities, including Senator John F. Kennedy, Elizabeth Taylor, Roy

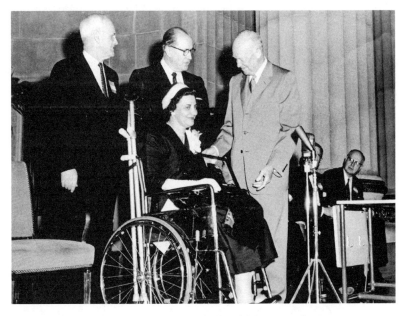

Senator Arthur Watkins, left, secretary of agriculture Ezra Taft Benson, center, and President Dwight D. Eisenhower, right, greet an unidentified woman at a speaking engagement, September 1958. Utah State Historical Society.

Campanella, Dean Martin, Jerry Lewis, Frank Sinatra, Harry Truman, and John Steinbeck. In 1954 Murrow asked to interview the Benson family. When Ezra mentioned the invitation to Flora, she strongly opposed the idea. She felt their children had been exposed too often to the public eye. Ezra initially agreed and dropped it. Their son Reed, though, was a returned missionary and college student who believed appearing on the show was an opportunity the family should not pass up. He suggested they could model a family home evening and emphasize the importance of family unity, prayers, and recreation. For a time, Flora remained opposed, stating, "If you insist on the show, have it down at your office. Leave the children out of it." Nevertheless, Reed persisted. He felt that his family could model a good American home life on prime-time television. Eventually, Flora not only agreed to the program but also put her energy into making the experience something special. Arrangements were made to record and air the program on Friday, 24 September 1954. Recalling the experience later, Ezra remembered, "Not only the family but, to a great extent, the Church would be on trial before the people."[67] On the day of the broadcast, the family prayed and fasted that everything would run smoothly and that they would represent the Church appropriately. Ezra reported,

> The show itself went off very satisfactorily. We ran through it once in a general way beforehand for timing; otherwise, there was no rehearsal. The children seemed very relaxed and Flora did an excellent job in talking about home and family. The girls' quartet sang, Barbara did a solo with Beverly at the piano and little Beth tap-danced. To make her tapping audible, we took my desk chair mat from my study. Reed and Mark explained our missionary work and Church program. We felt good when it was over, grateful to have had the opportunity.[68]

After the show, Murrow called Ezra from his offices in New York, letting him know that it was the best show he had ever done. Later, the United Press reported that Murrow's *Person to Person* program featuring the Bensons brought in more fan mail than any other show. Hundreds of letters also flowed into the Department of Agriculture and to the Benson home from across the country—from parents, clergy members, corporate personnel, and even children. The letters were positive and encouraging, leading President Eisenhower to say, "Ezra, besides all the rest of it, it was the best political show you could have put on."[69]

Perhaps President Eisenhower felt the conservative Christian values and the strong family ties the Bensons demonstrated were something our country needed to see and hear. Biographer Sheri L. Dew concluded, "The Murrow show brought the Bensons in front and center as spokesman for conservative religious thought."[70] Years later, President Thomas S. Monson remembered, "The entire Church found justifiable pride in the Edward R. Murrow telecast which featured the Ezra Taft Benson family at home. . . . America was starved to see a righteous family learning and living as a family should."[71] The Benson family had represented the Church and their family with dignity. Many people were positively influenced by their strong family values, unity, and love.

The Bensons continued their work of influencing many others throughout their time in Washington, DC. No matter where Elder Benson traveled, he was an ambassador of the gospel of Jesus Christ. Gibbons noted that Elder Benson's influence stretched far and wide:

> While in Washington, President Benson made hundreds of contacts, including contacts with foreign heads of state, which would ultimately be of great help to the Church in years to come. President Benson was aware of his influence, and he used it carefully for the blessing of the work. He knew that politics and influence could open doors for the Church. . . . He was a celebrity, both in and out of the Church, and he knew very well how to make good use of his celebrity. He seemed determined to use his experiences and status as a former Cabinet member for the good of the Church. For example, he was always ready to use that card to open doors to people of significance who might help the cause of the Church.[72]

As secretary of agriculture, Ezra Taft Benson made the cover of *Time* magazine twice, and his photograph appeared on the front covers of some of the most prolific news publications in the country, such as *U.S. News & World Report*, *Newsweek*, and the *New York Times Magazine*.[73] Even though Ezra Taft Benson was hounded and ridiculed, he did not react to the jeers. By the end of the Eisenhower administration, Ezra had become one of the most respected men in the cabinet. As the *Washington Star* reported, "Benson is regarded as the strongest member of the White House's inner circle. Undoubtedly, he is the most respected."[74] Columnist Rosco Drummond wrote, "Mr. Benson has emerged as the most influential member of the Eisenhower Cabinet, as the most secure figure in the Eisenhower administration."[75] Noted radio broadcaster Paul Harvey concluded, "Ezra Benson is a rare man in politics, thoroughly sincere, uncompromising, and above all, a good man."[76] Reed wrote that his father's "fine example and principled stand in a very controversial political role resulted in widespread favorable media coverage. That coverage blessed the Church as well as the nation and had worldwide ramifications for good. His influence touched the lives of many he met, including the heads of state, and prepared a way for missionary work on a broad scale."[77]

Ezra and his family had a profound influence on not only the individuals and families in their social circles, wards, branches, and neighborhoods but also on the elite of Washington, DC. Very few families, in or out of the Church, have been scrutinized like the Bensons. Even fewer families have had such a positive and lasting influence on those who knew them. Never has a Latter-day Saint been more influential on an American president than Ezra Taft Benson was on Dwight D. Eisenhower. Both men shared faith in God, love for family, and loyalty to the United States of America. As a presidential aide summarized, "The Boss [President Eisenhower] and Ezra have the same ability to stand up to an answer dictated by conscience and faith; no other men in the Cabinet are their equals in that respect."[78]

NOTES

1. Ezra Taft Benson, *God, Family, Country: Our Three Great Loyalties* (Salt Lake City: Deseret Book, 1974), 186.
2. Ezra Taft Benson, *Teachings of Ezra Taft Benson* (Salt Lake City: Deseret Book, 1988), 489.
3. Benson, *Teachings of Ezra Taft Benson*, 489.
4. Francis M. Gibbons, *Ezra Taft Benson: Statesman, Patriot, Prophet of God* (Salt Lake City: Deseret Book, 1996), 102–4.
5. Ezra only lacked a few months to complete his doctorate, but the University of Idaho—his employer—denied him adequate leave of absence to complete his degree.

6. Sheri L. Dew, *Ezra Taft Benson: A Biography* (Salt Lake City: Deseret Book, 1987), 123.

7. Oral History, Ezra Taft Benson, Part 1, 13, Church History Library, Salt Lake City.

8. Lydia Clawson Hoopes, "Ezra Taft Benson of the Council of the Twelve," *Improvement Era*, October 1943, 635.

9. Jay Richter, "Benson: Prayer, Persuasion, and Parity," *New York Times*, 14 June 1953, 58.

10. Ezra Taft Benson, *Ezra Taft Benson Remembers the Joy of Christmas* (Salt Lake City: Deseret Book, 1988), 8.

11. Oral History, Ezra Taft Benson, Part 1, 13, Church History Library, Salt Lake City.

12. Jerry P. Cahill, President Ezra Taft Benson: A Biographical Sketch, UA 5395, Series 2, Subseries 5, carton 19, folder 1, L. Tom Perry Special Collections, Harold B. Lee Library, Brigham Young University, Provo, UT.

13. Reverend Edward Everett, pastor of the Brattle Street Unitarian Church in Boston, was secretary of state under President Millard Fillmore from 1852 to 1853. Elder Benson surmised, "So far as I know, Dr. Everett and I are the only clergymen ever to serve in presidential Cabinets." Quoted in Ezra Taft Benson, *Cross Fire: The Eight Years with Eisenhower* (Garden City, NY: Doubleday & Company, 1962), 346.

14. David W. Evans, "Ezra Taft Benson—Agricultural Statesman," *Improvement Era*, January 1953, 28.

15. Evans, *Improvement Era*, "Agricultural Statesman," 28.

16. As cited in Evans, "Agricultural Statesman," 28.

17. Reed A. Benson, "Ezra Taft Benson: The Eisenhower Years," in *Out of Obscurity: The LDS Church in the Twentieth Century* (Salt Lake City: Deseret Book, 2000), 54.

18. Wesley McCune, *Ezra Taft Benson: Man with a Mission* (Washington, DC: Public Affairs Press, 1958), 13.

19. "Apostle at Work," *Time*, 13 April 1953, 27.

20. Dew, *Ezra Taft Benson*, 258.

21. Ezra Taft Benson, "The L.D.S. Church and Politics," as cited in Reed A. Benson, *. . . So Shall Ye Reap* (Salt Lake City: Deseret Book, 1960), 234.

22. "Bravo, Cousin Ezra! He Promises a Sane New Day for Agriculture," *Barron's National Business and Financial Weekly*, 16 February 1953, 1.

23. "Mr. Benson Called the Turn on the 'Farm Vote,'" *Saturday Evening Post*, 8 January 1955, 10.

24. Gibbons, *Ezra Taft Benson*, 186.

25. Dew, *Ezra Taft Benson*, 259.

26. Reed A. Benson, "Eisenhower Years," 55.

27. Gary James Bergera, "'Rising Above Principle': Ezra Taft Benson as U.S. Secretary of Agriculture, 1953–1961, Part 1," *Dialogue: A Journal of Mormon Thought* 41, no. 3 (2008): 88.

28. Edward L. Schapsmeier and Frederick H. Schapsmeier, "Eisenhower and Ezra Taft Benson: Farm Policy in the 1950s," *Agricultural History* 44, no. 4 (October 1970): 371.

29. Benson, *Cross Fire*, 53.

30. Schapsmeier and Schapsmeier, "Farm Policy," 371.

31. "Apostle at Work," *Time*, 13 April 1953, 25–28; see also Dew, *Ezra Taft Benson*, 272.

32. Patrick Q. Mason, "The Historic Conflicts of Our Time: Ezra Taft Benson and Twentieth-Century Media Representations of Latter-day Saints," in *Contingent Citizens: Shifting Perceptions of Latter-day Saints in American Political Culture* (Ithaca, NY: Cornell University Press, 2020), 208–9.

33. Mason, "Historic Conflicts of Our Time," 209.

34. Benson, *God, Family, Country*, 300.

35. Ezra Taft Benson, "Concerning Principles and Standards" (BYU commencement address, 4 June 1947), *Church News*, 14 June 1947, 5.

36. As cited in Bergera, "'Rising Above Principle,'" 86.

37. Elder Ezra Taft Benson, "A Witness and a Warning," *Ensign*, November 1979, 32.

38. "Ezra Taft Benson—He Beat the Farm Bloc," *U.S. News & World Report*, 27 April 1956, 74.

39. Ezra Taft Benson, "Farmers Can Prosper and Be Free," *Nation's Business*, January 1956, 1, 39, 44.

40. Bergera, "'Rising Above Principle,'" 94, as cited in Benson, "America: A Choice Land" (an address to the National Conference of Christians and Jews, May 11, 1953), 14, copy in Ernest L. Wilkinson Papers, Perry Special Collections.

41. Ezra Taft Benson, "Farmers Can Prosper and Be Free," *Nation's Business*, January 1956, 39.

42. Schapsmeier and Schapsmeier, "Farm Policy," 370.

43. Oral History, 21.

44. Bergera, "'Rising Above Principle,'" 93.

45. "Benson Baiters," *Time*, 4 November 1957, 18.

46. Schapsmeier and Schapsmeier, 377.

47. "Ezra & the Farm Vote," *Time*, 3 March 1958, 13.

48. Schapsmeier and Schapsmeier, "Farm Policy," 377.

49. Norman J. Ornstein, "Echoes of Benson's and Ike's Farm Debacle," *Christian Science Monitor*, March 11, 1985, 14.

50. "Benson Declares He Won't Resign," *New York Times*, 15 December 1959, 1, 44.

51. "Benson to Remain in Post Remainder of Ike Term," *Salt Lake Tribune*, 9 February 1959, 3.

52. Benson, *Cross Fire*, 328.

53. In 1957 Ezra was ready to quit again. The pressure was strong for him to resign. He told President Eisenhower that maybe it would be better if he stepped down. Eisenhower stated, "If I have to, I'll go to Salt Lake City and appeal to President McKay to have you stay on with me." Benson, *Cross Fire*, 221, 359.

54. "Ezra Taft Benson—He Beat the Farm Bloc," 77.

55. Francis M. Gibbons, *Remembering Seven Prophets: Ezra Taft Benson* (Holladay, UT: Sixteen Stones Press, 2015), 63.

56. Dew, *Ezra Taft Benson*, 292.

57. "President Ezra Taft Benson: A Faithful Servant," *New Era*, January 1986, 7.

58. Mason, "Historic Conflicts of Our Time," 214.

59. Benson, *God, Family, Country*, 175.

60. Derin Head Rodriguez, "Flora Amussen Benson: Handmaiden of the Lord, Helpmeet of a Prophet, Mother in Zion," *Ensign*, March 1987, 18.

61. Benson, *Cross Fire*, 199.

62. Benson, *Cross Fire*, 199.

63. Rodriguez, "Flora Amussen Benson," 18.

64. Rodriguez, "Flora Amussen Benson," 19. For one such example, see Benson, *Cross Fire*, 200–201.

65. Ezra Taft Benson, "Benson Family Papers, 1954–1957," Church History Library.

66. "Eisenhowers for Family Home Evening," *Church News*, 12 February 1955, 6.

67. Benson, *God, Family, Country*, 176.

68. Benson, *Cross Fire*, 215.

69. Benson, *Cross Fire*, 215.

70. Dew, *Ezra Taft Benson*, 299.

71. R. Scott Lloyd, "Happy Birthday: Televised Tribute Celebrates Rich Life of Service," *Church News*, 5 August 1989, 3.

72. Gibbons, *Remembering Seven Prophets*, 42–44.

73. Reed A. Benson, "Eisenhower Years," 56–57.

74. McCune, *Ezra Taft Benson*, 81–82.

75. Benson, *Cross Fire*, 405.

76. Dew, *Ezra Taft Benson*, 295–96, 528.

77. Reed A. Benson, "Eisenhower Years," 54.

78. Benson, *Cross Fire*, 317.

The J.W. and Alice Marriott family, ca. 1950. All photos in this chapter courtesy of Deseret Book. © Marriott International.

HOT SHOPPES, HOTELS, AND INFLUENCE: THE MARRIOTTS IN WASHINGTON

DALE VAN ATTA

Dale Van Atta is a New York Times *best-selling author and journalist who coauthored the world's most widely syndicated news column with Jack Anderson.*

John Willard Marriott, the son of a sheepherder, stepped off a train in Washington's Union Station on his twenty-first birthday, 17 September 1921.[1] Fresh from his Latter-day Saint mission to New England, J.W.[2] was dressed in a new tailor-made suit—a splurge of $47.50 for the near-penniless missionary. His parents wanted him home to work their farm north of Ogden, Utah, but first J.W. wanted to see his nation's capital. He never expected to return to the East Coast, so this would likely be his only opportunity.[3]

J.W. hopped on a tour bus that took him past the White House, Arlington Cemetery, and the monuments and the homes of some of Washington's notables, including Utah's controversial Senator Reed Smoot.[4] The senator had received a cold welcome in Washington in 1903 because of the polygamist heritage of his home state. Although his own monogamist marriage had been well established, Smoot was still the butt of local humor. The tour bus guide brought laughter when he pointed out that the senator's house had only one entrance because "he can only have one wife here."[5]

J.W. had no inkling at the time that he would someday make his home in Washington, DC, that he would found a restaurant and hotel empire there, or that his future mother-in-law would one day marry the widowed Senator Smoot—nor that he and his two sons would be able to use their prominent position in the nation's capital to *significantly* advance the cause of the Lord's restored church, The Church of Jesus Christ of Latter-day Saints.

While in Washington as a recently released missionary, J.W. spent an afternoon with Utah congressman Don Colton, whose son Hugh was one of J.W.'s best friends and a previous mission companion. Despite the buzz of the capital and the distinguished company, the one sight that remained in J.W.'s mind as he boarded the train for Utah was the hardworking street vendor selling ice cream, lemonade, and sodas to the sweltering tourists. If a man wanted to go into the food and beverage business, he thought, this would be the place to do it.[6]

Six years later, in the spring of 1927, J.W. left his family's farm behind and settled in Washington with his new wife, Alice (Allie) Sheets, his new business partner Hugh Colton, and a franchise agreement to build the first A&W Root Beer stand on the East Coast. J.W. and Colton's first tiny storefront operation opened downtown on Fourteenth Street, the same day that Charles Lindbergh took off for his solo flight across the Atlantic. J.W. rushed out that morning to buy a portable radio so customers would be lured into the shop to listen to news of Lindy's progress. Many years later when J.W. and Allie shared a dinner table at the White House with Lindbergh, J.W. joked, "You know, we went into business on the same day, but you got all the publicity!"[7]

Colton soon sold his share in the franchise and returned to Utah, leaving J.W. and Allie to turn the pop stand into a food operation. Allie collected recipes from her own Western upbringing and visited the Mexican Embassy to borrow ideas for Tex-Mex dishes. The popularity of the menu spread, and people began asking when they would open another "hot shop." The title stuck, and the couple rebranded from a root beer stand to sit-down restaurants they called Hot Shoppes, which were soon popping up all over Washington. The Hot Shoppe on Georgia Avenue was the first drive-in restaurant east of the Rocky Mountains.[8]

J.W. and Allie Marriott in DC.

The Hot Shoppe, 1927. J.W. is standing in the door.

As the first waves of the Great Depression were felt across the country, the Marriotts forged ahead with their Hot Shoppes chain. They opened their fifth restaurant on Connecticut Avenue on 2 July 1930, the same day Allie's widowed mother, Alice Sheets, married widower, Apostle, and senator Reed Smoot. The couple had met at church when Alice visited Washington, and their courtship was chronicled in the Washington newspapers. They planned to honeymoon in Hawaii, but President Herbert Hoover prevailed upon Senator Smoot to stay in town for an important vote. As consolation, Hoover invited the newlyweds to honeymoon for two weeks at the White House.[9]

Two years later, Smoot lost his reelection bid for a sixth term. He asked the Marriotts to move into his French provincial mansion on Garfield Street as caretakers (later buyers) so the Smoots could go back to Utah. J.W. and Allie moved in, along with their first child, John Willard Marriott Jr., born in 1932. He was called Billy and later Bill.

The Marriotts found their community of friends in the small Latter-day Saint branch, filled mostly with government workers drawn from Utah by Senator Smoot. One of their Sunday School teachers was the brilliant lawyer J. Reuben Clark Jr., undersecretary of state in the Coolidge administration and later an apostle. Another was the Church's most legendary FBI agent, Sam Cowley. It was Cowley who headed up the team that finally brought down America's "Public Enemy #1," John Dillinger, in July 1934. Four months later in a rural Illinois farm field, Cowley faced down George "Baby Face" Nelson in a submachine-gun battle, which ended in both their deaths.[10]

Washington D.C. Branch meetings at the time were held in an upstairs room of the Washington Auditorium at New York Avenue and E Street. In 1924, with help from Senator Smoot, the Church purchased land in the Embassy District on Sixteenth Street and Columbia Road, and construction began on a chapel. The Marriotts donated twenty-five hundred dollars to the building fund—a considerable sum at the time—and the chapel was dedicated by President Heber J. Grant in 1933 with more than a thousand people attending three separate dedication services.[11]

The dedication was a high point for the Marriotts in a year that brought troubling news. J.W. was diagnosed with Hodgkin's lymphoma—a conclusion confirmed by five doctors—and was told he had a year to live. Resigned to the news, the Marriotts took a long vacation along the East Coast. While visiting his former mission sites, it occurred to J.W. that the illness might be a test of his faith—a test that he was failing by giving up. Back in Washington, he called Edgar Brossard, a member of the U.S. Tariff Commission, and federal judge Gustave Iverson, both Church elders. They came to his house and gave him a priesthood blessing: "As elders of the church, we promise you in the name of the Lord that you will be healed. We rebuke this disease. We believe, and we ask you to believe with us, in your mission of service to your fellow man and to your church, and we promise that you will live to perform this mission." In a few weeks, J.W.'s symptoms were gone, thus ensuring the subsequent birth of his second son Richard (Dick) in 1939 and the future conversion from a restaurant to a hotel empire by his first son, Bill.[12]

Dick, J.W., and Bill in the office, ca. 1965.

In the 1930s and 1940s, the Washington community of Latter-day Saints was relatively small, so it was a natural thing that the Marriotts became very close with, among others, Ezra Taft Benson, before and after he was an Apostle and secretary of agriculture for President Dwight D. Eisenhower[13]; Mervyn Bennion, the captain of the USS *West Virginia* who went down with his ship in Pearl Harbor on 7 December 1941, becoming one of that war's first Medal of Honor winners[14]; Russell M. Nelson, who came to DC as a young lieutenant and doctor at Walter Reed Army Medical Center (1951–53);[15] and George Romney, president of American Motors, future presidential candidate, and governor of Michigan, who considered J.W. his closest friend[16]—so close, in fact, that he named his second son Willard Mitt, who would be known by his middle name.

Even though the Marriotts' wealth, connections, and reputation grew on the East Coast, when Bill went to the University of Utah as a freshman in the early 1950s, the Marriott name was still relatively unknown in the West. Donna Garff returned from a dinner date with Bill to meet his parents for the first time, and her sorority sisters filled her in. "Don't you know that they have a lot of money with all these Hot Shoppes back East?" they buzzed. "I didn't know anything about it, nor did I care," Donna recalled. "I just thought they [J.W. and Allie] were wonderful, down-to-earth people."[17]

After graduation, Bill joined the U.S. Navy—a brief career that J.W. tried to manage with his Washington connections. J.W. wanted Bill stationed in the capital, close to home. But Bill refused all special treatment and instead did a tour on the USS *Randolph* aircraft carrier. By telephone he proposed to Donna and invited her to spend December of 1954 with him and his family at the Marriott getaway—Fairfield Farm in Hume, Virginia. Elder Benson had invited another guest, President Eisenhower, to come to the farm at the same time for bird hunting.

Donna was *now* starstruck by her future in-laws, and Bill, the navy ensign, was stunned to be in the company of his commander-in-chief. When the temperatures outside dropped below freezing, the hosts asked Eisenhower if he still wanted to go hunting. The president turned to Ensign Marriott and said, "What do you think we should do?" Bill remembered the moment as an early lesson in leadership. "I was just the lowest form of life in the navy, and he was asking me what I wanted to do." Bill recovered his composure and said, "I think we should stay inside by the fire." The president replied with his big signature grin. "I think your suggestion is great. Let's do that." The guests settled down for dinner, followed by a "typical Latter-day Saint family home evening" led by Elder Benson, his wife Flora, and their children.[18]

Bill married Donna in the Salt Lake Temple in 1954, finished his obligation to the navy, and returned home to Washington, DC, to join the family restaurant business, which he quickly expanded by adding hotels. J.W. took some time to get on board with the idea, but when he did, he wanted to build grand lodgings—a hybrid between elegant downtown hotels of the day and mom-and-pop motor hotels that were the common suburban and highway fare. The first was the Twin Bridges Marriott on the Virginia side of the Fourteenth Street Bridge leading into Washington. Bill quickly proved proficient at running hotels. The Twin Bridges Marriott was a pioneer of many upscale motor-hotel features including room service, a reservation system, meeting rooms, ballrooms, restaurants, and a swimming pool that doubled as an ice skating rink in the winter. Special guests one Christmas Eve included Elder Benson, who took a fall on the ice and dislocated his shoulder.[19]

Uncertain about the long-term viability of the Hot Shoppes chain, Bill grew the hotel division, moving on to the Key Bridge Marriott in the DC suburb of Rosslyn, Virginia. The third Marriott—and the first outside of Washington, DC—was in Dallas. The first outside the United States was in Acapulco, Mexico. Eventually the company expanded into airline catering, industrial cafeterias, theme parks, cruise lines, fast food restaurant chains, fine-dining restaurants, full-service vacation resorts, and senior living facilities. The number of hotels grew from the hundreds to thousands as Marriott acquired other chains and applied its brand to existing hotels around the world.

Bill eschewed political entanglements, but his parents were drawn to them. Allie served as the first female treasurer of the Republican National Convention in 1964 and held the job again in 1968 and 1972. She rose to become vice chair of the Republican National Committee during the Nixon administration.[20] In 1966 J.W. joined the campaign advisory

Dick and Bill Marriott at Camelback for Bill's birthday party, 1997.

J.W. and Bill Marriott.

staff for George Romney's run for president until the stress of that highly charged campaign triggered a near-fatal heart attack for J.W. in 1967.[21]

Richard Nixon won that 1968 election and asked J.W. to chair the inaugural events. Allie and J.W. sat behind the Nixons at the inauguration and then led the inaugural parade to the White House in a convertible, with the Mormon Tabernacle Choir not far behind—an important appearance J.W. had arranged. Four years later, J.W. reluctantly chaired Nixon's second inaugural events in 1973. J.W. arranged for a thirty-member contingent from the Tabernacle Choir to perform at the White House church service before the inauguration. The choir brought the distinguished members of the audience to their feet with a rendition of the "Battle Hymn of the Republic."[22]

The balance of business and church was a demanding side of life for the Marriott family. But J.W. never forgot (and often passed along) the words his mother, Ellen, often said to her children: "I'd rather have a stone tied around your necks and have you cast into the ocean than to have you forget your religion and not live it every day of your lives." When J.W. had to make business decisions that involved his religious tenets, he was not shy about picking up the phone and calling an apostle or even a prophet for advice. In 1961 a prime opportunity arose to build a Marriott hotel in Philadelphia. The company's first three hotels had been in Virginia and Texas—both dry states that prohibited alcohol sales in hotels. But Pennsylvania was a wet state. Bill hired a consulting firm to give the bottom line on potential profits from the Philadelphia hotel; liquor sales in the restaurants would be key to the success of the venture, the consultants advised.[23] "Having a real struggle to expand and hold market without liquor. Must put in hotels. Will get a lot of criticism. I hate it," J.W. wrote in his journal.[24] He continued to agonize over the decision until he finally visited with President David O. McKay, who turned out to be surprisingly pragmatic.

"I will ask you as one brother to another," the eighty-seven-year-old prophet began, "suppose a sheepman, like you were, goes into a grocery store owned by a Mormon to buy supplies, and he wants cigarettes for his [non-LDS] men. If the storekeeper says, 'Sorry, we don't carry tobacco in any form because it's against our religion,' why, the customer won't come back the next time. If he wants coffee for his men and the storekeeper says, 'We disapprove of it, and we don't want your men to drink it either,' he won't come back again. He'll go to the store down the street not only for his tobacco and coffee, but for everything else he needs. In the long run, this could put the storekeeper out of business, don't you agree?" J.W.

agreed, and President McKay continued. "As I see it, Brother Marriott, if you don't satisfy your customers' wants and needs, you could be running the same risk. If liquor today is an essential part of the service that the hotel and restaurant industry offers to its patrons, it seems to me that you're obliged to sell it to them. To sell it to them doesn't mean that we approve of drinking, any more than to sell a gun means approval of using that gun to commit a crime. The patron who believes as we do is not compelled to buy liquor, nor, indeed, is anyone. But it is the patron's life, his money, his right to decide for himself, not ours."[25]

President McKay ended with a caution to J.W. against serving liquor in most of his other enterprises—particularly the family-oriented Hot Shoppes or any company eateries where children were regular customers. J.W. went back to Washington, DC, with a decision to allow liquor sales in his upscale hotel restaurants and lounges.

Gambling in Marriott hotels was a different matter. Bill and J.W. briefly considered a contract to manage a Las Vegas hotel-casino in 1972, but both were troubled by the moral and ethical repercussions, which at the time occasionally involved perks such as prostitutes and drugs for high rollers. Bill and J.W. passed on the deal.[26] In 1976, Bill toyed with the idea of buying part of the Del Webb Company. He wanted only the lodging portion of the company, excluding their four Nevada hotel-casinos. When rumors circulated that Marriott wanted all the Del Webb assets, Bill got a call from Church President Spencer W. Kimball. "I can't tell you how to run your business," the prophet carefully said, "but I would like to strongly suggest that you not get into gambling, that you not go into Las Vegas." He recounted his own sad experience with friends from his hometown in Arizona who had lost their meager fortunes to the lure of what some called "Sin City." Bill didn't need much convincing, and when he took the issue to the Marriott board, the board members agreed that gambling could tarnish the image of the company.[27]

The Marriotts' prominence and busy, globetrotting schedules did not exempt them from serving in the trenches of the Church. When Benson became the first Washington D.C. Stake president in 1940, he called J.W. to serve on the high council. Eight years later, in 1948, J.W. himself was called as stake president. Near the end of his nine-year service, on 30 October

1957, during a breakfast with Elder Harold B. Lee, J.W. was shocked to learn that the First Presidency wanted to consider him as a potential General Authority. According to J.W.'s journal, Lee said "there was no one outside the council as close to the brethren as I am. I should get my affairs in order as Chairman of (Marriott Corporation) Board so I could get away & take a church job (in Salt Lake City). This was quite a shock especially to Allie who feels we are now destined to a life-time job in the church." J.W. respectfully sent word back to President McKay that he felt he was of better use and influence for the Church in Washington, and the prophet agreed.[28]

Three years before his release, J.W. officially launched (with a letter) an intense lobbying campaign to persuade the First Presidency to authorize construction of a temple in the nation's capital, the first one east of the Mississippi River since the Nauvoo Temple burned down nearly a century before. Marriott and two others—prominent Latter-day Saint lawyer Robert Barker and successor stake president Milan Smith—were ultimately the local triumvirate most responsible for the acquisition of the site in 1962 and the subsequent 1968 decision to build the temple. But they would never have succeeded without the untiring advocacy of President Hugh B. Brown, first counselor in David O. McKay's First Presidency.[29]

When Bill was called to the Washington D.C. Stake's high council in 1974, his first assignment was to decide what to do with the aging Latter-day Saint chapel on Sixteenth Street—once a showplace with a statue of the angel Moroni on top of it. By the 1970s, however, it was a structural liability whose iconic status was now moot given the near-completion of the monumental temple in Kensington, Maryland. The following summer, in 1975, to everyone's surprise, Bill was called to be bishop of the Chevy Chase Ward. J.W. responded by doing something almost unheard of in the Church—he phoned President Kimball and asked him to cancel the calling because Bill was too busy running Marriott Corporation. The prophet responded, "This calling was approved by our First Presidency and we're not going to reverse it."

Bill's acceptance of the call may have been his greatest act of faith. He was CEO of a $732-million company in the middle of a recession, and now he had another full-time "job" overseeing a large congregation. Bill

J.W. Marriott's seventy-eighth birthday. Left to right: Bill, Donna, J.W., Allie, Nancy, and Dick Marriott.

coped by managing his ward as he did his business, but with a liberal dose of compassionate care. He scoured the ward to personally seek out the less-active members. He presided over worship services, weddings, funerals, social events, and—perhaps the most challenging—ward campouts. He dreaded camping, and he would outfit his station wagon with a mattress to avoid having to sleep in a tent. When a Hispanic congregation in the stake was disbanded, he absorbed the members into his largely Anglo and affluent Chevy Chase Ward, creating a translation booth and distributing headphones to Spanish speakers so they could participate in worship services. He was often one of the last to leave the church building after an activity and could be found doing dishes and mopping floors in the church kitchen.

Donna summed up her husband's life during that period: "First there were church meetings, and then he'd stay after church to counsel with people in his church office. After that, he'd make hospital visits or go to the members' homes to talk with them. Then he'd go to work Monday morning just wrung out. People couldn't understand why he was so tired on Monday. They'd all been out playing golf."

Bill was bishop for just two years before he was called as first counselor in the Washington D.C. Stake presidency, serving for five years. Then, in 1982, he was called to be the eighth president of the Washington D.C. Stake, a position he held for eight years during a period of the most unprecedented expansion of his hotel empire. Twice a year he flew to Salt Lake City to attend general conference. One year he formed a new friendship with a stake president from Germany, Dieter Uchtdorf, who would later become an apostle. Bill had met Uchtdorf first on business when Uchtdorf was chief pilot and senior vice president of Lufthansa Airlines, with responsibilities over airline catering, which was one Marriott sideline. Even before the two became friends, Uchtdorf strategically dropped Bill's name into curious or potentially hostile conversations in European business meetings about the Church. Once Uchtdorf mentioned Bill was a Mormon, conversations with associates about the Church turned positive. "He represented what the church stood for in a perfect, humble way, so there was never a risk of embarrassment using Bill as the example of Mormon values," Uchtdorf said.[30]

As stake president, Bill presided over the funeral of his father, who died in 1985. J.W.'s funeral was the closest thing to a state funeral ever hosted at a Latter-day Saint chapel, with speakers including not only apostles such as Ezra Taft Benson, Gordon B. Hinckley, and Boyd K. Packer but also former President Richard Nixon and the world's foremost Christian evangelist, the Reverend Billy Graham. The *Washington Post* devoted an editorial to the local hero's passing, casting it as the end of an era: "Pardon us for taking a slightly parochial view of J. Willard Marriott when we point out that with him died another bit of small-town Washington. A community's merchants give it much of its character. And the quality of its individual businesses reflects the quality of those who are responsible for them. [The city's] warm recollection of the Hot Shoppes institution is

Dick, Allie, and Bill at the annual meeting following J.W.'s death, 1986.

a tribute to Marriott. For many years, his little chain of restaurants helped give this capital something of the flavor of a courteous, pleasant, overgrown village before he became a towering business figure and the city also went on to bigger things."[31]

After the funeral, the Marriott family went to their Lake Winnipesaukee vacation homes in New Hampshire along with Elder Packer, who was to dedicate the small Latter-day Saint chapel in nearby Wolfeboro that Sunday. On Saturday morning, Bill was alone refueling his boat to give Elder Packer a ride on the lake, when a gas leak exploded into flames and engulfed him. Bill plunged into the lake, and his family dragged him to the beach. At the hospital, Elder Packer gave Bill a priesthood blessing, promising there would be no long-term repercussions from the severe burns that covered most of his body. He spent sixteen days in a hospital burn unit and endured months of skin-graft surgeries and rehabilitation, returning to work five months later. All the while, he retained his calling as stake president.

At the same time, he and his only sibling—younger brother Dick—had been depended upon by church leadership for not-so-well-known service. For example, serving under Elder Marvin J. Ashton, Bill became a key member of the board of the Polynesian Cultural Center in Laie, Hawaii, for eleven years (1977–88). Elder Dallin H. Oaks subsequently asked Dick to join the PCC board. Dick served eighteen years (1995–2013) in the voluntary position, the last four as chair.

Three decades after Bill was bishop, Dick was called—at age sixty-six—to the same position by then stake president Nolan Archibald, long-time CEO of Black & Decker. "I admire Nolan for doing it," recounted Elder Jeffrey R. Holland. "It probably would have been easy not to do it, to be fearful that 'you're just calling a Marriott again.' But what a tragedy it would have been for the Saints not to have had a bishop like Dick, and what a marvelous blessing it was for him. For six years, he was devoted to a fare-thee-well—an exemplary bishop."[32] President Russell M. Nelson agreed: "Can you imagine being called as the bishop at age sixty-six? I had nothing to do with that, of course. That was President Archibald. Bishop Marriott was faithful to every responsibility he had as bishop, even though it meant he had to give up a lot of his traveling. He never sloughed his responsibilities as a bishop."[33]

In part because the capital is home to more than 140 foreign embassies and international organizations, both Bill and Dick and their wives, Donna and Nancy, respectively, have been influential ambassadors for the Church for decades. President Nelson attributed a number of international goodwill successes for the Church to Bill, particularly in Eastern Europe before and after the Berlin Wall fell in 1989. "The Marriott name carried so much weight with these people," Elder Nelson said in a 2013 interview.[34] "They were doing cartwheels to get Marriott hotels in their countries, so when Bill hosted an activity, lending his good name and his great faith to the Lord's work, they came and they listened." President Nelson has specifically singled out Bill's assistance in making entrée for the Church in the Soviet Union (and now Russia), Bulgaria, Czechoslovakia, Hungary, the former Yugoslavia, and Poland, where the pioneering Warsaw Marriott (completed in 1989) was the safe meeting place for the Warsaw Saints.[35]

"It is always a joy to be able to accomplish something of unusual worth for the Church—and *you* have opened important doors, making it possible for us to walk through in the best possible light," seconded Beverly Campbell in a letter to Bill.[36] Campbell was the first director (1985–97) of the Church's key international affairs office in Washington, followed by directors Ann Santini (1997–2016) and Mauri Earl (2016–present). All three have gratefully engaged the Marriotts to host their primary international outreach events—the Christmas holiday Festival of Lights; the Western Family Picnic at the Marriott Ranch in Hume, Virginia; and the annual luncheon for the spouses of diplomats, which Donna Marriott hosted at least fifteen times (between 1994 and 2014) in her home, occasionally featuring a private tour of Bill's extensive antique auto collection.[37]

Because ambassadors could bring their families to experience an unforgettable piece of Americana at the annual fall picnic in the beautiful Virginia hills at the Marriott Ranch, the Western Family Picnic has been particularly popular among diplomats since 1991, when Dick and Nancy Marriott first began hosting the event. Barbecue, Native American dancers (from Brigham Young University), a short talk by a visiting General Authority, and various areas set up for western crafts and displays are often featured. "It was a lot of fun with a lot of things they could do there," recalled Santini. It's a "beautiful place" their families can enjoy, and "to meet Dick and Nancy Marriott is a big deal."[38]

The Festival of Lights began in December 1978, and dozens of diplomats are invited each year for the opening night when the dazzling display of four hundred thousand lights in the trees illuminates the Washington D.C. Temple grounds.[39] Bill has cohosted the popular Christmas event since it began, helping to select an ambassador to be honored each year. "Believe me, it has made a difference that Bill Marriott is at the top of the invitation and opens the program for us," said Santini.[40]

When Bill travels abroad to open a hotel, he routinely invites the area's mission president to be introduced to the country's leaders. Elder D. Todd Christofferson never forgot what a difference it made for Mexican government-Church relations when Bill introduced him to President

Ernesto Zedillo at the opening of a Mexico City Marriott. "I don't know how Bill knew Zedillo—he seems to know everybody in the world—but he was just so up front about the Church. Bill was not in the least reticent or embarrassed in any way about his membership and bringing it to the forefront." Elder Christofferson credited the introduction with helping to smooth over some visa issues regarding Latter-day Saint missionaries in Mexico. "I always appreciated Bill was upfront about the Church, and would so energetically use his influence on behalf of the Church."[41]

For many years, Latter-day Saint missionaries were banned from Thailand after an infamous photo of a missionary sitting on a Buddha was circulated. When Bill opened the JW Marriott in Bangkok in 1994 and was granted an audience with the king, he saw a chance to strengthen Church relations in the country. Son-in-law Ron Harrison was on hand for the visit. "He brought the mission president to that meeting, and it was a big deal. In the meeting, the king mentioned the incident from decades before, but became friendly in discussing future relations. . . . This is the kind of bridge building that Bill Marriott can do because he has these kinds of avenues to government leaders which enhance and accentuate the cause of building Zion."[42]

Finally, there is the placement of more than a million copies of the Book of Mormon in individual Marriott Hotel rooms around the world that has occurred for more than a half century—a major missionary effort by the Marriott family. Even though Marriott International owns few hotels—being primarily a hotel-management company—Bill mandates in a signed agreement that every owner will place a Book of Mormon in every hotel room, though the owners do not have to pay for them. The Marriott family foundation, headed by Dick Marriott since 1988, covers the cost of distribution and replacement of the scriptures, the latter being a substantial enterprise because the books are often borrowed by guests. When the satirical *Book of Mormon* musical ran on Broadway, so many guests were taking the book home from the New York Marriott Marquis hotel rooms to "learn the truth" that Dick's foundation could barely keep the books in stock, according to the late Elder Robert D. Hales.[43] Since 2016 the scriptures in the hotel rooms are embossed with the invitation "Please Accept with Our Compliments."[44]

In a letter to Bill and Dick in 1999, Elder David B. Haight wrote, "I remember when your father started this project many years ago, and how President David O. McKay heralded this unique and generous demonstration of the faith and devotion of the Marriott family." As the chair of the Church's Missionary Executive Council, Elder Haight added, "We will never know the amount of good that is accomplished through your continuing [of] this [program]."[45] Bill and Dick have received numerous letters from converts who initially learned about the Church from the Book of Mormon in their hotel room, but the letter from President Thomas S. Monson in 2000 was particularly moving. He wrote: "I had the privilege this past weekend to dedicate the Louisville Kentucky Temple. Featured in one of the dedication sessions was the testimony of Richard B. Vivian, second counselor in the temple presidency, a capable and sweet-spirited man. He spoke of his conversion and said that it commenced when he read from a copy of the *Book of Mormon* he found in a dresser drawer in his room in a Marriott hotel. As I listened to this outstanding leader speaking at the microphone in the celestial room of the temple, I thought of you [Bill] and Dick and your parents and of your untiring efforts and unswerving loyalty in behalf of the Church in all that you have done."[46]

NOTES

1. This article is adapted and expanded from Dale Van Atta, *Bill Marriott: Success Is Never Final; His Life and the Decisions That Built a Hotel Empire* (Salt Lake City: Shadow Mountain, 2019).

2. Though some called him J.W. or Willard, for most of his life he was known as Bill. For easier reading, the author has chosen to refer to the patriarch as J.W. and his son as Bill.

3. J.W. kept a journal for decades, beginning with his mission journal. This citation is from the September 17, 1921, entry. The journal, which will be referred to as JWM Journal, is kept in the archive room at Marriott International's Bethesda, MD, headquarters.

4. See chapter 11 herein, "The Seating of Senator Reed Smoot," by Casey Paul Griffiths.

5. JWM Journal, 18 September 1921.

6. JWM Journal, 19 September 1921; for Congressperson Colton's earlier visits to J.W.'s mission area, see JWM Journal of 1921: March 26 to 27 and August

14 to 15. Regarding the personal and business relationship between J.W. and Hugh Colton, see Lee Roderick, *Bridge Builder: Hugh Colton, from Country Lawyer to Combat Hero* (Washington, DC: Probitas Press, 2010).

7. JWM Journal, 28 January 1972.

8. "Connecticut Ave. Hot Shoppe Started the Marriott Empire," *Washington Post*, 14 June 1959; Sterling Slappey, "How Big Tamale Became J. Willard Marriott and Made Hard Work Pay and Pay," *Washingtonian*, January 1972, A18.

9. Robert O'Brien, *Marriott: The J. Willard Marriott Story* (Salt Lake City: Deseret Book, 1977), 142–47.

10. Bill Marriott, remarks, Washington D.C. Stake conference, 27 April 1986; Richard Emery, *Sam Cowley: Legendary Lawman* (Springville, UT: Cedar Fort, 2004); Steven Nickel and William J. Helmer, *Baby Face Nelson: Portrait of a Public Enemy* (Nashville: Cumberland House, 2002). J. Edgar Hoover repeatedly called Cowley the "bravest man I ever knew." The FBI director's most eloquent tribute to Cowley came two decades after the latter's death in a 7 May 1958 letter to J.W., with a seven-page attachment. Three decades later, Bill proudly delivered the tribute to President Gordon B. Hinckley, who gratefully acknowledged receipt in an 8 April 1986 letter.

11. See chapter 18 herein, "The Washington Chapel: An Elias to the Washington D.C. Temple," by Alonzo L. Gaskill and Seth Soha.

12. O'Brien, *Marriott*, 159–62. Brossard was the second president of the Washington D.C. Stake (after Benson), and J.W. was the third.

13. "No man ever had a better friend than J. Willard Marriott," Benson affirmed. Sheri L. Dew, *Ezra Taft Benson: A Biography* (Salt Lake City: Deseret Book, 1987), 158 and 164.

14. Howard S. Bennion (Mervyn's brother), "One of the Lord's Noblemen: Mervyn Sharp Bennion Captain, USS *West Virginia*, United States Navy" (unpublished manuscript, July 1943); Julian C. Lowe, "The Beginnings of Church Organization and Growth," *History of the Mormons in the Greater Washington Area* (Washington, DC: Community Printing Services, 1991), 30.

15. Elder Russell M. Nelson interview with author, 15 August 2013. As stake president, J.W. interviewed the young lieutenant and called him to be second counselor in the Washington Ward bishopric, which was "a very important part of my spiritual development." In fact, after J.W. died, Elder Nelson related to Bill in a 14 August 1985 letter that it was J.W. who gave him and his wife Dantzel "the opportunity, along with the encouragement and example, to seek first the kingdom of God knowing that all else would be appropriately taken care of."

16. When Romney returned home after his participation in J.W.'s 1985 funeral service, including offering the dedication of his grave, he wrote Bill on 19 August: "As you probably know while your father had many close personal friends I had only one and none really close now that he has departed temporarily."

17. Donna Marriott, interviews with author, 29 April 1982 and 18 April 2012.

18. "Elder Benson Family Plays Host: LDS Home Night Demonstrated to President and Mrs. Eisenhower," *Deseret News*, Church Section, 12 February 1955; Bill Marriott stake conference address, "A Sensitive Leader: Priesthood Leadership in Church and Home," 25 October 1981; Bill Marriott interviews with author, 19 December 2012 and 21 May 2013; Donna Marriott interview with author, 18 April 2012.

19. Bill Marriott interview about Christmas Eve 1957 incident with author, 30 April 2013; Dew, *Ezra Taft Benson*, 333.

20. Louie Estrada, "Alice Sheets Marriott Dies; Matriarch of Hotel Chain Was Active in Politics, Charities," *Washington Post*, 19 April 2000, B05.

21. O'Brien, *Marriott*, 279–81.

22. See chapter 6 herein, "'Make the Air with Music Ring': A Personal Perspective on the Tabernacle Choir at Temple Square," by Lloyd D. Newell.

23. J.W. Marriott to Milton A. Barlow, (Bill) Marriott, John S. Daniels, Frank Kimball, Wayne McAllister, Foster Kunz, and Alden Bowers, memorandum, 7 May 1959.

24. JWM Journal, 27 April 1959.

25. JWM Journal, 10 June 1961.

26. Minutes of Marriott Executive Committee Meeting, "Discussion of Las Vegas Hotel Proposal," 4 September 1972.

27. Bill Marriott, interview by Kathi Ann Brown, 17 October 1996; Bill Marriott, interview with author, 9 July 2013.

28. JWM Journal, 30 October 1957. Eleven years later, President McKay strongly approached J.W. about a General Authority position in June 1968. J.W. recounted, "Milan Smith—Pres. of (Washington D.C.) Stake—came to breakfast. The First Presidency asked him to check on me to see if my health would permit a 'big job' in the church. I told him I couldn't handle (such a) job with responsibility because of my heart trouble." JWM Journal, 13 June 1968.

29. See chapter 19 herein, "The Washington D.C. Temple: Mr. Smith's Church Goes to Washington," by Maclane E. Heward.

30. Dieter F. Uchtdorf, interview with author, 5 September 2012.

31. "J. Willard Marriott," *Washington Post*, 17 August 1985, A18.

32. Jeffrey R. Holland, interview with author, 26 June 2019.

33. Russell M. Nelson, interview with author, 26 June 2019.

34. Russell M. Nelson, interview with author, 15 August 2013.

35. Russell M. Nelson to Bill Marriott, 26 June 1990.

36. Beverly Campbell to Bill Marriott, 27 June 1990.

37. Beverly Campbell to Donna Marriott, 21 May 1996; 2006 "Invitation to the Ambassadorial & Congressional Dinner and Private Tour of His Premier Automobile Collection."

38. Ann Santini, interview by David Brent and Enid Smith for the North America Northeast Area, 11 October 2017.

39. Many *Deseret News* and *Church News* accounts, including Lee Davidson, "Temple Lights Up with Call for Peace: French Envoy Is Honored by LDS at Rites in D.C.," *Deseret News*, 4 December 2003 (online).

40. Santini, interview.

41. D. Todd Christofferson, interview with author, 9 August 2013; D. Todd Christofferson to Bill Marriott, 3 October 1996.

42. Ron Harrison (who served as Washington D.C. Stake president), interview with author, 2 August 2013. Bill has also been particularly helpful to Church relations with India and China, where, for example, he befriended Chinese ambassador Yang Jiechi, who was promoted to be China's tenth foreign minister from 2006 to 2013. Edward Cody, "China Names New Foreign Minister," *Washington Post*, 28 April 2007, A14.

43. Robert D. Hales, interview with author, 29 May 2012.

44. Mieka F. Wick (executive director, J. Willard and Alice S. Marriott Foundation) to author, email, 29 June 2020.

45. David B. Haight to Bill and Dick Marriott, 26 October 1999.

46. Thomas S. Monson to Bill Marriott, 21 March 2000.

The United States Capitol, photo by Caleb Perez, Unsplash.

AT THE CROSSROADS: T. H. BELL'S ROLE IN THE REAGAN ADMINISTRATION

ROGER G. CHRISTENSEN

Roger G. Christensen is an instructor of Church history and doctrine at Brigham Young University.

Several members of The Church of Jesus Christ of Latter-day Saints have served in various governmental roles in the United States, both as elected and appointed officials. Only six have served as cabinet officers, officials who directly advise the president on important issues of the day. T. H. Bell, a devout Latter-day Saint, served as secretary of education during the first four years (1981–85) of the Reagan administration. His appointment to serve came at a critical time in the early history of the Department of Education. This brief narrative account provides a case in contrast between Bell, a lifelong educator and administrator who focused on improving education, and the president and his advisers, who wanted to eliminate the department. It also illustrates how politics both helped and hindered Bell's efforts.

ROADS TO WASHINGTON

Terrel Howard Bell was born 11 November 1921 in Lava Hot Springs, Idaho, the eighth of twelve children born to Willard D. and Alta Martin

Bell.[1] His father passed away shortly after Bell's eighth birthday. As a result, he grew up in very humble circumstances during the Great Depression and saw education as his passport to the future.[2] After completing high school in his hometown, Bell attended Albion State Normal School, a small teachers college in Albion, Idaho.[3] World War II interrupted his education as he spent three and a half years serving in the Marine Corps, but he returned to Albion and completed a BA degree in 1946. He later received an MA (1954) from the University of Idaho and a PhD (1961) from the University of Utah.[4] He married Josephine Saunders in 1950. Their son, Jon, died in infancy, and they divorced in 1956. He later married Betty Ruth Fitzgerald on 1 August 1957. Together they had four sons.[5]

During his career as an educator, Bell worked as a coach, teacher, and professor at the secondary and postsecondary levels in Idaho, Wyoming, and Utah. He also served in various administrative positions at the district, state, and national levels; he was the commissioner of higher education for the state of Utah at the time of his appointment as U.S. secretary of education.[6] Bell noted that the basic tenets of his faith he had learned in his youth—hard work and self-sufficiency—influenced all aspects of his life, both personally and professionally.[7]

Ecclesiastically, Bell served much of his adult life teaching and working to improve teaching at the ward, stake, and general Church levels, serving on the Sunday School general board from 1972 to 1974. He was the Gospel Doctrine teacher of the Falls Church Ward while serving as secretary of education. Upon returning to Utah after his service in Washington, he served as a high councilor, stake president, and regional representative of the Twelve.[8]

Before his appointment as secretary of education, Bell had served in Washington on two previous occasions: first as associate commissioner (1970–71) in the Office of Education—a division of the Department of Health, Education, and Welfare (HEW)—under Richard Nixon and later as the commissioner (1974–76) under Gerald Ford. While serving as commissioner, Bell reported to Caspar Weinberger, secretary of HEW at that time. These two men got along well and respected one another.[9] Weinberger spent more than three decades in various political roles, including chair of the California Republican Party from 1962 to 1968. He was well-known by Reagan and served as secretary of defense during most of the Reagan administration.[10] Bell believed that it was Weinberger who recommended him to Reagan for consideration as secretary of education.[11]

During his early years in Washington, members of Congress and others within the administration recognized Bell for the keen administrative abilities and tact he exhibited when he addressed many challenging educational issues.[12] In his role as commissioner of education, he testified before Congress in support of creating a cabinet-level department for education.[13] Congress passed the act creating the U.S. Department of Education during the Carter administration, and it officially began operation in November 1979.[14] The department was the thirteenth cabinet office created and, as Bell noted, since the number thirteen is a notoriously unlucky number, its concerns and issues would indeed be last on the list for the Reagan administration's consideration.[15]

Ronald Reagan emerged as a political leader in the state of California. He was elected president of the United States on 4 November 1980 after serving as governor of that state from 1967 to 1975. His tenure as governor shaped his views on educational institutions and their leaders based, in part, on the turbulent circumstances of the times. Through the 1960s and extending into the early 1970s, negative reactions to U.S. involvement in the Vietnam War exploded across a number of university campuses.[16] The seedbed of discontent in California germinated at the University of California at Berkeley.[17] By the mid 1960s, however, the attitude of the public had not yet coalesced with that of the students. Many citizens were appalled at what was taking place in Berkeley (and later, on other campuses) and wanted leaders to put an end to the protests.[18]

One of Reagan's political strengths was his ability to assess popular sentiment, and he tapped into the anti-protest attitude in order to criticize educational institutions, administrators, faculty, and students for allowing the protests to occur.[19] His political mantra became, "It is time to clean up the mess at Berkeley."[20] Many believe he launched his political career based on his harsh criticism of higher education and, in particular, educational leaders.[21] He campaigned for governor on the platform of fiscal responsibility, limited government, welfare reform, and cracking down on student protests.[22] When Reagan won the nomination for the presidency,

Reagan's first official cabinet photo in the Oval Office, 1981. Ronald Reagan Presidential Library.

prominent planks in the Republican Party platform included similar themes: reduce taxes, limit government with corresponding reductions in federal spending, and eliminate the Department of Education.[23]

The stage was set for a political clash between the president-elect and his eventual nominee for secretary of education. Bell was officially nominated to become the U.S. secretary of education on 20 January 1981 by President Reagan and confirmed two days later by the U.S. Senate's vote of 90–2.[24]

ROUGH ROADS AHEAD

During the vetting process for his nomination as secretary of education, Bell met with members of the transition team, including Edwin Meese and his longtime friend Pendleton James. Meese served with Reagan during his years as governor of California (1967–75) and throughout his presidency, first as special counselor (1981–85) and then as attorney general (1985–88).[25] Meese knew well the president-elect's disdain for big government and educational institutions, including their leaders. He also was a leader of the "movement conservatives," a group that felt empowered to implement the president's agenda. James, president of an executive search firm, ultimately became director of the White House Personnel Office, which oversees hiring within departments of the administration, including the Department of Education. Both of these men proved to be antagonists in Bell's later efforts regarding the future of the department.[26]

The initial meeting focused on Bell's willingness to work toward eliminating the department. Pendleton James noted that, if appointed, Bell would have the distinction one day of walking into the Oval Office and stating, "Well, we've shut the abominable thing down. Here's one useless government agency out of the way."[27] The comment clearly expressed the environment and, presumably, the position Bell would assume if he accepted the nomination. Still, he felt he could make a difference in the national discourse around education and expressed his willingness to serve.[28]

Recruiting people to assume leadership positions in the department, however, became an arduous task due to the administration's stated objective. The most qualified and likely candidates declined being considered. Bell initially had to appoint temporary leaders into crucial positions from among the ranks of career civil service employees.[29] Key senior individuals in the administration—particularly Ed Meese, Pendleton James, and David Stockman, director of the Office of Management and Budget (OMB)—became central in all discussions Secretary Bell had regarding the administration of the department. Any actions having an impact on budgets or hiring of personnel had to be coordinated with these men, all of whom were movement conservatives and were firmly committed to abolishing the department.[30]

Fortunately, the president had assured his cabinet that they did not need to employ people in senior staff positions that they were not comfortable working with, which essentially gave each cabinet officer veto power over political appointees.[31] Bell used this delegated authority effectively, but it repeatedly created an impasse with White House staff in obtaining approval for his proposed candidates. For example, White House Personnel initially proposed that Bell consider Loralee Kinder to be the undersecretary of education. She had chaired a national educational task force and had high regard among the movement conservatives. Bell disagreed with many of the proposals of the task force and additionally felt that Kinder lacked the academic credentials to command the necessary respect within the academic community. Bell proposed Christopher Cross, a Republican educator, who was also a respected scholar. White House Personnel quickly rejected this recommendation, still angered over Bell's veto of Ms. Kinder.[32]

After extended (and at times contentious) negotiations, Bell secured a leadership team he could work with.[33] He noted, "It had been a rocky start, but I finally proved to my White House adversaries that I would not be intimidated or dominated. . . . I didn't win, but most importantly, I didn't lose either. . . . I had succeeded in assembling a staff that was a balance between moderates and ideologues, making it possible for me to have credibility in the education community as well as to do my job."[34]

AT THE CROSSROADS

Bell developed a level of credibility with educators, legislators, and the media while he navigated appointees through the approval process and some initial administrative actions he had taken regarding bilingual education and merit pay for teachers. In July 1981, *U.S. News & World Report* published an appraisal of the effectiveness of the Reagan cabinet based on a survey of 131 "Washington insiders"—White House administrators, Senators, members of Congress, key lobbyists, and others. Bell ranked fifth out of the thirteen cabinet secretaries. The article noted, "The ultimate surprise would be if Bell's Education Department, which has been slated for eventual elimination in Reagan's drive to trim the bureaucracy, escapes the ax—something that now seems a distinct possibility." He hoped to leverage his newfound standing to develop a measured proposal about the department's future.

Although he was determined to keep his commitment to the president, he also saw a need to maintain some role for the federal government in education, especially regarding "vital college-student-aid funding from loans, work-study opportunities, and grants to financially needy students."[35] In addition, he had regulatory obligations for other substantial programs, such as Title I funding for schools with large concentrations of low-income and educationally disadvantaged students, and enforcement of civil rights required by the education acts passed in the 1960s and 1970s. These matters weighed heavily on Secretary Bell, and he knew disrupting existing systems could be problematic if he didn't consider the long-term impact of any proposed changes. He needed time to assess the areas of greatest need in education across the country and how the department could best meet those needs.

Bell understood the impact of a timely message, one that could capture the attention of organizations and policy makers, as evidenced by the 1910 Flexner Report addressing the poor quality of medical education at that time in the United States and Canada.[36] He sensed the time was right for a landmark statement on the overall state of education in the United States, which could then inform long-term policy decisions (including recommendations on the department's future) and help define the role of the federal government in education.[37]

Bell discussed the idea of a presidential commission to study education with senior White House staff. His proposal met resistance from Ed Meese and other movement conservatives.[38] He therefore decided to move forward on his own and appointed a blue-ribbon commission to undertake a national study. He and his staff found qualified individuals to serve as members of the commission who would represent a broad spectrum of educational interests.[39]

The National Commission on Excellence in Education was formally organized by a charter Secretary Bell signed on 5 August 1981.[40] The charter included multiple responsibilities: (1) evaluating and synthesizing data and scholarly literature on the quality of teaching and learning across the country for all levels of education and types of educational institutions; (2) analyzing curriculum, academic standards, college admissions requirements, and student performance; (3) identifying educational programs that consistently attained higher than average results; (4) comparing academic requirements and outcomes for schools in the United States with those of other economically advanced countries; and (5) assessing major changes that had significantly affected educational achievement over the previous twenty-five-year period.[41] The commission also was to hold hearings to gather insights from experts and the public on perceived issues or concerns at all levels of education. It was then to provide a report defining issues and providing practical recommendations to help those serving in a capacity to influence change including parents, educators, governing boards, and local, state, and federal officials.[42]

Bell held a public orientation meeting to initiate the study and outline its objectives. Members of the media attended the session, which helped it garner national attention. He assured the commission that the department's support and resources would be available to it so that the tasks could be completed without interference. Bell also committed to holding a series of conferences across the country following receipt of the report in order to disseminate its findings, and he indicated that he would do all he could to get the president involved in those public meetings. In addition, Bell emphasized the importance of having the work of the commission be of the highest quality and insisted that any proposed recommendations be unanimous.[43]

The commission held a total of seventeen public meetings, panel discussions, hearings, and symposia in varying locations across the country. In addition, the commission solicited written papers on topics of concern from individuals who were experts in their respective fields.[44] Bell met with the commission on several occasions during the process in order to respond to questions and to offer encouragement.[45] As the deadline for submitting the report approached, Bell became concerned when the chair, David Gardner, called and requested an extension. Bell regarded Gardner highly and had previously worked closely with him when Gardner served as president of the University of Utah; he also knew they had a narrow window in which to get the report to the president if they hoped to have his involvement in any of the public meetings prior to the 1984 election season. Bell pressed hard, but Gardner was firm about needing the additional time to achieve full consensus of all eighteen members on all the recommendations. Bell relented and received the final report from the commission in April 1983.[46]

The report, entitled *A Nation at Risk: An Imperative for Educational Reform*, was direct, impassioned, and relatively short (only thirty-six pages long, not counting the appendices). The opening paragraph summarized the commission's concerns. It states, "Our Nation is at risk. Our once unchallenged preeminence in commerce, industry, science, and technology innovation is being overtaken by competitors throughout the world. . . . The educational foundations of our society are presently being eroded by a rising tide of mediocrity that threatens our very future as a Nation and as a people."[47] Additionally, the report presented the study's process, findings, recommendations, and its call to action. The summary comments were similarly poignant. The report concluded, "*Reform* of our educational system *will take time and unwavering commitment.* It will require equally widespread, energetic, and dedicated action . . . from groups with interest in and responsibility for educational reform."[48]

Secretary Bell was both pleased with and apprehensive about the commission's report. The day after receiving it, he transmitted a copy to the president, and it circulated among the White House staff. Within hours, Bell received calls from many who had read the report, and they commended the work. He was told that the president had also read the entire report and was pleased with it.[49]

Bell arranged to make the report public at a White House media event on 26 April 1983, where the president would receive an official copy.[50] The day before the meeting, Bell received an urgent call from a White House staffer who had seen a draft of the president's planned remarks and expressed concern about the tenor of his message. It said little about the work of the commission or of its report; the focus was on some key issues championed by the movement conservatives regarding education—tuition tax credits and school prayer. Bell immediately called the president's chief of staff, James Baker, to see if anything could be done to tailor the message appropriately. Baker assured Secretary Bell that the extraneous or irrelevant comments would be removed from the president's prepared notes.

Reagan's remarks on receiving the final report of the National Commission on Excellence in Education, 26 April 1983. T. H. Bell, David P. Gardner (chair of the commission), and President Reagan. Ronald Reagan Presidential Library.

On the morning of the press conference, emotions ran high. Everything was proceeding as planned, and the White House briefing room was packed—the back of the room was crowded with television cameras, invited guests occupied every available chair, and members of the commission sat up front. Bell welcomed everyone, gave a brief overview of the purpose of the work of the commission and invited the chair, David Gardner, to explain more about the process. Gardner delivered his comments and turned the microphone back to Bell. The president did not arrive as scheduled, so Bell continued making additional comments to fill the void. He tried to be positive, but it became apparent to everyone in the crowd that he was just buying time.[51]

When President Reagan finally entered the room, Bell turned over the podium to him. The president apologized for being late, pulled his note cards from his pocket, and started his remarks as prepared by his staff. Reagan waxed eloquent about aspects of the report, noting, "You have found that our educational system is in the grip of a crisis caused by low standards, lack of purpose, ineffective use of resources, and a failure to challenge students to push performance to the boundaries of individual ability." He continued, "We're entering a new era, and education holds the key. Rather than fear our future, let us embrace it and make it work for us by improving instruction." He then moved on to address the importance of school prayer as a fundamental freedom, the importance of competition and choice in education, and the value of tuition tax credits in accomplishing these aims. He also emphasized the need to abolish the department.[52]

Bell was stunned. These latter themes were the points he had hoped to excise from the president's comments. Although Bell did not take exception to most of these concepts in principle, this was not the proper setting for expressing these issues. As the president spoke, Bell looked down the corridor where Reagan had entered and saw Ed Meese and others of the movement conservatives smiling and giving congratulatory gestures to one another.[53]

Bell worried about how the press would treat the meeting and the report of the commission. Despite his worst fears, the president's peripheral comments fell flat with journalists covering the event; because everyone in the audience had received a copy of *A Nation at Risk* in advance, most news reports covered the content of the report, not the press conference related to its release.[54]

The importance of educational reform was now in the national spotlight. Nearly every broadcast media outlet and every newspaper across the country reported on the findings presented in *A Nation at Risk*. Secretary Bell became a popular interviewee on all the national news shows, and on the Sunday morning programs of *Meet the Press* and *Face the Nation*. Requests for copies of *A Nation at Risk* caused the U.S. Government Printing Office to run out of stock, and there were requests on backorder for months. Follow-up reports in the media kept the recommendations from the commission's report before the public for many days after its initial release.[55]

The issues raised in *A Nation at Risk* struck a national nerve. It became clear that addressing educational reform was high on the public agenda. This visibility given to the department also became a turning point on how it was perceived, for a time, within the administration. In a subsequent cabinet meeting to address budget proposals for the following fiscal year, David Stockman, director of OMB, emphasized the importance of reducing expenditures in each department with one notable concession: "The sensitive issue of education is an exception, of course. We will want to keep in front on this."[56] As a result, the department did not experience large budget cuts that year.

Bell had committed to organizing public dissemination meetings following the release of the commission's report. He coordinated twelve conferences in strategic areas around the country. Most members of the commission participated in these meetings, as did Secretary Bell. President Reagan also committed to help disseminate the findings of the report, and based on the national mood, it provided opportunities to address topics of importance during the pre-election season.[57] Reagan's involvement also gave greater visibility to the events and assured continuing media coverage.

Cabinet meeting, 23 February 1984. T. H. Bell, President Reagan, John A. Svahn (director, White House Office of Policy Development). Associated Press.

In these public meetings, President Reagan assured the people that he was working on plans to resolve the educational crisis. He was also involved in some of the question-and-answer sessions. However, in one question directed specifically to Reagan, "What was your rationale for wanting to abolish the Department of Education?" he was a bit awkward in his reply. He spoke of his keen interest in and support of education; however, he feared the federal government would take a stronger role in controlling education across the country if not carefully kept in check. Later, Reagan asked Secretary Bell, "Did I handle the question on the future of the Department of Education okay?" Given Reagan's prior commitment to abolish the department and the current public interest in improving education, Bell concluded, "The question of abolishing the Department of Education was an exercise in futility. He and I both knew that it would never happen."[58]

MOVING DOWN THE ROAD

Aligning with public sentiment, the tone of the Reagan administration toward education changed dramatically. In stark contrast to the wording of the 1980 Republican Party platform, the 1984 platform extolled President Reagan's leadership in shaping the national agenda on education. In part it read, "The Reagan Administration turned the nation's attention to the quality of education. . . . Ronald Reagan's significant and innovative leadership has encouraged and sustained the reform movement. He catapulted education to the forefront of the national agenda."[59] After much positive public attention, the president sent a personal note to Secretary Bell, praising him for his leadership in shaping the future of education in the country.[60]

Although pleased with what seemed to be a strong endorsement from the president, that support was short-lived. Bell soon realized the president's real interests were not in educational reform at all. It became apparent that the president was using the present enthusiasm for change in education to his political advantage.[61] He and many of his advisers leveraged the focus brought by the attention on education to advance other policy issues within their own political agendas.

After winning a landslide election in 1984, Reagan quickly moved on to other pressing issues. All of the traction gained around education quickly dissipated, and education reform again became a low priority. Those who had pushed for abolishing the department once again had the president's ear.

Confidential proposals Bell sent to the White House to address educational reform were leaked to the press and received unfavorable commentary in several conservative publications. Bell learned that Ed Meese and others among the movement conservatives had requested advanced copies of his proposals and were likely the source of these leaks. In a subsequent meeting to address budget requests, Bell confronted Meese and David Stockman directly. Both denied any knowledge of how the information became public. Although Bell continued to push his agenda on educational reform, senior White House staff repeatedly rebuffed his efforts; moving proposals on educational issues through the internal political process regularly stalled. Bell realized his effectiveness as secretary was compromised. As a result, he chose to resign from office to return to Utah, where he hoped to have an impact in formulating improvements in education at the state and local levels.[62]

Back in Utah, Bell received a professorship in the College of Education at the University of Utah and began teaching again.[63] According to a business associate, Bell loathed the idea of retiring, so in 1991 he also founded an educational consulting firm—T. H. Bell and Associates—and continued his advocacy for improving education across the nation.[64] During this time, Bell also served as a regional representative of the Twelve for two years (1990–92). He was released from that role in March 1992 to chair a special coalition against a proposed ballot initiative in Utah to legalize pari-mutuel betting.[65] T. H. Bell died on 22 June 1996 of pulmonary fibrosis at the age of seventy-four.[66]

AT THE END OF THE ROAD

As noted in *A Nation at Risk*, educational reform takes time and unwavering commitment. Without a consistent long-term policy, many issues raised in 1983 regarding education in America have persisted. Reflecting on his career, Bell lamented, "We would have changed the course of history in American education had the president stayed with us through the implementation of the school reform effort."[67] Although Bell was not successful in achieving the objectives he had hoped to realize, the immediate impact of his blue-ribbon report was extensive, and some positive steps were initiated. He helped set the tone for a national conversation, and he demonstrated the need for partnered efforts to raise the quality of education for every student.

Although T. H. Bell was tasked with abolishing the department, his background, vision, and role at a critical time allowed him to highlight national concerns about education and to elevate the image of the department in the eyes of many, especially in the eyes of the public. His leadership effectively saved the department from elimination. At that critical moment in history, he stood at the crossroads and helped influence the future direction that the U.S. Department of Education would take.

I chose to research the role of T. H. Bell because of a personal relationship I had with him. Bell served as secretary of education from 1981 to 1985 in the first Reagan administration. Shortly after returning to Utah from Washington, he was called as a regional representative of the Twelve. In 1990, while I was serving as a young counselor in a stake presidency, Elder Bell was assigned to work with the stakes in our area. During the time he met with our stake presidency, he started every meeting by sharing a political anecdote (generally humorous) about his experiences while serving in Washington. I also grew up in Northern California, near the University of California, Berkley, during the years Reagan served as governor of that state.

NOTES

1. Terrel Howard Bell, FamilySearch.org.

2. Terrel H. Bell, *The Thirteenth Man: A Reagan Cabinet Memoir* (New York: The Free Press, 1988), 6–8.

3. Bell, *Thirteenth Man*, 8–12.

4. Ronald Reagan, "Nomination of Terrel H. Bell to Be Secretary of Education," 20 January 1981, The American Presidency Project (website).

5. Bell, FamilySearch.org.

6. Reagan, "Nomination of Terrel H. Bell to Be Secretary of Education."

7. Bell, *Thirteenth Man*, 7–8.

8. Terrel H. Bell, biographical information provided to the Church History Department, 1990.

9. Bell, *Thirteenth Man*, 1–2.

10. Caspar W. Weinberger, "Biographical Information," https://history.defense.gov/Multimedia/Biographies/Article-View/Article/571286/caspar-w-weinberger/.

11. Bell, *Thirteenth Man*, 1–2.

12. *Hearing before the Committee on Labor and Public Welfare, United States Senate, Second Session on Terrel H. Bell, PhD, of Utah, to Be Commissioner of Education*, 93rd Cong. (1974).

13. Senator Jennings Randolph, "U.S. Commissioner of Education Leaves Significant Imprint on the Future of Public Education in America" (Congressional Record, 122:94, 30 July 1976), 28419–20.

14. Department of Education Organization Act of 1979. Pub. L. No. 96-88.

15. Bell, *Thirteenth Man*, ix–xi.

16. E. M. Schreiber, "Opposition to the Vietnam War among American University Students and Faculty," *British Journal of Sociology* 24, no. 3 (September 1973), 288–302.

17. William J. Rorabaugh, *Berkeley At War: The 1960s* (New York: Oxford University Press, 1989).

18. Gerard J. De Groot, "Ronald Reagan and Student Unrest in California," *Pacific Historical Review* 65, no. 1 (February 1996): 107–29.

19. Stuart K. Spencer, oral history, interviewed by Gabrielle Morris, 1979, "Developing a Campaign Management Organization" (Regional Oral History Office, Bancroft Library, University of California, Berkeley), 31.

20. Totton J. Anderson and Eugene C. Lee, "The 1966 Election in California," *Western Political Quarterly* 20, no. 2, part 2 (June 1967): 535–54. See also

Jeffrey Kahn, "Ronald Reagan's Political Career and the Berkeley Campus," *UC Berkley News*, 8 June 2004.

21. De Groot, "Ronald Reagan and Student Unrest," 107–9.

22. Anderson and Lee, "The 1966 Election in California," 535–54.

23. Republican Party Platforms, "Republican Party Platform of 1980," 15 July 1980, The American Presidency Project (website).

24. Reagan, "Nomination of Terrel H. Bell to Be Secretary of Education."

25. Edwin Meese III, "Biographical Information," Hoover Institution, Stanford University.

26. Bell, *Thirteenth Man*, 38–51.

27. Bell, *Thirteenth Man*, 2.

28. Bell, *Thirteenth Man*, 3–5.

29. Bell, *Thirteenth Man*, 40.

30. Bell, *Thirteenth Man*, 39–40, 67.

31. Bell, *Thirteenth Man*, 38.

32. Bell, *Thirteenth Man*, 40–41.

33. Bell, *Thirteenth Man*, 43–51.

34. Bell, *Thirteenth Man*, 48–50.

35. Bell, *Thirteenth Man*, 90.

36. The Carnegie Foundation, "Medical Education in the United States and Canada," A Report to the Carnegie Foundation for the Advancement of Teaching, by Abraham Flexner, Bulletin Number Four, 1910. See also Lester F. Goodchild and Harlod S. Wechler, eds., "Professional Education" and "Surveying the Professions," in *The History of Higher Education*, 2nd ed., ed. Lester F. Goodchild and Harold S. Weschler (Needham Heights, MA: Association for the Study of Higher Education, 1997), 379–402.

37. Bell, *Thirteenth Man*, 115.

38. Bell, *Thirteenth Man*, 116.

39. The National Commission on Excellence in Education was eventually composed of eighteen individuals. For a full list of members of the Commission, see USA Research, *A Nation at Risk: The Full Account* (Cambridge, MA: Murray Printing Company, 1984), appendix B: Members of the National Commission on Excellence in Education, 91–92.

40. USA Research, *A Nation at Risk*, appendix A: Charter: National Commission on Excellence in Education, 87–90.

41. This timeframe coincided with the period following the Russian launch of Sputnik I, the first artificial satellite, in October 1957 and the subsequent

emphasis placed on STEM (science, technology, engineering, and mathematics) education across the United States.

42. USA Research, *A Nation at Risk*, appendix A: Charter: National Commission on Excellence in Education, 87–90.

43. Bell, *Thirteenth Man*, 118–19.

44. For a full list of meetings, see USA Research, *A Nation at Risk*, appendix D: Schedule of the Commission's Public Events, 95–96. For a listing of participants and events at each location, see appendix E: Hearing Participants and Related Activities, 97–109. For a listing of those submitting commentary to the Commission, see appendix F: Other Presentations to the Commission, 111.

45. Bell, *Thirteenth Man*, 120.

46. Bell, *Thirteenth Man*, 120–22.

47. USA Research, *A Nation at Risk*, 5.

48. USA Research, *A Nation at Risk*, 84; emphasis added.

49. Bell, *Thirteenth Man*, 127.

50. Bell, *Thirteenth Man*, 123–31.

51. Bell, *Thirteenth Man*, 129–30.

52. Ronald Reagan, "Remarks on Receiving the Final Report of the National Commission on Excellence in Education," 26 April 1983, The American Presidency Project (website).

53. Bell, *Thirteenth Man*, 130–31.

54. Bell, *Thirteenth Man*, 131.

55. Bell, *Thirteenth Man*, 131.

56. Bell, *Thirteenth Man*, 131.

57. Bell, *Thirteenth Man*, 144.

58. Bell, *Thirteenth Man*, 148–49. After Bell's tenure in the department, the lack of a consistent education policy to address the issues initially raised in *A Nation at Risk* contributed to perceptions of the department's value in resolving these concerns. As a result, some politicians still question its purpose and the need for an ongoing role of the federal government in education.

59. Republican Party Platforms, "Republican Party Platform of 1984," 20 August 1984, The American Presidency Project (website).

60. Bell, *Thirteenth Man*, 159.

61. Bell, *Thirteenth Man*, 158.

62. Bell, *Thirteenth Man*, 157–58.

63. University of Utah, College of Education, Alumni Profiles, Terrell [*sic*] Howard Bell.

64. "Terrel Bell, Known for Defending Federal Role in Education, Dies," *Education Week*, 10 July 1996.

65. "LDS Leaders Attack Pari-Mutuel Betting," *Deseret News*, 1 June 1992.

66. "T. H. Bell, Ex-Cabinet Member and Educator, Dies at 74," *Deseret News*, 23 June 1996.

67. Bell, *Thirteenth Man*, 159.

Beverly Campbell in her office. Photos in this chapter courtesy of Thomas Campbell.

BEVERLY CAMPBELL: CHURCH PUBLIC AND INTERNATIONAL AFFAIRS DIRECTOR

MARY JANE WOODGER AND BROOKE ANDERSON

Mary Jane Woodger is a professor of Church history and doctrine at Brigham Young University. Brooke Anderson is a senior majoring in English at Brigham Young University.

Beverly Brough Campbell was an extraordinary woman known for her ability to open doors of communication and respect for The Church of Jesus Christ of Latter-day Saints. Among Latter-day Saint women, none has left a more indelible mark on world affairs than Beverly Campbell. Campbell's skills and gifts further developed and made a lasting impact on the international relations for the Church. She served as the director of the International Public Affairs Office in Washington, DC (1987–97), and her influence is still seen in Church organizations and the individuals who worked under her leadership.

For twelve years as she served as the director of International Affairs for the Church's Public and International Affairs Department in Washington, DC, she developed numerous programs and relationships still in place today. When asked how she was able to do all that she did, Campbell responded that she "had been prepared and trained from every step" of her life.[1]

MOVE TO WASHINGTON

When Campbell was thirty, she and her husband, Arwell Pierce Campbell, received job offers in New York, Los Angeles, and Chicago for positions in which Campbell felt certain their talents would be used. Despite the promise of these positions, she and her husband instead decided to move to Virginia to capitalize on a job offer for Pierce from a marketing firm. Campbell recalls the impracticality of their decision: "It made no sense. It made no sense at all. We just felt that was where we needed to be."[2]

REGIONAL PUBLIC AFFAIRS DIRECTOR

In 1984, Campbell was asked to be "the regional public affairs director for the Northeast Region" of the Church.[3] The Department of Public Affairs for the Church was created in 1970 by Spencer W. Kimball, President of the Quorum of the Twelve Apostles. In February of that year, President Kimball had met in New York with Church leaders and prominent Latter-day Saint businesspeople to discuss how the Church could respond to attacks and allegations regarding blacks and the priesthood and other issues. The result was the creation of two new departments: the Department of Internal Communications and the Department of Public Communications, later renamed the Department of Public Affairs. The purpose of Public Affairs was to "apprise the public of the policies, aims, and activities of the Church and to respond to questions raised about the Church and to attacks made on it."[4] The head of the department was located in Salt Lake City with regional directors located in each region of the Church. As regional director of the newly created office in Washington, DC, Campbell was responsible for developing contacts and fostering a "positive and accurate Church presence in the national and international media."[5] At first Campbell worked with the media in Washington to get stories about the Church into the news, but her work "quickly morphed" into the business of forming international relations.[6]

Change came when Campbell realized that "the shotgun approach of trying to reach individuals through media campaigns was less effective than getting accurate and useful information directly into the hands of policy makers in other countries." She found that because most countries

Pope Jean Paul II with Beverly Campbell in Rome.

viewed the Church as an American institution, when problems or questions arose concerning the Church in a particular country, government officials would consult their U.S. embassy for further information. The embassy staff, knowing little about the Church firsthand, would turn to the media, "often acquiring negative or misleading information that they did not have the means to adequately evaluate." Campbell determined that the best means of assuring that the Church was presented accurately would be to develop personal relations with the countries' ambassadors and provide them with firsthand knowledge. "Thus began the process of establishing personal contacts between ambassadors, prominent Church members in the Washington, DC, area, and the Church leaders responsible for various countries of the world"—a revolutionary approach for the Church.[7]

Initially, the hardest part of this approach was obtaining appointments with ambassadors and other government personnel[8] due to the Church's minimal ties. Fortunately, Campbell had previously been the director of the Joseph P. Kennedy Jr. Foundation, director of community relations for the Special Olympics, and the Church's spokesperson on the Equal Rights

Amendment. These previous positions provided her opportunities to form ties with many key people in the DC area. "I used members of Congress and senators, and CEOs—whoever I needed to get a door open."[9]

THE CHURCH'S UNOFFICIAL EMBASSY

One approach Campbell employed to form ties with necessary officials was to invite them one at a time to low-key dinners where they would meet well-known Church leaders, businesspeople, politicians, and others at her secluded home on the Potomac River in Virginia. The home was the fifth Campbell had designed and the largest, at 14,000 square feet.[10]

Campbell had begun building the home shortly before receiving her call to the Church Public Affairs Office. While the house was still under construction, Elder Royden G. Derrick of the First Quorum of the Seventy visited the house and told Campbell, "This house is being built for the Lord's purposes."[11] In fulfillment of Elder Derrick's pronouncement, Campbell's home became known as the unofficial embassy for the Church in Washington, DC. "I probably had a dinner party every ten days with one of the Brethren, a couple of CEOs, and nearly always a few congressmen, depending on what our objective was."[12] The dinners at her home provided the perfect atmosphere in which to develop personal relationships with her dinner guests. "They would often stay for long and substantive talks after dinner," she says. "That kind of interaction doesn't happen in more formal settings." As a result of these interactions, friendships and trust formed.[13] "It was amazing," Campbell recalls. "I saw a miracle a day."[14]

DIRECTOR OF INTERNATIONAL AFFAIRS

In 1987, Campbell's office gained the additional title of International Affairs.[15] The work of the International Affairs Department began in 1974 when President Kimball called David M. Kennedy "to assist the First Presidency with the explicit purpose of getting the Church into countries where it had no official presence." While Kennedy had worked with officials abroad, Campbell worked with the embassies in Washington, DC, to foster a positive media presence. When Kennedy's assignment ended, his work was absorbed by the Public Affairs Office, which was renamed the Office of Public and International Affairs. As director of that office, Campbell became "the key figure in obtaining for Church leaders an audience of government officials."[16] When international issues arose, they often found their way to Campbell's office,[17] where she would "marshal the resources and personnel necessary to address the issue,"[18] whether that issue was persecution of members, the inability of members to worship, or the forbiddance of missionaries in foreign countries.[19] She worked regularly with embassies and with the press and did a great deal of work with interfaith counsels, putting together interfaith events and conferences, all of which was "groundbreaking for the Church."[20]

PLANNING INTERNATIONAL EVENTS

With her new title and associated duties, Campbell's efforts to create contacts remained her primary focus. In addition to her home dinner parties, Campbell "nurtured relations with people internationally by having large events," developing many programs to acquaint ambassadors with the Church and to help them feel comfortable interacting with its members.[21] Among the most well-known events were the annual picnic at the Marriott Ranch, the annual Christmas parties at her home, and the temple lighting ceremony at the Washington D.C. Temple. Campbell would invite ambassadors from all over the world to these and other events.

Campbell began hosting the fall Western Family Picnic in October 1991. The event capitalized on the ambassadors' desires to have an event to which they could take their families. "There are so few opportunities for diplomatic families to participate together in the formal life of Washington," said Campbell to one newspaper reporter.[22] The annual event took place at the Marriott Ranch in Northern Virginia, where ambassadors and their families learned to dance the "Virginia Reel," rode ponies, played shuffleboard, and learned about the Church and its history—all while having an enjoyable day in the country.[23]

"This was one of the most beautiful days my family and I have spent in Washington," remarked Robert McClean, Peru's ambassador to the United States. Richard Marriott agreed to the annual event's success: "This gathering has produced more goodwill than countless Washington meetings."[24] The event was such a success that sometime later, several ambassadors at a reception approached Campbell with their personal calendars, wanting to "ensure their plans would not conflict with the annual barbecue picnic at the Marriott Ranch."[25]

Another popular event was the annual Christmas party that Campbell would host at her home with the Chinese embassy. Campbell "had an incredible number of very close relationships with Chinese government officials" and would invite the entire Communist Chinese embassy. "We'd have three to four hundred diplomats in the house singing Christmas hymns around the Christmas tree," recalls her son, Tom.[26] Campbell also had a tradition of making a birthday cake for Jesus on Christmas Eve, which she used as an opportunity to talk about Christmas and the beliefs of the Church. Tom says, "I'm sure there are thousands of Chinese that think that's part of the traditional Christmas ceremonies."[27] Campbell's Christmas party quickly became one of the most desired Washington invitations, second only to the Festival of Lights at the Washington D.C. Temple.

The Festival of Lights had its inauguration in 1978. The two-day Christmastime event began with a prayer at the visitors' center, after which eighty thousand lights would be turned on around the temple square. Campbell inaugurated a second ceremonial night of lighting in which a host ambassador would be asked to join a Church dignitary in turning on the lights. She also began the tradition of having Christmas trees decorated with traditional cultural items from countries around the world. The tradition began with each country being represented by a doll that was placed on a large Christmas tree in the visitors' center, which quickly mushroomed so that each country was represented with its own tree. The trees and the lighting ceremony helped to increase the visibility of the Church as an international organization.

The serene temple surrounded with lights also provided the perfect backdrop for introducing "international guests, members of the media, and local government, business and religious leaders," to the basic beliefs of the Church. [28] Campbell recalls one instance when Elder Neal A. Maxwell of the Quorum of the Twelve Apostles was the presiding Church dignitary. After the lighting, at a private reception for the ambassadors, an

African ambassador fell to his knees and cried, "You are an apostle. I know you are an apostle of the Lord."[29]

In addition to familiarizing others with the Church's beliefs, the event publicly confirmed the positive relations between the Church and foreign diplomats. Ten years after the first Festival of Lights, ambassadors and diplomats from more than fifty countries attended the 1988 Festival of Lights, including officials from Brazil, Columbia, Czechoslovakia, Guatemala, Hungary, South Africa, and the Soviet Union. "Also in attendance were numerous Congressmen, high officials in executive and judicial government positions, clergy from other churches, and reporters from local and international press organizations."[30] Campbell recalls, "I must have taken at least fifty or sixty ambassadors and their families to the temple. It got to be the big treat. When their children came they would call and say, "Will you take us to the temple?"[31]

Today, so many diplomats accept invitations to the Washington D.C. Temple lighting ceremony and other events that the occasions seem like UN sessions.[32] Through these large events and numerous more private meetings and interactions, Campbell "helped the ambassadorial community understand the Mormons were an integral part of the U.S. and that they weren't strange folk."[33] Following a day at the Marriott Ranch, Peru ambassador Robert Maclean remarked, "The Mormon people were warm and generous as anyone can imagine."[34]

As a result of Campbell's goodwill and hospitality, senators and representatives from Congress opened their doors to Church officials and representatives. Says Campbell, "My job was to create goodwill, to give them accurate, positive information so they would stand as our advocates in whatever court in their country they were standing in."[35] The task was not an easy one.

OPENING DOORS FOR THE CHURCH

During Campbell's time as director of the International Affairs office, the Cold War's iron curtain and the Communist suppression of religious activity seemed impenetrable barriers to the spreading of the Church and

Beverly Campbell, President George H. W. Bush, and Elder M. Russell Ballard.

the gospel. "Openings and opportunities were mercurial and fleeting," Campbell recalled.[36]

At first, getting just a finger in the door was a daunting and difficult task, but by 1985, "the Soviet empire's western edge had begun to slough the doctrine of Communism."[37] The Church got its hand in the door, then its foot, and then all at once it seemed, the door swung wide open. The tedious process of "first becoming acquainted with representatives of Eastern European nations in Washington, DC, and subsequently meeting their compatriots on the other side of the Atlantic had not only helped build bridges but also established trusting relationships that opened doors to the nations."[38] Working behind the scenes in the American embassies, Campbell was able to establish relations and set appointments for General Authorities to meet with the governing officials in Eastern Europe. "She paved the way for the entry of the gospel in Eastern Europe working with Bulgarians and East Germans and Albanians and Yugoslavians," her son recalls. "She was opening doors."[39]

OPENING CZECHOSLOVAKIA

Many, if not most, of the doors Campbell was able to open were due to the contacts she had made. One such connection was with Rabbi Arthur Schneier, head of an organization known as the Appeal of Conscience Foundation. Whenever leaders from European countries were in New York, Rabbi Schneier would invite Campbell to meet with them. Due to this network, in 1986 Campbell was able to arrange for Miroslav Houstecky, the Czechoslovak Soviet Socialist Republic's ambassador, to meet at her home with Elder Russell M. Nelson of the Quorum of the Twelve Apostles. After dinner, Houstecky and Elder Nelson retired to Campbell's study, where Elder Nelson was able to present the Church's desire to practice openly. Ambassador Houstecky agreed to lend his best efforts in arranging a consultation with the minister of religious affairs in Prague. The minister was a member of the Communist Party who oversaw religious activity within the Communist regime. He was the one to determine which churches could be recognized as legitimate organizations. Meeting with the minister was an essential step for the Church to gain recognition in the Czech Republic.[40]

Ambassador Houstecky was successful in arranging a meeting; however, it would be another four years of yearly meetings before, following the collapse of the Berlin Wall, the Church would be granted legal authority in the Czech Republic. The long-awaited call came from Ambassador Houstecky, who had been successful in arranging meetings soon to be held in Prague with the new deputy prime minister of the Republic of Prague. Within a month of the meeting, on 21 February 1990, papers were signed that granted the Church official recognition and ended forty years of waiting for the few and faithful Saints in the Czech Republic.[41]

OPENING ALBANIA

While the Saints in the Czech Republic had waited for recognition, the people of Albania had suffered similar depravations. During WWII, Albanian citizens lived in isolation under "a Communist tyrant as maniacal as any in history." In 1992 demonstrations and political unrest finally resulted in democratic developments and the election of a president, but when the door of the modern age opened on Europe, it slammed shut on Albania: "Over half the population did not have jobs, housing and food shortages forced two and three generations to live together in very small apartments, and the country's infrastructure was dilapidated and barely functioning."[42]

A year earlier, in 1991, Esat Ferra, an Albanian who defected, sought assistance for his country from the Austria Vienna Mission president Kenneth Reber. He provided the president with ten names of people that could assist the Church in helping Albania. These references later "proved to be the key in making contacts that gave the Church exposure at the highest levels of Albanian society."[43]

At the time, there were not yet any diplomatic relations between Albania and the United States. Campbell "contacted the Albanian UN delegation in New York to obtain permission for Church officials to enter the country" and made the necessary "arrangements with the Europe Area office in Frankfurt for the visit of Elder Dallin H. Oaks of the Quorum of the Twelve and Elder Hans B. Ringger, the area president. Nevertheless, when the two Church officials arrived at the Tirana airport in April 1991, they were not permitted to leave the plane." Campbell spent hours on the phone with Albania's UN office in New York and Albanian officials in Tirana. Through her efforts, the two were permitted to deplane.[44]

Six months later, Elder Ringger and others returned to Albania and explained to the Department of Agriculture their willingness to meet the nation's needs. Shortly thereafter, service workers flooded into the country. As a result of their presence, in 1992 Albania had its first convert to the Church. As Elder Ringger continued to meet with Albanian officials, he found them greatly impressed with the Church and its volunteers. In 1993, Elder Dallin H. Oaks flew to Albania to bless and dedicate the country for the spreading of the gospel.[45]

PICKING UP THE PACE AND OFFICE EXPANSION

After 1989, with the fall of the Berlin Wall, the pace at which the Church was welcomed into Europe grew exponentially. Campbell was at the home of her coworker Carolyn Ingersoll when she heard the news. "It's not possible!" she exclaimed. Campbell knew that the collapse of the wall would

Beverly Campbell hosting Nancy Reagan.

open up "many doors to the Church."[46] Indeed, many of the breakthroughs that Campbell was able to make for Church leaders came as a result of it. When asked which particular countries Campbell helped open, President M. Russell Ballard of the Quorum of the Twelve replied, "Every one that we had a challenge with."[47]

Changes were happening so fast that to keep aware and stay on top of them, Campbell and her office staff were reading newspapers daily. Every morning they would skim the *Washington Post*, the *Wall Street Journal*, and a couple other newspapers "to find out what was happening"[48] in each of the countries they were focusing on.

To help manage the influx of information and opportunities, Campbell began expanding the office and staff by identifying people who had expertise in certain areas. Each staff member was responsible for an area of the world based on the Church's assignment. They would keep Campbell abreast of the news in their assigned countries and help her arrange meetings and lunches with diplomatic representatives. She set a standard of high expectations for her staff. Said Carolyn Ingersoll, "She developed and ran in that office a very sophisticated, well-grounded, well-organized,

well-executed machine." She had developed a "procedure and a way of doing business for the Church that was very professional." With strong secre-
tarial support and hand-selected staff, Campbell was ready at the door for
the influx of diplomats that came in the wake of the fall of the Berlin Wall.

Always the visionary, Campbell understood that there would be many
new nations opening embassies in Washington and sending their ambassadors and that she would need to be prepared to meet them, saying, "All
these people are going to come and have ambassadorial or counselor presence in Washington, and we need to get to know them."[49] Over the next
few months, Campbell and her staff worked to locate the emerging embassies and become acquainted with the incoming ambassadors to Washington, DC.

Campbell's process of developing friendships with ambassadors and
other officials is still the program of the Church today. "Part of what we
still do is make friends for the Church that can be advocates for the Church
in their respective countries," remarked Elder Ralph W. Hardy Jr., an Area
Seventy who served as a stake president in DC at that time.[50] Throughout
the remainder of her life, Campbell still heard from people from all over
the world with whom she had worked during her time in the International
Affairs office. Nearly twenty years following her retirement, Campbell received an email from the deputy ambassador of the Soviet Union, who told
her how he still thought of his trips to Salt Lake City and their talks about
religion with great fondness.[51] Campbell also kept in touch with many ambassadors in China, Japan, the Soviet Union, and Ukraine.[52]

Campbell will be remembered as a pioneer, a dynamic leader, a powerful spokesperson, a wonderful representative of the Church, and a good
and faithful servant to the Lord and facilitator for leaders of the Church.[53]
During her tenure as director of International Affairs from 1987 to 1997,
the Church had "gained official recognition in thirty-nine countries and
new access to many more," with Campbell having fostered "many of the
initial contacts that opened those doors."[54] When Campbell had begun
work as director of the International Affairs office, "there were few ambassadors" that were known to the Church and "no established protocol for
gaining appointments with the government officials of foreign entities."

Now the Church has close ties with many ambassadors from a multitude of nations across Europe and the world.

At a time when international doors were mostly shut, Campbell had held a strong belief "that when the time is right for doors to open, they will open."[55] And open they did. President Ballard paid a fitting tribute when he said, "The Church of Jesus Christ of Latter-day Saints came out of the darkness publicly because of the great work of this good woman."[56]

NOTES

1. Beverly Campbell, interview by Mary Jane Woodger, 8 October 2010, Salt Lake City; transcription in author's possession.
2. Beverly Campbell, interview.
3. Susan Easton Black and Mary Jane Woodger, *Women of Character* (American Fork, UT: Covenant Communications, 2011), 59.
4. Francis M. Gibbons, *Spencer W. Kimball: Resolute Disciple, Prophet of God* (Salt Lake City: Deseret Book, 1995), 262.
5. Kahlile B. Mehr, "An LDS International Trio," *Journal of Mormon History* 25, no. 2 (Fall 1999): 114.
6. Carol Petranek, interview by Mary Jane Woodger, May 2019, Sandy, UT; transcription in author's possession.
7. Mehr, "LDS International Trio," 114.
8. Beverly Campbell, interview.
9. Beverly Campbell, interview.
10. Beverly Campbell, interview.
11. Beverly Campbell, interview.
12. Beverly Campbell, interview.
13. Lee Davidson, "'Ambassador' Opens Doors for LDS Church," *Deseret News*, 4 October 2010, 10.
14. Beverly Campbell, interview.
15. Mehr, "LDS International Trio," 114.
16. Kahlile B. Mehr, *Mormon Missionaries Enter Eastern Europe* (Salt Lake City: Deseret Book, 2002), 93, 158.
17. Mehr, "LDS International Trio," 118. See also Mark Campbell, interview by Mary Jane Woodger, May 2019, Sandy, UT; transcription in author's possession.
18. Beverly Campbell, interview.

19. Mark Campbell, interview.

20. Carol Petranek, interview.

21. Mark Campbell, interview.

22. Myrna Wahlquist, "Diplomats Get a Taste of Old West at Picnic," *Church News*, 26 October 1991, 11.

23. Black and Woodger, *Women of Character*, 59.

24. Wahlquist, "Diplomats Get a Taste of Old West," 11.

25. Davidson, "'Ambassador' Opens Doors for LDS Church," 10.

26. Mark Campbell, interview. See also Tom Campbell, interview by Mary Jane Woodger, May 2019, Sandy, UT; transcription in author's possession.

27. Mehr, "LDS International Trio," 114.

28. Kathryn Baer Newman, "Ambassador Helps Turn on Yule Lights," *Church News*, 12 December 1998, 6.

29. Beverly Campbell, interview by Mary Jane Woodger.

30. Lee Davidson, "Christmas Message Delivered through Tools of Goodwill," *Church News*, 17 December 1988, 9.

31. Beverly Campbell, interview.

32. Davidson, "'Ambassador' Opens Doors for LDS Church," 10.

33. Tom Campbell, interview.

34. Wahlquist, "Diplomats Get a Taste of Old West," 11.

35. Beverly Campbell, interview.

36. Spencer J. Condie, *Russell M. Nelson: Father, Surgeon, Apostle* (Salt Lake City: Deseret Book, 2003), 247.

37. Mehr, *Mormon Missionaries Enter Eastern Europe*, 111.

38. Condie, *Russell M. Nelson*, 255.

39. Tom Campbell, interview.

40. Condie, *Russell M. Nelson*, 250.

41. Condie, *Russell M. Nelson*, 252–53.

42. Mehr, *Mormon Missionaries Enter Eastern Europe*, 267.

43. Mehr, *Mormon Missionaries Enter Eastern Europe*, 267.

44. Mehr, "LDS International Trio," 118.

45. Mehr, *Mormon Missionaries Enter Eastern Europe*, 270–73.

46. Carolyn Ingersoll, interview by Mary Jane Woodger, May 2019, Sandy, UT; transcription in author's possession.

47. M. Russell Ballard, interview by Mary Jane Woodger, May 2019, Sandy, UT; transcription in author's possession.

48. Ingersoll, interview.

49. Ingersoll, interview.

50. Ralph W. Hardy Jr., interview by Mary Jane Woodger, May 2019, Sandy, UT; transcription in author's possession.

51. Beverly Campbell, interview.

52. Hardy, interview.

53. Petranek, interview. See also Wanda Franklin, interview by Brooke Anderson, May 2019, Provo, UT; transcription in author's possession. See also Mark Campbell, interview.

54. Davidson, "'Ambassador' Opens Doors for LDS Church," 10.

55. Petranek, interview.

56. M. Russell Ballard, interview.

Julian C. Lowe, Milan D. Smith, J. Willard Marriott, and Robert W. Barker, ca. 1970. Courtesy of Steven Lowe.

EIGHT LATTER-DAY SAINTS WHO MADE A DIFFERENCE IN WASHINGTON

RALPH W. HARDY JR.

Ralph W. Hardy Jr. is a former Area Seventy in the North America Northeast Area and a retired partner at Venable LLP who has lived more than seven decades in Washington, DC.

The 23 June 1940 formation of the Washington Stake (later the Washington D.C. Stake) by President Rudger Clawson and Elder Albert E. Bowen of the Quorum of the Twelve Apostles marked the beginning of a fifty-year era of substantial, sustained growth of The Church of Jesus Christ of Latter-day Saints in the greater Washington-Baltimore-Richmond metropolitan areas. A prime catalyst of this growth was the in-migration of several thousand Latter-day Saints from the West who came to serve in the burgeoning federal government operations, the many government servicing businesses, and the uniformed military services in connection with the United States' entry into World War II and its continuing Cold War aftermath. Another important catalyst was the direction and foresight of stake presidencies, bishoprics, mission presidents, and men's and women's auxiliary leaders who were called to plan for this growth and to lead the people.

This essay focuses on eight exceptional, interconnected Latter-day Saint leaders—all residents of Washington, DC—who occupied some of the most critical roles in planning for and implementing the growth, success, and recognition of the Church in the greater national capital area.[1]

These eight priesthood leaders are not the only Latter-day Saint leaders of undaunted faithfulness and distinction during that half century. They are, however, representative of the unusual quality and dedication of faithful Latter-day Saint leadership who made such a significant difference in the development and recognition of the Church during the fifty years between 1940 and 1990.

All of these eight men knew and respected each other; they worked together in many capacities; they learned from and supported each other; and each left an indelible mark on the rich history of what is today a significant concentration of Church membership in the eastern United States.

SNAPSHOT OF EIGHT LEADERS IN THE SPRING OF 1944

On 5 March 1944, **Ezra Taft Benson**, forty-five, raised in Whitney, Idaho, and having been ordained to the apostleship by President Heber J. Grant at the October 1943 general conference, was released as the first president of the Washington Stake of Zion, where he had served almost four years. That same day, **Edgar Bernard Brossard**, fifty-six, raised in Logan, Utah, was released as the first bishop of the landmark Washington Ward and set apart as second president of the Washington Stake. That year, **J. Willard Marriott**, forty-four, raised in Marriott-Slaterville, Utah, was serving as a member of the Washington Stake high council. Captain **Robert Whitney Barker**, twenty-five, from Ogden, Utah, of the U.S. Army's Second Armored Division and already a veteran of combat operations in North Africa and Sicily, waded ashore on Utah Beach through withering German fire on D-Day, 6 June 1944.[2] Two days later, first lieutenant **Julian Cassity Lowe**, twenty-six, from Orem, Utah, of the U.S. Army's 784th Automatic Weapons Battalion, waded chest deep through choppy waters in full battle gear toward Utah Beach on the Normandy Coast.[3] **Milan Dale Smith**, twenty-six, was a bishop in 1944, where he was supervising his family's significant canning and frozen vegetable operations in Pendleton, Oregon, packing harvested peas for the wartime American food supply and war effort. In March 1944, **J. W. Marriott Jr.**, twelve, was ordained a deacon in the Aaronic Priesthood in the Chevy Chase Ward of the Washington Stake.

William Donald Ladd, eleven, although not a member of the Church because of his Baptist father's stricture against his being baptized a Latter-day Saint, was attending the Palatka Ward in Florida in 1944.

EZRA TAFT BENSON (1899–1994)

When this great-grandson of Elder Ezra T. Benson (1811–69) of the Quorum of the Twelve Apostles arrived in Washington, DC, in 1939 to become executive secretary of the National Council of Farmer Cooperatives, an agricultural trade association, he brought with him his experience as the immediate former president of the Boise Stake in Idaho. In forming the new Washington Stake out of the Eastern States Mission, President Clawson and Elder Bowen extended a call to Ezra Taft Benson to be its first stake president, with Federal Reserve Board secretary Samuel R. Carpenter as first counselor and Washington attorney and future Brigham Young University president Ernest L. Wilkinson as second counselor. The geographical boundaries of the new stake included not only the Washington and Baltimore metropolitan areas but also extended south to Richmond, Virginia, and north to Fairview, Pennsylvania (close to Gettysburg).

With the benefit of his experience as stake president in Idaho, Ezra Taft Benson organized two wards in the District of Columbia as well as new wards in Chevy Chase, Maryland, and Arlington, Virginia, and new branches in Greenbelt, Annapolis, and Baltimore, Maryland.[4] In this fashion, President Benson created a basic, wide-area template for this vibrant new stake of the Church. In the aftermath of the Japanese surprise attack on Pearl Harbor, and as the nation's capital commenced preparations for the onset of the hostilities of World War II that had already engulfed Europe and Asia,[5] President Benson also set into motion a regimen of spiritual and temporal preparedness for the growing number of Latter-day Saints. This number included young people from the military who came to train and government workers who came to reside in the greater Washington area.[6] In this President Benson was assisted not only by his able counselors but also by other priesthood leaders of great capacity such as future treasury secretary David Kennedy and restauranteur J. Willard Marriott. Benson's

Ezra Taft Benson. U.S. Department of Agriculture.

service as an energetic stake president was only his first act in building the Church in the nation's capital. After Dwight D. Eisenhower was elected the thirty-fourth president of the United States in 1952, he brought Benson into his cabinet as the Secretary of Agriculture. This cabinet assignment required Elder Benson, now an Apostle, to return to Washington on a full-time basis for the entire eight years of Eisenhower's presidency and led him to become—like Senator Reed Smoot before him—Washington's resident Apostle. In this capacity, Secretary Benson was an encouraging presence in sacrament, stake conference, and other meetings. Those of us who grew up in Washington remember Secretary Benson well because we saw him often at our Church activities. In my own case, at a Boy Scout court of honor held in the Chevy Chase Ward, Elder Benson was on the stand and presented me with my Star Scout rank. In a quarterly Washington Stake conference meeting, stake president J. Willard Marriott made a humorous comment to the congregation that, because Secretary Benson was sitting on the stand, a *Washington Post* reporter was probably in the congregation. In fact, on Monday morning, the *Washington Post* carried a brief report of Secretary Benson's attendance and his remarks to the stake conference.

At a large 2015 fireside commemorating the seventy-fifth anniversary of the organization of the Washington D.C. Stake, Russell M. Nelson, then President of the Quorum of the Twelve Apostles, reminisced:

> President Ezra Taft Benson spoke at my farewell when I was released as a member of the bishopric [of the Washington Ward]. He was then in the Cabinet, as you know. And after the meeting was over, he said, "Brother Nelson, you're going to Boston, aren't you? Where are you going?" "To Massachusetts General Hospital to resume my surgical career and training." He said, "Well, when you go up there maybe you'll find a fine surgeon named Robert Walker. Look after him, would you?" So, I went up to Boston and looked after Robert Walker, who later married one of President Benson's daughters. So, there is a prophet, there is a seer![7]

EDGAR BERNARD BROSSARD (1889-1980)

Edgar B. Brossard succeeded Benson as the Washington Stake's president. Brossard was born in Oxford, Idaho, and grew up in Logan, Utah, where he graduated from Utah State University. He received his master's and PhD degrees from the University of Minnesota. Since the organization

Edgar Bernard Brossard, an economist, served as a member (and twice chairman) of the U.S. Tariff Commission. Public domain.

of the Washington Stake on 23 June 1940, Brossard had served as the first and much-loved bishop of the Washington Ward, located in the beautiful landmark chapel at Sixteenth Street and Columbia Road, N.W. In his professional career, President Brossard served as a member of the Federal Tariff Commission (now known as the International Trade Commission) from the time he was appointed by President Calvin Coolidge and subsequently reappointed by President Herbert Hoover (who designated him as chairman), Franklin D. Roosevelt, Harry S. Truman, and Dwight D. Eisenhower (who again designated Edgar Brossard as chairman). His thirty-eight years of continuous service made Edgar Brossard the longest-serving commissioner in the history of the Federal Tariff Commission.[8]

Edgar and Laura Cowley Brossard[9] lived in a comfortable apartment directly across Sixteenth Street from the Washington Ward Chapel. They opened their home—a "church crossroads"—as a gathering place for all, especially for the large number of young single adult members coming through Washington in connection with their service in the military, to work in the federal government, or to attend local universities. The Washington Ward was, to a large extent, what would today be referred to as the young single adult ward for the greater Washington area.

President Brossard was an affable, big bear of a man with a ready smile and a firm, friendly handshake. Both as bishop and then as stake president, President Brossard was very much a wise and loving pastoral leader in a stake with boundaries that stretched from Richmond, Virginia, on the south, to southern Pennsylvania on the north. During President Brossard's tenure, the Richmond Virginia Branch grew to be a ward. In May 1945, the membership of the Washington Stake was 2,928,[10] and the Capitol Ward in northeast Washington was organized; the construction of the Arlington Virginia Ward commenced; and a new branch was created in Fredericksburg, Virginia.[11] Following President Brossard's retirement from the Federal Trade Commission, he served as president of the New England Mission and the French Mission.[12]

J. WILLARD MARRIOTT (1900-1985)

John Willard "Bill" Marriott served in various Church roles, including full-time missionary in the Eastern States Mission, high councilor, counselor to stake president Edgar Brossard and, on 12 December 1948, third president of the Washington Stake. He served for nine years during a time of very substantial growth of the Church in Washington and its environs.

Marriott possessed enormous stature, was widely admired in the nation's capital, and was recognized not only as the Latter-day Saints' preeminent ecclesiastical leader but also as one of the region's most successful business entrepreneurs and popular employers. As stake president, and with his easy, affable, and rancher-like delivery, President Marriott spoke the language of the common member. Like a favorite wise uncle, he was easy to listen to, easy to follow, and easy to emulate.

Lee Roderick, a former Latter-day Saint president of the White House Correspondents Association, probably described President Marriott best:

> It would be difficult to overstate the contributions of J. Willard Marriott, Sr. to the growth of the Church. He and his young bride, the former Alice Sheets, came to Washington in 1927 to seek their fortune. Through hard work and adherence to high principles, they prospered and became a Washington legend. Today, the acorn of a root beer stand they planted over a half century ago has grown into the mighty oak of the Marriott Corporation, a multinational lodging and food service business that, in 1989, was one of the nation's top ten private employers. The Marriott family has contributed generously to the work of the Lord in Washington and throughout the Church, in-

cluding their contribution to the building of the Washington Temple and the Visitors Center.[13]

During Marriott's tenure as stake president, the Washington Stake continued to grow within its unchanged, broad geographical boundaries. The venue for stake conferences outgrew the Washington Ward Chapel and was moved to George Washington University's Lisner Auditorium.

One of President Marriott's sustained efforts was to urge the First Presidency to consider the future construction of a temple in the Washington area. In his March 1954 letter to the First Presidency, he noted there were seventy thousand members east of the Mississippi who would be served by such a temple. President Marriott concluded, "A temple would be a real strength and a blessing to all of us who live in the East."[14]

At the seventy-fifth anniversary of the creation of the Washington Stake held on 20 November 2015, President Nelson reminisced about his former stake president:

> Bill and Allie Marriott; what a surprise it was one day when I went to the stake president's office on the second floor of the Washington Ward (Sixteenth Street and Columbia Road) and there was President J. Willard Marriott who extended a call to me to be a counselor in the bishopric of that ward. How I love that man and his dear wife and their family! They're still very dear and close to me. President Marriott was ably assisted by two great counselors, Samuel Carpenter and Frank Kimball. We had such a wonderful experience in the bishopric.[15]

When President Marriott died in 1985, his funeral service was held in the Washington D.C. Stake Center, located next to the Washington D.C. Temple that he worked so hard to see come to fruition. Among the speakers at the funeral conducted by stake president J. W. Marriott Jr. were President Ezra Taft Benson of the Quorum of the Twelve Apostles, the Reverend Billy Graham, former president Richard M. Nixon,[16] and President Gordon B. Hinckley of the First Presidency.

MILAN DALE SMITH (1919-87)

On 30 November 1957, Elder Spencer W. Kimball of the Quorum of the Twelve Apostles called Milan D. Smith from the high council to succeed J. Willard Marriott as president of the Washington Stake, with Joseph Tippets and Robert W. Barker as counselors. President Smith was working as executive assistant to Secretary Benson. Previously Smith had served as president of the Union Stake in Le Grande, Oregon, then had left his frozen vegetable–packing company in the day-to-day care of a trusted assistant in order to commence his government service in Washington. He served a record thirteen years as stake president. When President Smith commenced his presidency, the Washington Stake still encompassed the same southern Pennsylvania to northern Virginia geography, with a growing number of wards and branches. Six new wards were created during the first five years of his presidency—the Fairfax, Mount Vernon, McLean, and Falls Church Wards in Virginia and the Baltimore Second and Rock Creek Wards in Maryland.

A historic change in the organization of the Church in the greater Washington metropolitan area occurred on 3 March 1963 when the Potomac Stake was created to include all of the wards and branches in Northern Virginia. This division, with its northern boundary along the Potomac River, launched a stake that would grow at a faster pace than the wards and branches on the Maryland and District of Columbia side of the Potomac River.

After concluding his duties as executive assistant to Secretary Benson, Milan Smith accepted several important leadership roles with the National Canners Association in Washington, where he eventually became its chief executive officer.

Robert W. Barker, his former first counselor and a regional representative of the Twelve, noted Smith's significant efforts to convince the First Presidency of the need to build a temple in the Washington area as soon as possible:

> At the first official meeting of the Washington Presidency in December 1957, Milan made known his desire to do all possible to have the church establish a temple in the nation's capital. There then was no

temple in the United States or Canada east of Salt Lake. The Salt Lake Temple was almost two thousand miles away. After obtaining permission to write all stakes and missions east of the Mississippi, we did so asking how they felt about a Washington Temple. The responses were all favorable, but many said the next temple should be in their hometown. It was certainly due to Milan's leadership and persistence that the First Presidency of the Church authorized us to acquire a site. Under Milan's leadership, our committee and church officials considered thirty-one sites. When we purchased the 57.4 acres in 1962, we were instructed to call it only a lot for future church use. President McKay made it clear that he did not wish to bind his successor to any project not started in President McKay's lifetime.[17]

After ground was broken for the Washington Temple on 7 December 1968, the First Presidency called President Smith to be chairman of the temple committee.

Additional wards and branches were created by President Smith in Aberdeen, Carrollton, Fort Meade-Laurel, Annapolis, Hagerstown, Frederick, Catonsville, Potomac, and Kensington, Maryland. In addition, the stake welfare farm holdings were changed in a significant way while President Smith presided over the Washington Stake. A dairy farm in suburban northern Virginia that was situated close to the planned Dulles International Airport was sold at an advantageous price, and a new dairy farm near Trappe, Maryland, on the Delmarva Peninsula was acquired. The farm was named Bountiful Farm and would become the largest dairy operation in the state of Maryland. Bountiful Farm was operating so successfully that it was later taken over directly and operated by the Church welfare system.

After Smith's release as stake president in September 1970, he was called by the First Presidency as president of the England London Mission.

When asked what he best remembers about his father's tenure as stake president of the Washington Stake, his eldest son, U.S. Circuit Court of Appeals Judge Milan D. Smith Jr., responded, "My father was a bishop at twenty-two in Oregon and then stake president twice. I remember that he was a builder—he loved finding suitable building sites and constructing new meetinghouses to address the Saints' needs."[18]

ROBERT WHITNEY BARKER (1919-87)

Robert W. Barker came to Washington from Ogden, Utah. His father and grandfather were significant figures in the law, his grandfather being a judge. During World War II, Bob Barker became an officer in the U.S. Army's 6th Armored Field Artillery Battalion. He was in heavy combat in North Africa and then in Sicily before going to England to train for the invasion of Normandy. He continued in combat operations under the command of General George Patton until Germany surrendered in 1945. When the war concluded, Bob Barker, then a major, left the army and returned to Ogden.

When he graduated from the Georgetown Law School in Washington, Bob received the Lucey Medal in recognition for graduating first in his class—where he was also an editor of the *Law Review*. After a short time practicing law with his father in Utah, Bob returned to Washington, joining the law firm headed by renowned attorney Ernest L. Wilkinson, where he specialized in various matters before the government, including significant claims filed by Native American tribes. Following Senator Wallace F. Bennett's election to the U.S. Senate in 1950, Bob Barker became his administrative assistant (chief of staff) for one year and then rejoined the Wilkinson law firm, where he became a name partner.

Stake president J. Willard Marriott called Bob Barker to be bishop of the Chevy Chase Ward until its division, when he became the first bishop of the new Silver Spring Ward. When Milan D. Smith was called to succeed Marriott as stake president, Smith called Bob as his counselor, where he served ten years. In 1967 Barker was called by the First Presidency to be in the first group of sixty-seven regional representatives of the Twelve, where he assumed oversight responsibilities with many of the stakes in the middle Atlantic area of the Church, which included the national capital area.

In connection with the efforts of Presidents Marriott and Smith to have the First Presidency approve the construction of a temple in Washington, Bob Barker assumed the principal role in the finding, due diligence, purchase negotiations, governmental approval process, and adjacent neighborhood acceptance of the placement of the proposed temple. The account of Barker's successful, herculean efforts to acquire this 57.4-acre wooded tract and secure all of the required governmental and neighborhood approvals was related by President Hinckley at Bob Barker's 6 January 1988 funeral service at the Washington D.C. Stake Center:

> As I came here from the Marriott Dulles Hotel this morning, I drove and saw the spires of the temple as they came into view. I said to myself, "That temple stands where it does because of Robert W. Barker." He was the one who negotiated the purchase of this acreage here. He was the one who fought the fight with the zoning commission. He was the one who set up neighborhood meetings with the people of this community who had some strong feelings against the construction of the temple here. Bob ameliorated those feelings and overcame the opposition and won the concurrence of those who reside in this vicinity. The temple stands where it stands in this beautiful section predominant and magnificent because of the labors of the man we honor today. That may not be widely known. That is the fact and we are all blessed by reason of that. How fitting it is that he should serve as temple president and finish out his life in that capacity. I am so grateful that he had that privilege and opportunity.[19]

Barker was a highly competent and influential attorney. He was part of a class of practitioners in the Washington legal establishment who were often referred to as "super-lawyers." Not only was Barker the senior partner of a prestigious Washington law firm, but he also represented with great skill many clients involved in complex matters of considerable moment. During the Watergate proceedings, for example, Barker was retained to represent, successfully, one of the defendants, former Nixon secretary of commerce Maurice Stans. For many years Bob Barker was also general counsel and senior vice president of Bonneville International Corporation, the Church's for-profit corporate entity that owns and operates radio and television stations KSL AM-FM-TV as well as other broadcast stations throughout the United States. He also served as general counsel of the Nixon presidential inaugurals held in 1969 and 1973.

In addition to his efforts to secure the purchase and approvals for the temple, it was through Bob Barker's eleven years as a regional representative and in his membership on the Church's Special Affairs Committee that he had a significant impact on the growth and development of the

Church in the eastern states, including the stakes proximate to the national capital area. His distinguished Church service concluded with his presidency of the Washington D.C. Temple.

JULIAN CASSITY LOWE (1917-2002)

Born in Provo, Utah, Julian Lowe spent his formative years in Orem. After returning from the Western States Mission and with the onset of World War II, he was inducted into the U.S. Army in June 1942, planning to be part of the Medical Corps. Instead, Julian was assigned to an antiaircraft training unit. When the Army sensed his maturity and leadership qualities, Julian was offered an invitation to attend the U.S. Army Officer Candidate School where he graduated, became a second lieutenant, and was assigned to the 784th Automatic Weapons Battalion. Thereafter, Julian was sent to England and prepared to be part of the Allies' D-Day Normandy invasion of France. After wading ashore on Utah Beach just after D-Day, his antiaircraft battalion commenced combat operations and engaged Luftwaffe aircraft that were threatening the Allied advance. His battalion fought its way through France, Belgium, Holland, and Germany until the war ended in April 1945. His unit had advanced as far as Hanover by the time of the German surrender.

On returning to the United States after the war ended, Julian Lowe, now a U.S. Army captain, married Nola Kotter. After receiving his master's degree from Brigham Young University, Julian was recruited to join the Central Intelligence Agency and moved to the Washington, DC, area, where he spent most of his professional career with that agency. Although originally living in Washington's Maryland suburbs, the Lowes moved in 1958 to northern Virginia. After several Church assignments, President Milan D. Smith called Julian Lowe in November 1961 as bishop of the newly formed McLean Virginia Ward. He immediately began to make plans and raise funds for the construction of the ward's new chapel.

In connection with the reorganization of the Potomac Stake presidency in January 1967, Elder Harold B. Lee of the Quorum of the Twelve Apostles called Julian Lowe to be the new stake president following the departure of President Miller Shurtleff to fulfill a National Science

Foundation assignment in India. The Potomac Stake covered all of the wards and branches in northern Virginia.

This was an era of exceptionally rapid Church growth in northern Virginia—which was still growing disproportionally faster than the stakes on the Maryland–District of Columbia side of the Potomac River.[20] During his ten-year tenure as president of the Potomac Stake,[21] Julian Lowe was deeply involved in the planning for the development of the church in Northern Virginia as new wards and stakes were created. He was released in September 1975 when President Marion G. Romney of the First Presidency extended a call to President Lowe to serve as a regional representative and was assigned responsibility for the Toronto Canada and New York–New Jersey Regions. In 1977, however, Elder Lowe's regional representative assignment was changed so that he had responsibility for the Capitol and Potomac Regions, which included the greater Washington area.

In connection with the construction of the Washington Temple, Julian Lowe was assigned in the late 1960s to serve as one of the eleven members of the finance committee charged with raising funds for the new edifice. In 1970, following the release of President Smith, Julian Lowe became chairman of the Washington Temple Committee.[22] His responsibilities as chairman were specified by the First Presidency as follows:

> (1) working with the Church Building Department in the preparation of the building plans and specifications, construction, landscaping, decorating, furnishing and equipping [of] the building; (2) making arrangements for the cornerstone services and laying of the cornerstone; (3) planning and managing the public preview, (4) planning and executing the dedicatory services; and (5) providing for the arrangements for all General Authorities and official visitors coming to the area for the completion ceremonies, for press conferences, for the public preview, and for the dedicatory services.[23]

Once the Washington Temple was dedicated, however, Julian Lowe reminisced that his responsibilities were not at an end:

> Although the opening of the Temple terminated the Washington Temple committee, I still had a role to play as chairman of the fi-

nance committee. By this time, we had raised all our monies for the construction of the Temple, but the Visitors' Center was yet to be built. The plans for the Center had already been completed, and the building was to cost $1,500,000. The Church was to pay a third, and the rest was to be collected from within the Temple District. J. Willard Marriott, Sr., who had already contributed heavily towards the construction of the Temple, volunteered to contribute one-half of the local share. This reduced our local assessment to $500,000. By the time the Visitors' Center was completed in June 1976, all our monies had been raised and the building was ready to be dedicated.[24]

J. W. (BILL) MARRIOTT JR. (1932-PRESENT)

In December 1982, thirty-four years after his father, J. Willard Marriott, became the third president of the Washington D.C. Stake, J.W. "Bill" Marriott Jr. was called by President Ezra Taft Benson, then President of the Quorum of the Twelve Apostles, as eighth president of the Washington D.C. Stake of Zion—like father, like son. J. W. Marriott Jr. had been first counselor to the previous stake president, Leonidas Ralph Mecham.[25]

Already one of America's most accomplished, visionary, and highly recognized business leaders, Bill served as president and chief executive officer of Marriott Corporation, a worldwide lodging enterprise founded by his legendary parents that operated hotels and restaurants and provided other commercial services such as airline food catering and industrial feeding facilities. In 1985, following his father's death at age eighty-five, Bill Marriott Jr. became chairman in

J. W. (Bill) Marriott Jr. Courtesy of the Marriott International Archives.

addition to his position as president and chief executive officer of Marriott Corporation.[26]

Like his distinguished father, Bill has been equally yoked and committed to the fulfillment of his many assignments to lead in The Church of Jesus Christ of Latter-day Saints. Beginning in 1975 until 2011, he was successively involved in Church leadership as bishop of the Chevy Chase Ward, stake president's counselor, president of the Washington D.C. Stake, regional representative, and Area Seventy. As a regional representative and member of the Seventy, in particular, Elder Marriott fulfilled his assigned responsibilities with the stakes in the greater Washington, DC, and Richmond, Virginia, regions of the Church as well as throughout the eastern part of the United States and Canada. In addition, for the past forty-two years since its commencement, Elder Marriott has been chairman, host, and speaker at all the Festival of Lights opening ceremonies held at the Washington D.C. Temple Visitors' Center at the beginning of each Christmas season. This program has become a well-recognized, signature Christmas event in the Washington metropolitan area where ambassadors and staff from the resident diplomatic community as well as members of Congress are in attendance.

During his eight-year stake presidency and thereafter as a long-term regional leader of the Church from 1990 to 2011, Elder Marriott has been one of the most influential and admired Latter-day Saints in the Washington community and throughout the country. On many occasions of importance to the Church, Elder Marriott has appeared on national television and been featured in print, electronic, and social media not only professionally in connection with his worldwide lodging business but also in support and defense of the Church and its prophetic leadership.[27]

Elder Marriott is a gifted, always well-prepared speaker and teacher of the restored gospel. Many years ago, Stephen Garff Marriott, his late eldest son, told me that he was sure very few people knew how hard his father worked to craft the many Church addresses he gave as bishop, stake president, regional representative, and Area Seventy. Stephen added that with many of his father's talks Elder Marriott would—even on long trips aboard his corporate aircraft—research the scriptures and then go through repeated drafts for as long as twenty hours until he was satisfied that he was well enough prepared to deliver the message he felt inspired to give to the Latter-day Saints.

WILLIAM DONALD LADD (1933–2009)

Don Ladd grew up in the rural Florida town of Palatka. His mother was a member of The Church of Jesus Christ of Latter-day Saints. His father was Southern Baptist and, although Don was allowed to attend Latter-day Saint meetings in the Palatka Ward, his father forbade him from being baptized into the Church. When Don turned nineteen and prepared to en- ter college at the University of Florida to pursue a degree in chemical engi- neering, he informed his father that, as a responsible adult, he intended to join the Church and be baptized. To a significant extent, Don Ladd cred- ited Woodrow W. Tilton, his wise Palatka Ward bishop, for his mentoring role and encouragement in the Church.[28]

After a European tour of duty with the U.S. Army, Don Ladd moved to Washington with a recommendation from Bishop Tilton and became a legislative assistant and then chief of staff to a Florida member of Congress. While in Washington Don Ladd attended the Washington Ward, where he met and married Ruth Pearson, who was working for U.S. sen- ator Wallace F. Bennett. After working on Capitol Hill, Don Ladd joined the U.S. Depart- ment of Agriculture, where he handled liaison with Congress and the White House.

In time, Don Ladd was called by President Milan D. Smith to serve on the Washington D.C. Stake high council. In June 1970 President Smith called Don Ladd as the first bishop of the new Po- tomac Ward in the Washington D.C. Stake; however, after less

William Donald Ladd as a stake president. Courtesy of Ralph W. Hardy Jr.

than a year, he was called as second counselor in the stake presidency to new stake president Wendell G. Eames.[29] When President Eames was released as stake president in 1974 to become first counselor in the first Washington Temple presidency, Don Ladd became the sixth president of the Washington D.C. Stake.

In 1973 Gordon B. Hinckley called President Don Ladd to serve as chairman of the newly organized Washington Special Affairs Committee. He was instructed to report directly to Elder Hinckley, who was chairman of the Special Affairs Committee at Church headquarters in Salt Lake City. This committee was later renamed Washington Public Affairs Committee. Over the years it has been staffed by Latter-day Saint men and women of stature with broad experience in and with government as well as in relationships with the resident diplomatic community of ambassadors and other international agencies in Washington. With the resources and experience of the Washington Public Affairs Committee, Don Ladd was able to convey information and advice to the Church's senior leadership with respect to matters in Washington that affected—or may affect—the vital interests of the Church. Elder Don Ladd chaired the Washington Public Affairs Committee for thirteen years, ending in 1994.

A significant task undertaken by Don Ladd was his due diligence and work with the Public Affairs Department and other senior General Authorities to expand the Public Affairs Office in Washington in order to address the opportunities to work more closely with the resident diplomatic community. In this connection, Elder Ladd worked closely with Beverly Campbell and others to acquire an office in the National Press Building as well as a full-time staff of capable people to handle liaison with congressional offices and Washington embassies.

As stake president Don Ladd also took a leading role in planning for the Church's 1976 bicentennial celebration, which involved all of the stakes in the greater Washington area. These efforts resulted in a special gathering of twenty thousand Latter-day Saints in the Capital Center and a concert presented by the Osmond family. Following his release as stake president in 1977, Don Ladd was called as a regional representative, where he assumed a more significant role in the leadership of the Church in the greater Washington, DC, area.

On 2 April 1994, Elder Ladd was called as a member of the Second Quorum of the Seventy.

CONCLUSION

Within a half century (1940–89), each of these eight men became exceptional Latter-day Saint leaders who were essential to the success of the Church in the greater Washington area. All were visionary builders who possessed the foresight to anticipate what the Church would need and could become. Of the eight leaders, two became General Authorities, four became regional representatives or Area Seventies, two became mission presidents, and two—father and son—came to be numbered among America's most successful entrepreneurial business leaders while, at the same time, contributing generously their time and means to the service, care, and leadership of the Church. Not one of the eight sought these responsibilities, because each knew he had been "called of God, by prophecy, and by the laying on of hands by those who are in authority, to preach the Gospel and administer in the ordinances thereof."[30]

APPENDIX

NINE APOSTLES WHO RESIDED
AND WORKED IN WASHINGTON, DC

Since November 1839, many Latter-day Saint leaders of apostolic rank have journeyed to Washington, DC, to meet with presidents of the United States, members of the United States Senate and House of Representatives, testify before congressional committees, attend receptions and presidential inaugurations, advocate on matters of vital interest to the Church, interact with foreign diplomats, and publish broadsheet tracts. These apostolic visitors include Joseph Smith Jr., Orson Pratt, George Q. Cannon, Joseph F. Smith, Heber J. Grant, George Albert Smith, David O. McKay, Spencer W. Kimball, Gordon B. Hinckley, Neal A. Maxwell, Dieter F. Uchtdorf, James E. Faust, M. Russell Ballard, and many others. Significantly, nine Apostles, including two future Presidents of the Church, have worked and resided in Washington.

1. **Reed Smoot** was a U.S. senator from Utah for thirty years (1903–33). He was a towering figure in the Senate and a confidant of Presidents Theodore Roosevelt, William Howard Taft, Warren G. Harding, Calvin Coolidge, and Herbert Hoover. Among other legislative assignments, he chaired the powerful Senate Finance Committee. Senator Smoot was a catalytic force in the development and establishment of The Church of Jesus Christ of Latter-day Saints in the Washington, DC, metropolitan area. His personal residence provided the initial venue for Latter-day Saint sacrament meetings and Sunday Schools. In addition, Reed Smoot was the moving force in identifying, negotiating, and helping the Church to acquire and construct the historic Washington Chapel on Sixteenth Street and Columbia Road, N.W.

Reed Smoot. © Intellectual Reserve, Inc.

2. **J. Reuben Clark Jr.** served as assistant so-
    licitor, solicitor (general counsel), and un-
    dersecretary of state before becoming U.S.
    ambassador to Mexico and then second
    counselor to President Heber J. Grant in the
    First Presidency of the Church in 1933. Pre-
    viously he had served on the general board
    of the Young Men's Mutual Improvement As-
    sociation. While serving as undersecretary
    of state, Clark authored the seminal *Clark*
    Memorandum on the Monroe Doctrine.

J. Reuben Clark Jr.
© Intellectual Reserve, Inc.

3. **Ezra Taft Benson** was executive secretary of
    the National Council of Farmer Cooperatives,
    a major Washington, DC-based farmers' trade
    association. He was the first president of the
    Washington Stake, serving for almost four
    years until released to devote himself full-time
    to the apostleship to which he had been called
    and ordained by President Heber J. Grant. In
    January 1953, while a member of the Quo-
    rum of the Twelve Apostles, Elder Benson
    was summoned to Washington by President
    Dwight D. Eisenhower to serve for eight years
    as the secretary of agriculture.

Ezra Taft Benson in 1955.
© Intellectual Reserve, Inc.

4. **Neal A. Maxwell** came to Washington, DC, in
    1952. His biographer, Elder Bruce C. Hafen,
    wrote that Neal Maxwell "wanted to find out
    for himself what it was like to be at the very
    center of political process, policy, and pow-
    er."[31] He worked first as an economic analyst
    with a government intelligence department. A
    little more than one year later, Neal Maxwell
    joined Senator Wallace F. Bennett's small
    staff, where he became an effective legislative

Neal A. Maxwell.
Photo by Boyart Studios,
Colleen Hinckley Maxwell.

assistant and learned the arts of crafting legislation, forging compromise, and political advocacy. During four years in Washington, the involvement of Elder Maxwell and his wife, Colleen, in the Washington Stake "would turn out to be an important bonus, expanding their vision and attitudes about life among a community of Saints."[32] Elder Maxwell served in the Washington Stake Young Men presidency and then in the stake mission presidency.

5.   **Russell M. Nelson** became an officer in the U.S. Army during the Korean War because of the desperate need for physicians in the military. With the benefit and experience of his surgical training, President Nelson was stationed in Washington, DC,[33] where he formed a surgical research unit at the Walter Reed National Military Medical Center.[34] During his tenure in the nation's capital, President Nelson was called to serve as second counselor in the bishopric of the Washington Ward.[35] Of this experience, President Nelson reminisced, "Bill and Allie Marriott; what a surprise it was one day

Russell M. and Dantzel Nelson. Photo by Eldon Keith Linchoten. © Intellectual Reserve, Inc.

when I went to the stake president's office on the second floor of the Washington Ward (16th Street and Columbia Road) and there was President J. Willard Marriott who extended a call to me to be a counselor in the bishopric of that ward."[36]

6. Following his graduation from law school, **Dallin H. Oaks** was law clerk to Chief Justice Earl Warren of the U.S. Supreme Court in Washington, DC. President Rex E. Lee of Brigham Young University (and former solicitor general of the United States) described President Oaks's twelve-month service at the U.S. Supreme Court: "Elder Dallin H. Oaks has had a brilliant professional career. He was the Editor-in-Chief of the *University of Chicago Law Review* and he served as a law clerk to Chief Justice [Earl] Warren on the United States Supreme Court—which is the equivalent of making All-American for a law student."[37] During his work at the Supreme Court, President Oaks, his wife, June, and their children were members of the Washington Stake.

Dallin H. Oaks, ca. 1971. University Archives, L. Tom Perry Special Collections, Harold B. Lee Library, Brigham Young University.

7. **Richard G. Scott** moved to Washington with his parents from Idaho when he was four years old and spent his growing-up years in Washington attending public schools and then George Washington University. He left for his mission to Uruguay from the Chevy Chase Ward. Professionally, Elder Scott became a member of the elite engineering staff in Washington run by Admiral Hyman Rickover, where he worked on nuclear propulsion systems for the U.S. Navy. Following his service as president of the Argentina North

Richard G. Scott in uniform. © Intellectual Reserve, Inc.

Young Richard G. Scott (left) with brothers Walter and Gerald. © *Intellectual Reserve, Inc.*

Mission (where he was Elder D. Todd Christofferson's mission president), Elder Scott returned to Washington to join some of his former Rickover colleagues working in submarine nuclear propulsion. Elder Scott served as a stake missionary, stake clerk, and first counselor in the Washington D.C. Stake presidency before being called as a regional representative of the Twelve and then as a General Authority.

8.   **D. Todd Christofferson** came to Washington, DC, following graduation from Duke University Law School (where he was an editor of The Duke Law Journal) to serve as law clerk to Chief Judge

U.S. District Chief Judge John J. Sirica, left, talks with his law clerk D. Todd Christofferson on 3 August 1974, in Washington. Intellectual Reserve, Inc.

John J. Sirica of the U.S. District Court for the District of Columbia. His tenure with Judge Sirica was extended beyond the usual one year to two and a half years because of the pendency of the epic Nixon Watergate case.[38] Elder Christofferson thereafter joined the Dow Lohnes & Albertson law firm in Washington, DC. After serving as a high councilor, Elder Christofferson became bishop of the Rockville (Maryland) Ward, Washington D.C. Stake. In 1980, Elder Christofferson relocated to Nashville, Tennessee, where he became senior vice president and General Counsel of Commerce Union Bank and, thereafter, Associate General Counsel of NationsBank (now Bank of America) in Charlotte, North Carolina, before his call as a General Authority Seventy in 1993.

9.   **Gerrit W. Gong** is a *summa cum laude* graduate of Brigham Young University and an Oxford University Rhodes Scholar, receiving his PhD and master of philosophy degrees in international relations. With this sterling academic background, Elder Gong spent more than twenty years living in Washington, DC. He served at the internationally preeminent defense and national security think tank, the Center for Strategic and International Studies (CSIS), where

he became Asia director and China chair. In addition, Elder Gong served as special assistant to the undersecretary of state as well as special assistant to two U.S. ambassadors to China. While in Washington, Elder Gong also served and traveled with congressional delegations visiting Asia. In addition, he served as special adviser to the chief justice of the U.S. Supreme Court during his official visit to Asia. During Elder Gong's long tenure in Washington, he served in the Church as an early-morning seminary instructor, high councilor in the McLean Virginia Stake, and bishop of the McLean First Ward.

Gerrit W. Gong.
Courtesy Susan Gong.

NOTES

1. Of course, there are many men and women who have contributed to the building of the kingdom in the Washington area over the decades. For this essay, I have chosen to discuss only eight of those notable individuals.

2. W. Dee Halverson and Micah J. Halverson, *The Life and Times of Robert W. Barker* (Salt Lake City: Heritage Associates, n.d.), 135–36.

3. Julian C. Lowe and Nola K. Lowe, *Our Lives and Family,* 2nd ed. (n.p.: self-pub., 1995), 169.

4. Julian C. Lowe and Florian H. Thayn, *History of the Mormons in the Greater Washington Area: Members of the Church of Jesus Christ of Latter-day Saints in the Washington, D.C., Area, 1839–1991* (n.p.: Community Printing Service, 1991), 35–36.

5. U.S. Navy Captain Mervyn S. Bennion, the son-in-law of President J. Reuben Clark Jr., of the First Presidency, skipper of the battleship USS *West Virginia* and a counselor in the bishopric of the Washington Stake's Chevy Chase Ward, was killed in the Japanese attack on Pearl Harbor—for which he received posthumously the Congressional Medal of Honor.

6. Sheri L. Dew, *Ezra Taft Benson: A Biography* (Salt Lake City: Deseret Book, 1987), 156, 162–63.

7. Transcribed text of remarks of President of the Quorum of the Twelve Apostles Russell M. Nelson to the Washington D.C. Stake 75th Anniversary Fireside, Kensington, MD, 20 November 2015 (quoted with permission).

8. John M. Dobson, *Two Centuries of Tariffs: The Background and Emergence of the U.S. International Trade Commission* (n.p., United States International Trade Commission, 1976), appendix A.

9. Laura Cowley Brossard was the sister of Elder Matthew Cowley of the Quorum of the Twelve Apostles.

10. In 2015, seventy-five years after the Washington Stake was organized, the aggregate membership of all twenty-four stakes whose boundaries, in whole or in part, were within the boundaries of the original Washington Stake in 1940, was ninety-three thousand.

11. See Lowe and Thayn, *Greater Washington Area*, 37–39.

12. See Eleanor Knowles, *Biography of Edgar B. Brossard: Government, Church & Civic Leader* (n.p., self-pub., 1979), 52–64.

13. Lowe and Thayn, *Greater Washington Area*, 39.

14. Lowe and Thayn, *Greater Washington Area*, 39.

15. Transcribed text of remarks of President of the Quorum of the Twelve Apostles Russell M. Nelson.

16. J. Willard Marriott was chairman of both Nixon inaugural celebrations in 1969 and 1973. When President Nixon stood up to speak at the Washington D.C. Stake Center, he did not carry a single sheet of paper or note to the podium. At the conclusion of the funeral service, however, he came to President J.W. Marriott Jr., opened his valise, and handed him six long yellow legal-length sheets with the text of his remarks written in his own hand on the airplane. Ralph W. Hardy Jr. telephone interview with J.W. Marriott Jr., 13 July 2020.

17. Remarks of Elder Robert W. Barker at the funeral of Milan D. Smith (24 October 1987), 8 (courtesy of President Smith's youngest son, former U.S. Senator (R-Oregon) and North America Northeast Area Seventy Elder Gordon Harold Smith).

18. Ralph W. Hardy Jr., interview with U.S. Circuit Judge Milan D. Smith Jr. (9th Circuit), 18 June 2020.

19. W. Dee Halverson and Micah J. Halverson, *Life and Times of Robert W. Barker*, appendix A.

20. At the end of 2019, there were nine stakes in northern Virginia and five stakes in the District of Columbia and suburban Maryland proximate to the I-495 Capital Beltway. Ralph W. Hardy Jr., interview with Area Seventy and former Oakton Virginia Stake president Kevin Calderwood, 21 June 2020.

21. Name subsequently changed to the Oakton Virginia Stake following the creation of the Annandale Virginia Stake.

22. Plans for the new Washington Temple evidenced that it would be among the three largest temples in the Church—after the Salt Lake and Los Angeles Temples.

23. Lowe and Lowe, *Our Lives and Family*, 266.

24. Lowe and Lowe, *Our Lives and Family*, 274–75.

25. President Ralph Mecham served as the second bishop of the Potomac (Maryland) Ward and was a regional representative. For twenty years President Mecham served as director of the Administrative Office of the United States Courts—effectively the general manager of the United States federal court system under the direction of the Chief Justice of the United States.

26. In 1993 Marriott Corporation was split into two publicly traded companies: Marriott International, Inc. (NASDAQ:MAR) and Host Hotels and Resorts, Inc. (NYSE:HST). Today, J.W. Marriott Jr. is executive chairman and chairman of the board of MAR; and his younger brother, Richard E. Marriott, former bishop of the Potomac Ward, Washington D.C. Stake, is chairman of the board of HST.

27. See, for example, Elder Marriott's rapid response to Hank Stuever's mocking *Washington Post* Style section article and the offensive illustrations on Latter-day Saints' sacred temple garments, *Washington Post* editorial page, 6 March 2002. Elder Marriott's published response on the newspaper's editorial page followed two days after his meeting with the newspaper's publisher, the editor of the Style section, and the article's writer. Another example is Bill Marriott's 7 April 1996 appearance on network television with President Hinckley and CBS *60 Minutes* investigative correspondent Mike Wallace.

28. Ralph W. Hardy Jr., interview with Ruth Pearson Ladd (Elder Don Ladd's widow), 5 June 2020.

29. The new first counselor in this stake presidency was recently returned Argentina mission president and Washington, DC, native Richard G. Scott—whom President Ezra Taft Benson, as President of the Church, would call in 1988 as a member of the Quorum of the Twelve Apostles.

30. Articles of Faith 1:5.

31. Bruce C. Hafen, *A Disciple's Life: The Biography of Neal A. Maxwell* (Salt Lake City: Deseret Book, 2002), 203.

32. Hafen, *A Disciple's Life*, 205.

33. The 7 February 1953 diary entry of a Washington Stake high councilor records: "I took Dr. Russell Nelson [age 29] with me to the Radio Correspondents Dinner for the President [Dwight D. Eisenhower] at the Statler Hotel.

It was a nice affair. Visited with many government officials and broadcasters." Diary of Ralph W. Hardy Sr., 1953.

34. Dallin H. Oaks, "President Russell M. Nelson: Guided, Prepared, Committed," supplement to *the Ensign*, May 2018, https://www.churchofjesuschrist.org/study/ensign/2018/05-se/president-russell-m-nelson-guided-prepared-committed.

35. Washington attorney and former McLean Virginia Second Ward bishop and lifelong Washington resident William B. Ingersoll recalls his fascinating encounter with Elder Nelson that took place at a diplomatic reception at Beverly Campbell's home in the late 1990s: "Introducing myself, I said, 'Elder Nelson, I am William Ingersoll.' Elder Nelson exclaimed, 'You mean you are Billy Ingersoll!' I responded, 'Well, that's what my mother called me.' 'You mean Loraine was your mother and your dad was Brown?' 'Yes.' Elder Nelson then said, 'Billy, I was your deacons quorum adviser in the Washington Ward!' Then, to my amazement, Elder Nelson proceeded to name and inquire about all ten of the young men who were members of that deacons quorum—more than forty years earlier!" William B. Ingersoll to Ralph W. Hardy Jr., email, 1 August 2020.

36. Transcribed text of remarks of President of the Quorum of the Twelve Apostles Russell M. Nelson to the Washington D.C. Stake 75th Anniversary Fireside, Kensington, MD, 20 November 2015, quoted with permission.

37. Transcription of President Rex E. Lee's introduction of Elder Dallin H. Oaks (Brigham Young University devotional, 17 January 1995), www.speeches.byu.edu/talks/dallin_h_oaks/adversity.

38. In my introduction of Elder Christofferson before his keynote address to the annual devotional of the J. Reuben Clark Law Society at the Conference Center in Salt Lake City, I provided the following background regarding his work as Chief Judge Sirica's law clerk: "During the long pendency of the *Watergate* case, the *Washington Post* described Elder Christofferson as 'a former Mormon missionary who serves as Judge Sirica's clerk and alter ego' and added that 'Todd, now a tall, soft-spoken, blond-headed young man,' had "served as a missionary in Argentina.' In its '1973 Person of the Year' cover story on Judge Sirica, *Time* magazine illustrated the exceptionally close relationship between this judge and his law clerk by observing that 'while the technicians continued their studies [for any evidence of tampering], [Judge Sirica] and his young law clerk, Todd Christofferson, listened to the [White House] tapes through headphones in a jury room.' Thirty years later I was privileged to be in the completely filled ceremonial courtroom of the United States Court of Appeals for the District of Columbia Circuit to attend a retrospective on the Watergate case that featured on the dais many of the still-living lawyers, television correspondents, and defendants

in that national drama. What was most interesting was the attention and great respect that was accorded to Elder Christofferson, whom everyone remembered well. He was, as you would imagine, the recipient of many questions—which he fielded with his trademark grace, humor, and good judgment. When Judge Sirica died in 1992, the family asked Elder Christofferson to speak at his funeral in Washington. What counsel would you have expected Elder Christofferson, then of the Seventy, to have given on that occasion? Yes! It was the doctrine of the plan of salvation. . . . I have dwelled somewhat on the early judicial clerkship of a young Elder Christofferson because this unique experience—occurring at the very epicenter of perhaps the greatest American political crisis since the Civil War—helped refine the key instincts, exceptional scholarship, sound judgment and advocacy skills that would enhance both his successful professional career and his ministry." Ralph W. Hardy Jr., introduction of Elder D. Todd Christofferson, J. Reuben Clark Law Society, BYU Law School Alumni Association, *Clark Memorandum* (Spring 2011), 49.

★ PLACES ★

Figure 1. *Joseph Smith portrait by Adrian Lamb in the Smithsonian National Portrait Gallery. Permanent exhibit. Used with permission.*

JOSEPH SMITH IN THE NATIONAL PORTRAIT GALLERY

ANTHONY R. SWEAT

Anthony R. Sweat is an associate teaching professor of Church history and doctrine at Brigham Young University.

In 1962 the United States Congress founded the Smithsonian National Portrait Gallery (NPG) in Washington, DC, with the commission to collect portraits of "men and women who have made significant contributions to the history, development, and culture of the people of the United States."[1] Its archives currently hold more than twenty-three thousand paintings, drawings, prints, photographs, sculptures, and other items. Of those twenty-three thousand, only about fourteen hundred portraits (roughly 6 percent of the collection) are on permanent display for the museum's visitors—over one million annually.[2] A prominent portrait of Joseph Smith in a warm cherry frame is displayed on the first floor in the permanent East Gallery of the "American Origins" exhibit near a bust of Booker T. Washington (figure 2).

The purpose of this paper is to explore how this particular portrait of Joseph Smith became part of the National Portrait Gallery's permanent display. This story follows a chronological flow that briefly outlines the development of portraiture in Western art and America, Joseph Smith's portraits he sat for during his life, the establishment of the NPG in 1968, the

Figure 2. *Joseph Smith portrait (left wall) in the National Portrait Gallery's "American Origins" exhibit. Photo by author.*

events surrounding the inclusion of a Joseph Smith portrait in the NPG's opening, and the Joseph Smith portrait that currently hangs in the NPG permanent display along with its origins. This paper will conclude with an analysis of the likeness of the NPG Joseph Smith portrait and what its presence may say about Joseph Smith and the Restoration's place in the American nation.

THE PROMINENCE OF PORTRAITURE

Portrait painting is one of the most popular genres of Western art. Before photography, portraiture was used for thousands of years as the primary means to capture, idealize, and propagate the likeness of important or beloved individuals. A portrait "contains a divine force which not only makes absent men present . . . but moreover makes the dead seem almost alive," Leon Alberti said in his classic 1435 work, *On Painting*.[3] Even Jesus makes a reference to portraiture when he referred to Caesar's likeness on a Roman coin and instructionally asked, "Whose is this image and superscription?" (Matthew 22:20).

According to art historian Joanna Woodall, although portraiture has been popular for millennia, "the 'rebirth' of portraiture is considered a definitive feature of the Renaissance" (AD 1300–1600) and is characterized by paintings with "closely observed facial likeness, including idiosyncrasies and imperfections, to represent elite figures. . . . By the turn of the sixteenth century, the 'realistic' portrait was widespread."[4] For popes, royalty, military leaders, politicians, scholars, and the beautiful, wealthy, and influential, a painted portrait was often a social status symbol. President John Adams quipped, "No penance is like having one's picture done,"[5] yet—aware of portraits' public import—he sat for no less than six portraits in his lifetime.[6] President Andrew Jackson knew and leveraged the power of personal portraiture to the extreme: he hired a full-time painter, Ralph Earl, to live with him at the White House, who "churned out Jackson portraits as quickly as possible."[7]

Portraiture is the first artistic "genre to appear among the Saints," writes Terryl Givens,[8] and it played a prominent role in early Latter-day Saint history. As an example, to help solidify his new position as the leader of The Church of Jesus Christ of Latter-day Saints after Joseph Smith's death, Brigham Young commissioned and posed for a seven-foot-tall, full-body portrait by Selah Van Sickle in July of 1845. Brigham stands in the painting, staring directly at the viewer, with a filled bookshelf behind him. The Book of Mormon and Bible sit on a table in the foreground, and Brigham's hand holds up a third book—Joseph's book containing the names of the faithful called the "Book of the Law of the Lord." This painting was hung on the east wall in the celestial room of the Nauvoo Temple so that when members directly entered the room, this "life-sized portrait sent a powerful message that Joseph Smith's personal record book had passed to the hands of Brigham Young and only Brigham Young had the authority to *deliver* the law of the Lord to the Church."[9]

JOSEPH SMITH'S PORTRAITS FROM LIFE

Like John Adams, Andrew Jackson, and many others, the Prophet Joseph Smith sat for a few artistic portraits during his lifetime. Joseph's journal for 25 June 1842 says, "Set for the drawing of his profile. for Lithographing on city chart."[10] This profile image, done by Sutcliffe Maudsley, was intended for inclusion in the bottom corner of the map of Nauvoo. The original painting was sent to the lithographer to re-create for the map (and thus the image on the map is a copy by another artist copying Maudsley's drawing). The original Maudsley life drawing was lost until 1982, when it was redis-covered with some old books at a garage sale in Salt Lake City.[11] Joseph posed again (perhaps for Maudsley, although the artist is uncertain) for a profile drawing of the Prophet in a white suit. Desdemona Fullmer Smith, who donated the drawing to The Church of Jesus Christ of Latter-day Saints in 1881, wrote, "This portrait of the Prophet Joseph Smith I saw taken while he stood up in Nauvoo with the white suit on that I made for him."[12] Just a few months after his initial sitting for Maudsley, on 16 Sep-tember 1842, the Prophet posed for another portrait: "Friday 16th. With brother [David] Rogers at home. bro R painting." In comparison to his profile drawing by Maudsley (who may have used a pantograph technique to physically trace Joseph's profile[13]), this Brother Rogers sitting was for a multiday portrait, likely an oil painting given the amount of time it re-quired. Joseph's journal continues: "Saturday 17th. At home with brother [David] Rogers, painting. . . . Monday 19th. & Tuesday 20th. With brothers [David] Rogers. painting at his house."[14]

Glen Leonard, former director of the Church History Museum, con-cludes that the painting attributed to David Rogers from September 1842 is the well-known front-view oil painting of Joseph Smith (with a compan-ion painting of Emma Smith) owned by the Community of Christ (for-merly the Reorganized Church of Jesus Christ of Latter Day Saints), which hangs in their Temple Museum in Independence, Missouri (see figure 2).[15] The Community of Christ also attributes this painting to Rogers.[16] No-tably, the Rogers portraits of Joseph and Emma have strong provenance. During Joseph's life, the portraits hung in the sitting room in the lower southwest corner of the Mansion house and were later moved upstairs. Emma Smith then moved the portraits into the Nauvoo House when she

Figure 3. *Portrait of Joseph Smith, attributed to David Rogers, 1842. The Community of Christ.*

moved there in the 1870s. When Latter-day Saint missionary Junius F. Wells visited Emma Smith in the winter of 1875–76, he recollected that Emma "entertained me very hospitably and showed me the painting [of Joseph], then hanging in her bedroom at the Nauvoo House."[17] Elder Wells wrote that this "first and only full face portrait is an oil painting made by an artist named Rogers."[18] However, there are some who debate whether this front-view image (or a profile oil painting of Joseph and a companion of Hyrum) is the "Brother Rogers" painting in question.[19] For ease of reference, however, I will refer to this well-known image attributed to David Rogers as the Rogers portrait throughout the remainder of this paper (figure 3).

The Rogers portrait of Joseph Smith has been reproduced numerous times. Two copies were made in 1899 for the Community of Christ. In the 1950s Israel Smith had it copied again by artist Harold Bullard. Another reproduction copy currently hangs in the bottom floor of the Salt Lake Temple. The original Rogers portraits of Joseph and Emma now hang in the Community of Christ Temple Museum in Independence, Missouri.[20] If the original Rogers painting of Joseph Smith hangs in Independence, Missouri, then which copied version of it hangs in the National Portrait Gallery in Washington, DC?

ESTABLISHING THE NATIONAL PORTRAIT GALLERY

As the new American nation grew in the eighteenth to twentieth centuries, prominent American portraits began to be collected by museums and institutions to preserve historic individuals and works of art. Portraits tell a story and serve to both preserve and create history. When the National Portrait Gallery in London opened in 1859, there was a general sentiment among some Americans to establish a similar gallery in the United States. As of the1920s, however, there was yet no established U.S. portrait gallery. In 1921 the Smithsonian—in conjunction with the National Gallery of Art—commissioned twenty portraits of World War I notables, which formed the nucleus of the nation's first gallery of portraits.[21] In 1957 the old Patent Office in Washington, DC, was proposed to be demolished, but due to public opposition Congress decided to turn the building over to the

Smithsonian and make it into a museum. In 1962 the U.S. Congress authorized the founding of the National Portrait Gallery, approved by President John F. Kennedy. Title 20 of the U.S. Code, section 75b for the "Establishment of National Portrait Gallery," reads as follows: "There is established in the Smithsonian Institution a bureau which shall be known as the National Portrait Gallery . . . for the exhibition and study of portraiture and statuary depicting men and women who have made significant contributions to the history, development, and culture of the people of the United States and of the artists who created such portraiture and statuary."[22]

Over the next six years, the National Portrait Gallery (NPG) labored to acquire its initial body of portraits and opened first to the public in 1968 with around six hundred portraits.[23] Many of the initial portraits were on loan. Brandon Fortune, chief curator of the NPG in 2019, said, "When the National Portrait Gallery was founded in 1962, it had no collection. During the next decade, as the museum staff gathered works by gift and purchase and transfer for the collection, they also researched available portraits of Americans who had great impact on our history and culture. Occasionally, the staff commissioned a copy of a painting in order to fill a gap when it was unlikely that the museum would ever be able to acquire an original portrait from life."[24] *Washington Post* journalist Bob Thompson says, "Sometimes they [the NPG] tracked down portraits, and sometimes portraits came to them. Sometimes they scraped together money for purchases, and sometimes they pleaded for donations," claiming that the opening show for the NPG could have been titled "Won't Someone Give Us Some Pictures Like These—Please?"[25]

As portraits were originally acquired by the National Portrait Gallery, no portrait was obtained unless it or the artist was considered historically significant by the NPG staff and the NPG Commission, which commission—composed of curators and historians appointed by the Smithsonian regents—voted in each new addition.[26] The addition of new portraits continues today. Each month the commission meets to vote in or reject potential images. Other than portraits of U.S. presidents and their spouses, no portrait can be added to the permanent collection unless the subject has been deceased for ten years. The process of who gets admitted into the NPG can be contested. Bob Thompson continues, "The culling of notable

Americans for admission to the National Portrait Gallery can feel at times like the construction of history itself: sometimes logical and fair-minded, but just as often idiosyncratic or skewed."[27]

JOSEPH SMITH IN THE NATIONAL PORTRAIT GALLERY

Joseph Smith's portrait was included from the very beginning of the National Portrait Gallery. His portrait's inclusion is related to the history of the NPG's 1968 opening, which was limited by funding and largely based on loans. Based on a request from the NPG staff, in 1968 Wallace B. Smith (the then president of the Reorganized Church of Jesus Christ of Latter Day Saints) loaned the original Rogers portrait of Joseph Smith for the gallery's grand opening. [28] Lewis McInnis, a member of the curatorial staff at the NPG, received the painting from Wallace Smith. In an unpublished manuscript provided to the author, Ronald Romig and Lachlan Mackay tell the story of what happened next:

> After [the] return [of the original Rogers portrait] to Independence in December of 1968, the National Portrait Gallery made a proposal to provide the RLDS church a copy of the portrait of Joseph in exchange for the original. As an alternative, the National Portrait Gallery agreed to accept a sensitively done copy of the portrait, if the RLDS church would fund the project. After a group of members of the Washington, D.C., Congregation responded to the challenge and raised the funds, a copy of the original was produced by artist Adrian Lamb of Washington, D.C. On 14 November 1971, President W. Wallace Smith presented the Lamb copy to the National Portrait Gallery.[29]

In other words, the National Portrait Gallery wanted Joseph Smith's original Rogers painting and offered to pay for a duplicate to replace it for the RLDS Church. The RLDS Church did not accept that offer and the NPG, it seems, turned the tables, placing the burden on the RLDS Church to fund a new portrait if Joseph Smith's portrait was to be included in the NPG's permanent collection. Those who see Joseph Smith today on permanent display in the NPG are indebted to generous, forward-thinking members of the RLDS Church in 1971 who paid to have this replica portrait of the Prophet produced.

Thus the painting in the National Portrait Gallery on permanent display is not the original 1842 painting attributed to Rogers, nor a copy made by the RLDS Church in 1899 or the 1950s, but rather it is a reproduction of the original Rogers image and was reproduced in 1971 by an artist named Adrian Lamb.

ARTIST ADRIAN LAMB

Adrian Lamb (1901–88) was born in New York City and studied at its Art Students League in the mid-1920s. He also studied art at the Julien Academy in Paris, completing his studies in 1929. Afterward he traveled to England and other European nations to practice, refine, and employ his capacities as a portrait artist.[30] Lamb became successful not only as an original artist but also as an artist with the technical ability to reproduce popular portrait paintings. For example, Lamb's paintings are on display at George Washington's Virginian estate, Mount Vernon. Lamb reproduced English painter Robert Edge Pine's portraits of Washington's grandchildren and John Trumbull's portrait of Washington at the victory in Yorktown.[31]

Lamb's portraits are found in many collections, including in collections from the State Department, the National Gallery of Art, The White House, the U.S. Naval Academy, Harvard University, and the Supreme Court of the United States.[32] Lamb was selected as the artist to paint Daniel Webster's portrait in the Senate Reception Chamber.[33] Lamb also has multiple paintings in the National Portrait Gallery, including portraits of John Pierpont Morgan Sr., John D. Rockefeller Sr., and Theodore Roosevelt. When he died of a heart attack at eighty-seven, Lamb was prominent enough that his death was announced in the *New York Times*[34] and *Chicago Tribune*.[35]

Chief NPG Curator Brandon Fortune said, "Adrian Lamb was a well-regarded artist in New York who made several copies for the museum, including the painting of Joseph Smith, which was a copy of a painting owned by the Reorganized Church of Jesus Christ of Latter Day Saints in Independence. He made the copy at the request of a private donor."[36]

Lamb's reproduction painting of the Rogers portrait was done with oil on canvas, is 33 × 29 inches in size, and was completed in 1971.

COMPARING THE ROGERS AND LAMB PORTRAITS

When comparing the original Rogers painting with Lamb's National Portrait Gallery reproduction, the skill used in Lamb's portrait is evident. Joseph's pose, the right hand up with its wedding ring, the folds of the clothing, the background landscape with its dark and brewing sunset, Joseph's pompadour hair, and his high upturned collar are all faithfully reproduced. It is difficult to detect substantial differences in these particulars. Although Adrian Lamb was a gifted technical reproduction artist, however, inconsistencies are introduced almost any time a reproduction is made. This is particularly true in the finer facial features. In general, Lamb's NPG reproduction of Joseph Smith makes his facial features thinner. Joseph's nose is narrower than the original in Rogers's portrait. Thus Joseph's eyes are closer together (since the outside of the nostrils generally line up with the inside of the eyes on the average human face), and therefore his mouth is slightly smaller (since the edges of the mouth generally line up with the middle of the eyes). Joseph's forehead is higher in Lamb's reproduction, as is Joseph's hair. Also, Joseph's nose appears slightly longer, and his cheekbones are lower in Lamb's reproduction. All these small changes add up to show noticeable differences between the original and the reproduction, which are especially prominent to the trained eye.

These subtle changes between the Rogers original and the Lamb National Portrait Gallery reproduction are compounded by the fact that the original Rogers portrait differs from the Maudsley life profile drawings of Joseph Smith and from Joseph's death mask. According to Junius F. Wells's later reminisce of his visit with Emma Smith in 1875–76, when Wells asked Emma "if it [the RLDS portrait] were a good likeness of the Prophet," Emma responded, "No. He could not have a good portrait—his countenance was changing all the time." Wells then asked Emma what Joseph thought about this portrait of himself, to which Emma reportedly responded, "I can tell you that, for I asked him, and he said: 'Emma that is a nice painting of a silly boy, but it don't look much like a Prophet of the Lord!'"[37]

| Community of Christ, 1842 | National Portrait Gallery, 1971 | Death Mask, 1844 |

Figure 4. *Side-by-side comparison of the Community of Christ, National Portrait Gallery, and death mask images of Joseph Smith. Photos by author.*

As Ephraim Hatch, author of *Joseph Smith Portraits*, writes about the Rogers original, "Either Joseph was not the model, or if he was, the artist was not very accurate [when compared to the death mask]. The mouth of the subject in the painting is too small, the upper lip is not high enough, the nose is too narrow at the base, and the eyes are too close together."[38] In other words, the Rogers original is narrower in the nose, eyes, and lips than the death mask, and the Lamb NPG reproduction is narrower in those same areas than the RLDS Rogers original. There's a *double narrowing* of Joseph's features in the Lamb NPG portrait, as can be seen in figure 4.

CONCLUSION: JOSEPH'S LIKENESS IN THE NATIONAL PORTRAIT GALLERY

Although there are some notable facial differences between the death mask of Joseph Smith and the Rogers original, Romig and Mackay note, "Joseph Smith III, and successive RLDS leaders . . . [expressed] belief that the oil portrait was the most authentic representation of Joseph Smith, Jr. . . . Its continuing acceptance may relate in some sense that, as a result of the artist's evident skill, the portrait captures a portion of the emotional feel of Joseph's character."[39] I agree. While Maudsley's profiles may be more consistent with the outline of the death mask, Maudsley's images are more static stylized caricatures than true portraits that attempt to capture the spirit of individuals. Like the death mask itself, Maudsley's images can lack the charisma and inspiration of Joseph that the Rogers portrait seems to carry. Similarly, although the Lamb NPG reproduction differs more narrowly in Joseph's facial features from the Rogers original, it seems to similarly convey a strong spirit. Most notably, the characteristic unconscious smile of Joseph Smith,[40] seen in the Rogers original, is also captured in Lamb's NPG reproduction. Many are unaware there is even a difference between the Rogers original and the Lamb NPG reproduction, thinking the NPG is the actual nineteenth-century original. Good portraiture, even if at times not precisely accurate, aims to communicate the potency of a person. There is a difference between a *picture* and a *likeness*. Most great paintings of Jesus fall into this category: they may not be historically accurate (such as Rembrandt's Dutch model or Del Parson's American one), but the artist *represents* the Redeemer and *communicates* the Christ to the viewer.

Noting my admitted bias toward Joseph Smith's role in American history, it is remarkable that the Joseph Smith portrait hangs in a cherry-orange frame on a prominent wall in NPG's permanent display, staring out at 1.3 million viewers who pass by him annually. The hall of "American Origins," where Joseph's portrait is located, is surrounded by authors, inventors, and educators who typically get much more wall space than prophets and preachers. Joseph is displayed near Washington Irving, Alexander Graham Bell, Samuel Morse, Thomas Edison, Frederick Douglass, Isaac Singer, Ira Aldridge, and Walt Whitman. Out of fourteen hundred images on permanent display, Joseph's portrait is one of only a few religious leaders perpetually hung in the National Portrait Gallery.[41] Joseph's inclusion in the NPG's permanent display suggests a public recognition, as historian Robert V. Remini wrote at the 2005 "Worlds of Joseph Smith" conference at the Library of Congress in Washington, DC: "Mormonism is a very American religion . . . [which] has expanded, has been accepted, and has become part of the Christian tradition," with the Book of Mormon being "a typically American story" that "Americans can easily appreciate."[42]

Joseph's NPG portrait accurately represents the gallery's mantra of "poets and presidents, visionaries and villains, actors and activists whose lives tell the American story."[43] All who are interested in the prophetic mission and influence of Joseph Smith upon America and the world are indebted to both the National Portrait Gallery and the Community of Christ for their efforts and foresight to include Joseph's portrait in a permanent display.[44] As the effects of Joseph Smith's prophetic mission continue, it is hoped that his portrait will remain permanently and prominently displayed in the Smithsonian's National Portrait Gallery so that its visitors can consider his "significant contributions to the history, development, and culture of the people of the United States."[45]

NOTES

1. "About Us," National Portrait Gallery (website).

2. In 2017, 1.3 million people toured the portrait gallery, https://newsdesk .si.edu/factsheets/national-portrait-gallery.

3. Leon Alberti, *On Painting* (1435).

4. Joanna Woodall, *Portraiture: Facing the Subject* (Oxford: Manchester University Press, 1997), 1–2.

5. As cited in David McCullough, *John Adams* (New York: Simon & Schuster, 2001), 638.

6. Adams sat for portraits by Benjamin Blythe in 1766 (when Adams was only thirty), Mather Brown in 1788, John Singleton Copley in 1783, John Trumbull in 1793, Gilbert Stuart in 1798, and again for Stuart in 1824 at the age of eighty-nine, just a year and a half before Adams died.

7. Peter Grier, "The Semi-Secret History of Trump's Andrew Jackson Portrait," *Christian Science Monitor*, 9 February 2017.

8. Terryl Givens, *People of Paradox: A History of Mormon Culture* (Oxford University Press, 2007), 181.

9. Jill C. Major, "Artworks in the Celestial Room of the First Nauvoo Temple," *BYU Studies Quarterly* 41, no. 2 (2002): 50.

10. "Journal, December 1841–December 1842," 125, The Joseph Smith Papers, https://www.josephsmithpapers.org/paper-summary/journal-december -1841-december-1842/30.

11. See Don L. Searle, "Painting of the Prophet Is Probable Source of Likeness on Map," *Ensign*, April 1985, 78.

12. "Sutcliffe Maudsley Exhibit," https://history.churchofjesuschrist.org/exhibit /sutcliffe-and-elizabeth-foxcroft-maudsley?lang=eng#mv6.

13. Glen M. Leonard, "Picturing the Nauvoo Legion," *BYU Studies Quarterly* 35, no. 2 (1995): 96.

14. "Journal, December 1841–December 1842," 205, The Joseph Smith Papers. https://www.josephsmithpapers.org/paper-summary/journal-december-1841-december-1842/82.

15. Sarah Jane Weaver, "What Did Joseph Smith Really Look Like?," *Church News*, 6 December 1997.

16. Community of Christ Apostle Lachlan Mackay says that based on his research, "We are quite comfortable going with 'attributed to David Rogers.'" Email communication with the author, 9 August 2019.

17. Junius F. Wells, "Portraits of Joseph Smith the Prophet," *Instructor*, February 1930, 79.

18. Junius F. Wells, *Instructor*, 79.

19. Author S. Michael Tracy, in his book *Millions Shall Know Brother Joseph Again: The Joseph Smith Photograph* (Salt Lake City: Eborn Books, 2008), concludes, "It is our opinion after much study that the side view oil painting of Joseph and its companion portrait of Hyrum are done by the artist named 'Brother Rogers,'" 21. See also William B. McCarl, "The Visual Image of Joseph Smith" (master's thesis, Brigham Young University, 1962), who also concludes that "Rogers painted a profile view of the Prophet and his brother, Hyrum . . . [and] the artist of the front view portrait owned by the Reorganized Church cannot be determined," 65, 68.

20. Summarized from Ronald Romig and Lachlan Mackay, "Hidden Things Shall Come to Light: The Joseph Smith, Jr., Family Visual Record" (unpublished manuscript in the author's possession and used with permission).

21. National Portrait Gallery—Agency History," Smithsonian Institution Archives, http://siarchives.si.edu/research/ah00008npg.html.

22. https://www.law.cornell.edu/uscode/text/20/75b.

23. Erin Williams, "Beverly Jones Cox, Former Director of Exhibitions and Collections Management for the National Portrait Gallery, Reflects on Her Past 43 years with the Museum," *Washington Post*, 13 June 2011.

24. Email communication between Brandon Fortune and the author, 19 June 2019, cited with permission.

25. Bob Thompson, "Face Off," *Washington Post*, 13 June 1999.

26. Thompson, "Face Off."

27. Thompson, "Face Off."

28. Although the current exhibition label summarizing Joseph Smith's life is expertly written, the first label prepared for the grand opening was unflattering: https://npg.si.edu/object/npg_NPG.71.43. Shortly before the opening of the National Portrait Gallery, the original text accompanying the portraits of Joseph Smith and Brigham Young was shared with Elder Ralph W. Hardy,

Area Seventy with a Church public affairs assignment for the District of Columbia. Recognizing that the text contained inaccuracies and even potentially offensive summaries of their lives, Elder Hardy quickly worked with museum officials to rectify the wording prior to the gallery's opening. Biographer and historian Richard Lyman Bushman revised the text, producing what accompanies Joseph Smith's portrait today.

29. Romig and Mackay, "Hidden Things Shall Come to Light," 3.

30. "Adrian Lamb Biography," askART (website).

31. Mount Vernon Museum Collections, Mount Vernon Museum Official Website.

32. "Adrian Lamb," American Art Collaborative (website).

33. "Daniel Webster," United States Senate Art and History Archive (website).

34. "Adrian S. Lamb, Artist, 87" (obituary), *New York Times*, 4 January 1989.

35. "Adrian S. Lamb, 87, Portrait artist" (obituary), *Chicago Tribune*, 6 January 1989.

36. Email communication between Brandon Fortune and the author, 19 June 2019, cited with permission.

37. Wells, "Portraits of the Joseph Smith the Prophet," 79.

38. Ephraim Hatch, *Joseph Smith Portraits: A Search for the Prophet's Likeness* (Provo, UT: Religious Studies Center, Brigham Young University, 1998), 50.

39. Romig and Mackay, "Hidden Things Shall Come to Light," 3, 1.

40. Parley P. Pratt wrote of Joseph Smith, "His countenance was ever mild, affable, beaming with intelligence and benevolence; mingled with a look of interest and unconscious smile, or cheerfulness." *The Autobiography of Parley Parker Pratt* (New York: Russell Brothers, 1874). 47.

41. A search of "religious leaders" on the NPG website returns forty-six portraits such as Martin Luther, George Whitefield, Martin Luther King Jr., Ayatollah Khomeini (five of them), Dalai Lama, Billy Graham, Pat Robertson, and Brigham Young (seven portraits).

42. Robert V. Remini, "Biographical Reflections on the American Joseph Smith," *The Worlds of Joseph Smith: A Bicentennial Conference at the Library of Congress*, ed. John W. Welch (Provo, UT: BYU Studies, 2005), 23, 25.

43. "About Us," National Portrait Gallery (website).

44. Over the years, the NPG has also collected other images of Joseph Smith (as well as Brigham Young), although they are not on permanent display: an 1847 lithograph of Joseph and Hyrum (NPG.79.159), an 1842 Oliver Pelton engraving copy of Sutcliffe Maudsley's drawing (NPG.82.102), and seven images of Brigham Young (NPG.81.75; NPG.80.284; NPG.76.100; NPG.78.47; NPG.97.105; NPG.80.279; NPG.67.57).

45. "About Us," National Portrait Gallery (website).

The Washington Chapel. L. Tom Perry Special Collections, Harold B. Lee Library, Brigham Young University.

THE WASHINGTON CHAPEL: AN ELIAS TO THE WASHINGTON D.C. TEMPLE

ALONZO L. GASKILL AND SETH G. SOHA

Alonzo L. Gaskill is a professor of Church history and doctrine at Brigham Young University. Seth G. Soha is a practicing physician assistant and an independent researcher who is an alumnus of Brigham Young University.

The original Washington Ward's chapel is unique among meetinghouses in The Church of Jesus Christ of Latter-day Saints. From its architecture to its history, the chapel stands out as one of the most distinctive Church buildings constructed since the restoration of the gospel began.[1]

Prior to 1920, there was no "formal organization" of The Church of Jesus Christ of Latter-day Saints—no wards or stakes—in the DC area.[2] The few Latter-day Saints who lived and worked in DC met on Sundays in homes or other buildings—but not as an organized branch of the Church.[3] When Elder Reed Smoot of the Quorum of the Twelve Apostles became a U.S. senator (in 1903), his move to DC made him the de facto leader of the few Latter-day Saints living in that part of the world.[4] As numbers increased, and as members could no longer all meet in a living room or hotel room, the Church began renting various properties in the DC area so that members could comfortably gather together in one place to worship.[5] Starting in May 1920, the Washington Branch was officially organized—with an average Sunday attendance of somewhere between fifty and sixty members.[6]

Robert M. Stewart, son-in-law of Elder George Albert Smith (of the Quorum of the Twelve Apostles), was the impetus behind getting a chapel built in DC. As he walked to work each day, he would pass the vacant lots (on Sixteenth Street) on which the Washington Chapel would eventually be built, and he was consistently impressed with what an ideal location that would be for the Church's first chapel in Washington.[7] Elder Smith approached President Heber J. Grant about this and also encouraged Robert Stewart (who had previously worked in real estate) to make inquiries with regard to what it would cost to acquire the lots.[8] When Mary Foote Henderson—the wealthy widow of former Missouri senator John B. Henderson—learned that someone was interested in purchasing the two adjoining lots, she quickly purchased them.[9] Mrs. Henderson owned a significant amount of property in the area and thus was "quite anxious to control whatever buildings" might be erected in the vicinity.[10] Robert Stewart, on behalf of the Church, met several times with Mary Henderson in an effort to convince her to sell the lots. After several meetings, she made a verbal agreement to let the Church purchase the properties, as the following source relates:

> According to Brother Stewart, when Mrs. Henderson told her architect, a Mr. Totten, that the Mormon Church was the purchaser of the lots, "he told her the sale was a mistake, that a Mormon Church in that vicinity would tend to depreciate the value of all property in the neighborhood, and foreign governments would refuse to rent her properties then used as embassies." This was particularly important to Mrs. Henderson because she wanted to make 16th Street the most beautiful neighborhood in the city. She likewise told William Corcoran Hill, the real estate man, who became enraged and threatened to stop the sale if possible.
>
> So, when Brother Stewart returned to Mrs. Henderson with the final form of the contract to be signed, she had to admit that she was sorry she had sold the property to the Mormon Church. Yet it remains to her credit that she kept her oral promise to them and signed the papers.[11]

It is said that, upon learning of the interest of the Church in the prop-erty, "a delegation of Protestant ministers" approached Mrs. Henderson in an attempt to discourage her from selling it to the Church.[12] Despite the very strong admonitions against selling the property to the Latter-day Saints (which she received from seemingly all sides), Mary Henderson moved forward with the deal for two primary reasons. First, because of her very "high regard for Senator [Reed] Smoot."[13] Second, because of the Church's position on the Word of Wisdom. (Mrs. Henderson was strongly against the use of tobacco and alcohol—and Senator Smoot is said to have explained the Word of Wisdom to her.)[14] In addition to Mrs. Henderson's two lots (purchased on 9 April 1924[15]), the Church also purchased a third lot (which adjoined the other two on their south sides) on 9 April 1930.[16] On the combined 18,300-square-foot property, the Church would build its first chapel in DC.[17]

In many ways, this chapel would stand as a symbol to the people of Washington that truth had been restored and that the gospel of Jesus Christ was taking root in the nation's capital.[18] Not everyone was thrilled about that message or the building that would symbolize it. Thus, shortly before construction began on the new building (in December of 1930), a group of investors approached the Church—offering to purchase the combined lots for forty thousand dollars more than the Church had paid for them; this, in an apparent last-ditch effort to keep the Church from having a building in the upscale neighborhood. President Heber J. Grant's "curt response," sent via telegraph, was simply this: "Property not for sale."[19]

The groundbreaking for the Washington Chapel was held on 13 De-cember 1930.[20] The cornerstone was laid on 21 April 1932. The capstone atop the spire was placed on 21 March 1933. And, finally, the building was dedicated by President Heber J. Grant on Sunday, 5 November 1933—with the entire First Presidency and five members of the Quorum of the Twelve Apostles present.[21] Considering the tenuous relationship between the Church and the U.S. government during the nineteenth century, the construction and ultimate dedication of this edifice was a significant sym-bolic statement.

Stained glass window of Book of Mormon temple in the Washington Chapel. Photo by Richard J. Crookston.

The new building had a number of unique features that set it apart from other nearby buildings and from other houses of worship built by the Church. The Washington Chapel has the singular honor of being the first building ever built with travertine, or what is commonly referred to as "birdseye marble," that was taken from the Mount Nebo Quarry.[22] The beauty of this substance is that "at different times of the day [it] reflects various hues. After a heavy rain the effect is that of highly polished marble which changes, as it dries, into [a] hazy purple."[23] The disadvantage is that it is a porous substance and thus not ideal for the humid climate of DC, thereby causing it to severely deteriorate over time.[24] On the north, south, and east sides of the chapel, there are also nine beautiful stained glass windows—unique to that building.[25] They depict various scenes in Church history, including the Hill Cumorah (where the plates of the Book of Mormon were buried), the migration of the Saints westward, and even ancient temples of the Western Hemisphere.[26]

To some outside of the Church, the Washington Chapel was perceived as "the 'Mormon Temple' in Washington, D.C."[27] Architecturally,

The Torleif Knaphus angel Moroni statue being prepared for placement atop the spire of the Washington Chapel, where it was displayed from 1933 through 1976. L. Tom Perry Special Collections, Harold B. Lee Library, Brigham Young University.

many have noticed the design parallels between the chapel and the Salt Lake City Temple.[28] For example, the Washington Chapel's singular 160-foot spire is remarkably similar in its design to the Salt Lake Temple's six spires.[29] Indeed, one source states, "The chapel's tower intentionally echoes the style and image of the six virtually identical towers on the Salt Lake City Temple, offering an architectural and cultural connection between the two buildings."[30] The building has the unique distinction of being the only Sunday house of worship to ever have an angel Moroni atop its tall spire.[31] The Washington Chapel's Moroni was similar to the angel Moroni statue atop the Salt Lake Temple and was sculpted by Torleif Knaphus.[32] Like many temples of the Restoration (including the Washington D.C. and Salt Lake Temples), the Washington Chapel faces east.[33] One source noted, additional "elements" on the Washington Chapel "recalling the [Salt Lake] Utah temple are the book and scroll design on the tower, urns, round arched windows, and the spire terminating in a ball, on which stood the figure of the angel Moroni."[34] Elsewhere we read, "The [chapel's] tower has two arched rectangular windows with a small vertically oriented oval window on each of its four elevations. . . . These openings . . . are mainly decorative and reminiscent of the windows found on the Salt Lake Temple."[35] On the building's exterior are engraved a number of inscriptions, including the words of Isaiah 2:2, Psalm 85:11, and the declaration of Doctrine and Covenants 93:36, "The glory of God is intelligence"—which is also inscribed over the doorway to the celestial room of the Mesa Arizona Temple.[36] Like the various temples of the Church, the Washington Chapel had a cornerstone ceremony during which certain items were placed in the cornerstone prior to it being sealed.[37] The placement of the Washington Chapel also seems to mimic the Church's approach to placing their temples in conspicuous locations and, often, on elevated lots. For example, one source pointed out, "The [Washington] temple is located in Kensington, Maryland, just north of Washington, D.C., and is on top of the wooded hill in a beautiful suburban section."[38] The Washington Chapel was also built "on one of the higher elevations of the city (two hundred feet above the base of the Washington Monument)."[39] Even the fact that the President of the Church signed off on the design of the Washington Chapel seems parallel with latter-day temples—since individual chapels do not traditionally need the approval of the prophet.[40]

A number of elements associated with the dedication of the Washington Chapel seem reminiscent of a temple dedicatory service. First, the entire First Presidency and five members of the Quorum of the Twelve Apostles attended and spoke at the dedicatory sessions—something that is simply unheard of as it relates to the dedication of a ward meetinghouse.[41] The President of the Church dedicated the building; again, a rarity for local chapels—and, in doing so, he used language that has been used in other temple dedicatory prayers.[42] After the dedicatory prayer, the choir sang the "Hosanna Anthem," which happens to be the song composed for and sung at the dedication of the Salt Lake Temple.[43] In addition, during the dedicatory services, the congregation sang "The Spirit of God," which was sung at the dedication of the Kirtland Temple.[44] Finally, there were three different dedicatory services held for the Washington Chapel; again, something the Church typically only does for the dedication of a temple.[45]

Isaiah 2:2 carved on one of the exterior walls. Photo by Richard J. Crookston.

Doctrine and Covenants 93:36 carved on an exterior wall. Photo by Richard J. Crookston.

Like the Washington D.C. Temple that would follow it, the chapel was unique enough that it drew the attention of those who passed by. For example, one non–Latter-day Saint source—speaking of the chapel's unique architecture—noted that "the golden figure on the spire . . . bids us pause for reflection."[46] Unquestionably, "there was . . . an evangelical [or missionary] component to the building. . . . The exterior may be viewed in this light as well (attracting curious passers-by)."[47] In addition to the focus on the redemption of the dead and salvific ordinances for the living, temples often serve a missionary purpose. Their unique design and manicured grounds consistently draw the attention of those who are unfamiliar with the Church. The Washington Chapel is known for having this same effect. Once dedicated, it became a "beehive of missionary activity."[48] Church members perceived the chapel as a sort of "showplace" that would draw nonmembers in and would provoke curiosity about the Church and its teachings.[49] The 5,000-plus pipe organ and its regular recitals, for example, facilitated the missionary work the building was designed to provoke.[50] "Elder [Edward P.] Kimball played organ recitals nearly every night except Sundays, giving 1001 recitals between November 5, 1933, and March 15, 1937, which 45,000 persons had enjoyed, and by his lovely music and spoken presentations learned of the Gospel and the history of the Church."[51] The staff from various countries' embassies would be invited to the building on specific nights during which Kimball would give "special recitals of the music of their own country."[52] This served as a strong draw, bringing members of other faiths into the building every week. Elsewhere we read, "Following the organ recitals and after each of the regular meetings, tours were conducted throughout the chapel, which had become a major sight-seeing attraction of the city."[53] Like many of the Church's temples throughout the world, the Washington Chapel even had as part of it a bureau of information—akin to a visitors' center—that answered investigators' questions and coordinated building tours.[54] The Washington Chapel was a visual landmark that drew people in and prepared them for the further light and knowledge the gospel had to offer. Just as those who drive the Capital Beltway for the first time are often shocked when they see the Washington D.C. Temple rising up out of the trees, in many ways, those who saw the Washington Chapel for the first time were drawn in by its uniqueness and beauty. Both have served as great missionary tools for the Church, and the Church's "leadership perceived the Church's image as improving in light of the new chapel."[55]

In the Church, we sometimes use the name Elias as a title, referring to something or someone that serves as a "forerunner."[56] In some ways, the Washington Chapel was a kind of proto-temple and an "Elias," or forerunner, of the Washington D.C. Temple.[57] Even though it may not have been intended as such, the chapel seemed to prepare the people for the temple. DC-area resident Page Johnson noted that "the Washington Chapel prepared people of other faiths and backgrounds for the arrival of the temple. Washington area residents . . . first began to know and accept the 'Mormons' because of the Washington Chapel. That building prepared them for an even more special place—situated on a hill for all to see—that would represent the continuation and expansion of the Lord's work."[58]

As the chapel's window of use drew to a close, and as members of the Church living in the area began to prepare for the open house and dedication of the Washington D.C. Temple, missionary work centered on both buildings became very important.[59] Indeed, in a way, the construction and dedication of the Washington D.C. Temple functioned as a transition—a passing of the mantle. What was once the historic centerpiece, symbolic of the Church's presence in the area, would fade into the background as a new edifice, also reminiscent of the Salt Lake Temple,[60] took the chapel's place as the official symbol of the restored gospel's presence in the nation's capital. As a former member of the Washington Ward pointed out, "The opening of the temple ushered in a new era of the Church in Washington. Before, the Washington Ward chapel was the center of activity and the symbol of the Church in the Washington area; now, the temple and the visitors center filled those roles."[61]

The final meeting of Latter-day Saints in the Washington Chapel was held on 31 August 1975.[62] The building had been deteriorating over a number of years, needed extensive repairs, and the costs to restore and maintain it were prohibitive. [63] In addition, post-WWII, many members had moved out of the city, preferring the suburbs.

The neighborhood in which the chapel stood, once considered an upper-class portion of DC, was now run-down and had an escalating crime rate.[64] The building had served its purpose but was now no longer ideal for the Church's needs in that part of the world. Thus, on that last day of August in 1975, stake president Donald Ladd announced that the Washington Ward was being dissolved and that its members would in one week begin to attend the various other chapels in the areas in which the members resided.[65] President Ladd also announced that the Church would be selling the Washington Chapel.[66] Needless to say, many members were saddened by the announcement.[67] Less expected was the anger that some felt. "One group, the Historical Washington Chapel Preservation Committee, became fairly well organized in opposition to the Church's selling the chapel. They prepared an extensive report against the action, which they sent to the First Presidency of the Church; and they received some publicity in the news media, making it necessary for the Church to respond."[68] In the end, such efforts didn't change things, and the Church moved forward with its preparations to sell the historic edifice.

It took nearly two years to sell the building, in part because of zoning, but also because of its need for extensive repairs, and because of its unique and elaborate architecture—which made it appealing to a limited clientele.[69] "On September 9, 1977, the Mormon Church sold the land rights to Columbia Road Recording Studios, Inc. who allegedly planned to use it for a radio/music headquarters but instead turned around and sold it the next day to the Holy Spirit Association for the Unification of World Christianity."[70] The president of the Columbia Road Recording Studios, Mitchell NewDelman, paid the Church $300,000 for the property but then immediately sold it to the Unification Church (or "Moonies," as they are sometimes called in the United States) for $475,000—a whopping $175,000 profit.[71]

Before the Church formally turned the building over to the Unification Church, a crane was utilized to remove the statue of the angel Moroni, and the Latter-day Saints also opened the building's cornerstone to remove its contents.[72] "The Angel Moroni statue was . . . stored until 1984, when it was displayed in Salt Lake City in the new Museum of

Church History and Art," now known as the Church History Museum, "where it has been since that time."[73] After taking possession of the property, the Unification Church made major changes to the interior and added their own identifying symbol to the spire where the angel Moroni once stood.[74]

Though many members of the Church are unfamiliar with the history and use of the old Washington Chapel, it is an important part of the history of the Church. For example, many members will be unaware that we once had a Sunday meetinghouse that displayed a statue of the angel Moroni atop its spire, that two future Presidents of the Church, an Apostle, and a future Apostle, served in the leadership of the congregations meeting in the Washington Chapel,[75] or that the Houston Texas Temple was architecturally modeled after the chapel.[76] There is so much history wrapped up in this important and yet forgotten edifice. Though no longer in the hands of the Church, it remains a monument to an important part of the Church's history—particularly its history in the nation's capital. As one source noted, "The Washington Chapel joins in with the monumental landscape of national churches while simultaneously distinguishing itself as a unique, distinct entity. . . . The building's symbolic legacy of permanently establishing Mormonism in Washington would outlast the ownership of the Mormon Church."[77]

NOTES

1. As one source noted, "The Church did not build chapels like this elsewhere." Samuel R. Palfreyman, *Washington Chapel, Church of Jesus Christ of the Latter Day Saints (Unification Church), 2810 Sixteenth Street Northwest, Washington, District of Columbia* (Washington, DC: National Park Service, U.S. Department of the Interior, n.d.), Library of Congress, HABS No. DC-539, 8. Another source referred to the chapel as "one of the most beautiful church edifices . . . ever seen." P. V. Cardon, "A Vacant Lot at the Crossroads," *Improvement Era*, September 1935, 546.

2. See Lee H. Burke, *History of the Washington D.C. LDS Ward: From Beginnings (1839) to Dissolution (1975)* (Salt Lake City: Publishers Press, 1990), 1; Palfreyman, *Washington Chapel*, HABS No. DC-539, 6; Edgar B. Brossard, "The Church in the Nation's Capital," *Improvement Era*, February 1939, 119.

3. Unofficial meetings such as those held in DC were common during that era. See Brossard, "Church in the Nation's Capital," 120.

4. See Burke, *Washington D.C. LDS Ward*, 14; F. Ross Peterson, "Washington, D.C.," in *Encyclopedia of Latter-day Saint History*, ed. Arnold K. Garr, Donald Q. Cannon, and Richard O. Cowan (Salt Lake City: Deseret Book, 2000), 1314. One source noted that "the branch perhaps owes more to Senator Reed Smoot . . . than to any other one person. In a general way the branch is a memorial to the able and persistent Church work of Elder Smoot." Brossard, "Church in the Nation's Capital," 120.

5. In addition to various hotel rooms and living rooms, from the early 1900s until November 1933, Church meetings were held in a hall owned by the National Board of Farm Organizations and in the Washington Auditorium Building's Assembly Hall.

6. See Burke, *Washington D.C. LDS Ward*, 14, 20; Palfreyman, *Washington Chapel*, HABS No. DC-539, 6; Milton Barlow and Margaret Cardon, comps., *Washington Chapel* (Washington, DC: self-pub., 1943), 4. DC resident Brent Smith noted that there are records "that refer to the branch organization in May 1920, thus showing a discrepancy to Edgar Brossard's published reference to the branch having been organized in June of that year. . . . Reed Smoot's diary (which states [that the branch was organized] May 30 [1920]), as well as [the] Eastern States Mission . . . records . . . noted that 'the Washington Branch was partly organized (on the evening of May 30th). Elder Reed Smoot presented the name of J. Bryan Barton to act as branch president . . . until the branch becomes well established. . . . Elder Barton will look after the affairs of the branch until all of the organizations are completed, when he will [then] be relieved of part of the responsibility.' . . . [It] would have taken a few weeks to issue callings and get the auxiliaries up and running, which is probably what Brossard was remembering." Brent Smith, correspondence, 15 July 2020. On a related point, "When the chapel was dedicated in 1933, [the] Washington Branch was within the Capitol District of the Eastern States Mission." The Washington D.C. Stake was organized on 30 June 1940 with Ezra Taft Benson as its first stake president. See Burke, *Washington D.C. LDS Ward*, 82, 83. The Washington Branch became a ward this same year. Sue A. Kohler and Jeffrey R. Carson, *Sixteenth Street Architecture* (Washington, DC: The Commission of Fine Arts, 1988), 2:525; Reed Russell, "The Washington, D.C. Chapel," http://www.keepapitchinin.org/2012/09/26/guest-post-the -washington-d-c-chapel/comment-page-1/. Two years before the organization of the Washington Branch, the Capitol Branch was organized just outside of DC—in the state of Maryland. We express appreciation to Brent Smith for pointing this out.

7. See Burke, *Washington D.C. LDS Ward*, 40. One source pointed out that the location was ideal because it was "in the very heart of the embassy district." See Gladys Stewart Bennion, "Impressions," in "Washington Ward Calendar—10th Anniversary, Vol XI, No 2 (Feb. 1942)," in Edgar B. Brossard Collection, Utah State University Archives, COLL MSS 4, box 37, folder 10, p. 22.

8. See Palfreyman, *Washington Chapel*, HABS No. DC-539, 7; Burke, *Washington D.C. LDS Ward*, 41.

9. The lots were originally owned by Westmoreland Davis, the governor of Virginia. See Palfreyman, *Washington Chapel*, HABS No. DC-539, 7. At the time Robert Murray Stewart noticed them, the lots were empty. One source notes, "there were four small frame buildings located on the property facing Columbia Road in 1896; however, they seem to have been cleared shortly thereafter—at [the] latest by 1919—in order to widen Columbia Road." See Palfreyman, *Washington Chapel*, HABS No. DC-539, 3.

10. See Burke, *Washington D.C. LDS Ward*, 41–43.

11. Burke, *Washington D.C. LDS Ward*, 44. See also Kohler and Carson, *Sixteenth Street Architecture*, 2:521; Barlow and Cardon, *Washington Chapel*, 5. The Church was to be built "in the historical Meridian Hill neighborhood among embassies, churches, and well-to-do residences. . . . On either side of Sixteenth Street, wealthy homeowners gravitated to the corridor for its proximity to power, and an eclectic mix of congregations would follow including Baptists, Episcopalians, Jews and Buddhists." The street became "the *de facto* setting for many foreign embassies and national churches." See Palfreyman, *Washington Chapel*, HABS No. DC-539, 1, 5. Elsewhere we read, "Other churches in the area were at first reluctant to have the Mormons in their neighborhood, as were also some of the permanent residents living near the chapel." Burke, *Washington D.C. LDS Ward*, 69.

12. See Kohler and Carson, *Sixteenth Street Architecture*, 2:521; Russell, "Washington, D.C. Chapel."

13. See Burke, *Washington D.C. LDS Ward*, 43. See also Palfreyman, *Washington Chapel*, HABS No. DC-539, 7; Barlow and Cardon, *Washington Chapel*, 5.

14. See Barlow and Cardon, *Washington Chapel*. See also Burke, *Washington D.C. LDS Ward*, 43–44; Kohler and Carson, *Sixteenth Street Architecture*, 2:521–22.

15. Henderson agreed to the sale of the property on 28 March 1924 and signed the paperwork on 9 April of that same year. See Palfreyman, *Washington Chapel*, HABS No. DC-539, 7. DC-area resident Page Johnson suggested: "Mrs. Henderson's conditions for selling the lots to the Church give insight into the architectural planning of the chapel: It had to be a church that was

appropriate for the location and which fit the type of architecture she would approve.... [Not] only did the Church want a beautiful structure, but so also did the seller, who conditioned the sale on" the promise of an aesthetically pleasing design. Page Johnson, correspondence, 6 July 2020.

16. The third lot belonged to Lucy E. Moten. See Palfreyman, *Washington Chapel*, HABS No. DC-539, 3, 7; Kohler and Carson, *Sixteenth Street Architecture*, 2:522. Her name is sometimes erroneously given as "Jucey E. Moten."

17. See Burke, *Washington D.C. LDS Ward*, 45; Palfreyman, *Washington Chapel*, HABS No. DC-539, 2, 4. On 20 May 1924, Elder Reed Smoot sent a letter to Isaac Russell (of Chicago). In that letter, Elder Smoot noted, "We have purchased the best corner in Washington. It cost the Church $54,000. I expect the Church to put up a magnificent building here, one that will be . . . an honor to the Church. . . . I know nothing that will advertise the Mormon people better than a magnificent structure on the corner of Columbia Road and Sixteenth Street." A transcript of this letter can be found in Russell, "Washington, D.C. Chapel." It should be pointed out that "the Washington Chapel only served as the dedicated meetinghouse for *all* members of the Church in Washington from 1933–1938, when church leaders divided the congregation [in 1938] into the Arlington Branch (Virginia) and the Chevy Chase Branch (Maryland). Members [then] started building and attending other chapels in the area." Page Johnson, correspondence, 6 July 2020, emphasis added.

18. See editor's comment in J. Reuben Clark Jr., "Beware of False Prophets," *Improvement Era*, May 1949, 268. Page Johnson wrote, "A great mission of the Washington Chapel was to herald the presence of the Church in Washington. It did that very well for four decades." Page Johnson, correspondence, 6 July 2020.

19. "Washington Ward Calendar—10th Anniversary, Vol XI, No 2 (Feb. 1942)," in Edgar B. Brossard Collection, Utah State University Archives, COLL MSS 4, box 37, folder 10, p. 27. See also Palfreyman, *Washington Chapel*, HABS No. DC-539, 7; Burke, *Washington D.C. LDS Ward*, 45.

20. Inscribed on the cornerstone of the building is the name of the three architects who designed the chapel: Don Carlos Young Jr., Ramm Hansen, and Harry P. Poll—all from the firm of Young & Hansen. This same firm built other noteworthy buildings, including the Mesa Arizona Temple and the Salt Lake Federal Reserve Building, in addition to being responsible for the remodels of "all LDS temples in Utah between 1935 and 1953." See Palfreyman, *Washington Chapel*, HABS No. DC-539, 8. See also Burke, *Washington D.C. LDS Ward*, 45.

21. See Palfreyman, *Washington Chapel*, HABS No. DC-539, 2, 9, 10, 11; Brossard, "Church in the Nation's Capital," 122; Barlow and Cardon, *Washington Chapel*, 5; Kohler and Carson, *Sixteenth Street Architecture*, 2:525; Burke, *Washington D.C. LDS Ward*, 45, 50–51, 54; "Beautiful Washington D.C. Chapel of the Church of Jesus Christ of Latter-day Saints (Mormon)," Church History Library MS 3642, 2; Russell, "Washington, D.C. Chapel." There were three dedicatory sessions and, according to Burke, approximately 1,200 people total attended. Burke, *Washington D.C. LDS Ward*, 54. Another source claims that "approximately 3,000 people total . . . attended the three dedicatory services." See Palfreyman, *Washington Chapel*, HABS No. DC-539, 10. See also "3,000 Attend Mormon Rite in Dedication," *Washington Post*, 6 November 1933, classified section, 13; Russell, "Washington, D.C. Chapel." In addition to dignitaries from the Church, the President of the United States was also invited to the chapel's dedicatory services. "Although President Franklin Delano Roosevelt was invited and responded that he would try to make it if his schedule allowed him, he proved to be too busy to leave the White House that day." Palfreyman, *Washington Chapel*, HABS No. DC-539, 10.

22. See "New Mormon Chapel in Washington," in *Boston Evening Transcript*, 18 November 1933, magazine section, 4; Kohler and Carson, *Sixteenth Street Architecture*, 2:523. One can only conjecture why the Church chose to use Utah birdseye marble instead of using local East Coast materials. Nevertheless, this creates a parallel between the Salt Lake Temple and the Washington Chapel; both buildings using stone from the Utah mountains. Of birdseye marble, one website sponsored by the state of Utah explains, "Approximately 58 to 66 million years ago (Paleocene epoch), a large body of water known as Lake Flagstaff covered parts of northeastern and central Utah. This lake deposited a sequence of sediments that formed rocks known as the Flagstaff Formation. Although these rocks are technically a limestone, the building stone industry has termed this deposit a 'marble.' The rocks are rich in algal ball structures commonly known as 'birdseyes.' These birdseye features were formed by algae that grew around snail shells, twigs, or other debris. The algae used these objects as a nucleus, forming into unusual, elongated, concentric shapes." https://geology.utah.gov/popular/places-to-go/rock-mineral-collecting-sites/the-rockhounder-birdseye-marble-in-the-manti-la-sal-national-forest-utah-county/. Another source states, "The so-called 'marble' is technically a limestone, and thus, its porosity has left it vulnerable to weathering." Palfreyman, *Washington Chapel*, HABS No. DC-539, 23. See also "Washington Ward Calendar—10th Anniversary, Vol XI, No 2 (Feb. 1942)," in Edgar B. Brossard Collection, Utah State University Archives, COLL MSS 4, box 37, folder 10, p. 27.

23. "New Mormon Chapel in Washington," in *Boston Evening Transcript*, 18 November 1933, magazine section, 4. See also Kohler and Carson, *Sixteenth Street Architecture*, 2:523.

24. See Palfreyman, *Washington Chapel*, HABS No. DC-539, 1; Kohler and Carson, *Sixteenth Street Architecture*, 2:525, 528.

25. Harry Kimball, of Salt Lake City, was the artisan who created the stained-glass windows for the Washington Chapel. See *Washington Ward Calendar*, March 1939, CHL LR 9948 25, 2. DC resident Brent Smith pointed out, "[An] August 2011 earthquake in the DC area . . . damaged the chapel itself[,] including its sanctuary and its 'South America/Book of Mormon' stained glass window." Brent Smith, correspondence, 6 June 2020.

26. See Barlow and Cardon, *Washington Chapel*, 6; Burke, *Washington D.C. LDS Ward*, 62; Palfreyman, *Washington Chapel*, HABS No. DC-539, 34; Kohler and Carson, *Sixteenth Street Architecture*, 2:525, 535; "Beautiful Washington D.C. Chapel," 1. "The foyer also has stained glass windows. Its semicircular-headed window on the north elevation has stained glass depictions of books of scripture; the five books represent the Book of Mormon, the Old Testament, the New Testament, the Doctrine and Covenants, and the Pearl of Great Price. The top book is larger than the other four and inscribed in a circle." Palfreyman, *Washington Chapel*, HABS No. DC-539, 34. One source noted that these windows depicting the standard works of the Church "so attracted the attention of passers-by that I have seen them stop, look, turn around and slowly mount the steps of the chapel to learn their meaning." Gladys Stewart Bennion, "Impressions," in "Washington Word Calendar—10th Anniversary, Vol XI, No 2 (Feb. 1942)," p. 24. See also Burke, *Washington D.C. LDS Ward*, 48–49.

27. "Washington Ward Calendar—10th Anniversary, Vol XI, No 2 (Feb. 1942)," in Edgar B. Brossard Collection, Utah State University Archives, COLL MSS 4, box 37, folder 10, p. 9. While it was absolutely *not* designed nor intended to be one of our temples, that it was commonly mistaken as one is suggested by the following comment by DC resident Brent Smith: "Since 2016, Church Public Affairs, other DC-area Church members/former Washington Ward members, and the Church History Department [have been] involved in ongoing contacts with . . . the current occupants of the chapel, what is called the Washington Family (Unification) Church. . . . In this connection we have particularly worked to help them correct/dispel their mistaken notion (spelled out on their website) that their chapel was originally a smaller LDS temple—with the transfer of the angel Moroni statue and construction/dedication/move to the new Kensington, MD, temple at the time the chapel was sold." Brent Smith, correspondence, 6 July 2020.

28. See, for example, "New Mormon Chapel in Washington," in *Boston Evening Transcript*, 18 November 1933, magazine section, 4; Dave Clemens, "Inner Circle of LDS Church Debating Fate of Historic Structures," in *Ogden Standard-Examiner*, 9 November 1975, 14A.

29. See Barlow and Cardon, *Washington Chapel*, 6; "Beautiful Washington D.C. Chapel," 2; J. Michael Hunter, "I Saw Another Angel Fly," *Ensign*, January 2000, 32.

30. Palfreyman, *Washington Chapel*, HABS No. DC-539, 1. See also 8, 23. In addition, see Barlow and Cardon, *Washington Chapel*, 6; Kohler and Carson, *Sixteenth Street Architecture*, 2:528. Another wrote, "its design was intended to symbolize the spirit of the temple at Salt Lake City." Kohler and Carson, *Sixteenth Street Architecture*, 2:522. See also Russell, "Washington, D.C. Chapel."

31. See Palfreyman, *Washington Chapel*, HABS No. DC-539, 10. See also Russell, "Washington, D.C. Chapel."

32. See Barlow and Cardon, *Washington Chapel*, 5; "Mormon Faith Heads to Join in Dedication," *Washington Post*, 29 October 1933, p. M; "New Mormon Chapel in Washington," in *Boston Evening Transcript*, 18 November 1933, magazine section, 4. John Gerritsen, the grandson of Torleif Knaphus, suggested that the reason a Moroni statue was placed atop the Washington Chapel was because of the importance of the location of this building in the nation's capital. His understanding was that the Church wanted the chapel to be easily recognized. John Gerritsen, interview, 27 November 2019. Lee Burke similarly explained that "they wanted this chapel to be a showplace to the nation's capital; one that functioned as a gathering place in a city of dignitaries and ambassadors of other countries." In hindsight, the fact that it looked to many so much like a temple may have helped to facilitate this. Lee Burke, interviews, 3 November 2019 and 20 July 2020. Elder Reed Smoot's 20 May 1924 letter, cited above, confirms this. See Russell, "Washington, D.C. Chapel." Sometime after the statue was removed from the top of the Washington Chapel, LaVar Wallgren "made two castings of the Knaphus replica. One was placed on the Atlanta Georgia Temple; the other was placed on the Idaho Falls Idaho Temple." See Hunter, "I Saw Another Angel Fly," 32. This version of the statue is ten feet high and weighs 645 pounds. It is covered in 23-karat-gold leaf.

33. See Palfreyman, *Washington Chapel*, HABS No. DC-539, 8.

34. Kohler and Carson, *Sixteenth Street Architecture*, 2:522–23. See also "New Mormon Chapel in Washington," in *Boston Evening Transcript*, 18 November 1933, magazine section, 4. For additional parallels between the Washington Chapel and the Salt Lake Temple, see Kohler and Carson 2:530; "Beautiful

Washington D.C. Chapel," 2; Palfreyman, *Washington Chapel*, HABS No. DC-539, 25; "A Union Service with Mormons," the *Christian Leader* (a national periodical of the Unitarian Church in America), cited in *Latter-day Saints' Millennial Star*, 30 May 1935, 339–40.

35. Palfreyman, *Washington Chapel*, HABS No. DC-539, 28.

36. See Burke, *Washington D.C. LDS Ward*, 67; and Barlow and Cardon, *Washington Chapel*, 6. See also http://ldspioneerarchitecture.blogspot .com/2017/05/mesa-temple-interior.html. Reynolds and Sjodahl associated this phrase with the temple: "In the *Doctrine and Covenants*, the divine element is called 'the light which now shineth.' (Sec. 88:11–33) . . . It is the Glory of God, the manifestation of the divine presence; the fire and smoke, which made Sinai tremble; the glory which rested on the Mercy Seat in the tabernacle and the temple; the wind which filled the house on the Day of Pentecost. It is divine intelligence, since 'the glory of God is intelligence.' It is the force before which mountains flee and worlds perish, for 'the presence of the Lord shall be as a fire that burneth, and as a fire which causes water to boil.' (*Doctrine and Covenants* 133:41)." George Reynolds and Janne M. Sjodahl, *Commentary on the Book of Mormon* (Salt Lake City: Deseret Book, 1976), 2:169–70.

37. See Kohler and Carson, *Sixteenth Street Architecture*, 2:525–26. See also Russell, "Washington, D.C. Chapel."

38. Burke, *Washington D.C. LDS Ward*, 131–32.

39. Palfreyman, *Washington Chapel*, HABS No. DC-539, 4. See also "Beautiful Washington D.C. Chapel," 1.

40. While we do not know the extent of his involvement, President Heber J. Grant personally signed one of the architectural drawings of the building, and above his name he wrote "Approved." See "Washington Chapel Rendering" dated 1925, CHL MS 27892.

41. See Kohler and Carson, *Sixteenth Street Architecture*, 2:525. See also CHL LR 9948 20, "The Chapel Beautiful," 26; Franklin S. Harris Jr., "Washington Chapel Dedicatory Services," *Latter-day Saints' Millennial Star* 95, no. 49 (14 December 1933): 801–2; "3,000 Attend Mormon Rite in Dedication," 13; "New Mormon Chapel in Washington," in *Boston Evening Transcript*, 18 November 1933, magazine section, 4; Burke, *Washington D.C. LDS Ward*, 51. In his remarks (at the dedication), Elder Stephen L. Richards of the First Presidency described the chapel as "a beautiful prediction of the future." Burke, *Washington D.C. LDS Ward*, 57. One can only conjecture as to what exactly President Richards meant or saw. Did he foresee the day when the temple would be built there? Or were his words simply meant as a prediction that the Church would grow significantly in the DC area in the coming years?

42. For example, President Grant prayed, "Father, we thank Thee for this beautiful chapel and we now dedicate it to Thee for Thy Holy purposes." "3,000 Attend Mormon Rite in Dedication," 13. Similarly, in the Birmingham, Alabama Temple dedication, President Gordon B. Hinckley prayed, "We are met to present unto thee this sacred house, a temple of the Lord dedicated for purposes according to Thy will and pattern." "Dedicatory Prayer," Birmingham Alabama Temple, 3 September 2000. https://www.churchofjesus christ.org/temples/details/birmingham-alabama-temple/prayer/2000-09 -03?lang=eng.

43. Richard O. Cowan, *Temples to Dot the Earth* (Springville: Cedar Fort, 1997), 112.

44. Barlow and Cardon, *Washington Chapel*, 7; Burke, *Washington D.C. LDS Ward*, 55.

45. See Burke, *Washington D.C. LDS Ward*, 54; "3,000 Attend Mormon Rite in Dedication," 13. They had a special dedication for the cornerstone of the chapel; something unheard of for a chapel, but similar to a Temple. Elder Reed Smoot offered the prayer of dedication, stating the following, among other things: "Bless, O Lord, this effort. Help us to complete with all possible speed the erection of this building that it may be *dedicated to Thy holy name.* . . . May the stone laid here this day be a corner stone to a place of worship where truth and light may be always uppermost in the mind of those who come within *its sacred portals.*" Reed Smoot Cornerstone Dedicatory Prayer, CHL LR 9948 20, 1–2, emphasis added.

46. *Washington Evening Star*, cited in *Improvement Era*, April 1957, 250.

47. Palfreyman, *Washington Chapel*, HABS No. DC-539, 14–15.

48. Burke, *Washington D.C. LDS Ward*, 37. See also "Washington Ward Calendar—10th Anniversary, Vol XI, No 2 (Feb. 1942)," in Edgar B. Brossard Collection, Utah State University Archives, COLL MSS 4, box 37, folder 10, pp. 4–5, 7. During that era, the Washington and Potomac Stakes— which shared a border—were among the five highest baptizing stakes in the Church. See "Proposal for a Washington D.C. Temple," in Edgar B. Brossard Collection, Utah State University Archives, COLL MSS 4, box 37, folder 15, p. 13.

49. Burke, *Washington D.C. LDS Ward*, 70. Having a chapel in DC was a unique opportunity for making national and international contacts, as the building would be built in the heart of the embassy district. In fact, the chapel was listed in all major hotel and guidebooks of the era. Even cab drivers were familiar with the iconic edifice, and approximately ten thousand guests per year visited the building and toured its facilities. Such was not the case for most DC churches of the era, but the Washington Chapel

was architecturally unique. Edgar Brossard explained, "A Church that has no National Chapel in Washington cannot be adequately represented in the religious life of the Capital. The Latter Day Saints have felt keenly the need of a spiritual center. . . . A superb building adds to the dignity of religious services, and a monumental church in Washington adds to the dignity and prestige of a religious organization." Church leaders in the area wanted to build a "National Chapel," which would be a showplace for the Church. It has been said that the unique Utah birdseye marble made the Church building "reminiscent of the Salt Lake Temple." The distinctive exterior stone and gold Moroni statue would add to the uniqueness of the building and facilitated drawing attention to its unusual features. See Edgar B. Brossard Collection, Utah State University Archives, COLL MSS 4, box 37, folder 10, pp. 17, 22, 23, 28.

50. See Burke, *Washington D.C. LDS Ward*, 63–64. Writing about the chapel's remarkable organ, George D. Pyper—once a member of and "manager" of the Mormon Tabernacle Choir—wrote, "next to the great Salt Lake Tabernacle organ there was installed in the Washington chapel the finest instrument in the Church." See George D. Pyper, "Church Music—LDS Church Music at the Nation's Capital," *Improvement Era*, December 1933, 863.

51. Brossard, "Church in the Nation's Capital," 122. Another source noted, there were "public organ recitals six days a week (every day except for Sunday) for the first year, recording more than 18,000 visitors." Palfreyman, *Washington Chapel*, HABS No. DC-539, 15. See also Kohler and Carson, *Sixteenth Street Architecture*, 2:525. Edward P. Kimball was the organist for the Tabernacle Choir for nearly three decades prior to becoming the organist for the Washington Chapel. In response to a call from the First Presidency of the Church, he remained the organist at the chapel until his death (in 1937). Handwritten note regarding Kimball, in Edgar B. Brossard Collection, Utah State University Archives, COLL MSS 4, box 37, folder 7; "Washington Ward Calendar—10th Anniversary, Vol XI, No 2 (Feb. 1942)," in Edgar B. Brossard Collection, Utah State University Archives, COLL MSS 4, box 37, folder 10, p. 4.

52. Brossard, "Church in the Nation's Capital," 123.

53. Burke, *Washington D.C. LDS Ward*, 74. See also "Washington Ward Calendar—10th Anniversary, Vol XI, No 2 (Feb. 1942)," in Edgar B. Brossard Collection, Utah State University Archives, COLL MSS 4, box 37, folder 10, p. 7.

54. See handwritten note about Edward Kimball, in Edgar B. Brossard Collection, Utah State University Archives, COLL MSS 4, box 37, folder 7. See also Burke, *Washington D.C. LDS Ward*, 57–58, 59, 62, 71. The Salt Lake Temple Square Visitors' Center was originally called "The Bureau of Information," and functioned much like the one operated at the Washington Chapel. See

"Washington Ward Calendar—10th Anniversary, Vol XI, No 2 (Feb. 1942),"
in Edgar B. Brossard Collection, Utah State University Archives, COLL MSS
4, box 37, folder 10, p. 30; Edward H. Anderson, "The Bureau of Information," *Improvement Era*, December 1921, 130–39. One source noted, "At the
close of the services, announcement was made that strangers who cared to
remain would be shown through the building by Brother Kimball." Cardon,
"Vacant Lot," 584. Kimball was originally the director of the bureau. See
"Washington Ward Calendar—10th Anniversary, Vol XI, No 2 (Feb. 1942),"
in Edgar B. Brossard Collection, Utah State University Archives, COLL MSS
4, box 37, folder 10, p. 4.

55. Palfreyman, *Washington Chapel*, HABS No. DC-539, 13. "On March 1,
1976, the *New York Times* described how the chapel's completion in 1933
was 'seen as a testament to the end of Washington's hostility toward the
Mormons.'" Palfreyman, *Washington Chapel*, HABS No. DC-539, 18. Not
many members lived in the DC area (in the late-nineteenth and early-
twentieth centuries), in part because of the Church's emphasis on gathering
to Utah and, quite possibly, because perceptions of the Church were not
great in those early years, particularly in Washington. President Heber J.
Grant (1856–1945), eighth President of the Church, pointed out, "for years
and years not a single person from Utah was ever able to secure employment in Washington, and . . . the delegates from Utah were expelled" from
the United States Senate. Heber J. Grant, in Conference Report, April 1930,
186. See also Heber J. Grant, *Gospel Standards* (Salt Lake City: Bookcraft,
1998), 90. The *Encyclopedia of Latter-day Saint History* similarly notes,
"During the nineteenth century, numerous Latter-day Saint leaders visited
the [U.S.] capital to seek federal support for the move west and for statehood, although the Church and the federal government were at odds over
a variety of issues from 1857 until 1907." Peterson, "Washington, D.C.,"
1314. See also Brossard, "Church in the Nation's Capital," 119. In more
recent years, "the LDS Church has maintained a positive and respected position in Washington, D.C. The relationship with the federal government
has evolved from one of antagonism and prejudice to one of participation
and influence." Peterson, "Washington, D.C.," 1315. Thus, even though the
Church would begin to grow rapidly in various parts of the world, starting
with its official organization in 1830, it would be many decades before it
gained any footing in the DC area. However, things would change. The
Washington Ward would eventually include notables, such as a member
of the United States Tariff Commission, the head of the Publication Division of the U.S. Department of Agriculture, the director of agricultural
extension and industries for all Native Americans in the United States,
the head of the Sugar Manufacturers' Association of America, two future

presidents of the Church, and several individuals holding various elected offices. Cardon, "Vacant Lot," 583–84. The makeup of the congregation seems significant owing to all that the Church had gone through in that city over the years—particularly in light of a twentieth-century tradition of a supposed prophecy made by Joseph Smith after visits with President Martin Van Buren. After the president rebuffed the prophet, Joseph is said to have prophesied not only of the demise of Van Buren's political career but also of a time when the Saints would be influential in DC. One source gives the prediction as follows: "The Mormons would return to Washington and occupy responsible positions in the affairs of the state and become a respected people." Wendell B. Anderson, "Mormons in Washington," *Latter-day Saints' Millennial Star*, 3 September 1942, 563. Elsewhere, this same prophetic declaration is given as: "Some day [*sic*] the Mormon people will be held in renown in the nation's capital." See "The Church Moves On," *Improvement Era*, July 1938, 415.

56. See "Elias," in LDS Bible Dictionary (2013), 634; Robert L. Millet, "Elias," in *LDS Beliefs: A Doctrinal Reference*, ed. Robert L. Millet, Camille Fronk Olson, Andrew C. Skinner, and Brent L. Top (Salt Lake City: Deseret Book, 2011), 177.

57. It should be understood that we are not claiming that the Washington Chapel was *intended* as a "placeholder" for the future temple, nor are we claiming that the Church necessarily intended it as a "forerunner" to the future temple—only that it ultimately functioned as such.

58. Page Johnson, correspondence, 6 July 2020.

59. Burke *Washington D.C. LDS Ward*, 107.

60. One source noted, "Similar to the Chapel before it in 1933, the [Washington D.C.] Temple sought to pay homage to the Salt Lake Temple, but it did so in a more formal gesture rather than a stylistic one. The six-spire design recalls that of the flagship temple in the Great Basin, but the architectural style is radically modern and dramatically vertical. The one feature shared by all three buildings . . . is having their highest point capped by as statue of the angel Moroni." Palfreyman, *Washington Chapel*, HABS No. DC-539, 17. Elsewhere we read, "The temple towering over the trees near the Washington Beltway, . . . gives the appearance of the Salt Lake Temple with similar shape and six towers. It is a breathtakingly lovely building—sometimes looking almost unreal, so white and tall above the trees." Burke, *Washington D.C. LDS Ward*, 132.

61. Burke, *Washington D.C. LDS Ward*, 134. The groundbreaking for the Washington D.C. Temple was held on 7 December 1968. See Burke, *Washington D.C. LDS Ward*, 131.

62. See Kohler and Carson, *Sixteenth Street Architecture*, 2:525; Palfreyman, *Washington Chapel*, HABS No. DC-539, 2, 18.

63. See "Mormons' historic chapel for sale as parish dissolves in Washington," *Battle Creek Enquirer* (Battle Creek, MI), 3 April 1976, 7, where it suggests that repairs needed on the building would have cost the Church $450,000— and that figure excluded the cost of needed masonry work. See also "Mormons Selling Historic Chapel," in *New York Times*, 1 March 1976, 42. The building was also lacking adequate parking. "Car ownership" when the building was built "was uncommon, and the later essential parking lot was not even considered in constructing the chapel. Street cars were the accepted mode of travel" when the building was first built. Burke, *Washington D.C. LDS Ward*, 69.

64. See Burke, *Washington D.C. LDS Ward*, 136–39.

65. According to Burke, the Washington Ward was dissolved *before* the building was sold, largely because of dissension in the ward regarding the selling of the building. Thus, there was a directive that the Washington Ward members begin to attend family wards in the suburbs of DC. At the time, the ward was made up of singles, sort of a mishmash attending from all over the area. Burke, similarly, lived in Virginia but attended the Washington Ward. Lee Burke, interview, 3 November 2019. Page Johnson pointed out, "In the last years the building was owned by the Church, a Spanish branch also met there." Page Johnson, correspondence, 6 July 2000.

66. See Burke, *Washington D.C. LDS Ward*, 135.

67. See Burke, *Washington D.C. LDS Ward*, 135.

68. Burke, *Washington D.C. LDS Ward*, 140; see also Palfreyman, *Washington Chapel*, HABS No. DC-539, 18; Russell, "Washington, D.C. Chapel." The *Ogden Standard-Examiner* reported, "Some critics" of the Church's "preservation practices say the church lacks a guiding policy on historical buildings and has based the future of its edifices too much on financial expediency and on architecturally uninformed decisions by local leaders. The Church responds that its business is saving souls, not buildings, and that it can't preserve all the structures others might think merit saving." Two architects, Allen Roberts and Paul Anderson, conducted a "study" of the Church's "historical buildings" and counseled the Church that the "Washington, D.C., chapel" should be considered "untouchable." The *Standard-Examiner* added, "A group of local [DC] Mormons joined in to oppose the sale." See Dave Clemens, "Inner Circle of LDS Church Debating Fate of Historic Structures," in *Ogden Standard-Examiner*, Sunday, 9 November 1975, 14A.

69. Mitchell NewDelman, president of Columbia Road Recording Studios, "said he contracted in April 1976 to purchase the chapel from the Mormon Church, but because of zoning and other difficulties, including a restrictive covenant in the deed, he was unable to reach a final settlement." "The Mormon Media Image," *Sunstone*, November–December 1977, 24. See also Laura A. Kiernan, "Unification Church Buys Former Mormon Chapel," *Washington Post*, 16 September 1977. https://www.washingtonpost.com/archive /local/1977/09/16/unification-church-buys-former-mormon-chapel/62ab e9de-3ab1-456e-91b4-63b2214a4346/.

70. Kohler and Carson, *Sixteenth Street Architecture*, 2:525; Palfreyman, *Washington Chapel*, HABS No. DC-539, 3–4; see also 1 and 19; Russell, "Washington D.C. Chapel." Burke claims it was sold the very same day. See Burke, *Washington D.C. LDS Ward*, 141.

71. Burke, *Washington D.C. LDS Ward*, 141; Russell, "Washington, D.C. Chapel."

72. See Kohler and Carson, *Sixteenth Street Architecture*, 2:525–26. See also Russell, "Washington, D.C. Chapel." Ariel Thomson, then a member of the high council, was given the assignment to clear out the building and remove the contents of the cornerstone. Thompson tried using a number of different chisels and four types of hammers in order to get the cornerstone open. He worked on opening it for three hours, with absolutely no progress (because the mortar was so hard). He finally took his biggest hammer and smashed the sides of the cornerstone. That enabled him to access the metal box inside. Within that box was a triple combination and a 1933 *New York Times* and *Washington Post*. According to Thomson, Don Ladd, who was at that time president of the Washington Stake, kept the triple combination that had been retrieved from the cornerstone. Ariel Thomson, interviews, 14 March 2019 and 2 November 2019.

73. Burke, *Washington D.C. LDS Ward*, 140.

74. See Palfreyman, *Washington Chapel*, HABS No. DC-539, 19–23.

75. President Ezra Taft Benson was the first president of the Washington Stake, serving in that capacity from 30 June 1940 until 5 March 1945. President Russell M. Nelson served as the second counselor in the DC Ward bishopric from 29 December 1951 until 15 March 1953. Apostles Reed Smoot and Richard G. Scott also served in the leadership of the Church in DC, the latter of the two serving as a counselor in the stake presidency (in the early 1970s), and the former being the one who first presided at gatherings of the Church in the area (prior to the official organization of a Church unit in DC). In addition, Religious Education professor Reed A. Benson—son of President Ezra Taft Benson—served as the second counselor in the bishopric

from 13 February 1955 until January 1956. See Burke, *Washington D.C. LDS Ward*, 147, 149, 156.

76. See Russell, "Washington, D.C. Chapel," comments 51, 52, 54.

77. See Palfreyman, *Washington Chapel*, HABS No. DC-539, 14, 10. Another source similarly stated that the Washington Chapel has been called "so rare a jewel, even among the magnificent churches of Washington." Brossard, "Church in the Nation's Capital," 122.

The Washington D.C. Temple. Photo by Richard C. Clawson.

THE WASHINGTON D.C. TEMPLE: MR. SMITH'S CHURCH GOES TO WASHINGTON

MACLANE E. HEWARD

Maclane E. Heward is a Seminaries and Institutes instructor and was a visiting professor at Brigham Young University when this was written.

Sacred space is among the most visible aspects of religion and functions as a location of interaction between believers, interested onlookers, and the divine.[1] The Washington D.C. Temple (formerly the Washington Temple) functions as a prominent and unique example of sacred space for The Church of Jesus Christ of Latter-day Saints because of its location in the nation's capital. It has become a location shared by the Church and its members as well as the national and international communities located in the area. This shared location was purposefully created by the Church and has facilitated important relationships between the Church and national and international leaders throughout the world. The following pages will discuss the vision the leadership of the Church had for the temple, how interaction with God sacralized the temple and how the Church and the community have utilized the location for their own purposes. This will facilitate an understanding of the uniqueness of the Washington D.C. Temple in fulfilling its intended purposes.

THE UNIQUE MISSION OF THE TEMPLE

Church leaders saw the temple as not only beneficial to the membership but also a symbol that the Church had entered a new phase of respectability. The temple was also seen as an opportunity to inform the world about the tenets of the faith. Elder Ezra Taft Benson (then of the Quorum of the Twelve Apostles) and President Hugh B. Brown (of the First Presidency) both indicated that the building of the temple was a symbol that the Church had outgrown persecution. Speaking at the dedication of the ground for the temple on 7 December 1968, Benson reflected on the history of the Church in the DC area: "I thought last night . . . of the days of persecution when the Saints were being driven—many of them murdered, and their homes burned." Along with recounting President Martin Van Buren's famous response to Joseph Smith, Benson also discussed the Reed Smoot hearings with a sense of bewilderment that Smoot's senate seat was called into question after he was "elected by the people of the sovereign state of Utah." "Well, there have been great changes," which Benson attributed partially to the specific efforts of the Saints in the DC area. "I'm so pleased," Benson continues, "that a temple of God is to be erected in the nation's capital, the capital of the greatest nation under heaven." So Benson saw the temple as a symbol that the Church had overcome its persecuted past and looked forward to the continued establishment of the Church in the United States. His concluding thoughts leave little room to misunderstand that a primary benefit of the temple in Washington, DC, is for the neighbors of the Church in that area. "A temple in Washington will be inspiration not only to the Latter-day Saints, but to people of many faiths, our friends, our neighbors, and thousands upon hundreds of thousands who will come here and receive inspiration as they view this structure which will light this hill." Benson concluded with an invitation for those present to "appreciate what this project means."[2]

President Hugh B. Brown began his remarks at the dedication of the temple site by indicating that President David O. McKay, the President of the Church, made a special effort to ensure that a message of his love was brought to the people in the Washington area. Brown then quickly transitioned and paralleled Benson's remarks: "To me," he began, "this is one

The Washington D.C. Temple and fountain. Courtesy of author.

of the most significant moments in the history of the Church—a moment when we came back east from which we were driven years ago. . . . But now we come back and we propose to build a temple on this site—a temple to the Lord, our God. I had a thrill as I think of its significance, what it portends." Thus, for both Benson and Brown, the temple symbolized the Church coming to a time in its development when it had overcome the persecutions of the past and was now a part of the nation. Later in his remarks Brown discussed the gospel being taken to the nations of the earth in anticipation of the day of peace. He seemed to suggest that this temple will have a significant role in that development and thanked God in the dedicatory prayer, saying, "We thank thee for what it portends."[3]

According to Brown, the temple seemed to be a significant part of that development.

President Brown made his understanding of the purpose of the temple even more clear as he invited the selected group of architects to begin their work designing the building. Keith Wilcox, one of the architects, remembered meeting with Brown and hearing Brown's emphasis on sharing with those who would design the building the unique feelings of the First Presidency regarding this particular temple. Brown emphasized the specific "missionary impact" of the building, further stating that Washington, DC, was the capital of the country but that some viewed it as the "capital of the world." The architecture should therefore match the intended missionary impact as well as fit in with the other architecturally significant buildings in the area. It ought to be beautiful and be a credit to the Church.[4] Though the Church leaders wanted the architecture to be meaningful and powerful, no one knew how iconic the temple would become. After the route of the Capital Beltway was finalized and before the groundbreaking, the location of the temple was adjusted sixty feet to line up perfectly with the Capital Beltway. This small adjustment has had repercussions for missionary work as many people, due to its visibility and beauty, stop by the temple seeking information about its purpose.[5]

The approach of the Church in actively seeking public participation in the events of the temple completion and open house represents a transition for the Church. Historian J. B. Haws indicated that this transition had roots at Brigham Young University. In 1969 Ernest Wilkinson, the president of BYU, faced a difficult decision to either stay quiet regarding the exploding racial conflict growing out of BYU athletics and the Church's racial policies or to defend the university and the Church. Wilkinson accurately expressed the previous approach of the Church when he expressed worry that "our story is being told—by our detractors, by those who are uniformed, by almost everyone except us. . . . In the past our lips have been largely sealed." Wilkinson was advised by N. Eldon Tanner of the First Presidency to use his "best judgment" in the situation. With the help of Heber Wolsey, the head of public relations for the school, the school began to tell its own story and control its own message. Though an aberration from previous patterns, this approach was incredibly successful. Wolsey, just three short years later, became the chief assistant in the newly formed Public Communications Department. This development, growing out of the newly organized administration of President Harold B. Lee, dramatically altered the public communication strategy of the Church, leaving it professionalized and progressive. The shift went from an approach of "we don't, in effect, want media publicity to the idea that we'll hire the best people we can possibly hire to help us with the public relations program."[6]

The approach of the Church in introducing the temple to the community in Washington, DC, evidences this significant shift. Not only did the Church seek after the "best people" for their public relations efforts regarding the opening of the temple, but the Church sought to use the temple to proactively educate the public about its core beliefs and create relationships with key constituencies. Though the temple gave evidence for the vitality of the diaspora of Latter-day Saints and the effectiveness of the missionary program, information gathered by the newly formed Public Communications Department indicated that Americans at large did not understand who the Saints were, what the Church was, or what its doctrines were. Just before the opening of the temple, the Public Communications Department assessed the attitudes and understanding of Americans regarding the Church in six metropolitan areas. The department members' main takeaway was summarized by Boyd K. Packer of the Twelve Apostles on one of the final pages of the report: "The problem faced by missionaries ordinarily is not opposition, but *obscurity*."[7] The temple and the open house associated with it became an opportunity for the newly formed, professionalized Public Communications Department to make an impact on public perception and to try and establish "family unity" as the brand of the Church.[8] They did this, in large measure, by inviting individuals to come and experience the temple before its dedication and to feel of the power of the sacred space after its dedication through annual events. Thus visitors were welcomed to the grounds to sense the sacredness of the place, a sacredness that was manifest to and created by local members of the Church even before the final purchasing agreement was signed and the location was approved as a temple site.

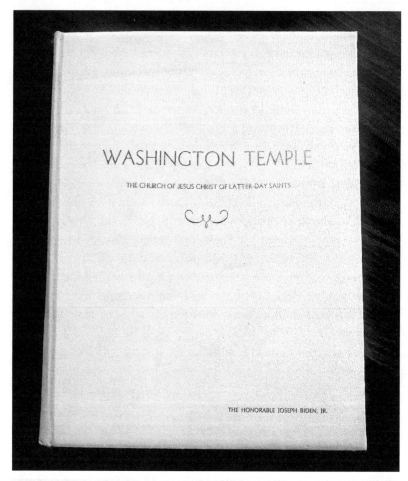

Members of the United States Senate and House of Representatives, along with many other government officials, were given special copies of a special issue of the Ensign *magazine with their names embossed on the cover. Joseph Biden Jr.'s personalized copy is shown above. Photo in possession of the author. This* Ensign *is currently in the possession of Flora McConkie and was given to a local stake president by a member of Senator Biden's staff.*

MAKING THE TEMPLE SACRED SPACE

What makes space sacred? Sacred space can commemorate past events, look forward to future events, or be a conscious effort to invite the sacred into a space. Sacred space is formed through the commemoration and anticipation of theophanies. Mount Sinai, the Mount of Olives, the Sacred Grove, and Adam-ondi-Ahman are examples of such spaces. Mircea Eliade, a religious historian and philosopher, suggested that if a "sacred location" is not directly attached to hallowed historic events, the performance of sacred rites and rituals can "provoke" or create sacred space. In effect, Eliade argued that men and women could create a space and, through ritual, invite God to inhabit the location. "Since religious man cannot live except in an atmosphere impregnated with the sacred," explains Eliade, "we must expect to find a large number of techniques for consecrating space." One such technique is engaging in ritual that "*reproduces the work of the gods.*"[9] Latter-day Saint theology sacralizes temples for each of these reasons: The temple is a location that both commemorates and anticipates interaction with the divine. It is a place where individuals participate in ritual to invite the divine. And men and women participate in the "work of the gods" at the temple. The following anecdotes will illustrate the unique spirit of the Washington D.C. Temple and how that connection with the divine developed through lived experience.

The location of the temple and the designation of the area as sacred space came even before the land was officially selected as the location of the temple. Initially, the land in Kensington, Maryland, where the Washington D.C. Temple rests was unavailable for purchase by the Church. The eventual purchase of the land was a result of a mutual understanding and respect for sacred space shared by Latter-days Saints and Jews. For many Church members who understand the details, the acquisition of the land for the temple illustrates God orchestrating and facilitating the accomplishment of his will.

In 1962 the title to the coveted land was owned by a group of investors who authorized three of its group to proceed with negotiations for the sale of the property.[10] Renowned lawyer and local Church leader Robert Barker was given approval by Church leadership to purchase the land. Barker was met with repeated rejection as the sale of the land was already being negotiated for by a real estate developer who wanted to build homes on the property. The investors had given their word that the land would be sold to the developer. In a moment of despair, Barker expressed his frustration to his wife, Amy, and explained that he felt strongly that the temple needed to be in this particular location, but it seemed the way was being hedged up. At this point in time, the Capital Beltway had been approved, but the plans and location were not finalized. Amy's response to her husband's frustrations and determinations was to direct him to tell the investors exactly what temples mean to Latter-day Saints and why it was so important that this spot of land be purchased. Barker decided to make one final attempt, asking one of the three leading investors to have lunch with him. This investor flatly refused and indicated that the land was not for sale. Barker, in an act of desperation, promised the investor that if he would come to lunch and hear what he had to say, Barker would never contact him again; this was just the motivation the investor needed!

During his lunch with this Jewish investor, Barker sought to build on common ground and to speak from his heart. He connected the love Latter-day Saints feel about the temple with the temple-building tradition of the Jewish people. Barker assured the investor that the temple ceremonies that Latter-day Saints participate in have similarities with the ceremonies with which the Jewish people were familiar. In the end, Barker shared the Church's doctrine about temples and the Church's commitment to building them in a personal, heartfelt way. The end of the lunch left Barker uncertain about the impact of his attempt, but that uncertainty did not last long. Just two hours later, the investor called Barker to indicate that the requested land would be sold to the Church. The investors decided that to stand in the way of a religious group wanting to build a house to God would not align with the individual beliefs of the investors, who were significant contributors in the Zionist movement.[11]

Years later when Diane Holling, a DC-area architectural student, was tasked with collecting historical documents regarding the temple, she interviewed the two surviving Jewish investors and found that if Barker's final plea would have been three days later, the land would have been tied up in the purchasing process and unavailable for the Church. Utah senator David S. King, former president of the Washington D.C. Temple and author of *Come to the House of the Lord*, concluded his summation of this story by declaring that in the details of the acquisition of the land, "the hand of the Lord was felt in the accomplishment of his purposes." King remembered that at the dedicatory service, President Spencer W. Kimball "declared . . . that the selection of the temple site . . . had been inspired of God."[12] Thus Saints interpreted the purchasing of the land as a moment in which they were working with God to bring about his purposes, a work that helped make the temple sacred space.

The development of the architectural plan for the temple also evidenced God's hand. Keith Wilcox remembered the significant emphasis President Brown placed on the shoulders of those who were assigned to design the building. The temple was to be a symbol of the Church and its presence in the nation and the world. Along with his emphasis on the reality that the temple structure ought to fit the purpose and missionary aims of the Church, he added one final measure of importance to the project by indicating that President David O. McKay had a "keen interest in this project."[13]

The men immediately began holding meetings to solidify the plans for the temple. In a meeting on 5 February 1969, one of the architects chided Wilcox for not yet submitting a drawing of the temple to the committee for consideration. Knowing the significance of the task, Wilcox cleared his schedule that Friday and Saturday and commenced the creation of a plan. "As I sat and pondered this challenge, I decided to make the problem a matter of deep, personal prayer." The inspiration that came to him came in the form of a single word: "enlightenment." Unaware of the time, Wilcox worked through the night, recalling that ideas "seemed to flow out of my fingertips without effort," visualizing the building's appearance even before drawing it. "I began to feel a great surge of the Spirit and a creative desire. It was a glorious feeling. I felt as if I were being lifted up; my mental faculties sharpened. I lost awareness of where I was. Truly, I felt full of 'enlightenment.' My mind and spirit were in tune with the challenge. A power beyond my own gave me strength."[14] At one point, Wilcox explained that he almost felt that he was in the presence of "Heavenly Beings."[15] He was deeply humbled by the experience and professed that the inspiration of heaven brought about the temple design. The building therefore came to represent for Wilcox a visible reminder of a sacred moment when he felt that God had parted the heavens and inspired an architect to create his house. Wilcox had participated in the "work of the gods."[16]

The sacrifice of individual members in donating money for the Washington D.C. Temple also helped to sacralize the edifice. During this time, members of the Church who would benefit from the construction of new buildings were asked to financially contribute to a building fund.[17] For the temple, members were asked to contribute more than four million dollars. Nicholas Perry, a wealthy convert, became the first to donate to the temple building funds. Perry had moved to Eastern Europe with his company before WWII commenced. During the war, Perry's business was confiscated by the Nazi Regime in Eastern Europe, and he and his family fled for their lives back to the United States. Perry had received funds from the Alien Property Custodial Act but donated the funds to the building of the temple instead.[18]

Other anecdotes illustrate the degree to which the Washington D.C. Temple was sacralized in the minds of the Latter-day Saints. Marsha Sharp Butler and her husband, Karl D. Butler, were able to attend the temple dedication ceremony and described it as a magnificent experience. Marsha expressed her feelings that the temple had a special aura around it and that she "just knew that it was a special place and that it was meant to be there at that particular time." After attending the temple dedication, Karl and Marsha noticed that a Brother Zimmer, a member of their local congregation, looked as if he was having a difficult time walking to his car from the temple. His walking was so labored that he needed assistance from his family, something unusual for Brother Zimmer. The next week at their local meetings, Marsha was informed that Brother Zimmer had experienced a theophany while in the temple. This experience further sacralized the temple for the Butlers. Later, when Karl was preparing to participate in ordinances in behalf of his deceased grandfather, his grandfather appeared to him as if to verify to Karl that the work he was doing was exactly what God and his grandfather wanted. These experiences bound the Butlers' hearts to this location as a sacred place where God manifested himself to his people.[19]

The Butlers' experiences are not unique. Other oral histories mention the realities of visitations or experiences where individuals felt the presence of those who had died. Doreen Taylor and her husband, Bramwell, went to the Washington D.C. Temple to be sealed. Because they were living in New Brunswick, Canada, they stayed in a hotel and spent a few days participating in ordinances for their deceased ancestors. While Doreen participated in the initiatory ordinances for her mother and grandmother, she "knew" that they had accepted the gospel, and she felt that they were by her side. She reported that all who were helping her through these ordinances were emotional, and, to this day, she still gets emotional thinking about the experience.[20]

Harold Ranquist, a local member who worked on the temple and served at that time as a major in the Army Reserves, believes God miraculously provided a miracle that facilitated the opening of the temple open house. At the last minute, the day before President Gerald Ford, his family, his cabinet, and many foreign diplomats were scheduled to attend the temple open house, the fire marshal refused to allow the open house to take place unless a separate emergency standby generator was ready to operate the sprinkler fire-suppression system in the event of a power outage. Having connections with military personnel in the area, Ranquist spent eight hours on a Sunday calling his military associates, including vacationing generals, to locate a generator that could be borrowed. As attendance was limited, virtually everyone that he spoke to asked for tickets to the open house. After significant effort, a generator was found and arrived on location just twenty-five minutes before the open house's scheduled starting time. After connecting the generator to the building systems and receiving the approval of the fire marshal, the open house began with minutes to spare. "That day," recalled Ranquist, "30 tickets were committed to the various colonels and generals with whom I had spoken. I have received several letters of appreciation from them commenting on their excellent experience and thanking me for making it possible."[21] In Ranquist's mind, God had provided a miracle that further facilitated the sacralization of the temple and an understanding that the Saints were engaged with God in sharing the temple with their neighbors.

INVITING THEIR NEIGHBORS
TO EXPERIENCE SACRED SPACE

The Church organized an executive committee to plan and carry out activities designed to allow the members of the Church and the public to learn about and experience the sacred space of the temple. This helped

President Gerald Ford and First Lady Betty Ford talk with President Spencer
W. Kimball and Sister Camilla Kimball at the Tabernacle Choir concert held
in the John F. Kennedy Center for the Performing Arts in conjunction with
the dedication of the Washington D.C. Temple and open house. Kimball–Ford
Photos, Church History Library.

accomplish the leadership's vision for the temple. The following anecdotes
illustrate the Church's deliberate efforts to invite key constituencies to

experience the temple and also show the impact of the Church's efforts. The committee orchestrated four main planned events to accomplish their purpose. They first facilitated completion and cornerstone-laying ceremonies. Next, they held an exclusive temple preview in which special guests participated in a tour of the interior of the temple. The invited guests included all General Authorities and local church leaders, the president of the United States and the White House staff, all members of the Senate and House of Representatives, the Supreme Court justices, and national and international leaders and their spouses.[22] The third event, the public preview, which was originally scheduled for four weeks, was extended an additional two weeks, which resulted in more than 215,000 additional attendees. In all, more than 758,000 people attended the temple open house, more than all previous temple open houses combined, a reality that partially evidences the contributions brought about through the Church's Public Communications Department.[23] Tickets to attend the open house, according to *Christianity Today*, became "as scarce as those for the home games of the Washington Redskins football team."[24] The dedication was the final event and included ten dedicatory sessions with each session accommodating 4,200 individuals.[25]

President Gerald Ford and his wife, Betty, were scheduled to attend the open house on the first morning of the special preview. Due to unforeseen circumstances, President Ford was required to reschedule his attendance, but the First Lady reported having an excellent experience.[26] Upon leaving the temple, Mrs. Ford gave a statement to the press in which she indicated that the open house was a wonderful experience for her and that the temple was "one of great beauty and a great addition to our surroundings here in Washington." She then explained that the temple "is really an inspiration to all of us. I don't know when I have enjoyed anything quite so much." Mrs. Ford also complimented the Church on allowing individuals to tour the building, saying that the Church was "very generous letting us attend and having it open to the public before they have their own services." She concluded with the statement that the Church's actions "shows a great generosity on their part."[27] Mrs. Ford's focus on the inspiration that the temple provided to all and the great generosity of the Church in allowing individuals to participate evidences the good-will built through the efforts of the Church.

The experiences in the temple facilitated further interactions between the Church leaders and the First Lady. As President Kimball and other political and religious leaders escorted the First Lady and some of the White House aides through the temple, they explained that the ordinances of the temple required preparation and that admittance to the temple was limited. While in the solemn assembly room, Betty Ford asked how temple officials were able to distinguish between those who were prepared and those who were not. As one of the party explained that each individual who met the qualifications was given a "recommend," Senator Wallace Bennett took out his recommend and showed it to Ford. One by

First Lady Betty Ford signs the temple open house guest book with Sister Kimball and President Kimball. Kimball–Ford Photos, Church History Library.

one, each individual in the group leading the tour showed his or her recommend, except for President Kimball who rifled through his wallet three or four times before finally finding his recommend. Ford, with some mischief in her voice, said, "I'm so glad you've got one, too. You had me worried."[28] Interactions like this removed barriers and created friendships with national influencers.

Other governmental leaders expressed similar feelings to Ford's at the conclusion of their tours. Supreme Court justice Warren E. Burger remarked that the temple "certainly will be a tremendous addition to the great religious monuments of Washington along with the other great cathedrals that are here." Maryland governor Marvin Mendel said, "I think the temple itself is probably one of the most beautiful buildings I have ever seen in my life, and we are absolutely delighted that it is located here in Maryland. It certainly adds something to our state."[29]

The temple attracted widespread favorable publicity across the nation from news organizations, churches, and church members.[30] The National Catholic News Service issued a news release that in part read the following: "In the Temple which bears the Mormon name, Catholics and members of many other faiths will be getting a rare insight during the weeks ahead of how another religion is practiced. It will be a fascinating discovery." In addition to these encouraging remarks, the news release attributed sacred meaning to the building, saying, "the three-story celestial room stands as a symbol of the exalted state [men and women] may achieve through the gospel of Jesus Christ."[31] A Methodist woman remarked on the feeling in the temple by saying, "It is a place of worship, and of course we worship the same God, and we worship the same Christ. For that reason I felt a worshipful attitude as I walked through the temple today."[32]

The temple open house clearly made an impact on visitors, as was evidenced with the number of individuals who requested additional information. As part of the tour, participants were handed a card that they could fill out if they desired additional information. Some 15 to 20 percent of visitors returned the cards to request additional information, a significant figure, said one of the missionaries involved, when one "considered that most persons who filled out cards brought their whole families with them."[33]

The temple continues to be a location that the Church uses as a way of building goodwill. Just a few years after the temple was completed, the Church organized its first Festival of Lights at the adjacent visitors' center. Each year since 1978, the Church has invited ambassadors from across the globe who are in Washington, DC, to participate in the temple Christmas lighting ceremony. One ambassador is selected to give remarks and to turn on the Christmas lights. These experiences have promoted significant understanding and have created relationships and opened doors for the Church. Utah senator Orrin G. Hatch has attended many of these events, being that he arrived in Washington the year before the lighting ceremonies began. Hatch described the benefit of these ceremonies by recalling an experience he had with the Russian delegation that had been invited to the temple lighting ceremony. Hatch indicated that a few days after the ceremony, the Russian ambassador took the chance to meet with Hatch and ask him questions regarding the Church, allowing Hatch to share general information about the Church and its desire to strengthen families and nations. Hatch expressed that these relationships have benefited the Church and even helped to facilitate countries being willing to officially receive the Church.[34]

The lighting ceremonies helped to create a situation in which relationships were formed in natural and significant ways. In 1998, for example, the *Deseret News* began an article about the Festival of Lights at the Washington D.C. Temple by saying, "Not many years ago, few would have dared imagine a high official of China publicly praising The Church of Jesus Christ of Latter-day Saints, embracing a general authority and inviting the church to work more with his Communist country. But the impossible dream of Cold War years was a reality Wednesday as Li Zhaoxing, ambassador to the United States from the People's Republic of China, did all of that." The article indicated that Senator Hatch introduced the ambassador and that Zhaoxing, after the kind introduction, hoped that all those "good words were overheard by God and by my boss." The article concludes by indicating that over the past decades, the ambassadors that have been honored in the tree lighting ceremonies have "later helped open the doors to LDS missionary work in their nations—including numerous formerly Communist countries."[35] Clearly, from these experiences, the temple has become a location from which the Church has symbolically stated that they are a permanent part of the national and international religious marketplace.

The temple has also become a location for comedic and political commentary. One early news article suggested that the temple looked like a "bleached Emerald City of Oz."[36] Even before the dedication of the temple, a comedic artist created a signage on one of the underpasses approaching the temple that read "Surrender Dorothy."[37] Some thirty-four years later,

President Spencer and Camilla Kimball talk with First Lady Betty Ford on the grounds of the Washington D.C. temple after Ford completed a tour of the Temple, 12 September 1984. Kimball Ford Photos, Church History Library.

a similar sign appeared with comedic value and political motives. The vandalism came at the end of a week in which President Donald Trump's former campaign manager was convicted of eight felony counts and his former attorney pled guilty to campaign finance violations. The sign read simply "Surrender Donald."[38]

The temple is an accepted part of the landscape of the DC area and a landmark to which individuals are drawn. This is a calculated and intended outcome driven by the desire of Church leaders to create a place in which national and international leaders may feel the spirit of the place and create relationships of mutual respect and understanding. This location is a significant place to help the Church overcome "obscurity" and positively impact the Church's missionary efforts. Thus it is not unusual to have individuals enter the visitors' center indicating that they have long seen the temple on their commute and have finally come for information. Likewise, a picture of the DC metropolitan area phone book even donned a picture of the temple on its cover.[39] The related experiences have shown that the Church consciously used the temple to create relationships with national and international leaders and the local public. In large measure, the tactics of the Church have succeeded in showing that the Church has come to stay, both nationally and internationally.

NOTES

1. Alonzo L. Gaskill, "Religious Ritual and the Creation of Sacred Space," in *Sacred Space, Sacred Thread: Perspectives across Time and Tradition,* ed. John W. Welch and Jacob Rennaker (Eugene, OR: Pickwick Publications, 2019), 103.

2. Ezra Taft Benson, "Remarks at the Washington D.C. Temple Site Dedication," 7 December 1968, CR 633 1, Church History Library, Salt Lake City. Hugh B. Brown, address, 7 December 1968, photocopy of typescript, MS 3305, Church History Library.

3. Hugh B. Brown, address, 7 December 1968, photocopy of typescript, MS 3305, Church History Library, 1–4.

4. Further illustrating the leadership's emphasis on using the temple to take the message of the restored gospel not only to the nation but to the world, a radio broadcast in 1972 called "The World of Religion" reported a Church spokesmen as saying, "We have a message for the world. We want the world to hear it. We want the world to have the opportunity of understanding the gospel—the Restored Gospel. We are happy to attract people to our message. We hope the *design* does attract a great deal of attention so people will investigate the Church." Clearly the target audience went far beyond the nation. As quoted in Keith W. Wilcox, *The Washington DC Temple: A Light to the World* (Kensington, MD: self-pub., 1995), 5. Stewart M. Hoover, a professor of religion and media studies, indicated that "The World of Religion" radio broadcast was, in 1998, America's longest-running radio broadcast focused on religion. It was produced at KMOX in St. Louis. Stewart M. Hoover, *Religion in the News: Faith and Journalism in American Public Discourse* (Thousand Oaks, CA: SAGE Publications, 1998), 156.

5. Mark Garff, Church Building Committee chair; Emil Fetzer, Church architect; and Tim Timmerman, construction architect, were the architects who

made the adjustments to the location of the temple by sixty feet. These adjustments were made during the planning phase, before the commencement of construction. Diane L. Holling, interview by Maclane Elon Heward, 10 and 12 July 2019.

6. The campaign consisted of radio appearances, campus visits and traveling presentations among other things. J. B. Haws, *The Mormon Image in the American Mind: Fifty Years of Public Perception* (New York: Oxford University Press, 2013), 62, 75.

7. "Attitudes and Opinions Towards Religion: Religious Attitudes of Adults (over 18) Who Are Residents of Six Major Metropolitan Areas in the United States: Seattle, Los Angeles, Kansas City, Dallas, Chicago, New York City—August 1973," 33, L. Tom Perry Special Collections, Harold B. Lee Library, Brigham Young University, Provo, UT. See also Haws, *Mormon Image*, 76–77.

8. Orson Scott Card, "Wendell Ashton Called to Publishing Post," *Ensign*, January 1978, 73–4. "Attitudes and Opinions Towards Religion," 33. See also Haws, *Mormon Image*, 76–77. A number of factors led to the flood of curious visitors during the open house. The Church had been in the news at an unprecedented rate in the previous five to seven years for things like the death of President David O. McKay, George Romney's presidential campaign, and the protests directed at BYU regarding the Church's racial policies. The excitement around the Church at the end of the 1960s and into the 1970s coincided with the Church's participation in the New York World's Fair, a success that convinced Church leaders of the untapped potential of outreach on a grander scale. The result was the replacement of the Church Information Service with the Public Communications Department. The leader of the newly formed communications department, Wendell Ashton, was an advertising executive and a journalist. He pulled Heber Wolsey (BYU's public relations officer who had played a significant role in the proactive stance of the university in the protests at the turn of the decade) into the newly formed organization as Ashton's chief assistant. See Jon Ben Haws, "The Mormon Image in the American Mind" (PhD diss., University of Utah, 2010), 170–76. Wolsey's graduate training and professional experience centered in radio and television broadcasting. Between the two, the culture of the department was set. Ashton reported that the "whole thrust of our department was to take the initiative and not wait to respond to people seeking information." See Wendell J. Ashton oral history, 1984, 173, Church History Library, as cited in Public Affairs Department, unpublished departmental history, cited in Haws, *Mormon Image*, 77.

9. Mircea Eliade, *Sacred and Profane: The Nature of Religion*, trans. Willard R. Trask (Orlando: Harcourt, 1957), 28–29; emphasis in original. Sacrifice can also create sacred space. Members of the Church were asked to raise significant funds for the building of the temple ($4.5 million). Frank Miller Smith, "Monument to Spirituality: Sacrifice, Dreams, and Faith Build the Washington Temple," *Ensign*, August 1974, 8.

10. Wilcox, *Washington DC Temple*, 5.

11. David S. King, *Come to the House of the Lord* (Bountiful, UT: Horizon, 2000), 12–14. See also Holling, interview, 10 July 2019.

12. King, *Come to the House of the Lord*, 12–14. See also Holling, interview, 10 July 2019.

13. Wilcox, *Washington DC Temple*, 5.

14. Wilcox, *Washington DC Temple*, 9–10.

15. Wilcox, *Washington DC Temple*, 13.

16. Mircea Eliade, *Sacred and Profane*, 28, 29. The temple rests on forty-eight concrete caissons, which were sturdy enough to help the temple withstand a 5.8 magnitude earthquake forty miles northwest of Richmond, VA, in 2011. Though minor damage occurred, the temple remained open. See Joseph Walker, "'Minor Damage' to D.C. Temple in Earthquake," *Deseret News*, 24 August 2011.

17. During his brief remarks at the dedication of the land for the temple, Hugh B. Brown voiced his opinion that he hoped the Church never stopped asking the members to help pay for buildings. He clearly recognized the benefits to the membership of the Church in sacrificing to create sacred space. He also shared his own experiences sacrificing to contribute to Church buildings. Hugh B. Brown, address, 7 December 1968, photocopy of typescript, Church History Library.

18. Smith, "Monument to Spirituality," 8.

19. Marsha S. Butler, oral history, interview by Karl D. Butler Jr., Salt Lake City, 25 April 2014, Church History Library.

20. See Bramwell W. Taylor and M. Doreen Taylor, oral history, interview by Arnon Livingston, New Brunswick, Canada, 12 August 2014, Church History Library.

21. See Harold Alexander Ranquist, reminiscence, 1999, typescript, Church History Library.

22. Special guests were given a special edition of the *Ensign* magazine with their names embossed on a special cover. The author is in possession of a picture depicting the cover of one magazine embossed with "THE HONORABLE JOSEPH BIDEN, JR."

23. "Washington Temple: Missionary Tool," *Ensign*, December 1974, 73.

24. See Harold Alexander Ranquist, reminiscence. For the citation regarding the Washington Redskins, see Edward E. Plowman, "Ford's First Month: Christ and Conflict," *Christianity Today*, 27 September 1974.

25. Jesse R. Smith, "Washington Temple," in *History of the Mormons in the Greater Washington Area: Members of the Church of Jesus Christ of Latter-day Saints in the Washington, D.C. Area, 1839–1991*, ed. Julian C. Lowe and Florian H. Thayn (Washington, DC: Community Printing Service, Inc., 1991), 168.

26. For information regarding President Gerald Ford's attendance at the temple open house, see Edward L. Kimball and Andrew E. Kimball Jr., *Spencer W. Kimball: Twelfth President of The Church of Jesus Christ of Latter-day Saints* (Salt Lake City: Bookcraft, 1977), 419.

27. "Statement of Mrs. Betty B. Ford to the Press, 11 September 1974, upon leaving the Washington Latter-day Saint Temple, 11 September 1974," typescript, Church History Library.

28. Jesse R. Smith, "Washington Temple," 169. See also Holling, interview, 10 July 2019.

29. *The Washington Temple: A New Landmark* (video), Church History Library.

30. Richard O. Cowan, *Temples to Dot the Earth* (Springville, UT: Cedar Fort, 1997), 177. The open house also attracted widespread publicity. Favorable articles appeared not only in national periodicals but also in newspapers in all fifty states and abroad. Surprisingly, controversies relative to the Church from just a few years previous were either not mentioned or mentioned only obscurely. See Haws, *Mormon Image*, 70–71.

31. Tom Lorsung, "Mormon Temple Tour Is a Rare Insight," Catholic Research Resources Alliance, Catholic News Service-Newsfeeds, 5 September 1974.

32. *The Washington Temple: A New Landmark* (video).

33. "Washington Temple, Missionary Tool," *Ensign*, December 1974, 73–74.

34. Orrin G. Hatch, interview by Maclane Heward, Salt Lake City, 29 May 2019.

35. Lee Davidson, "Chinese Envoy Illuminates D.C. Temple: He Offers Warm Praise for the LDS Church," *Deseret News*, 3 December 1998.

36. "Behind the Temple Walls," *Time*, 16 September 1974, 110.

37. "Wicked Witch of the Beltway?" *Montgomery Journal*, 31 October 1974.

38. John Kelly, "'Surrender Donald': A Highway Overpass along the Capital Beltway Goes Political," *Washington Post*, 24 August 2018.

39. John Laing, interview with Maclane Heward, Salt Lake City, 1 March 2019.

Over four-hundred thousand men, women, and children have been interred at Arlington National Cemetery. Photo by author.

LATTER-DAY SAINTS AT ARLINGTON NATIONAL CEMETERY

KENNETH L. ALFORD

Kenneth L. Alford is a professor of Church history and doctrine at Brigham Young University and a retired colonel in the U.S. Army.

People die only when we forget them . . .
If you remember me, I will be with you always.
—Isabel Allende[1]

A prominent sign at the entrance to Arlington National Cemetery identifies it as "our nation's most sacred shrine." Visitors are directed to "please conduct [them]selves with dignity and respect at all times" and to "remember these are hallowed grounds."[2] While most Americans are familiar with the Tomb of the Unknown Soldier, there are also memorials to the Unknown Dead of the War of 1812 and Unknown Civil War Dead. The cemetery is dotted with numerous monuments—from the USS *Maine* to the Rough Riders and to the space shuttle memorials of both *Challenger* (1987) and *Columbia* (2004). Less well known is the fact that hundreds of Latter-day Saints are among the honored dead at Arlington.

Enlisted soldiers guard the Tomb of the Unknown Soldier every hour of every day. All photos by author unless otherwise noted.

OVERVIEW

Located adjacent to the Pentagon and across the Potomac River from the Lincoln Memorial, Arlington is the only national cemetery that includes burials from every major conflict in our nation's history.[3] Arlington is the final resting place of U.S. presidents John F. Kennedy and William H. Taft; generals John J. Pershing, Philip Sheridan, Philip Kearny, Henry "Hap" Arnold, James "Jimmy" Doolittle, and Maxwell Taylor; admirals William "Bull" Halsey, Grace Hopper, and Hyman Rickover; Supreme Court justices Oliver Wendell Holmes, Thurgood Marshall, William H. Rehnquist, and Earl Warren; explorers John Wesley Powell, Richard Byrd, and Robert E. Peary; astronauts Roger Chaffee and Virgil I. Grissom, who died in the Apollo 1 fire; other revered individuals like Walter Reed, Pierre Charles

L'Enfant, George Westinghouse, Joe Louis, and Abner Doubleday; and more than four hundred thousand other men, women, and children.

The story of Arlington National Cemetery began during the American Civil War. The cemetery occupies the grounds of Arlington House, the still-standing nineteenth-century mansion and eleven-hundred-acre estate owned by Confederate general Robert E. Lee and his wife, Mary Anna Custis. Four days after Fort Sumter surrendered in 1861, Virginia seceded from the Union. The following day—18 April—Lee was offered command of all Union forces. In declining the offer, Lee stated, "If I owned four millions of slaves in the South I would sacrifice them all to the Union; but how can I draw my sword upon Virginia, my native state?"[4] With Arlington House being situated two hundred feet above and looking down on Washington, DC, "it did not take a military genius to appreciate the strategic importance of the old plantation."[5] On 24 May 1861, federal forces occupied the house and grounds at Arlington, just a few days after Mary Anna Lee had left.

A federal statute enacted in June 1862 authorized federal tax commissioners to assess and collect taxes on Confederate-owned property.

This is the main entrance to Arlington National Cemetery. Arlington House, Robert E. Lee's home prior to the Civil War, can be seen on the hill in the background.

McClellan Gate in the heart of Arlington National Cemetery.

The law required owners to pay the tax in person or forfeit their property. In 1863 a tax of $92.07 was levied on the Lees' Arlington property. Mary Anna Lee sent a cousin to pay the tax, but federal tax commissioners refused to accept payment from him. The Arlington estate was purchased by the federal government in February 1864.[6]

Union brigadier general Montgomery C. Meigs, who had a great personal dislike for Robert E. Lee, turned the property into a military cemetery—partially to ensure that the Lees would not be able to return.[7] On 13 May 1864, William Christman was the first soldier buried there, a twenty-one-year-old private in the 67th Pennsylvania Infantry Regiment who died of peritonitis and never saw combat. Over a decade after the Civil War, the Lees' oldest son, George Washington Custis, successfully sued the federal government to return the property. He then sold it back to the federal government in 1883 for $150,000.[8]

Memorial Day, originally called Decoration Day when it was conceived by the Grand Army of the Republic (an influential fraternal organization for Union Civil War veterans), was first celebrated at Arlington National Cemetery on 30 May 1868. The day was "designated for the purpose of strewing with flowers or otherwise decorating the graves of comrades who died in defense of their country during the late rebellion [the Civil War]."[9] Today, service members and other volunteers place flags at every burial site in the entire cemetery every Memorial Day.

Arlington National Cemetery is 624 acres of rolling hills, grass, and gardens—approximately half of Robert and Mary Anna Lee's original Arlington estate. In the first sixty years of its existence, there were just over thirty thousand interments.[10] Today, the cemetery averages between twenty-seven and thirty funeral services every weekday and between six and eight services on Saturdays throughout the year.[11] Arlington National Cemetery is divided into eighty-five consecutively numbered sections. Some of the higher numbered sections are still vacant. There is no more land available for the cemetery to easily increase in size, and there is concern that it will be filled in the next few decades if rules regarding interments are not modified.[12]

ARLINGTON GRAVE MARKER EMBLEMS

Following World War I, a board of officers—which included the secretary of war and the army's chief of staff, General John J. Pershing—"adopted a new [headstone] design to be used for all graves except those of veterans of the Civil and Spanish-American Wars." The grave markers, known as "general" type, were to be "slightly rounded at the top, of American white marble, 42 inches long, 13 inches wide and four inches thick." And, for the first time, a religious emblem was authorized for inclusion on the general-type headstones. Only two emblems were authorized at that time—"the Latin Cross for the Christian faith and the Star of David for the Jewish faith."[13]

The federal government provides marble grave and columbarium markers for every veteran interred at Arlington National Cemetery. At the top of the marble marker is room for an emblem to be carved above the

This angel Moroni grave marker was approved by the Veterans Administration Monument Services in 1980. Veterans Administration.

name of the deceased. The Department of Veterans Affairs and the National Cemetery Administration have currently authorized seventy emblems. In order to be approved, each design must represent "the sincerely held belief of the decedent that constituted a religion or the functional equivalent of religion and was believed and/or accepted as true by that individual during his or her life. The belief represented by an emblem need not be associated with or endorsed by a group or organization. Emblems of belief for inscription on Government headstones and markers do not include social, cultural, ethnic, civic, fraternal, trade, commercial, political, professional or military emblems."[14]

The most common grave marker emblem at Arlington is the simple Christian (Latin) cross. Emblems are included for several Christian denominations: Lutheran, Presbyterian, Episcopal, Unitarian, Methodist, Seventh-day Adventist, Catholic, Church of God, the Polish National Catholic Church, and the Community of Christ. Other approved emblems denote the Jewish, Buddhist, Muslim, Hindu, Sufi, Baháʼí, Sikh, and Shinto faiths. There are also emblems for atheism, humanism, Wicca, Druidism, Eckankar, and Farohar as well as some nondenominational emblems such as a guardian angel, a heart, a pomegranate, a Maltese Cross, a medicine wheel, an eagle, a crane, and an infinity sign.[15] No other graphics or symbols are authorized on the government-furnished markers except the Civil War Union Shield, the Civil War Confederate Southern Cross of Honor, and the Medal of Honor insignia.[16]

Until 1980, Latter-day Saints had no distinctive emblem to clearly identify Church affiliation of the deceased. Donald L. Wardle, a Latter-day Saint director of Monument Services for the Department of Veterans

The angel Moroni grave marker of Jacklyn Lucy, wife of Captain Norman Owens, U.S. Navy.

Affairs, "noticed the lack of an LDS grave marker emblem in his position at the V.A. and began corresponding with Church leaders about it. They agreed the Church should have one. Several designs were considered but most were too intricate for headstone in[s]cription. Finally, [an] angel Moroni design was submitted, and it met all requirements." The First Presidency approved the design, which "profiles the Angel Moroni blowing his trumpet. The bell end extends upward through an oval-shaped border." The angel Moroni design was accepted by Veterans Affairs soon after.[17]

IDENTIFYING LATTER-DAY SAINTS

A project to identify members of the Church interred at Arlington was conceived several years ago. After learning from the cemetery historian's office that no public records regarding religious affiliation or headstone emblems exist, the challenge to identify Latter-day Saints became more

Lloyd P. Shipley and Lottice Bledsoe, who were reinterred in Arlington National Cemetery in 2019, were married at Mobile, Alabama, on 8 February 1945 during the closing months of World War II. Courtesy of the Lloyd and Lottice Shipley family.

daunting. After visually inspecting tens of thousands of individual grave markers and markers in the cemetery's ten columbaria for the angel Moroni emblem, seventy-two Latter-day Saint interments had been identified.[18] A research team of Brigham Young University undergraduate students systematically checked 1980-and-later grave markers in all the remaining sections of the cemetery using an online database of grave marker photos.[19]

The research team identified 262 interments at Arlington National Cemetery with the angel Moroni emblem or who have been confirmed as members of The Church of Jesus Christ of Latter-day Saints—172 military service members (70 U.S. Army, 45 U.S. Navy, 40 U.S. Air Force, 16 U.S. Marine Corps, and 1 U.S. Coast Guard), 72 military spouses, and 18 dependent children (see table 1). There is an almost equal number of officers and enlisted service members. Latter-day Saints are buried in thirty-three sections of the cemetery and nine sections of the columbaria. Section 60 has the most Latter-day Saint interments, with forty-three burials. Five sections have between twelve and nineteen Latter-day Saint graves, and the remaining twenty-seven sections have fewer than ten burials each.

CATEGORY	COUNT
U.S. Army	**70**
Officer	28
Warrant Officer	5
Enlisted	37
U.S. Marine Corps	**16**
Officer	7
Enlisted	9
U.S. Navy	**45**
Officer	22
Enlisted	23
U.S. Air Force	**40**
Officer	23
Enlisted	17
U.S. Coast Guard	**1**
Officer	1
Family Members	**90**
Spouse	72
Child	18
Total	**262**

Table 1. Summary of Latter-day Saints interred at Arlington National Cemetery.

Arlington National Cemetery grave markers include information regarding which wars the military members served in. Fifty-six of the Latter-day Saint veterans had no wartime service listed on their headstones. Sixty-seven served in one war, thirty-three served in two wars, and sixteen served in three wars (see tables 2 and 3).

WARTIME SERVICE	COUNT
World War II	62
Korea	50
Vietnam	56
Gulf War	4
Afghanistan	6
Iraq	3
Total	181

Table 2. Wartime service summary of Latter-day Saints interred at Arlington National Cemetery.

For several years near the end of the twentieth century, individuals and families could provide their own headstones at Arlington in place of the white marble markers that are mandatory today. Some of those personalized grave markers include the angel Moroni emblem. The grave marker for Sergeant Major Richard Brown Wilson and his wife, Elizabeth Jeanne Marceau Wilson, for example, includes the phrase "Sealed in the Swiss Temple for Time and all Eternity" beneath their names. The marker for Colonel Ross Lee Carson and his wife, June Elizabeth Lydamore, includes Doctrine and Covenants 132:46: "Whatsoever you seal on earth shall be sealed in heaven; and whatsoever you bind on earth, in my name and by my word, saith the Lord, it shall be eternally bound in the heavens."[20]

WARTIME PARTICIPATION	COUNT
Three Wars	16
Two Wars	33
One War	67
No wartime service	56
Total	172

Table 3. Summary of wartime service of Latter-day Saints interred at Arlington National Cemetery.

With forty-three burials, Section 60 has the most Latter-day Saint interments at Arlington National Cemetery.

LATTER-DAY SAINTS BURIED AT ARLINGTON

Each Latter-day Saint interred at Arlington National Cemetery has a unique story. What follows is one of the many possible stories that could be told. Private First-Class Lloyd P. Shipley, from Cache County, Utah, was deferred from the 1940 draft because he lost most of two fingers on his right hand in a lawn mower accident as a six-year-old. After Pearl Harbor was attacked, he was reclassified and drafted. His military service began on 11 February 1942, and he served honorably for the next three years, two months, and eleven days. A farmer before the war, he was trained as a rifleman and served in Europe as a communications messenger in the 137th Infantry Regiment of the 35th Division. Seriously wounded by machine gun fire during the Normandy Campaign seven weeks after D-Day, he was hospitalized for the next nine months. He received a Purple Heart and earned a Combat Infantry Badge.[21] Of his service in France, he wrote, "It

This 1910 patriotic postcard includes a few lines from Theodore O'Hara's poem "Bivouac of the Dead" that are engraved on the McClellan Gate at Arlington National Cemetery.

took about half a day in France to cool our ardor for the war. It was just like maneuvers, but the enemy was shooting back with real bullets and some of us were being killed. . . . It was a trying experience, but I wouldn't trade it for anything. It gives you the best opportunity to see men at their worst and to see the best come out in them under the worst circumstances."[22] He passed away in 1999. On the hundredth anniversary of his birth—17 December 2018—he was reinterred with his wife at Arlington National Cemetery with all his living grandchildren in attendance to witness the event.[23]

SUMMARY

Arlington National Cemetery has reached 80 percent of its capacity. There are only a hundred thousand burial sites left. To extend how long the cemetery "can be used as the final resting place for American service members," federal officials are "moving to limit the number of individuals eligible for burial at Arlington National Cemetery in Virginia, restricting below-ground sites to combat heroes, battle casualties and a small pool of notable dignitaries."[24] In the future, Latter-day Saints buried in Arlington National Cemetery will most likely be buried without any accompanying family members.

In the nineteenth century, Theodore O'Hara, a Kentucky veteran of the Mexican War, penned an elegiac poem entitled "Bivouac of the Dead." The quatrain that ends the first stanza appears on the large and imposing McClellan Gate in the center of Arlington National Cemetery:

On Fame's eternal camping-ground
Their silent tents are spread,
And Glory guards, with solemn round,
The bivouac of the dead.[25]

Due to the incompleteness of available burial records, we may never know how many Latter-day Saints are buried in Arlington National Cemetery. This research is an initial effort to identify and honor them and their service to our nation.

APPENDIX
ARLINGTON NATIONAL CEMETERY
LATTER-DAY SAINT INTERMENTS

The following list is not complete (no burial database listing religious preferences is currently available for review, and a Latter-day Saint grave marker image was not available until 1980). Additional details about these people are available through the free ANC Explorer app, the ANC Explorer website (https://ancexplorer.army.mil), and FamilySearch.org.

Table explanatory notes:

1. **STATUS** entries are: "USA" (U.S. Army), "USAF" (U.S. Air Force), "USCG" (U.S. Coast Guard), "USMC" (U.S. Marine Corps), "USN" (U.S. Navy), "Spouse," or "Dep" (which denotes a service member's legal guardianship, usually for a child).

2. **RANK** abbreviations vary by both military service (for example, Captain is "CPT" in the U.S. Army and "CAPT" in the U.S. Air Force and U.S. Navy) and time period. Military rank definitions are available at https://www.cem.va.gov/cem/hmm/abbreviations.asp.

3. **WARTIME SERVICE** abbreviations are: "WWII" (World War II), "KOR" (Korea), "VN" (Vietnam), "GW" (Gulf War), "AFG" (Afghanistan), and "IRQ" (Iraq). A dash denotes no wartime service is recorded on the grave or columbarium marker.

4. **ANC LOCATION** information is either "S##–####" (Section number – Grave number), "C#–##–##–#" (Columbarium Court number – Section number – Column number – Niche number), or "CN#–##–##–#" (Columbarium Niche Wall number – Section number – Column number – Niche number).

NO.	NAME	STATUS	RANK	BIRTH	DEATH	WAR-TIME SERVICE	ANC LOCATION
1	ACKERSON, Lyona Larsen	Spouse	—	1912	2001	—	S38-4221
2	ADAMS, Thomas J.	Child	—	2013	2013	—	S60-10113
3	ADAMSON, Dale Joseph	USAF	MSGT	1920	2013	WWII, KOR	S51-2677
4	ALLAIN, Barbara Jean	Spouse	—	1928	2014	—	S71-359
5	ANTHONY, Carrie R.	Spouse	—	1956	2017	—	C9-N85-20-5
6	ARCENEAUX, Kathy Lee	Spouse	—	1942	2011	—	S69-480
7	ARCENEAUX, Stanley John, Jr.	USAF	TSGT	1945	2018	VN	S69-480
8	ARNOLD, Richard, Jr.	USAF	COL	1913	2000	WWII, KOR	S65-865
9	ARNOLD, Vivienne	Spouse	—	1915	2005	—	S65-865
10	BACON, Jack Gates	USN	ETCS	1915	1997	WWII, KOR	S60-953
11	BADGER, Phyllis	Spouse	—	1913	2008	—	S66-6902
12	BADGER, Rodney Jenkins	USN	CAPT	1912	2002	WWII, KOR, VN	S66-6902
13	BALLADARES, Samuel J.	USMC	PFC	1982	2002	—	S68-1628
14	BEACHUM, Anne Hampton	Spouse	—	1922	2002	—	S66-6853
15	BEAMAN, Gordon	USAF	TSGT	1926	2002	WWII, KOR, VN	S67-1829
16	BEASON, Richard Wallace	USMC	LT COL	1936	2010	VN	S54-3045
17	BEGOLE, Patricia C. R.	Spouse	—	1922	1997	—	S37-2333
18	BELCHE, Brintice E	Spouse	—	1928	2013	—	S55-396

NO.	NAME	STATUS	RANK	BIRTH	DEATH	WAR-TIME SERVICE	ANC LOCATION
19	BELCHE, Homer Robert	USA	LTC	1923	2013	WWII, KOR, VN	S55-396
20	BENISHEK, Richard Paul	USA	SGT	1928	2014	KOR, VN	S60-3183
21	BENNETT, Lavor Dolph	USA	SFC	1922	1999	—	C5-EE-51-2
22	BENNETT, Lola Mae	Spouse	—	1929	2017	—	C5-EE-51-2
23	BERG, Attellia Ann	Spouse	—	1922	2016	—	S28-3333
24	BERG, Gordon H.	USAF	LT COL	1916	1995	WWII, KOR	S28-3332
25	BERG, Sydney Louise	Child	—	1944	1961	—	S28-3332
26	BIGELOW, Andrew Curtis	Child	—	1961	1961	—	S46-650
27	BIGELOW, Avalon C	Spouse	—	1922	2003	—	S46-650
28	BIGELOW, Joseph Alfonso	Child	—	1961	1961	—	S46-650
29	BIGELOW, Lavell	USN	CAPT	1917	2007	WWII, KOR	S46-651
30	BLAMIRES, Jesse Allen	USA	SGT	1981	2007	AFG	S60-8769
31	BLANCHARD, Glendon F.	USN	LCDR	1914	1997	WWII, KOR	S64-1778
32	BOAZ, Monroe Thomas, Jr.	USN	ACC	1953	1988	VN	S69-3506
33	BOUDREAUX, Mona Joan	Spouse	—	1937	2014	—	S60-11334
34	BOUDREAUX, Robert Matthew	USMC	CAPT	1924	2015	WWII, KOR	S60-11334
35	BRADLEY, Kenneth Dylan	Child	—	2002	2017	—	S55-510

NO.	NAME	STATUS	RANK	BIRTH	DEATH	WAR-TIME SERVICE	ANC LOCATION
36	BRADY, Arlo James	USN	LT	1917	2001	WWII, KOR, VN	S68-1929
37	BRADY, Delores Jensen	Spouse	—	1916	2005	—	S68-1929
38	BRINGLE, Vilate A.	Spouse	—	1897	1988	—	S10-10609-WS
39	BRITTON-MIHALO, Andrew Trevor	USA	SSG	1986	2012	AFG	S60-10097
40	BROWN, Vera K.	Spouse	—	1924	2011	—	S69-3489
41	BROWN, Wilbur Ronald	USAF	MAJ	1936	1966	VN	S60-8933
42	BULL, Robert George, II	USAF	CAPT	1939	1969	-	S46-690-1
43	BULL, Virginia	Spouse	—	1946	2012	—	S46-613
44	BULLOUGH, Bruce Lynn	USN	CAPT	1948	2003	VN	S69-5178
45	BYINGTON, Carlyle Owens	USAF	TSGT	1941	2018	VN	S57-1541
46	CALHOUN, Norman Douglas	USA	CPL	1933	2013	—	C7-W-4-5
47	CARDON, Eli P.	Child	—	1993	1993	—	S60-4971
48	CARDON, Marvin Barlow	USA	LTC	1934	1997	—	C4-Z-8-1
49	CARSON, Andrew David	USA	CPL	1921	1998	WWII	S64-3375
50	CARSON, Dora E. Maloy	Spouse	—	1923	2009	—	S64- 3375
51	CARSON, June Elizabeth Lydamore	Spouse	—	1928	1994	—	S10-10780-A
52	CARSON, Ross Lee	USAF	COL	1926	2010	—	S10-10780-A
53	CHEEVER, Kelly	Child	—	1986	1986	—	S69-158

NO.	NAME	STATUS	RANK	BIRTH	DEATH	WAR-TIME SERVICE	ANC LOCATION
54	CHILDERS, Providence Carol	Spouse	—	1922	2008	—	S68-2554
55	CLARK, Allyn Lee	USA	LTC	1930	2016	KOR, VN	S55-1862
56	CLARK, Doris May II	USA	MAJ	1940	2012	—	S64-1320
57	COCKRILL, Robert L. Jr.	USN	CS1	1927	2004	WWII, KOR, VN	S51-2949
58	COFFEY, Claudia C.	Spouse	—	1939	2009	—	C8-SS-17-3
59	COLE, Veronica Ponchey	USN	HM2	1951	2012	—	S54-1913
60	COLEMAN, Roy Elmo	USA	PFC	1928	2017	KOR	C9-N85-28-1
61	COLLIER, William W.	USN	LCDR	1921	1993	WWII, KOR	S4-3317-A
62	COOK, Robert E.	USAF	SSGT	1935	2005	—	C6-QQ-27-5
63	CORRY, Donna Krecklau	Spouse	—	1932	2017	—	C9-N85-9-1
64	COX, Daniel Emitt	USN	CCS	1916	1992	—	C6-Q-11-1
65	COYLE, Mark A.	USA	LTC	1946	2009	—	S64-3427
66	CREMEEN, Jason L.	Child	—	1978	1978	—	S59-1291
67	CREMEEN, Joy Lyn	Spouse	—	1955	1998	—	S59-1291
68	DALY, Florence B.	Spouse	—	1918	2010	—	S68-1828
69	DALY, John W.	USA	LT COL	1912	2001	WWII	S68-1828
70	DAVIDSON, William Stanley	USN	BM3	1945	2011	—	C8-UU-18-3
71	DEANE, Robert W.	USMC	L CPL	1971	1991	GW	S70-1409
72	DECOSTA, Guerene Merita	Spouse	—	1939	2003	—	S69-5263
73	DEFABIO, John L.	USA	CPL	1913	1997	—	C4-MM-5-2

NO.	NAME	STATUS	RANK	BIRTH	DEATH	WAR-TIME SERVICE	ANC LOCATION
74	DEFABIO, Josephine A.	Spouse		1912	2006	—	C4-MM-5-2
75	DEFRANK, Vincent Aaron	USA	SP4	1988	2015	IRQ	S62-722
76	DEGOOYER, Franzetta R.	Spouse	—	1913	1997	—	S6-9299-A
77	DENHOLM, Nancy	Spouse	—	1948	1990	—	C2-PP-27-3
78	DERWIN, Drew Alan	USAF	AIC	1988	2014	—	S70-2383
79	DOAN, James Milton	USAF	SMSGT	1940	2014	VN	S71-501
80	DUEHRING, Ottillia E.	Spouse	—	1893	1981	—	S39-402
81	DUNKEL, Walter E. JR.	USA	SGM	1938	1995	VN	S60-3414
82	ESPINOZA, Alfonso Stevan	USAF	MSGT	1930	1986	KOR, VN	S69-5149
83	FAIRBOURN, William T.	USMC	MG	1914	1987	WWII, KOR, VN	S34-510-A
84	FARROW, Mary Chesney	Spouse	—	1952	2009	—	S53-1860
85	FARROW, Timothy Bradford	Child	—	1977	1977	—	S53-1860
86	FARWELL, Gary M.	USA	CW5	1970	2010	—	S60-9668
87	FAST, Rodrick S.	USAF	LT	1945	1995	VN	S60-3013
88	FERGUSON, Sean Ray	USA	SSG	1982	2011	AFG, IRQ	S60-9883
89	FINCH, Donald Malcom Benton	USMC	SGT	1943	2015	VN	S62-657
90	FOECHTERLE, Edward R.	USAF	LT COL	1941	1995	VN	S67-259
91	GEORGE, Charles W.	USA	MAJ	1914	1996	WWII, KOR	S67-2899

NO.	NAME	STATUS	RANK	BIRTH	DEATH	WAR-TIME SERVICE	ANC LOCATION
92	GEORGE, Muriel L.	Spouse	—	1922	1980	—	S67-2899
93	GIBB, Rulon Stewart	USAF	LT COL	1946	2014	—	S55-827
94	GIESE, Juanita B.	Spouse	—	1924	2004	—	S51-904
95	GIESE, Kenneth W.	USA	CSM	1923	1975	WWII	S51-904
96	GILBERT, George Francis Jr.	USMC	MSGT	1924	2000	WWII, KOR, VN	S59-277
97	GOFF, Pamela M.	Spouse	—	1948	2011	—	S51-3374
98	GOLDSMITH, Andrew H.	USA	CW3	1934	1989	KOR	S69-3082
99	GORE, Louis Elmore	USN	HM1	1923	2012	WWII, KOR, VN	S55-3726
100	GRASSMEIER, Kathleen Frances	USAF	MAJ	1942	2001	VN	S54-5461
101	GRIFFITH, Myrna Hazel	Spouse	—	1909	1980	—	S53-1200
102	GRIMES, Shaun M.	Child	—	1995	1995	—	S60-3403
103	GROESBECK, Mac S.	USA	SGT	1916	1942	WWII	S60-8245
104	GUILD, Marlin T.	USA	COL	1948	2008	VN, GW	S60-8471
105	GUILD, Misako	Spouse	—	1937	2010	—	S60-8471
106	HAGEMAN, Helen Josephine	Spouse	—	1922	2012	—	S54-2731
107	HAIGHT, Chauncy P.	USA	LTC	1920	2009	WWII, KOR, VN	S60-9244
108	HAIGHT, Gayle Alice Baker	Spouse	—	1927	2012	—	S60-9244
109	HAJNY, Zdenek	USA	2LT	1922	1949	WWII	S34-2476
110	HALL, Harold Byron	USAF	LT COL	1922	2013	WWII, KOR	S60-10334

NO.	NAME	STATUS	RANK	BIRTH	DEATH	WAR-TIME SERVICE	ANC LOCATION
111	HALL, Hazel J.	Spouse	—	1924	2013	—	S60-10334
112	HAMEL, Fred Mack	USMC	SGT	1918	1997	WWII	S60-1726
113	HAMMAR, Carl Erik	USA	SSG	1987	2012	AFG	S60-10225
114	HAND, Lee Merrill	USA	COL	1930	1995	KOR, VN	S60-7089
115	HANSEN, Alice M.	USMC	MAJ	1911	1986	—	C2-A-16-1
116	HARDING, William J.	USA	PFC	1925	2002	WWII	S68-4673
117	HARTUNG, Lill Irene	Spouse	—	1939	2005	—	S69-1971
118	HAWK, Hawkins	Child	—	1989	1989	—	S68-1705
119	HILDUM, James McDowell	USAF	MAJ	1920	2017	WWII	S76-1626
120	HILTON, Lawrence David	USN	LT	1968	2004	—	S69-190
121	HINES, Jordan B.	Child	—	1997	1997	—	S67-4616
122	HOFFMAN, Frederick D. Jr.	USAF	A1	1929	1986	—	C2-H-22-3
123	HOLSTON, Alice	Spouse	—	1921	2013	—	C4-S-14-2
124	HOLSTON, Henry	USN	SD2	1925	1996	—	C4-S-14-2
125	HOLZWARTH, Rodney F.	USA	SGT	1933	2007	—	C7-CC-3-2
126	HUGHES, Arville Lyle	USA	LTC	1938	2012	VN	S64-4430
127	ILER, John Robert	USN	CAPT	1922	2011	—	CN70-B-9-1
128	JACK, Robert Lee	USA	SSG	1948	2011	VN	S55-3021
129	JANIAK, Kenneth Philip	USA	ILT	1947	2009	—	S60-9319
130	JAROSS, James	USMC	COL	1928	2009	—	S60-9245

NO.	NAME	STATUS	RANK	BIRTH	DEATH	WAR-TIME SERVICE	ANC LOCATION
131	JENNINGS, Donald Earl	USAF	AD2, TSGT	1931	2014	VN	S33-12089
132	JENNINGS, Elizabeth A.	USN	SA	1944	1987	—	C2-CC-13-1
133	JOHANSEN, Carl Oscar	USMC	PSGT	1921	2004	WWII	S69-3546
134	JOHNSON, Curtis Lee Jr.	USA	COL	1929	2016	KOR	S55-3601
135	JOHNSON, Dean L.	USA	CAPT	1945	2010	VN	S54-5898
136	JOHNSON, Esther I.	Spouse	—	1926	2005	—	S54-360
137	JOHNSON, Joyce B.	Spouse	—	1921	1984	—	S65-3642
138	JOHNSON, King D.	USA	PVT	1920	1989	—	C2-DD-2-2
139	JOHNSON, Walter Irving	USN	YNT2	1922	2010	WWII	S54-360
140	JOHNSON, Yvonne M.	Child	—	1968	1968	—	S12-8121-2
141	KANE, Robert Joseph	USN	SK1	1932	2000	KOR, VN	S54-3848
142	KELLY, Cedric I.	USAF	TSGT	1924	2009	KOR	S38-2494
143	KELLY, Ola J.	Spouse	—	1927	1977	—	S38-2494
144	KNIGHT, Nathan K.	USA	SGT	1918	1991	—	S43-2939
145	KUTA, Fred	USA	SGT	1924	2015	WWII	S54-81
146	LAMMONS, Hugh A.	USA	WO3	1950	1982	—	S53-2196
147	LANDRY, James Peter	USA	CPT	1922	2012	WWII, KOR	S64-4529
148	LANDUA, Oliver H.	USN	CAPT	1919	2010	WWII	S8-7244

NO.	NAME	STATUS	RANK	BIRTH	DEATH	WAR-TIME SERVICE	ANC LOCATION
149	LANEY, Ira L.	USA	LTC	1927	2007	WWII, KOR, VN	S60-132
150	LAWTON, Timothy Gardner	USAF	COL	1936	2014	VN	S37-2070
151	LEWIS, Marjorie Hennigan	USA	2LT ANC	1920	2008	WWII	S11-373-NH
152	MACDONALD, Jonathan L.	USA	SP4	1983	2005	—	S64-1425
153	MANNING, Glenda	Spouse	—	1919	2004	—	S60-4142
154	MANNING, Harry Keith	USN	BMI	1923	1993	WWII, KOR	S60-4142
155	MARSHALL, John Lloyd	USA	LTC	1944	2015	VN	S57-2983
156	MARTIN, George Teo	USAF	COL	1957	2008	—	S60-8882
157	MAYFIELD, Agnes R.	Spouse	—	1922	1965	—	S37-3286
158	MAYFIELD, Darrell Ware	USAF	COL	1921	2011	WWII, KOR, VN	S37-3286
159	McDERMAID, Marion	Spouse	—	1912	2004	—	S59-101
160	McDERMAID, Richard	USAF	COL	1914	1999	WWII	S59-101
161	McLEAN, Max C.	USN	LCDR	1923	2004	WWII, KOR	S66-6203
162	McLEAN, Virginia	Spouse	—	1923	2001	—	S66-6203
163	McMAHAN, DeAnn T.	Spouse	—	1954	2005	—	S69-2224
164	McPHERSON, William D.	USN	CDR	1958	2013	—	CN70-H-41-3
165	McREYNOLDS, Stephen Wayne Jr.	USA	SSG	1949	2011	VN	S59-150
166	MEILING, Jaque L.	USN	LCDR	1937	1986	VN	S64-131

NO.	NAME	STATUS	RANK	BIRTH	DEATH	WAR-TIME SERVICE	ANC LOCATION
167	MERRILL, Alvin S.	USMC	1ST SGT	1930	2004	KOR, VN	S54-73
168	MILLAR, Jack W.	USN	CAPT	1922	1994	WWII, KOR, VN	S68-4004
169	MILLER, John Frederick Jr.	USN	CAPT	1915	2015	WWII	S55-6118
170	MILLER, Kim Hunter	USA	PFC	1947	2016	—	S71-1591
171	MILLER, Thelma C. Jamison	Spouse	—	1920	2010	—	S55-6118
172	MOATS, Evelyn C	Spouse	—	1916	1999	—	S66-2788
173	MOATS, Paul Daniel	USN	EMC	1913	2008	WWII, KOR	S66-2788
174	MOORHEAD, Cecil Allen	USA	CWO2	1931	2006	KOR, VN	S64-5153
175	MORGAN, Keisha M.	USA	SPC	1982	2008	—	S60-8561
176	MORGAN, Paul Roy	USA	CPT	1946	2008	VN	S60-8272
177	MORRISON, Joseph John	USA	MAJ	1918	2011	WWII	S54-1713
178	MOSS, Linda Louise	Spouse	—	1955	2017	—	S62-1245
179	NELSON, Johnathan L.	USA	SP4	1945	2002	VN	S67-2629
180	NESMITH, Anna Elizabeth	USA	PFC	1950	2011	—	C8-VV-11-1
181	NEWCOMB, Fred J.	USN	MRC	1919	1982	WWII, KOR	S69-4735
182	NORDIKE, Brian David, Sr.	USN	OSC	1968	2005	—	S69-2198
183	OKERLUND, Edward C.	USAF	MAJ	1932	1989	KOR	S65-3970
184	OKERLUND, Janet R.	Spouse	—	1932	2017	—	S65-3970

NO.	NAME	STATUS	RANK	BIRTH	DEATH	WAR-TIME SERVICE	ANC LOCATION
185	OSTENBERG, John Michael	USAF	MSGT	1952	2014	VN, GW	S71-202
186	OSTENBERG, Michelle Marie	Spouse	—	1956	2017	—	S71-202
187	OWENS, Jacklyn Lucy	Spouse	—	1937	2016	—	S60-11054
188	PENDLETON, Alvin F. Jr.	USA	TEC4	1924	2007	WWII	C8-R-5-3
189	PENDLETON, Donna B.	Spouse	—	1925	2015		C8-R-5-3
190	PERRY, Robert Lee	USN	HMC	1925	2004	WWII, KOR, VN	S69-3807
191	POULSEN, Bryant Edmond	USA	1LT	1921	1944	WWII-10925	S60
192	PYEATT, Lucas Todd	USMC	SGT	1986	2011	AFG	S60-9605
193	QUINN, Larry G.	USA	LTC	1937	1999	VN	S68-2514
194	RAMPLIN, Patrick C.	USN	YNT3	1924	1998	—	C6-EE-26-2
195	RASMUSSEN, Floyd Alton	USA	CPT	1942	2011	VN, GW	S64-6593
196	REX, Sandra L.	USAF	MSGT	1949	2010	—	S54-3526
197	RICHARDS, Catherine S.	Child	—	1984	1984	—	S12-8510-7
198	RICHARDS, Jody L.	Child	—	1984	1984	—	S12-8510-7
199	RICHARDS, Merlon F.	USA	MAJ	1920	1998	WWII	S70-663
200	RUSSO, Reeta Ann	Spouse	—	1931	2014	—	S64-7014
201	SANDERSON, Albert F. Jr.	USA	COL	1911	1983	WWII	S65-4101
202	SAVARD, Ryan	USA	SFC	1983	2012	AFG	S60-10129
203	SAYLOR, Horace A.	USA	1SGT	1920	1997	—	C4-LL-9-1

NO.	NAME	STATUS	RANK	BIRTH	DEATH	WAR-TIME SERVICE	ANC LOCATION
204	SCARBOROUGH, Daniel Paul	USMC	1SGT	1923	2016	WWII, KOR, VN	S69-4198
205	SCHNEIDER, Matthew Evan	USA	SPC	1983	2006	—	S60-8422
206	SCHOFIELD, Sondra Sue	Spouse	—	1940	2017	—	S60-11286
207	SENGSTACK, Cinda Murdock	USN	LT	1931	2012	—	C7-X-9-3
208	SEVILLANO, Diana L.	Spouse	—	1953	2010	—	S40-106
209	SHEA, Clair Val	USA	SSG	1923	1990	—	C2-NN-24 3
210	SHEA, Estella Mae	Spouse	—	1921	1991	—	C2-NN-24 3
211	SHIPLEY, Lloyd Price	USA	PFC	1918	1999	WWII	S55-1499
212	SHIPLEY, Lottice Bledsoe	Spouse	—	1921	1991	-	S55-1499
213	SHURTLEFF, Carlyle Hegsted	USA	COL	1915	1994	WWII, KOR	S64-2111
214	SHURTLEFF, Mary Jane Tomlinson	Spouse	—	1921	2007	—	S64-2111
215	SMITH, Florence J.	Spouse	—	1907	2000	-	S67-384
216	SMITH, Glenn Lowell	USCG	CAPT	1923	2018	-	S60-11895
217	SMITH, John E.	USN	FTCM	1925	2010	WWII	S59-175
218	SMITH, Marjorie Ann	Spouse	—	1926	2017	—	S60-11895
219	SPENCER, Loren James	USAF	LT COL	1924	2013	WWII, KOR	S54-1361
220	SQUIRE, Boyd E.	USAF	LT COL	1930	1967	VN	S34-3830
221	STEWART, Glenn S.	USA	LTC	1919	1996	WWII, KOR	S67-3235
222	STIRLING, Beth Ellis	USN	YN2	1921	1997	—	C4-W-14-3

NO.	NAME	STATUS	RANK	BIRTH	DEATH	WAR-TIME SERVICE	ANC LOCATION
223	STOCKS, Maurice L.	USAF	COL	1947	2014	VN	S57-2908
224	STYLER, June Marie	Spouse	—	1961	2004	—	S69-3348
225	THOMPSON, Mack Eugene	USA	WOJG	1921	2014	WWII	C3-V-6-4
226	TOLMAN, David Elden	USN	LT	1910	1953	—	S8-5425-A
227	TONER, Francis L. IV	USN	LT(JG)	1982	2009	—	S60-8876
228	TORRY, John Archibald Hyde Jr.	USN	CDR	1919	2000	WWII, KOR, VN	S54-5295
229	TOTH, Joseph Charles Andrew	USAF	A2C	1936	2016	—	C9-S42-5-3
230	TUCKER, Edwardean A.	USN	CDR	1912	1993	WWII, KOR	S67-81
231	TURNER, Raymond V., Jr.	USN	SA	1952	2009	—	S64-26
232	TYLER, Claude G.	USAF	SSGT	1918	1943	—	S60-9712
233	UNGER, Cody Harold	USAF	MSGT	1920	2011	WWII, KOR	S55-3130
234	VAN DAM, Geraldine Stokes	Spouse	—	1916	2006	—	S7-8152-1
235	VAN DAM, Norman	USMC	COL	1912	1994	WWII, KOR	S7-8152-2
236	VAUGHAN, George F.	USN	LCDR	1931	2000	VN	S46-1176
237	VAUGHAN, Timothy K.	Child	—	1959	1959	—	S46-1176
238	VAUGHN, Thomas W.	USN	MM3	1961	1981	—	S68-3644
239	VOSS, Richard A.	Child	—	1992	1992	—	S69-264
240	VZATEK, Stanley Stephen	USN	DSC	1950	2013	VN	S55-535

NO.	NAME	STATUS	RANK	BIRTH	DEATH	WAR-TIME SERVICE	ANC LOCATION
241	WADE, Gordon R.	USMC	CPT	1929	2010	—	S39-5-25
242	WADE, Joy	Spouse	—	1926	2010	—	S39-5-25
243	WALKER, Rulon Anthony	USN	LCDR	1907	1992	—	C3-O-6-3
244	WALQUIST, Ronald LeLand	USA	SGT	1945	2018	VN	S76-1616
245	WANNEBO, Peter E.	USA	CPL	1917	1984	—	S65-2164
246	WEBB, Allen K.	USA	1st SGT	1915	2007	—	C8-XX-29-3
247	WEISS, Gary Alan	USA	PFC	1950	2016	VN	CN70-N-36-3
248	WELTI, Conrad Joseph	USAF	LT COL	1917	1991	WWII	S68-2506
249	WHITAKER, Mike	USAF	TSGT	1941	2010	—	C8-YY-4-1
250	WHITE, Nathan Dennis	USN	LT	1972	2003	IRQ	S60-7873
251	WILLIAMSON, Boyd Dean	USAF	LT COL	1924	2010	WWII, KOR, VN	S40-101
252	WILLIAMSON, Norah Dawn	Spouse	—	1925	2010	—	S40-101
253	WILSON, Elizabeth J. Marceau	Spouse	—	1955	1998	—	S10-10889
254	WILSON, Frances Gail	Spouse	—	1936	2014	—	S71-965
255	WINTER, Galen C.	USA	TEC 3	1911	1986	—	C2-H-13 4
256	WINTER, Virginia H.	Spouse	—	1913	2003	—	C2-H-13 4
257	WOOD, James Frederick	Child	—	1953	1953	—	S10-10883-B
258	WOOD, Robert A.	USAF	LT COL	1918	1999	WWII, KOR	S10-10883-B
259	YOUNG, Bertha W.	Spouse	—	1914	2001	—	S46-264

NO.	NAME	STATUS	RANK	BIRTH	DEATH	WAR-TIME SERVICE	ANC LOCATION
260	YOUNG, Fay Hubert	USN	CM2	1912	2002	—	C6-Z-13-4
261	YOUNG, Helen Ehlers	Spouse	—	1920	2011	—	C6-Z-13-4
262	ZEMLICKA, Frank Kenneth	USAF	LT COL	1936	2015	VN	S71-1239

NOTES

1. Isabel Allende, *Eva Luna: A Novel*, trans. Margaret Sayers Peden (New York: Atria Paperback, 1987), 50.

2. Arlington National Cemetery is one of 150 national cemeteries maintained by federal agencies. The Department of Veterans Affairs maintains 136 cemeteries, the Department of the Interior manages fourteen, and the Department of the Army maintains two cemeteries—Arlington National Cemetery and Soldiers Home. See "General History," National Cemetery Administration, https://www.cem.va.gov/history/.

3. Ten Revolutionary War soldiers were reinterred at Arlington National Cemetery from other cemeteries. See Linda Witt, "Introduction," in Lorraine Jacyno Dieterle, *Arlington National Cemetery: A Nation's Story Carved in Stone* (Rohnert Park, CA: Pomegranate Communications, Inc., 2001), 11.

4. Doris Kearns Goodwin, *Team of Rivals* (New York: Simon & Schuster, 2005), 350.

5. Robert M. Poole, *On Hallowed Ground: The Story of Arlington National Cemetery* (New York: Walker & Company, 2009), 22.

6. Poole, *On Hallowed Ground*, 54–55.

7. Robert M. Poole, "The Battle of Arlington," *Smithsonian* 40, no. 8 (November 2009): 52.

8. Ruth Tam, "8 things you didn't know about Arlington National Cemetery," *PBS News Hour* (website).

9. General Orders No. 11, Headquarters Grand Army of the Republic, Washington, DC, 5 May 1868. "Memorial Day Order," National Cemetery Administration, U.S. Department of Veterans Affairs, https://www.cem.va.gov/cem/history/memdayorder.asp.

10. *History of Arlington National Cemetery* (postcard, Washington, DC: B. S. Reynolds Co, 1921).

11. "About Arlington National Cemetery," Arlington National Cemetery, https://www.arlingtoncemetery.mil/about.

12. According to the 2010 census, there are 21.8 million living military veterans who have earned the honor of being buried in a national cemetery. According to the National Cemetery Administration, "Veterans with discharges other than dishonorable, their spouses and dependent children may be eligible for burial in a VA national cemetery. Those who die on active duty may also be buried in a national cemetery." See "General History," National Cemetery Administration, https://www.cem.va.gov/history/.

13. "History of Government Furnished Headstones and Markers," National Cemetery Administration, https://www.cem.va.gov/cem/history/hmhist.asp.

14. "Types of Emblems Available," National Cemetery Administration, https:// www.cem.va.gov/cem/hmm/emblems.asp.

15. "Available Emblems of Belief for Placement on Government Headstones and Markers," National Cemetery Administration, https://www.cem.va.gov /cem/hmm/abbreviations.asp; emblems available as of July 2018.

16. "Types of Emblems Available," National Cemetery Administration, https:// www.cem.va.gov/cem/hmm/emblems.asp.

17. "Gravestone emblem approved," *Church News*, 31 May 1980, 13.

18. A columbarium is a place where funeral urns are stored. An increasing percentage of interments at Arlington National Cemetery are in a columbarium.

19. ANC Explorer, https://ancexplorer.army.mil.

20. You can look up these and other burials at "FindAGrave," Arlington National Cemetery (website).

21. Lloyd P. Shipley, Honorable Discharge, WD AGO Form 53-55, Army of the United States, 20 April 1945; Army Separation Qualification Record, WD AGO Form No. 100, 20 April 1945.

22. Lloyd P. Shipley, Life History, September 1991, copy in author's possession.

23. Spencer Burt, "Utah-raised WWII veteran to be interred at Arlington Cemetery on 100th birthday," *Deseret News*, 15 December 2018.

24. Leo Shane III, "New Eligibility Rules for Arlington Cemetery Would Exclude Most Non-Combat Veterans," Military Times (website), 25 September 2019.

25. Major Sidney Herbert, "Col. Theodore O'Hara, author of 'The Bivouac of the dead'—Soldier, Orator, Poet and Journalist." *Register of Kentucky Historical Society* 39, no. 128 (July 1941): 231. Tradition says it was General Meigs who ordered the lines be added to the McClellan Gate. "In fall 2001, the National Cemetery Administration . . . install[ed] a new cast-aluminum tablet featuring the first stanza of 'Bivouac of the Dead' in all the existing national cemeteries where they are missing . . ." https://www.cem.va.gov /cem/history/BODpoem.asp.

The Nauvoo Temple. Photo by Gogogoff, Pixabay.

CHURCH AND STATE: THE NATIONAL PARK SERVICE AND NAUVOO

SCOTT C. ESPLIN

Scott C. Esplin is a professor of Church history and doctrine at Brigham Young University.

There is a rich history of Latter-day Saint interaction and influence in Washington, DC, as the essays in this volume have demonstrated. Dictated by revelation and implemented through decades of practice, The Church of Jesus Christ of Latter-day Saints has sought redress from the federal government (Doctrine and Covenants 101:76) and, more recently, has provided "honest . . . wise . . . and good" men and women to serve in public and private ways in various capacities within the federal district (Doctrine and Covenants 98:10). The stories of its history, people, and places make Washington an overlooked but important part of the larger Church narrative. But the relationship between the Church and Washington is reciprocal. One federal agency in particular that has had important interactions with the Church has been the National Park Service, a significant curator of national memory and one of several agencies that shapes life in the nation's capital and beyond.[1]

Washington, DC, is a monument city. The District of Columbia boasts as many as twenty-five national parks, trails, and monuments, seventy-four national historic landmarks, and more than six hundred sites on the

National Register of Historic Places, all of which attract more than forty million visitors each year.[2] The National Mall, frequently referred to as "the nation's front yard" and "a center of our collective history and art," hosts more visitors than Yellowstone, Yosemite, and Grand Canyon National Parks combined and—like these and many other American treasures—is administered by the National Park Service.[3] Disproportionate to other cities nationwide, sites occupying as much as 27 percent of the total land area in the District of Columbia are managed by Park Service employees, patrolled by Park Service police, maintained by Park Service crews, and ultimately overseen by the National Park Service director officed in the city itself.[4] In many ways, the Park Service may be among Washington, DC's most visible federal entities.

As a federal agency, however, the influence of the National Park Service extends far beyond the bounds of the federal district. Charged with preserving "unimpaired the natural and cultural resources" of the United States,[5] the National Park Service has an expansive mission that often intersects with the interests of private groups. Designating historic sites for

National Park Service information booth in front of the Washington Monument. Photo by Fred Bell, National Park Service History Collection.

preservation can be controversial, especially when it overlaps with religious history. Throughout the twentieth century, the Park Service partnered with the Church to develop historic sites celebrating a shared history. By this means, the federal government touched the lives of hundreds of thousands of Latter-day Saints.

This essay examines the involvement of the Church with the federal government, primarily through National Park Service directors Conrad Wirth (1951–64) and George Hartzog (1964–72), in designating and preserving Latter-day Saint sacred space. Also, the support provided for the development of Church historic sites is explored, as are the reasons the partnership was dissolved. Additionally, the manner in which Church leaders engaged in the country's larger historical narrative through organizations like the National Park Service is traced.

OVERVIEW OF THE NATIONAL PARK SERVICE

Formal preservation of natural and historic space within the United States by the federal government began in 1872 when Yellowstone National Park was designated "as a public park or pleasuring-ground for the benefit and enjoyment of the people" and placed "under exclusive control of the Secretary of the Interior."[6] Expanding the reach of the federal government, the Antiquities Act of 1906 granted the president of the United States authority to designate "historic landmarks, historic and prehistoric structures, and other objects of historic or scientific interest" as national monuments.[7] The National Park Service, a federal bureau under the direction of the Department of the Interior, was formed in 1916 by the Organic Act. The legislation dictated that "the service . . . shall promote and regulate the use of the Federal areas known as national parks, monuments and reservations . . . to conserve the scenery and the natural and historic objects and the wild life therein and to provide for the enjoyment of the same in such manner and by such means as will leave them unimpaired for the enjoyment of future generations."[8] Beginning in 1916, the Park Service took control of the thirty-five existing national parks and monuments. Seventeen years later, two executive orders issued in 1933 consolidated additional properties including national military parks, battlefield sites, monuments, and

National Park Service Director Conrad L. Wirth (1951–64) at Glacier National Park. Photo by Jack E. Boucher, National Park Service History Collection.

miscellaneous memorials under the head of the National Park Service, creating "today's truly national system of parks—a system that includes areas of historical as well as scenic and scientific importance."[9]

The Historic Sites Act of 1935 significantly expanded the Park Service's areas of focus, declaring that "it is a national policy to preserve for public use historic sites, buildings, and objects of national significance for the inspiration and benefit of the people of the United States." The act specifically charged the National Park Service to identify historically important locations and to "restore, reconstruct, rehabilitate, preserve, and maintain historic or prehistoric sites, buildings, objects, and properties of national historical or archaeological significance and where deemed desirable establish and maintain museums in connection therewith."[10] At present, more than one hundred years after its founding, the National Park Service manages an extensive network of more than four hundred properties, including parks, monuments, trails, sites, and recreational areas.

In addition to actively managing properties, the National Park Service oversees federal recognition of historic significance for thousands of additional sites. In 1960 the agency initiated the National Historic Landmarks program, a designation reserved for the sites of greatest significance. To qualify, sites and their stories must be important to the history of the entire nation rather than to individual communities or states. Additionally, the sites must possess a high level of historic integrity. Nearly twenty-six hundred properties currently enjoy the designation of National Historic Landmark.[11] In 1966 the National Park Service also began curating an expansive list of locations, known as the National Registry of Historic Places. Less exclusive than the Landmarks program, the National Registry contains more than ninety-five thousand properties deemed worthy of preservation.[12]

In a country founded by religiously motivated settlers that enshrined freedom of religion, it is inevitable that the federal agency charged with identifying, preserving, and celebrating the nation's history would overlap with faith. The Park Service has a longstanding relationship with religion and religious organizations. Several sites that are part of the National Park System have a connection to faith through the history they preserve.[13] "Most of the national parks are cultural sites," Kathy Kupper, Park Service spokesperson observed. "They tell the story of who we are collectively as a people and as a society." Therefore, "though the U.S. governmental agencies operate within the guidelines of separation of church and state, there are sacred symbols in many of the national parks, mainly because . . . religious institutions are a part of the nation's story."[14]

While America's story includes actors and actions that are significantly religious, not all of the historically religious sites are directly owned by the federal government. Importantly, the Historic Sites Act of 1935 charged the National Park Service to "contract and make cooperative agreements with States, municipal subdivisions, corporations, associations, or individuals . . . to protect, preserve, maintain, or operate any historic or archaeologic building, site, object, or property used in connection therewith for public use," regardless of who held title to the property.[15] As a result, partnerships between church and state exist, allowing for federally supported historical designation and even the sharing of religious space in some instances. These designations include Latter-day Saint historical sites across the country.

FEDERAL INTEREST IN LATTER-DAY SAINT SITES

Federal interest in the historical sites of the Church emerged during the early decades of the National Park Service. The interest coincided with significant focus on site development by the federal government in the years immediately after the twentieth century's two world wars. During the "aggressive patriotism post–World War I, followed by the highly nationalistic New Deal—in which the national parks participated through [Civil Conservation Corps] projects," the nation's historic sites and parks became "symbols of American greatness" and "contributing factors to [a] nation-centered discourse."[16]

This flourishing of park-centered patriotism in the early twentieth century coincided with Latter-day Saint interest in emerging from its mountain exile in the American West to step out on the national stage. Through participation in the nation's politics, its armed conflicts, and its commemorations, Latter-day Saints sought a greater role in American discourse.[17] Memorials to a shared past, as Kathleen Flake describes them, "signaled the church's intent to come out from behind its mountain barrier and claim a place in America at large."[18] During the early decades of the twentieth century, the Church acquired and developed properties in Sharon, Vermont; Palmyra, New York; and Carthage, Illinois, as a way to stake a claim to the telling of its story.

The use of national parks and historic sites for patriotic political purposes was repeated following World War II, "a time when Americans flocked to the parks in greater numbers and the Park Service had few resources to deal with them."[19] This coincided with the golden age of American family vacations, when Cold War fears contrasted with robust consumerism in a summertime tradition of crisscrossing the country on its expanding federal highways.[20] Conrad Wirth, the country's longest-tenured National Park Service director (1951–64), developed "Mission 66," an ambitious ten-year agenda aimed at celebrating the system's fiftieth-year jubilee in 1966 by revamping a park program that was woefully overrun and simultaneously underfunded. For Wirth, the development of the National Park system was both patriotic and religious. "It is an investment in good citizenship," he wrote. "Where else do so many Americans under the most pleasant circumstances come face to face with their Government? ... Where else but in the great out-of-doors as God made it can we better recapture the spirit and something of the qualities of the pioneers? Pride in their Government, love of the land, and faith in the American Tradition—these are the real products of our national parks."[21]

Historic Nauvoo, Illinois, was a place where God, patriotism, and pioneers came together for Director Wirth. Throughout the 1950s and '60s, private individuals—as well as organizations such as the state of Illinois and the Church—explored the idea of developing historic Nauvoo. In May 1962, representatives from these parties gathered in Nauvoo to formalize a plan. Joining Presidents Henry D. Moyle and Hugh B. Brown of the Church's First Presidency; A. Edwin Kendrew, senior vice president and chief historical architect for the restoration of Colonial Williamsburg; J. LeRoy Kimball, visionary restorer of Nauvoo's Heber C. Kimball home; and J. Willard Marriott, hotel developer and entrepreneur, was Conrad Wirth, director of the National Park Service.[22]

As the party toured Nauvoo's surviving historical structures from its Latter-day Saint past, the group discussed possibilities for a restored future. This fact-finding mission aimed "to discover the possibilities for the restoring of the historic significance of Nauvoo as one of the major bases of overland migration from the Mississippi into the American West,"[23] a mission which was of interest to the National Park Service. As part of his visit, Wirth declared that "we are custodians of this land only for a few years, we must preserve our heritage, sort out important things to be accomplished and not stray from this purpose, all important historical places should be preserved for posterity."[24] With this declaration, Wirth effectively connected Nauvoo's restoration to his agency's vision for historic preservation.

Federal interest in Nauvoo as an important national historic site extended beyond Wirth's high-profile visit in the city. Even before Wirth's visit, the National Park Service had been actively exploring Nauvoo as a site of national significance. Studying overland migrations west of the

Mississippi River, the Park Service settled on the story of the Latter-day Saints and, by association, Nauvoo. "The fifth decade of the nineteenth century was America's most expansive period," noted a Park Service report conducted under the authority of the Historic Sites Act. "Within the space of a few years, the boundaries of the United States were pushed across half the continent. The most significant aspect of this expansionism was the overland movement of emigrants. The optimistic pioneer farmer, moving with his family to Oregon, the persevering Mormon, searching for a home in which he might live in peace, and the adventurous forty-niner, hurrying to the new El Dorado with visions of the wealth that awaited him there, all carried American civilization westward and building in the Great West the foundations for a new society." Nauvoo was touted "as a site of exceptional value commemorating and illustrating the history of the United States."[25] As a result of this conclusion, the National Park Service nominated Nauvoo as a National Historic Landmark in January 1961.[26]

In Salt Lake City, J. LeRoy Kimball, a physician and visionary who had been urging Church leadership to restore Nauvoo, capitalized on this national recognition for the City of Joseph. In December 1961, he drafted a report entitled "An Outline for the Restoration of Nauvoo," which cited the National Park Service study extensively. Importantly, Kimball linked his vision for Nauvoo to that of the National Park Service. In addition to rebuilding and rededicating the temple, Kimball echoed the findings of the federal study, proposing that the city be restored "to provide an historically authentic physical environment for awakening a public interest in, and an understanding and appreciation of, the story of Nauvoo and the mass migration of its people to the valley of the Great Salt Lake; and to dramatize the interpretation of that story, not only as a great example of pioneering courage and religious zeal, but also as one of the vital forces in the expansion of America westward from the Mississippi River."[27] Thus an informal partnership between the Church and the Park Service was born.

After his lengthy tenure, Conrad Wirth was replaced as National Park Service director in 1964 by George B. Hartzog Jr., who led the Park Service from 1964 until 1972. Hartzog assumed leadership from his position as superintendent of the Jefferson National Expansion Memorial (known today as the Gateway Arch National Park) located in St. Louis, downriver from Nauvoo. Interestingly, like Nauvoo, the Jefferson National Expansion Memorial served as a site to commemorate American expansion.

Like his predecessor, George Hartzog expressed support of the Nauvoo project. In his first year as Park Service director, Hartzog visited Nauvoo and "reaffirmed his desire and the desire of the National Park Service to cooperate in every way, stating it was their intention to include Nauvoo in their over-all plan of development, to furnish such information as will aid in the project, and to include Nauvoo in their literature in connection with the Jefferson Arch Memorial and their Mission 66 program." Arrangements were made to ensure that the "Great River Road," which was then under development and followed the Mississippi River through portions of ten states, would "best serve the [Nauvoo] project's interests."[28]

Hartzog maintained correspondence with Nauvoo Restoration leaders, calling himself "an enthusiastic supporter of the project from its inception" while accepting invitations to represent the National Park Service at significant events in the city.[29] In 1969 Hartzog attended the groundbreaking for the Church's visitors' center in Nauvoo, joining Church and national dignitaries including Nauvoo Restoration trustee and U.S. Secretary

National Park Service director George B. Hartzog (1964–72). National Park Service History Collection.

of the Treasury David M. Kennedy; U.S. Secretary of Housing and Urban Development George W. Romney; Belle S. Spafford, president of the National Council of Women and of the Church's General Relief Society; Hugh B. Brown; Harold B. Lee; Delbert L. Stapley; and Neal A. Maxwell. Two years later, Hartzog joined a similar cast for the building's dedication, where he also spoke. On that occasion, Director Hartzog publicly revealed National Park interest in Nauvoo. "We of the National Park Service have watched with growing interest and admiration the unfolding restoration of this historic town," Hartzog declared. "You have re-created here a vivid reminder of an important part of our national heritage—the setting not only of significant people and events of history but of a past way of life too. You have harmoniously combined old and new in a model exhibition of enlightened historic preservation." Speaking of his own organization's interest in historic preservation, Hartzog continued, "It is informative as well as inspiring to me to see what you have done here, for each year the National Park Service becomes more heavily involved in historic preservation. Although our image in the eyes of many still centers on the great natural parks, such as Yellowstone and Grand Canyon, fully two-thirds of the areas of the National Park System—about 180—were set aside because of historical value."[30] He noted that this interest in historical sites would necessitate partnerships like the one created in Nauvoo. "Our interest in historic preservation extends far beyond the historic sites we administer. In line with what has been termed the 'new federalism,' we are also able to give help and encouragement to state, local, and private efforts. Our cooperative programs, featuring a partnership between the National Park Service and the private sector, are demonstrated right here in Nauvoo."[31]

"The Secretary of the Interior has designated Nauvoo a National Historic Landmark, one of about 900 sites so honored to date as possessing exceptional value in illustrating the cultural heritage of our Nation," Hartzog continued. "The determination of national significance—as opposed to state or local significance—required for Landmark status is the same criterion applied to prospective additions to the National Park System. . . . Few places in the United States deserve this distinction more than Nauvoo."[32] As the million-dollar visitors' center was being dedicated, the partnership between the National Park Service and the Church seemed strong.

SEPARATING CHURCH AND STATE

So what happened? Why would a visitor to Latter-day Saint historic sites today find little representing the National Park Service? Similarly, why would someone studying the National Park Service or federal interaction in historic sites find few references to Nauvoo today?

Strain that drove the two organizations apart emerged shortly after Nauvoo's designation as a National Historic Landmark in 1961 and the public appearance of the National Park Service director in town the next year. A week after his high-profile visit to Nauvoo in May 1962, Director Wirth received a complaint from an Illinois resident about National Park Service involvement. "Where in the U.S. is a like project? Where taxes from local, state & national sources are solicited to restore a religious temple or provide an extensive park around it? Do you believe in separation of church and State? We do. Therefore we oppose the restoration of Nauvoo by using taxes."[33] In a more cordial way, the managing editor for the Reorganized Church's press, Herald House, inquired later that summer "about the extent of federal government participation in the restoration work and the amount of federal financing involved in the project."[34] Additionally, Herbert H. Kahler, chief of the division of history and archeology of the Park Service, was forced to respond to discussion that Nauvoo might be elevated as "a national historic site in nonfederal ownership." He stressed that Director Wirth "wanted this to be considered not in terms of religious implications but rather as one of the great westward migrations."[35] Nevertheless, questions persisted, with the Nauvoo Planning Commission inquiring in 1963 about "rumors that the National Park Service may be planning to take over part of Nauvoo as a National Historic Shrine." Director Wirth quickly squelched the rumor.[36]

Following the public holding of hands by the Church and the National Park Service in restoring Nauvoo during the 1960s, both projects eventually took dramatically different turns. In July 1972, George Hartzog wrote a complimentary letter to Harold B. Lee, offering his "heartiest congratulations and good wishes . . . on the occasion of [his] election as President of the Church of Jesus Christ of Latter Day Saints. . . . It has been a pleasure, indeed, for me to know and work with you in Nauvoo," Hartzog noted. "If there is any way in which I may serve you at any time, please let

Director George B. Hartzog speaking at a National Park Service Summer in the Parks program. Photo by Cecil W. Stoughton, National Park Service History Collection.

me know."[37] Lee responded, "I sincerely appreciated your note. . . . I have come to value not only friends within the Church but friends like yourself outside whose counsel and whose fellowship we seek and appreciate very much. It was with pleasure that I had the brief meeting with you with reference to work now being done in Nauvoo." Lee continued, "I believe that the beautiful visitors center with the few buildings which have been restored as near as possible to their original state, will provide not only a monument to the westward march of the early pioneers, but also to indicate to the visitors that those early members of the Church were indeed people of refinement and culture as their buildings and the work of their hands attested. Please be assured that we would appreciate any further counsel you may wish to give us with reference to this or other projects which come under your supervision."[38]

Despite overtures for continued cooperation, within eighteen months neither Hartzog nor Lee was directing their respective organizations. By late 1972, Hartzog was embroiled in several political controversies. Earlier in his administration, Hartzog enacted the practice of shuttering parks and monuments for two days a week in response to Vietnam War–era budget cuts. At the same time, Hartzog repeatedly butted heads with U.S. president Richard Nixon over issues relating to the parks, personally alienating him when the Park Service revoked a permit for a close friend of the president to have special access to facilities at Biscayne National Monument.

Hartzog later wrote, "The bell had begun to toll on my tenure as director."[39] In December 1972, Hartzog was relieved of duty, replaced by an official from the Nixon White House, signaling for some a shift from civil service to partisan politics within the Park Service.[40]

In the case of the Church, leadership changes, including the deaths of early Nauvoo supporter President David O. McKay in 1970 and President Harold B. Lee in 1973, led to a shift in views for a restored Nauvoo. Even in Nauvoo Restoration's founding, participants sensed that not all shared the strong connection between Nauvoo and American westward expansion, preferring instead that the site be used for more traditional proselytizing purposes. In 1964, T. Edgar Lyon, historical consultant to Nauvoo Restoration, wrote, "The road ahead does not look too cheery—some opposition is arising within the Church."[41] Nauvoo Restoration secretary Rowena Miller summarized the challenge. "It will take the wisdom of a Solomon," Miller cautioned, "to walk the tight-rope of historic interpretation [and] proselyting you people . . . have confronting you."[42] Some of the concern centered around the high costs of restoration and the desire to place greater focus on proselytizing efforts.

In 1971 the board of Nauvoo Restoration was restructured, establishing even greater Church control. Project secretary Rowena Miller summarized the impact of the reorganization. "The restoration was administered as an historical project, as outlined in the Articles of Incorporation, and the purpose for which the corporation was set up. With two non-members on the Board of Trustees, the corporation had a standing in the nation as an historical restoration project. . . . After the death of President David O. McKay, who had supported the corporation in all of its activities, there were some in the officialdom of the Church who did not believe in the historical approach of the restoration."[43] A year later, a Nauvoo Mission was created. The national narrative of westward expansion was pushed to the margins, replaced with proselytizing approaches that were, at times, at odds with the mission of the National Park Service.

CONCLUSION

For several years, the reach of Washington, DC, and one of its federal agencies extended directly to a historic rural Illinois town on a bend of the Mississippi River. During the tenures of National Park Service directors Conrad Wirth and George Hartzog as well as Church Presidents David O. McKay, Joseph Fielding Smith, and Harold B. Lee, the National Park Service and The Church of Jesus Christ of Latter-day Saints maintained a shared active relationship regarding Church historic sites. The arrangement was mutually beneficial for each organization. From the perspective of the National Park Service, Latter-day Saints represented a clean-cut counterpoint to the culture wars that engulfed America during the 1960s and '70s. The Latter-day Saint story of bravely stepping out into the frontier during the nineteenth century melded with modern efforts to defend American exceptionalism while exploring space-age frontiers. For the Church, cooperation with a federal organization like the National Park Service brought expertise and credibility to its historic site endeavors. National standing and interpretive control were especially important in a place like Nauvoo, where the faith's story was inserted into the narrative of westward expansion but also framed against alternate historical interpretations offered at neighboring sites by the Reorganized Church of Jesus Christ.

The relationship's demise reflects realities within both organizations and changing dynamics between the Church and the federal government. The National Park Service became more political, removing one of the strongest proponents for the partnership, making it increasingly problematic to cooperate in overtly religious projects. At the same time, Church historic sites like Nauvoo became more religious, pushing evangelizing messages and later, through the reconstruction of the temple, shaping the site as a spiritual retreat for the faithful. However, for at least a decade during the twentieth century, the National Park Service and the Church worked hand-in-hand to make Church historic sites "a resting-place for the weary traveler" where they could "contemplate the glory of Zion" (Doctrine and Covenants 124:60).

NOTES

1. In addition to the National Park Service, agencies that merit examination for their federal and Church interactions include the Bureau of Land Management, the Bureau of Indian Affairs, and the Departments of Justice and Education, among others.

2. National Park Service, "District of Columbia," nps.gov.

3. Lisa Benton-Short, *The National Mall: No Ordinary Public Place* (Toronto: University of Toronto Press, 2016), 69, 94, 241; James F. Cooper, "Foreword," in *The National Mall: Rethinking Washington's Monumental Core*, ed. Nathan Glazer and Cynthia R. Field (Baltimore: Johns Hopkins University Press, 2008), vii.

4. Brooke Sabin, "5 National Parks in D.C. That the Locals Love," Where traveler.com.

5. National Park Service, "About Us: Our Mission," nps.gov. See also *An Act to Establish a National Park Service*, 25 August 1916, 39 Stat. 535.

6. *An Act to Set Apart a Certain Tract of Land Lying Near the Headwaters of the Yellowstone River as a Public Park*, 1 March 1872, 17 Stat. 32.

7. *An Act for the Preservation of American Antiquities*, 8 June 1906, 34 Stat. 225.

8. *An Act to Establish a National Park Service*, 25 August 1916, 39 Stat. 535.

9. National Park Service, "Quick History of the National Park Service," nps.gov.

10. *Historic Sites Act of 1935*, 16 U.S.C. sec. 461–62.

11. National Park Service, "The National Register of Historic Places and the National Historic Landmarks Program," nps.gov; see also National Park Service, "Roots of the National Historic Landmarks Program," nps.gov.

12. National Park Service, "What Is the National Register of Historic Places?," nps.gov. All National Historic Landmark sites are automatically included in the National Register of Historic Places.

13. Examples include the Roger Williams National Memorial in Rhode Island and the San Antonio Missions in Texas.

14. Nancy Wiechec and Chaz Muth, "National Parks: Places of Wonder, History, Spiritual Refuge," *National Catholic Reporter*, 29 October 2016.

15. *Historic Sites Act of 1935*, 16 U.S.C. sec. 462.

16. Lynn Ross-Bryant, *Pilgrimage to the National Parks* (New York: Routledge, 2013), 153.

17. Among many areas, Latter-day Saints actively engaged in military service in the Spanish-American War and World Wars I and II, in political activism like women's suffrage, and in business and educational pursuits.

18. Kathleen Flake, "Re-placing Memory: Latter-day Saint Use of Historical Monuments and Narrative in the Early Twentieth Century," *Religion and American Culture: A Journal of Interpretation* 13, no. 1 (2003): 80. Supporting this view, Latter-day Saint Apostle Francis M. Lyman declared at the dedication of the monument to Joseph Smith's birth in Sharon, Vermont, "And now we come back. The west and the east meet here on this blessed occasion. . . . We want your friendship; and you have ours." *Proceedings at*

the Dedication of the Joseph Smith Memorial Monument (Salt Lake City: self-pub., 1906), 17.

19. Lynn Ross-Bryant, *Pilgrimage to the National Parks* (New York: Routledge, 2013), 153.

20. Susan Sessions Rugh, *Are We There Yet? The Golden Age of American Family Vacations* (Lawrence: University Press of Kansas, 2008), 2–5.

21. Cited in Lynn Ross-Bryant, *Pilgrimage to the National Parks* (New York: Routledge, 2013), 161.

22. "Nauvoo Restoration Studied by Church and Federal Experts," *Nauvoo Independent*, 10 May 1962, NRI Historical Files, Nauvoo, Illinois. While beyond the scope of this study, J. Willard Marriott and his involvement is a significant connection between Washington, DC, and Latter-day Saint historic sites. Marriott served as an original trustee for Nauvoo Restoration, Incorporated. For additional information about the restoration of Nauvoo, see Scott C. Esplin, *Return to the City of Joseph: Modern Mormonism's Contest for the Soul of Nauvoo* (Urbana: University of Illinois Press, 2018).

23. "City Co-operation A Necessity," *Nauvoo Independent*, cited in Journal History, 10 May 1962, 6.

24. "Nauvoo Restoration Studied by Church and Federal Experts," *Nauvoo Independent*, 10 May 1962, NRI Historical Files, Nauvoo, IL.

25. J. LeRoy Kimball, "An Outline for the Restoration of Nauvoo," 11 December 1961, NRI Historical Files, Nauvoo, IL.

26. National Park Service, "Illinois NHL Nauvoo Historic District," Record Group 79, National Archives, College Park, MD.

27. J. LeRoy Kimball, "An Outline for the Restoration of Nauvoo," 11 December 1961, NRI Historical Files, Nauvoo, IL.

28. "Report of Progress and Development by the President to the Board of Trustees of Nauvoo Restoration, Incorporated," 25 June 1964, 4–5, NRI Historical Files, Nauvoo, IL. Following the formation of Nauvoo Restoration, Incorporated, the National Park Service issued a grant to David E. Miller, professor of history at the University of Utah, to conduct a yearlong historical survey of Nauvoo. David E. Miller, *Westward Migration of the Mormons with Special Emphasis on the History of Nauvoo* (Salt Lake City: University of Utah, 1963).

29. George B. Hartzog Jr. to L. LeRoy Kimball, 1 May 1969, Clemson University Archives, Clemson, SC.

30. In a draft version of this address, Hartzog added, "As the System expands in the future, the ratio will become even more disproportionate. Opportunities

to acquire unspoiled natural parks will decrease, but history—and thus historic sites—will continue to be made."

31. George B. Hartzog Jr., "Remarks of George B. Hartzog, Jr., Director of the National Park Service, at Dedication of Visitor Center at Nauvoo, Illinois," 4 September 1971, Clemson University Archives.

32. Hartzog Jr., "Dedication of Visitor Center at Nauvoo."

33. Minnie Prior to Director of the National Park Service, 14 May 1962, "Illinois NHL Nauvoo Historic District," Record Group 79, National Archives. Herbert E. Kahler, Park Service chief of the division of history and archaeology, responded and said that recognition of Nauvoo was "not on the basis of religious contributions but on the role this group played in the settlement of the West." Herbert E. Kahler to Minnie Prior, 31 May 1962, "Illinois NHL Nauvoo Historic District," Record Group 79, National Archives.

34. Roger Yarrington to the National Park Service, 27 August 1962. "Illinois NHL Nauvoo Historic District," Record Group 79, National Archives. Park Service officials clarified that they were "not participating in the restoration work itself."

35. Herbert H. Kahler to Regional Director, Region Five, 31 May 1962, "Illinois NHL Nauvoo Historic District," Record Group 79, National Archives.

36. John T. Moffitt to the National Park Service, 3 May 1963; Conrad L. Wirth to John T. Moffitt, 22 May 1963, "Illinois NHL Nauvoo Historic District," Record Group 79, National Archives.

37. George B. Hartzog Jr. to Harold B. Lee, 20 July 1972, Clemson University Archives.

38. Harold B. Lee to George B. Hartzog Jr., 10 August 1972, Clemson University Archives.

39. George B. Hartzog Jr., *Battling for the National Parks* (Mount Kisco, NY: Moyer Bell, 1988), 237–38.

40. Conrad L. Wirth, *Parks, Politics, and the People* (Norman: University of Oklahoma Press, 1980), 365.

41. T. Edgar Lyon to William E. Berrett, 13 November 1964, in Lyon, *Teacher in Zion*, 280.

42. Rowena Miller to Rex Sohn, 26 April 1967, NRI Historical Files, Nauvoo, IL.

43. Rowena Miller to J. Alan Blodgett, 6 July 1981, NRI Historical Files, Nauvoo, IL.

IN THIS TEMPLE
AS IN THE HEARTS OF THE PEOPLE
FOR WHOM HE SAVED THE UNION
THE MEMORY OF ABRAHAM LINCOLN
IS ENSHRINED FOREVER

Dedicated in May 1922, the iconic Lincoln Memorial is a favored destination of visitors to the nation's capital. This memorial has become a symbolic location for speeches on many important national issues, including Dr. Martin Luther King Jr.'s "I Have a Dream" speech on race relations in August 1963. All photos by Richard B. Crookston unless otherwise noted.

HISTORIC SITES IN WASHINGTON, DC: A PHOTO ESSAY

RICHARD B. CROOKSTON AND R. DEVAN JENSEN

Richard B. Crookston is the IT Manager for Religious Education at Brigham Young University. R. Devan Jensen is the executive editor for the Religious Studies Center at Brigham Young University.

This photo essay briefly documents a few buildings and artifacts in or around the nation's capital that inform the history of The Church of Jesus Christ of Latter-day Saints.

President George Washington laid the first cornerstone of the United States Capitol Building on 18 September 1793. Both wings were completed and connected by a wooden passageway in 1813. Although British troops set fire to the structure during the War of 1812, a rainstorm prevented its total destruction. During reconstruction in 1815, Benjamin Latrobe changed the interior design and introduced new materials, including marble from the Potomac.[1]

Boston architect Charles Bulfinch finished restoring the north and south wings and created chambers for the Supreme Court, the House, and the Senate by 1819. He completed updates to the central dome, landscaping, and decoration by 1826. Later Greek-Italian artist Constantino Brumidi painted *The Apotheosis of Washington* fresco.[2]

After Latter-day Saints were driven from the state of Missouri in 1838, they gathered in Illinois and decided in 1839 to send Sidney Rigdon to ask national leaders to gain redress for their losses. Judge Elias Higbee and Joseph Smith joined the expedition. Higbee reported in a letter to Hyrum Smith, "We arrived in this City on the morning of the 28th of November, and spent the most of that day in looking up a boarding house which we succeeded in finding. We found as cheap boarding as can be had in this city." Smith and Higbee lodged just west of the U.S. Capitol Building on the corner of Missouri and 3rd Streets, a site that today would be located on Washington's National Mall. Higbee recorded their visit to the White House thus: "[President Martin Van Buren] looked upon us with a kind of half frown and said, what can I do? I can do nothing for you,—if I do any thing, I shall come in contact with the whole State of Missouri."[3] The Latter-day Saints, who were bitterly disappointed with his refusal to compensate their losses, eventually migrated to the Great Basin.

Latter-day Saints in the United States honor George Washington as one of the most important Founding Fathers. Mount Vernon is the former estate of George and Martha Washington and twenty other Washington family members. It overlooks the banks of the Potomac River in Fairfax County, Virginia. George Washington died at Mount Vernon on 14 December 1799. His last will provided for a new brick tomb to be constructed to replace his original tomb, which was already deteriorating.[4]

Arlington National Cemetery is built on the former plantation of George Washington Parke Custis, grandson of Martha Washington and step-grandson of President Washington. In 1857 Custis willed the property to his daughter, Mary Anna Randolph Custis, the wife of Robert E. Lee. The cemetery is the burial ground for more than four hundred thousand active-duty service members, veterans, and family members, including many Latter-day Saints.[5]

The Tomb of the Unknown Soldier or the Tomb of the Unknowns is dedicated to deceased U.S. service members whose remains have not been
identified. Tomb guards are soldiers of the U.S. Army. The soldier "walking
the mat" wears no rank insignia so as not to outrank the Unknowns.[6]

The Three Soldiers (also called *The Three Servicemen*; see photo above) is a bronze statue by Frederick Hart. Installed a few feet from the Vietnam Veterans Memorial Wall at the National Mall (below), the sculpture was unveiled on Veterans Day, 11 November 1984, and portrays a Caucasian, an African American, and a Latino American.[7]

ᔿᏃᎾ ᎴᏋ ᎤᎾᏉᏗᎷᏋ:

ᎴᏉ ᏃᎾᏋᏓᏝ ᏗᏗᏕ ᏋᏛ

ᚤ ᏛᏉᏓᏟ ᎴᏋ ᎤᎾᏉᏗᎷᏋ,

ᏝᏗᏌ

ᏔᏝᏋᏗᏕ ᏐᏋᎾᏓ ᏛᏗᏉᎠ ᚤ ᏔᏝᏋᏗᏕ ᎴᏋ ᏌᎠᏛᏝ.

The Rare Books room in the Library of Congress's Thomas Jefferson Building houses important Latter-day Saint publications, such as an 1830 Book of Mormon, an 1833 Book of Commandments, an 1851 Pearl of Great Price, and a Book of Mormon in the Deseret Alphabet (shown here). Additional important documents and publications from American history reside here—such as a copy of the Emancipation Proclamation signed by Abraham Lincoln, a handwritten letter by Abraham Lincoln, and the first Bible published in America—as well as other rare items from the Library of Congress's extensive collections, including a life mask of Abraham Lincoln.

NEW YORK:
PUBLISHED FOR THE DESERET UNIVERSITY
BY RUSSELL BROS.
1869.

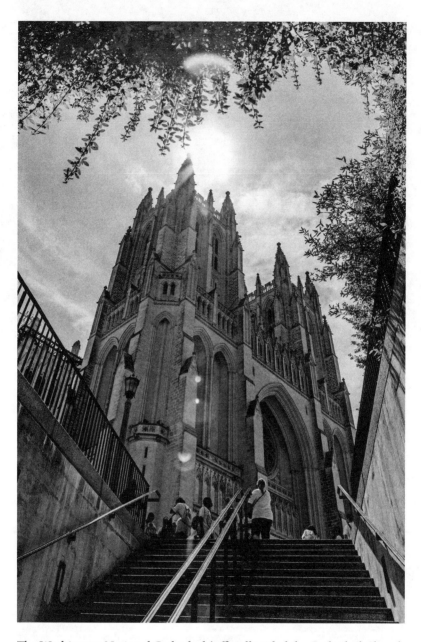

The Washington National Cathedral (officially titled the Cathedral Church of Saint Peter and Saint Paul in the City and Diocese of Washington), is the second-largest cathedral in the United States and the sixth-largest in the world.[8]

The Lincoln Bay of the Washington National Cathedral is an alcove with a massive bronze statue of President Abraham Lincoln, a gift from his great-grandson Lincoln Isham. The statue portrays the nation's sixteenth president kneeling in prayer before leaving his home in Springfield, Illinois, on his way to the presidency.[9]

The Museum of the Bible houses ancient Hebrew artifacts such as a scroll containing commentary on the book of Habukkuk dating to 30 BC–AD 30. Such artifacts honor the ancient Hebrew origins of the Bible.

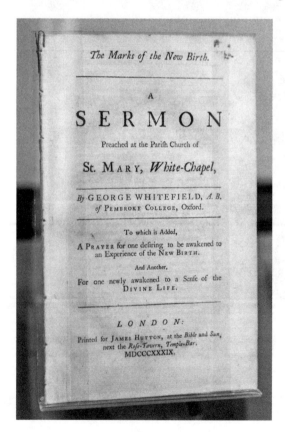

The museum offers a substantial gallery on the Great Awakening in America (1730s–1760s). The Great Awakening was a wave of religious fervor gripping the American colonies. Its most popular leader was the Anglican priest George Whitefield, who preached a message of new birth.

The Joseph Smith Translation and 1979 Latter-day Saint edition of the Bible appear on display at the Museum of the Bible in Washington, DC.

The Washington Chapel on Sixteenth Street was built to serve the original Washington D.C. Ward and was patterned after the Salt Lake Temple. A statue of the angel Moroni was originally on top of the 160-foot spire. The chapel is still standing, although it was sold to the Unification Church. A mosaic of the Sermon on the Mount still welcomes visitors at the entrance. Different floral depictions grace the windows, including the sego lily.

In the main room of the Washington Chapel, the east windows picture the North American continent, the Hill Cumorah, and the Rocky Mountains, where the Saints established themselves after their long persecutions. The south windows show the South American continent and an ancient temple, recalling the early history of the Western Hemisphere as told in the Book of Mormon. The north windows portray the continent of Europe, sailing vessels of the early immigrants, and the barren plains crossed by the pioneers, symbolic of the gathering of Saints to Zion.[10]

Auditorium of Daughters of the American Revolution Constitution Hall, 1934. Harris and Ewing photograph collection, Library of Congress.

The Daughters of the American Revolution's Constitution Hall accommodated stake conferences for the Washington Stake after the membership proved too large for the Washington Chapel and George Washington University's Lisner Auditorium.

Elbert D. Thomas, a Latter-day Saint senator from Utah, was the chairman of the Thomas Jefferson Memorial Commission. He had a lifelong fascination with Jefferson and made lasting contributions toward the memorial. His research prompted him to write *Thomas Jefferson: World Citizen* (published in 1942), and he selected the quotes that graced the memorial wall in 1943. He became chair in 1944 and oversaw the final stages of the memorial, including the creation of the Jefferson statue.

On panel 3, Thomas amalgamates four Jefferson sources into one quote, making it seem as if Jefferson were "a believer in emancipation, if not abolition, rather than a slave owner."[11] To the left of the entrance is a carved inscription about the memorial with the name of Elbert D. Thomas listed as "Chairman 1944" (in small print to the right of his name).

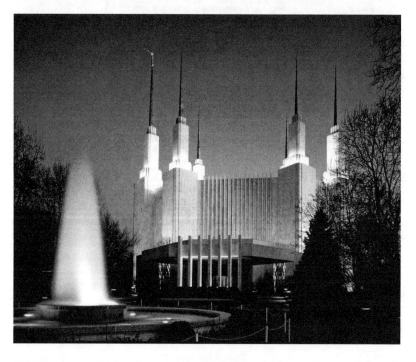

Washington D.C. Temple in Kensington, Maryland. Carol M. Highsmith Archive, Library of Congress.

The Washington D.C. Temple is an important house of worship for Latter-day Saints in the area and the world. This cutaway model in the visitors' center shows the interior layout. At the time of the temple's completion, its district included Church members in thirty-one U.S. states and the District of Columbia, seven Canadian provinces, Cuba, Haiti, Puerto Rico, the Bahamas, and the Dominican Republic. It is the Church's third-largest temple and the tallest; its easternmost spire is 288 feet tall (88 meters).[12]

In May 1999 the Church bought a four-story, 1920s-era brick building that once housed offices of the nearby George Washington University Medical School. The Church then renovated and expanded the building, renaming it the Milton A. Barlow Center.[13] During the dedication ceremony in 2002, Kathleen B. Morgan, said that her father, Milton, dreamed of a "reverse migration" from the West and felt that creating a "Washington Center" could help in that goal.[14] The building is an important gathering place for DC-area Saints, housing the Church's Office of International and Government Affairs, a chapel and other religious facilities for a church congregation, classes for an institute program for young adults, and apartments and classrooms for Washington Seminar interns from Brigham Young University.

NOTES

1. "History of the U.S. Capitol Building," Architect of the Capitol (website).

2. "History of the U.S. Capitol Building," Architect of the Capitol (website).

3. Joseph Smith and Elias Higbee to Hyrum Smith, "Corner Missouri and 3d Street," Letterbook 2:85–88, Church History Library, Salt Lake City.

4. "Mount Vernon," History.com.

5. History.com editors, "Arlington National Cemetery," History.com.

6. "Tomb of the Unknown Soldier (Arlington)," Wikipedia.

7. Frederick Hart, "Vietnam Veterans Memorial, Three Soldiers," *Histories of the National Mall*, Mallhistory.org.

8. "National Cathedral," Sacred Destinations (website).

9. "Lincoln Bay," Cathedral.org.

10. "Washington D.C. Ward," Historic LDS Architecture (blog).

11. Hahna Cho, *Notes on the State: Jefferson Beyond Jefferson*, 12 July 2008, https://notesonthestate.wordpress.com/2018/07/12/misleading-quotation/.

12. "History of the Washington DC Temple," https://www.dctempleupdates.org/history.

13. Lee Davidson, "New D.C. Home for LDS Offices," *Deseret News*, 13 April 2002.

14. Mauri Earl, "Barlow Center Dedicated in Washington, D.C.," *Church News*, 18 April 2002.

ACKNOWLEDGMENTS

We are pleased to recognize the publishing expertise and professionalism of the faculty and staff who serve in Brigham Young University's Religious Studies Center, including the publications director Scott Esplin; publications coordinator Joany Pinegar; editors Devan Jensen, Shirley Ricks, Meghan Rollins Wilson, Cara Nickels, and Sarah Johnson; production supervisor Brent Nordgren; and designer Emily Strong. We are grateful for everyone who reviewed and edited draft essay manuscripts.

The editors gratefully acknowledge our colleagues who have contributed their time and talents to researching and writing the essays in this volume. The authors also acknowledge the assistance provided by Beverly Yellowhorse, who directs the Religious Education Faculty Support Office, and the able assistance of the following student research assistants: Ally Fronk Bichsel, Anna Pomares, Annie Mangus, Bradley McCormick, Camdyn Barney, Ciera Anderson, Deanna Nielson, Drew Carson, Emma Thornock, Jena Burgess, Laynie Calderwood, Liel Maala, Madison Godfrey, Maren Davis, Nathan Hubert, Savannah Jardine, Scott Garrett, and Ward Hedges.

We appreciate the willingness of Dale Van Atta and Ralph W. Hardy Jr. to contribute essays to this volume. Their intimate knowledge of Church-related people and events in Washington, DC, has made this a more comprehensive volume. Dale Van Atta acknowledges the assistance of Daryl Gibson, his longtime editor and collaborator, on his essay. He is appreciative of the oversight and encouragement for the Marriott book project from Sheri Dew, as well as Chris Schoebinger and his team at Shadow Mountain, a Deseret Book subsidiary, as well as the book's editor, Emily Watts. Ralph Hardy thanks the family members and friends of those featured in his summary who contributed to his research.

INDEX